Gabler Theses

In der Schriftenreihe „Gabler Theses" erscheinen ausgewählte, englischsprachige Doktorarbeiten, die an renommierten Hochschulen in Deutschland, Österreich und der Schweiz entstanden sind. Die Arbeiten behandeln aktuelle Themen der Wirtschaftswissenschaften und vermitteln innovative Beiträge für Wissenschaft und Praxis. Informationen zum Einreichungsvorgang und eine Übersicht unserer Publikationsangebote finden Sie hier.

Tobias Baumgärtner

A Software Framework for Mobile Apps in the Museum Application Domain

Springer Gabler

Tobias Baumgärtner
University of Passau
Bavaria, Germany

Publication of the Dissertation
submitted by Tobias Baumgärtner
to the School of Business, Economics and Information Systems
of the University of Passau, in Passau on 17.07.2023
Disputation Date: 23.08.2023
Primary Reviewer: Prof. Dr. Franz Lehner, University of Passau
Secondary Reviewer: PD Dr. Michael Scholz, Deggendorf Institute of Technology

ISSN 2731-3220 ISSN 2731-3239 (electronic)
Gabler Theses
ISBN 978-3-658-44366-5 ISBN 978-3-658-44367-2 (eBook)
https://doi.org/10.1007/978-3-658-44367-2

This Springer Gabler imprint is published by the registered company Springer Fachmedien Wiesbaden GmbH, part of Springer Nature.
The registered company address is: Abraham-Lincoln-Str. 46, 65189 Wiesbaden, Germany

Paper in this product is recyclable.

Preface

This section ties together the particular structures surrounding the overall research project. It summarizes the intent of the ViSIT project, the relevance of the overall undertaking, and the transposition between the practical and scientific perspectives. The stage for the dissertation is set by highlighting the contiguity between the domains and communities involved.

Domains and Communities

The inevitable influence of information technology and digital devices has reached most sectors of today's society. When researching the impact of such systems, the perspective needs to be adjusted for the characteristics of a specific field's contextual environment and its stakeholders. This has led to multiple transdisciplinary actors trying to absorb the emerging possibilities and their dependencies into their own domain knowledge.

Putting the focus on the context at hand—museums—Marty and Burton Jones (2008) describe the field of *Museums Informatics* to examine the "socio-technical interactions of people, information, and technology in museums" (Marty and Burton Jones, p. 274, 2008). In doing that, they try to capture the complexity and govern the flow of information at the conjuncture between experts and visitors on both theoretical and practical levels. The relevant aspects are representation, organization, and access to information as well as the enabling technologies.

Those insights were connected to only the individual data layer for a long time. However, that drastically changed with the introduction of the internet. It was no longer possible to conceal those considerations to just one singular institution. The aspects of sharing and interaction became inevitable. That makes it mandatory to build strong communities and to develop ways to enable automated exchange between their members.

The progress on this end is already quite far advanced from the technical perspective, as data models, platforms, and task-specific systems are available. Advances in standards in the data persistence and exchange layer may help to incorporate smarter systems, but that does not account for institutions on the strategic or operational level. The transfer of the lessons learned, extracting existing best practices, and accessing available knowledge should be more of a concern to making them widely available for as many members within the domain as possible (Marty & Burton Jones, 2008).

Similarly, the focus of *Digital Humanities* initially has been pointed toward incorporating digital tools and archives as well as advanced analytical methods to the increasing demand of their respective fields. However, the scope opened up by the rapid advances in technology and its general availability. Now "it can at times be difficult to determine with any specificity what, precisely, digital humanities work entails" (Gold & Klein, 2016). That leads to the construct referred to as the "big tent" accounting for the interdisciplinary influence and the growing emphasis on information and communication technology in practice, outside of archives (Warwick, et al., 2011).

With the further evolution of technology, ubiquitous user-centered systems and applications need to get even more attention. The conception, development, and implementation of these are core components of *Information System Research*. Knowledge and process management are advanced in this field alongside human-computer interaction. Supplying users and technical systems with information by incorporating application programming and graphical user interfaces, this field tries to develop and connect the economic questions to their technological solutions (Mertens, et al., 2001) (Stormer, Meier, & Lehner, 2005).

Information Systems Research, therefore, provides the ideal methodological foundation if the goal is to design a holistic and sustainable Software Framework for Mobile Apps in the Museum Application Domain (Stein, Galliers, & Whitley, 2016).

This dissertation has been accompanied by four paper publications and one demonstration, highlighting the practical relevance and scientific foundation of the conducted research. In that regard, both the intrinsic entity of the scientific domain within Information Systems Research and the practical community of museum professionals surrounding the online presence of cultural heritage institutions have been included:

- 'Museums and the Web' (MW) is the largest international conference devoted to the exploration of art, science, and natural and cultural heritage online. It was founded by 'Archives & Museum Informatics' in 1997 and is still hosted annually by the 'MuseWeb Foundation' an offshoot of the 'Museum and the Web LLC.' with the goal of transforming the business of culture.
- The European Conference on Information Systems (ECIS) is considered the premier Information Systems event in the European region. It is affiliated with the Association for Information Systems (AIS) and has been held annually since 1993.

Preceding Publications and Presentations

The following publications were accepted by their peers, and each has been presented to the respective audiences of the practical and/or scientific community. The results of these manuscripts are, in part, included within this dissertation.

The Technical Aspects of Museum Information
vs.
the Museum Professional's Point of View:
A Conceptual Change of Perspective on Data Processing.

Baumgaertner, T. & Lehner F. (2017).
Proceedings of the 21st Museums and the Web conference (MW17),
Cleveland, Ohio, USA, April 19–22, 2017.
Published February 16, 2017.

Entwicklung mobiler Applikationen
im Anwendungsbereich von Museen—
Customer Experience Value Chain.

Baumgärtner, T. & Lehner, F., (2017).
HMD Praxis der Wirtschaftsinformatik: Vol. 54, No. 5.
Springer Fachmedien Wiesbaden. (S. 808-820).
https://doi.org/10.1365/s40702-017-0350-1

HMD

Introducing Socio-Technical Changes through "Mobile First" in the Museum Application Domain.

Baumgaertner, T. (2018).
Proceedings of the 22nd Museums and the Web conference (MW18),
Vancouver, British Columbia, Canada, April 18-21, 2018.
Published February 15, 2018.

A Software Framework for Mobile Apps within the Museum Application Domain.

Baumgaertner, T. (2019).
Demonstration at the 23rd Museums and the Web conference (MW19),
Boston, Massachusetts, USA, April 2–6, 2019.

Conceptualizing a Mobile App Framework For the Museum Application Domain.

Baumgärtner, Tobias. (2019).
Proceedings of the 27th European Conference on Information Systems (ECIS), Stockholm & Uppsala, Sweden, June 8–14, 2019.
ISBN 978-1-7336325-0-8 Research Papers.

The ViSIT Project

This dissertation has been accompanied by the project with the title 'Virtuelle Verbund-Systeme und Informations-Technologien für die touristische Erschließung von kulturellem Erbe' (ViSIT). The project has been funded by the INTERREG programme 'V-A Bayern-Österreich 2014–2020' enabled by the 'European Regional Development Fund' (ERDF).

That fund focuses its investments on the 'thematic concentration' within these priority areas:

- Innovation and Research
- The Digital Agenda
- Support for Small and Medium-Sized Enterprises (SMEs)
- The Low-Carbon Economy

ViSIT highlights the cultural area lined out by the three rivers Inn, Salzach, and the Danube. That territory has been historically defined by the salt trade, dating back to the beginning of the 11th century, as well as the Prince-(Arch-)Bishoprics of Salzburg and Passau. Thus, the territory has a strong connection, characterized by its rich historico-cultural heritage.

Within the focal scope of ViSIT was the visitor experience to be generated, especially in alignment with the development of partnerships between institutions. Among other integral projects, the development of *A Software Framework for Mobile Apps in the Museum Application Domain* has been a pivotal element.

Tobias Baumgärtner

Executive Summary

The popularity of mobile applications has been ever-increasing since their conception in 2007. Structural changes related to digital transformation and tourism significantly impact the expectations of and toward cultural heritage institutions associated with the subject of apps. The overall role of museums has shifted from a keeper of artifacts to a provider of information.

The intention of those apps is to generate added value for the visitor, who therefore is mainly seen as the primary element of any associated reflection related to the experience that is created while interacting with that mobile application. Nevertheless, the cohesion between an application's creator, the application's content, and the consumer operating the app in a designated context needs to be appropriately examined.

Looking at the specific customer touch-point provided by mobile applications, it is not trivial to create such an integrated user experience. Those apps can be drivers for digital transformation and strategic alignment of historico-cultural institutions. However, the mandatory insights and know-how necessary to create such experiences are not at all related to the core skill set of museum professionals or the existing processes within those institutions. That makes it quite challenging to implement an overall (digital) strategy that enables institutions to provide interactive applications based on structured data in addition to their core tasks.

Especially in the context of museums, it is necessary to simultaneously cater to different perspectives to provide a coherent digital experience to both the visitor and the museum professional. Based on insights gained during this examination and under the utilization of design science research, human-centered design, and domain-driven design, *A Software Framework for Mobile Apps in the*

Museum Application Domain is created, and a prototype implementation using web technologies is developed throughout this dissertation.

The resulting Page CUBE Content Representation (PCCR) application framework intends to act as an entry point to the digital realm for museum professionals. The development of mobile applications is the anchor for digitization and acts as a starting point to further examine the properties of mobile applications, specifically within the Museum Application Domain, in the future.

Contents

Abbreviations

ACID	Atomicity, Consistency, Isolation, and Durability
AIS	Association for Information Systems
AJAX	Asynchronous JavaScript and XML
API	Application Programming Interface
AR	Augmented Reality
ARIA	Web Accessibility Initiative's Accessible Rich Internet Applications
BASE	Base Availability, Soft state, and Eventually consistent
BITA	Business-IT-Alignment
BYOD	Bring Your Own Device
CBT	Computer-Based Training
CRM	Conceptual Reference Model
CRUD	Create, Read, Update, and Delete
CUBE	Composition Ubiquity Building Element
DBMS	DataBase Management System
DDD	Domain-Driven Design
DOM	Document Object Model
DSR	Design Science Research
ECIS	European Conference on Information Systems
GUI	Graphical User Interface
HCI	Human-Computer Interaction
HTTP	HyperText Transfer Protocol
ICOM	International Council of Museums
ICT	Information and Communication Technology
IDE	Integrated Development Environment
JSON	JavaScript Object Notation

LIDO	Lightweight Information Describing Objects
LOD	Linked Open Data
MAD	Museum Application Domain
MoMA	Museum of Modern Art
MRT	Magnetic Resonance Tomography
MV*	Model-View-Star
MVC	Model-View-Controller
MVP	Minimal Viable Prototype
MVVM	Model-View-ViewModel
MW	Museum and the Web
OLAP	OnLine Analytical Processing
OLTP	OnLine Transaction Processing
OS	Operating System
PC	Personal Computer
PDA	Personal Digital Assistant
RDF	Resource Description Framework
REST	Representational State Transfer
SDK	Software Development Kit
SEO	Search Engine Optimization
SME	Small and Medium-sized Enterprises
SOA	Service-Oriented Architecture
SOAP	Simple Object Access Protocol
SQL	Structured Query Language
UNESCO	United Nations Educational, Scientific and Cultural Organization
URI	Uniform Resource Identifier
UX	User Experience
ViSIT	[Project Name Recronym]
VR	Virtual Reality
W3C	World Wide Web Consortium
WHATWG	Web Hypertext Application Technology Working Group
WWW	World Wide Web
WYSIWYG	What You See Is What You Get
XML	Extensible Markup Language
XSS	cross-site scripting

List of Figures

List of Tables

List of Listings

1 Introduction and Structure of the Thesis

The dissertation entails nine chapters. In this introduction, each chapter is briefly described to provide a general overview of the manuscript and its fundamental structure, presented in **Figure 1.1**. The reasoning and motivation for the investigation in the context of the Museum Application Domain (MAD) are provided. The proposed research setup is underlined along the conceptual foundation of the Software Framework for Mobile Apps in the Museum Application Domain and the resulting prototype implementation.

Across all domains, information and communication technology (ICT) exerts its influence on value-oriented institutions, on how they operate, and on the manner, they interact with their customers. The impulses involved often create a precedent to spill over demand into other domains. Like the case within cultural heritage institutions, those may initially not be equipped to adopt certain innovations. Proposals are often not reflected in their intended situation or are obstructed by other intrinsic or extrinsic restrictions, like societal implications or the capabilities accessible within the target domain.

To shape an understanding of the current landscape and possible issues, data available from German museums gathered between 2008 and 2018 has been analyzed. The greatest impacts today originate from digitization, mobile technologies, and tourism. These factors contribute to the field of tension surrounding the institutions in question (*Chapter 2—Motivation*).

The identity coined by the historic role of cultural heritage institutions and the inherently embedded collection-based processes museum professionals were primarily occupied with in the past do not reflect the modern profile established by the shift of focus within their societal tasks. While museums were able to provide technology-based aid for their visitors in the past, the increasing complexity and pace of innovation make it difficult to keep up with the state of the art. These issues weigh even greater in smaller institutions, which struggle to provide

T. Baumgärtner, *A Software Framework for Mobile Apps in the Museum Application Domain*, Gabler Theses, https://doi.org/10.1007/978-3-658-44367-2_1

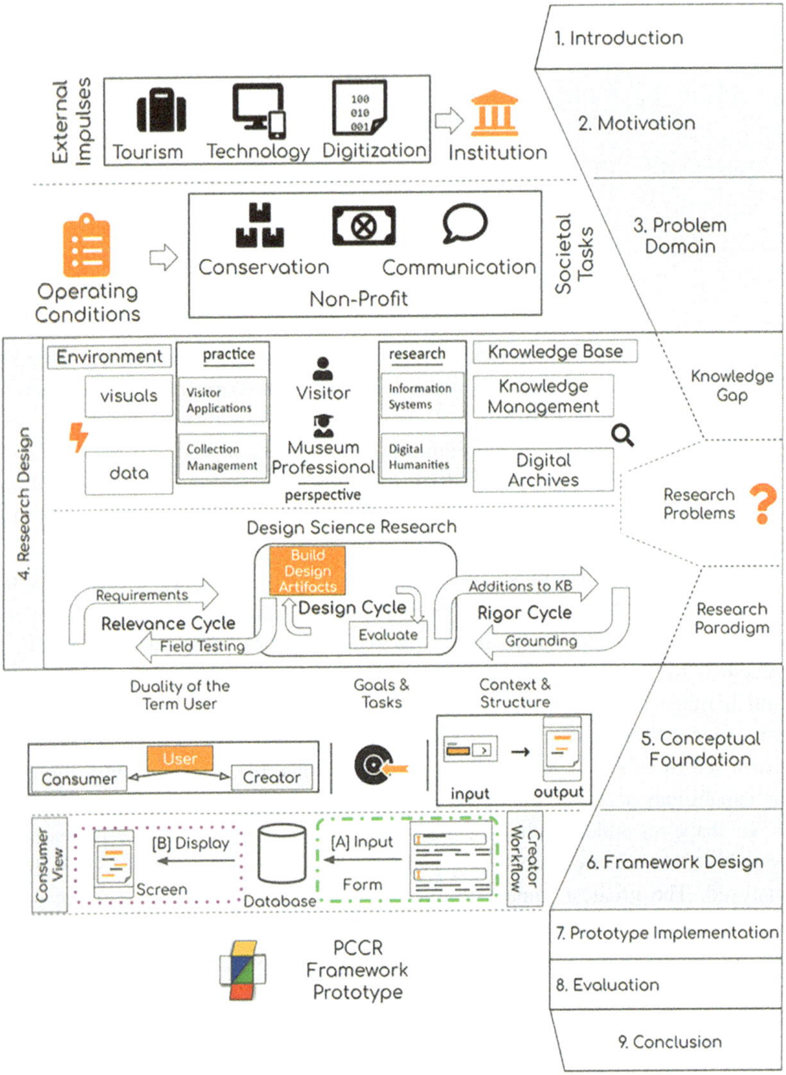

Figure 1.1 Visual Abstract

the required resources to maintain a holistic strategy because they do not have access to an entry point to introduce digital products like mobile applications, nor the required aides to access or obtain the knowledge to develop, deploy, and distribute potential solutions (*Chapter 3—The Problem Domain*).

The conflicts within the MAD are multi-dimensional. The most obvious is the usual barrier between research and practice, which might not appear to be most relevant in the application-oriented scenario, but perfectly illustrates the skew of perspective as well as the existing gaps and deficits within the domain. While the internal processes of museum professionals are primarily motivated by the conservation of knowledge and artifacts for the purpose of scholarly work, they tend to focus on tasks to fit their agenda, involving organizing their findings and archiving their existing collections. From the outside view, the museum audience, by contrast, desires to experience collections in an informative and entertaining fashion, being able to interact more directly with the artifacts decoupled from the associated scientific foundation. Thus, data must be collected in a manner to satisfy both perspectives without creating overhead on top of the processes necessary between data inquiry and presentation (*Section 4.1—Problem Areas*). Those challenges are reflected in the leading research motive:

"How to provide guidance for small cultural heritage institutions to govern digital transformation, and how to align the possibilities with the available capabilities by creating A Software Framework for Mobile Apps in the Museum Application Domain?"

This question is dissected into three separate research problems (*Section 4.2—Research Problems*) to be approached by applying a design science research approach with the intent to build a robust domain artifact (*Section 4.3—Research Paradigm*).

To instigate the process, certain important terms need to be distinguished. That includes defining the conceptual idea of a framework, how content is perceived in relation to information, which is to be presented to the consumer, and the elements of human-centered design. To further advance that holistic inspection, those conceptual components need to be extended by the psychological foundation obligatory for genuine user experience design. One of the most central postulations is the conceptual difference in how the term user is applied to the observation, which influences application design. It is crucial to understand that the needs related to information systems involved in mobile content delivery do not only include the consumer but the creator as well. The attention usually exclusively put on the consumer-facing product needs to be extended to the structure and the context of the data entry process itself, which the creator is bound to interact with initially. Facilitating the dedicated understanding of the conceptual foundation the whole system is based upon creates immediate opportunities for the individual and produces long-term benefits for the whole organization. Finally, the essence of the presented composition is aligned with the conceptual foundation characteristic for system development (*Chapter 5—Conceptual Foundation*). This does conclude the purely theoretical inspection of the underlying issues and commences the transition toward the design and development of the Software Framework for Mobile Applications in the Museum Application Domain.

The concepts of domain-driven design are introduced to set up the framework design process. The central ideas behind the initial design iterations and the insights gained within each of those loops are summarized before the final design is introduced. The foundation for the realization of the framework is discussed based on the processes and roles involved. The architectural model chosen for the framework is used as a scaffold for introducing the fundamental concepts, which tie together the user interface and the data model. The core system design accommodates the resulting consumer app pages as an anchor for all creator tasks. That makes it possible to approach the available features from each perspective independently (*Chapter 6—Framework Design*).

The technology necessary for the prototype implementation of the framework as a web application is introduced alongside the tools and services applied and used during the entire development process (*Chapter 7—Prototype Development*).

The episodes of the evaluation process are then described, supported by the pivotal guidelines from within the research approach. The suggestions received by different users and the related improvements achieved during the trial are compiled to represent the adaptability and extensibility of the framework scope (*Chapter 8—Evaluation*).

To conclude the thesis, the main findings are summarized. Further research potential is pointed out and is encouraged based on the presented results (*Conclusion*).

2 Motivation

This chapter presents the central impressions surrounding the subject environment of the Museum Application Domain. To warrant the investigation and provide a frame of reference, first, some longitudinal data about museum visits in Germany over the past decade is being analyzed (*Section 2.1—Museum Visits in Germany*).

The motivational setup for the thesis is provided by analyzing the three central themes between digital transformation (*Section 2.2—Digital Transformation*), mobile technologies (*Section 2.3—Mobile Technologies*), and tourism (*Section 2.4—Tourism*). These three external impulses are most relevant for the perception of the subject environment and how its assignments are being framed, approached, and processed. Those topics are presented in **Figure 2.1** and further described below.

The major impact of digital transformation does affect the inside view (Section 3.1), controlled by inherent domain processes (Subsection 3.1.1) as well as the goals and tasks of the museum professional (Subsection 3.1.2). Historically the museum identity has been dominated by collecting and conserving historic artifacts, while in the 20th century, the focus of the societal tasks stemming from the institutional assignments has shifted toward communication. Systemically, that does lead to a conflict today in the 21st century.

T. Baumgärtner, *A Software Framework for Mobile Apps in the Museum Application Domain*, Gabler Theses, https://doi.org/10.1007/978-3-658-44367-2_2

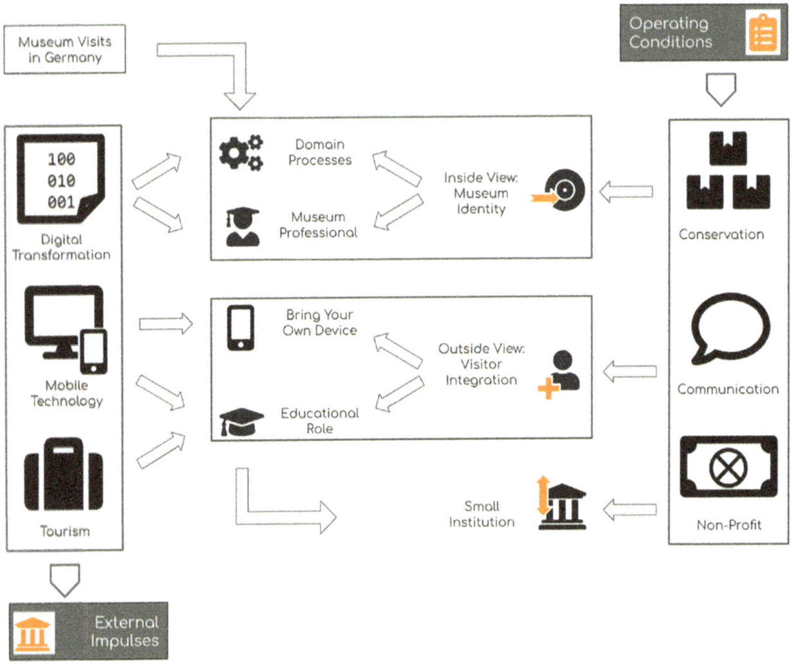

Figure 2.1 Relationship between External Impulses and Operating Conditions

On the one side, the museum professional's inside perspective and the domain processes are coined by conservation, which often translates to digitization projects being directed toward archiving and similar purposes or fully disregarded without establishing any middle ground.

Conversely, the audience structure grows increasingly heterogeneous and becomes more conscious while less centered. In general, the outside view (Section 3.2) shifted from a historically academic circle focused on scholarly work to a more casual consumer. These visitors, who approach the learning environment provided by the museum's educational role (Subsection 3.2.1) seeking entertainment, need to be integrated with the institutional context. They are still motivated by the physical museum experience. However, the shifts touristic encounters have experienced across the board as well as recent developments in mobile technology, exert immense pressure on the content authored and published by cultural heritage institutions. Visitors have developed the desire to have access to additional digital information. The support of the visitor with technology-based means has been pursued for a long time in the Museum Application Domain. The increasing complexity and pace of innovation, however, makes it difficult to keep up with the state of the art and expectations. Obstacles caused by the dependency upon digital devices can be reduced by invoking a Bring Your Own Device (BYOD) strategy to deliver information directly to the smart mobile devices carried by the visitor (Subsection 3.2.2).

Especially smaller institutions struggle to integrate their societal tasks with those new driving forces because of the financial restrictions applied by the non-profit nature of museums (Section 3.3). They need to have access to an entry point to adopt the available technology, to reevaluate the modern interpretation of the museum identity, and to engage their own strategy by building up the necessary knowledge to articulate their desires.

2.1 Museum Visits in Germany

The 'Institut für Museumsforschung' in Germany conducts an annual statistical inquiry among German museums. Some of the results are presented in **Table 2.1** (Museumsforschung, 1981–2018). Analyzing the data of the last decade, some general observations can be extrapolated, which indicate the fundamental characteristics that motivate the perspective of reflection regarding cultural heritage institutions within this dissertation. Small museums with limited resources often are operated by non-profit organizations or public bodies. While, on average, the visitor count per institution is increasing, smaller institutions struggle to generate growth or cannot monetize the increasing visitor count to begin with. The basic elements are further illustrated within this section.

Operations

In 2018 over two-thirds of museums were located in the territorial states of Southern Germany. These two states, Baden-Württemberg (1243 | ~18%) and Bavaria (1184 | ~18%), are then followed by Nordrhein-Westfalen (741 | ~11%). One-fifth of recorded visits occur in Bavaria (~20%). Overall, the vast majority of these institutions are operated by public or non-profit bodies.

Over half of those museums located in Germany are operated by public bodies (51—55%), financed by the state or the federal government. Out of the museums in private leadership, two-thirds (~65%) are operated by non-profit societies (Vereine). Thus, the overwhelming majority of the field has restricted access to financial resources, as seen in **Figure 2.2**.

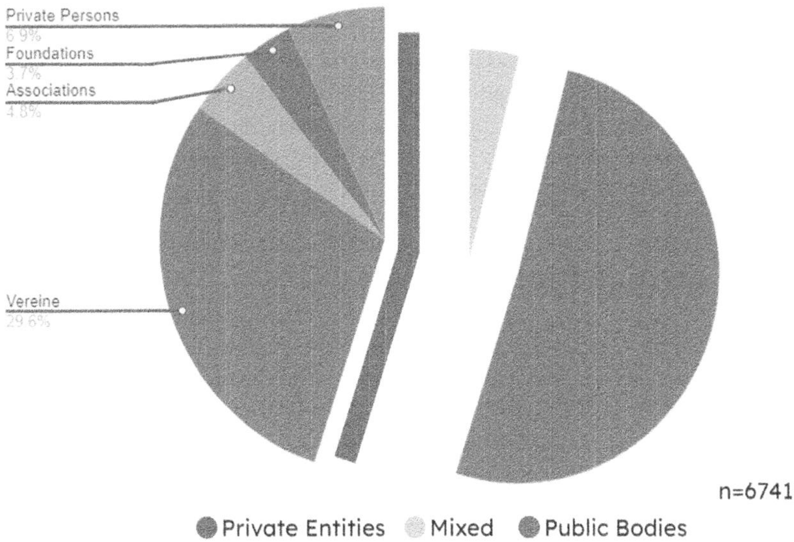

Figure 2.2 Operators of Cultural Heritage Institutions

Demographics

The seasonality of the cultural heritage sector is likely caused by the critical dependency on tourists, which account for the largest visitor group in around 40% of institutions. That includes pre-booked groups as a part of chartered trips. In 30% of institutions, which track visits by student groups, those appointments account for over 50% of group visits. Overall, around 30% of all museums are predominantly visited by pre-booked groups. The majority, however, remains the independent visitor, which includes groups of friends and families. More than a third of museums experience over 75% of independent visitors. **Figure 2.3** visualizes these indications.

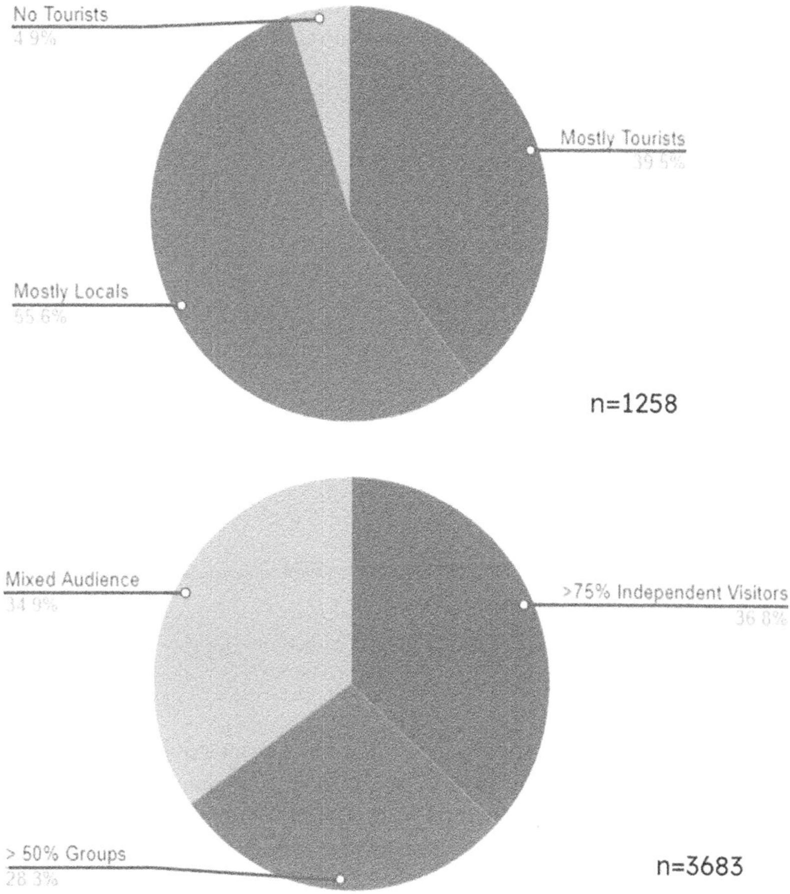

Figure 2.3 Visitor Structure

Visitor Numbers

The total number of visitors per institution has been steadily increasing over the past decade. The overall number of visitors to German cultural heritage institutions increased from 104 852 334 to 111 662 229, which equates to a 6% growth. On a per-institution level, the increase accounts for 4.5% or around 100 visitors per museum.

Noteworthy is that this increasing trend from 2008 onwards has been broken and has been declining since 2016, as shown in **Figure 2.4**.

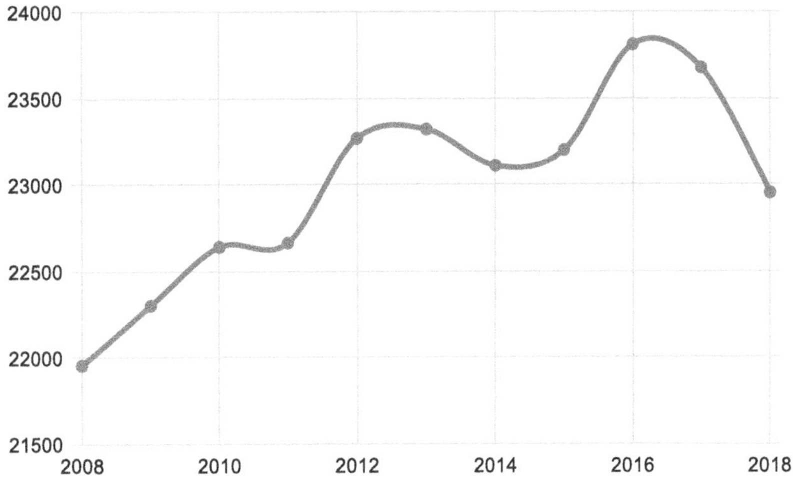

Figure 2.4 Visitors per Institution

Visitor Distribution

As shown in **Figure 2.5**, the smallest museums, which count less than 5 000 visitors per year, make up for ~ 41% of all museums in Germany. Medium-sized institutions between 5 000 and 100 000 visits occupy another 30% of the market. Only 3.75% of museums are able to attract more than 100 000 visitors each year. Of those, only three to six individual museums are able to each maintain over one million visitors per year. Of the 25% that could not provide their visitor numbers, most are assumed to belong to the first group of the smallest museums, which further increases the importance of those institutions.

Miscellaneous

Some additional notes regard the versatility necessary to drive growth. Museums with the capacity to carry out special exhibits attributed the growth to these limited-time installations throughout the decade. At the beginning of the period under review,

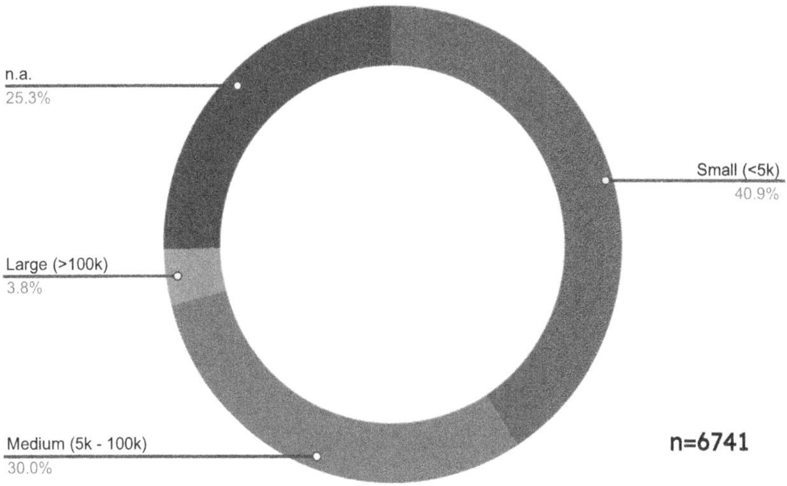

Figure 2.5 Visitor Distribution

structural expansion projects and extending opening hours were mostly deemed responsible for growth. Over time, the measures shifted toward public relations, including museum education programs and special events. That puts additional pressure on those museums that cannot afford any extra expenses, including over one-third of institutions (35%) that do not even generate a return on investment on the visitor level, as they do not charge any entrance fees. Thus, the goal must be to identify a way for them to participate.

The following sections attend to the three primary external impulses for the introduction of mobile applications within the Museum Application Domain, accounting for the international audience, the recent decline in visitors, and the financial burden museums face today.

Table 2.1 Inquiry Results of German Museums by the Institute of Museum Research (2008–2018) (Museumsforschung, 1981–2018)

Year		2008	2009	2010	2011	2012	2013	2014	2015	2016	2017	2018
Museums	Population	6,190	6,256	6,281	6,304	6,355	6,358	6,372	6,710	6,712	6,771	6,741
Operators	Public Bodies	3,419	3,444	3,449	3,438	3,443	3,368	3,371	3,455	3,457	3,479	3,463
	Nonprofit Societies	1,713	1,742	1,749	1,778	1,796	1,779	1,786	1,951	1,943	1,978	1,989
Visitor Numbers	Response Visitors Numbers	4776	4790	4823	4835	4848	4735	4846	4932	4699	4831	4865
	Total Visitors	104,852,334	106,820,203	109.196.469	109,581,613	112.807.633	110,425,002	111,984,006	114,423,192	111,877,085	114,375,732	111,662,229
	Visitors per Institution	21,954	22,301	22,641	22,664	23,269	23,321	23,109	23,200	23,809	23,675	22,952
	YoY change per Institution (abs.)	-	347	340	23	605	52	-212	92	609	-133	-723
	YoY total change (%)	-2.30%	1.90%	2.20%	0.35%	2.90%	-2.10%	1.40%	2.20%	-2.20%	2.20%	-2.40%
Demographics	Response Demographics	3,288	3,361	3,486	3,452	3,514	3,542	3,589	3,369	3,418	3,515	3,683
	Single (>75%)/Group (>50%)	33.4%/29.9%	34%/30.7%	34.5%/29.5%	35%/28.7%	34.7%/29.2%	34.6%/28.1%	36.0%/27.4%	34.3%/30.0%	34.3%/28.4%	34.5%/28.7%	36.8%/28.3%
	Tourist Majority	42.10%	40.20%	41.30%	40.40%	39.70%	40.40%	39.00%	38.80%	39.60%	39.50%	39.50%
Visitor Distribution	Small Museums (<5k)	42.00%	41.60%	42.20%	41.80%	42.10%	40.60%	41.60%	40.60%	38.30%	38.80%	40.60%
	Medium Museums (5k - 100k)	31.50%	31.20%	30.80%	31.20%	30.40%	30.10%	30.70%	29.20%	28.10%	28.70%	27.80%
	Large Museums (>100k)	3.70%	3.80%	3.80%	3.70%	3.80%	3.80%	3.80%	3.70%	3.60%	3.80%	3.80%
	n.a.	22.80%	23.40%	23.20%	23.30%	23.70%	25.50%	23.90%	26.50%	30.00%	28.70%	27.80%

2.2 Digital Transformation

Technological advances and the availability of digital infrastructure have an overwhelming impact on many organizations. To underline how the interaction with data affects enterprises and how the approach to digital content has changed over time, examining the two main components that bolster today's transformational processes is mandatory. While often used interchangeably, the terms digitization and digitalization address two very different stages of said process. In the 1970s, emerging technology trends were enabled by the internet and relational databases, which facilitated services such as search. That permitted institutions to dislodge and replace paper-based archiving systems and access information in completely new ways (Stam, 1996).

The availability of digital archiving allowed the translation of analog records to their digital counterparts. That is described as *digitization*, a process that exerts itself only on a descriptive level (Marty & Burton Jones, 2008) (Jeurgens, 2013).

Within the following decades, technology like digital photography, 3D scanning, and increasingly affordable hardware made it possible to create digital replications of physical objects. This is expressed as *digitalization*, operationalizing processes on a representational level (Marty & Burton Jones, 2008).

Today new transformational drivers are about to change IT infrastructure as a whole, with both mobile devices and on-demand access to infrastructure, platforms, and software via the internet, commonly referred to as *cloud computing* (Stormer, Meier, & Lehner, 2005) (Fernando, Loke, & Rahayu, 2012) (Floerecke & Lehner, 2016).

The emerging ramifications of these ubiquitous digital technologies need to be recognized. The socio-technical implications related to these developments and their implementation are often summarized under the umbrella term of *digital transformation*, which has been omnipresent across all industries over the last decade (Capgemini Consulting, 2011) (Westerman, Bonnet, & McAfee, 2014).

In 2014 Westerman, Bonnet, and McAffee proposed nine core elements of said digital transformation. These are meant as building blocks to support the executive decision-making process. Those elements are structured within three groups containing three elements each. The digital transformation framework formulated by Matt, Hess, and Benalin (2015) highlights the importance of these factors by underlining four key dimensions by differentiating operational and functional strategies for such endeavors (Hess, Matt, Benalian, & Wiesböck, 2016).

The first group of Westerman et al. (2014) aims at 'customer experience' and contains 'understanding customers', 'top-line growth', and 'customer touchpoints'. They argue that deploying tools for analytics enables companies to understand the behavior of the existing customer base, develop brands, and derive concepts to enhance their interaction with customers, new and old (Westerman, Bonnet, & McAfee, 2014).

The ability to explore and exploit the 'use of digital technologies' is determined by operational alignment. It establishes whether to independently develop solutions or rely on existing standards, if available (Hess, Matt, Benalian, & Wiesböck, 2016).

The second group described by Westermann et al. (2014) is centered on the 'transformation of operational processes' and consists of the elements 'process digitization', 'worker enablement', and 'performance management'. Automation can help to refocus on core tasks and reduce overhead, not only by focusing on static processes but also by enabling collaborative employee structures. The goal should be to detach the physical working environment from the associated task wherever possible while simultaneously improving reporting systems. The latter boosts the capabilities of strategic decision-making, while the first allows for more flexibility (Westerman, Bonnet, & McAfee, 2014).

Hess et al. (2016) concur on these 'structural changes' and advise specifically looking at affected products, processes, or skills within the organization or its teams.

The third group of Westermann et al. (2014) addresses 'transforming business models' and consists of the 'digitally modified business', 'new digital business', and 'digital globalization'. The outline of their reasoning is that it might not be enough to adapt and augment existing structures and workflows but to disrupt and reinvent them continuously. Service integration, digital products, and multinational operations underline the need for social strategies once again. The authors clearly see the primary responsibility within the leadership of the organization to frame and deploy clear strategies (Westerman, Bonnet, & McAfee, 2014) promoting sustainability. These 'changes in value creation' can lead to higher risks depending on the derivation from the classical core business's service portfolio and the demand to increase knowledge accordingly (Hess, Matt, Benalian, & Wiesböck, 2016).

Westerman et al. (2014) urge focusing on areas most prevalent in the specific environment to be transformed. Hess et al. (2016), however, attribute the selection to the 'financial aspects' and the implications the decision invokes as these constitute "both a driver of and a binding force of the transformation" (Hess, Matt, Benalian, & Wiesböck, p. 4, 2016). They overall suggest strategic alignment of all four of those dimensions.

Bughin et al. (2017) mainly focus on the economic implications of these new technologies. Goals need to be utilizing technologies readily available, and resources are supposed to be shifted toward future drivers, not only focusing on the obvious customer-centered benefits but also considering the internal transformation of processes without getting lost in trends. This enables organizations to concentrate fully on the execution and learn from the success of others by simultaneously avoiding pitfalls that might punish a first-mover in the long run (Bughin, LaBerge, & Mellybye, 2017) (Baumgärtner, 2019.1) (Baumgärtner, 2019.2).

This shows, as Kohnke (2016) also indicates, that these procedures do not just hinge on technology. Furthermore, 'organizational change management' and 'the people side of digitization' must be considered at each step along the way. Employees need to be enabled to cope with occurring changes. Creating a digital mindset can aid businesses in identifying and communicating their requirements. Programs to educate and train them are pivotal to developing necessary digital skill sets. Agile and collaborative tasks can support them to react to the continuously shorter intervals in which change occurs and counteract other issues, like the generation divide. At a higher level, it is important not to alienate information technology from the associated business functions when innovation causes conflicts but to re-engineer the underlying processes. Embracing those changes is inevitable if the vision is to maintain a sustainable working environment, even if short-term business benefits cannot be realized immediately (Kohnke, 2016).

However, these approaches cannot solve all root problems encountered in many situations. Increasing demand regarding the expertise among employees and the infrastructure within the institution, crucial to implement such strategies, may be limited. Especially in small and medium-sized enterprises, a lack of focus causes investments to be distributed too broadly, which may invalidate spending into digital and the associated return on investment (ROI) or simply the perception of progress. The setting in which those changes occur has to be adapted, while technology needs to be adjusted toward the existing environment. Hence, that transformational force has substantial managerial implications for resolving these dilemmas (Heavin & Power, 2018). Those implications also apply to non-profit organizations.

Digital technology, while being a driver of change, overall needs to keep its role as an enabler and not take priority over the core business model (Lassnig, Stabauer, & Friebel, 2019). Especially if new tools or concepts are introduced, their purpose and the connected benefits need to be clearly communicated by management or, even better, be directly visible on an individual level related to the task involved.

2.3 Mobile Technologies

The continuous improvement of access points to the internet, i.e., LTE and Wi-Fi hotspots, contributed to innovating information and communication technologies (Bullinger, Auernhammer, & Gomeringer, 2004) (Zheng, Li, Lou, & Hou, 2017). Smart mobile devices have supercharged this momentum. The possibilities of ubiquitous information access and interactions independent of time and location have permanently altered many aspects of daily routines, be it in private or at work (Jose & Davies, 1999) (Zheng, Li, Lou, & Hou, 2017).

The dawn of these innovations dates back to June 2007. With the release of the first iPhone running the operating system iOS by Apple Inc. (Apple Inc., 2007) began the conquest of smartphones. It was joined shortly after by Android—Google's Linux-based mobile operating system—first shipped on the HTC Dream (T-Mobile G1) in October of 2008 (HTC, 2008). Continuous advances in hardware and computing technologies enable smaller and more powerful devices (Adepu & Adler, 2016). With the decision to open their platforms to third-party developers, mobile devices are capable of accessing diverse services and running complex mobile applications (Open Handset Alliance, 2007) (Snell & Cohen, 2008).

Small programs, referred to as *apps,* are typically distributed through virtual stores linked directly to the vendor of the respective operating system (OS). In 2019 over 200 billion apps were downloaded from these stores (Takahashi, 2020). While around 90% of those applications can be downloaded for free, most of these free apps are monetized via advertising (56%) or in-app purchases (39%), including subscription-based business models (smaato.com, 2020).

In the beginning, multiple additional competitors were able to establish significant OS market shares, namely Nokia (SymbianOS, Series 40), Research in Motion (BlackberryOS), and Windows (Windows mobile); today, only the two aforementioned brands—Android and iOS—remain. Android by Google, owned by Alphabet, dominates the global market with around 74%, and Apple (iOS) occupies 24% (Statcounter, 2019), while others do not play any significant role within the global mobile ecosystem.

Today, smartphones are a daily companion for many people. While around 40% of the global population owns a smartphone (Statista, 2019), in Germany, the rate of smartphone users exceeded three-quarters of the population in 2016 and recently surpassed 80% (Bitkom, 2019). The global revenues of mobile applications reached over $90 billion in 2018 and are projected to grow immensely by 2022 (Appel, Libai, Muller, & Shachar, 2018) supported by cloud infrastructure

(Fernando, Loke, & Rahayu, 2012), enabling around 16 billion connected mobile devices worldwide (The Radicati Group, 2020).

This adoption is a valuable appliance for companies across all domains to build customer touch-points and create engagement opportunities that can be individually tailored and managed on a per-customer level. Thus, businesses have become capable of supplying their clients with innovative information offerings and services that are aware of context and location. This opens up an ecosystem introducing new roles and business models (Stormer, Meier, & Lehner, 2005) (Hufenbach, 2014). On average, consumers spend over 200 minutes daily on their mobile devices, dominated by social networks and video streaming services (Takahashi, 2020).

Commercial companies use these opportunities quite effectively. Because of certain restrictions, other institutions, like those found in the Museum Application Domain, struggle to keep up with new mobile business opportunities (Marty & Burton Jones, 2008) (Atkinson, 2013) (Hufenbach, 2014) (Decker, 2015). Museums in the past were able to provide technology-based aid to provide additional information within exhibitions for their visitors, which is further discussed in subsection 3.2.2. Increasing complexity, financial implications, and other restrictions make it more challenging to develop and maintain solutions that comply with both the expectations of the visitors and the goals of the museum professional.

2.4 Tourism

The expanding interconnectedness of the world, enabled by technology, integrates regional and national economies, societies, and cultures into a global community. Political, demographic, economic, social, and technological drivers permit the trend of globalization to determine that development. The consequences—including fewer constraints regarding visas, decreasing travel costs, increasing availability of education, and the growth of the leisure society—create immense opportunities for the tourism industry. General connectivity fueled by information and communication technology facilitates the customization of services (Dwyer, 2015). On a larger scale, this brings forth a positive impact on destination productivity and visitor flow as well as an overall increase in quality of life for the local population (Plaza, 2006) (Knežević Cvelbar, Dwyer, Koman, & Mihalič, 2016) (World Tourism Organization, 2019).

On the other hand, ethical questions emerge, and the very identity of the tourism sector has to be audited regarding environmental impact and the established industrial mindset to achieve long-term viability. The needs of the tourist must be considered, but without surrendering self-identity and marginalization of local stakeholders (Dwyer, 2015). Since digitization reduces economic friction, it enables competition, pressuring both revenue and profit growth (Bughin, LaBerge, & Mellybye, 2017).

The World Tourism Organization (UNWTO), a United Nations specialized agency, is concerned with the development of responsible, sustainable, and universally accessible tourism. The findings of their 2019 report state that the sector managed to realize growth in nine consecutive years and is consistently outpacing the global economy with a growth of 4.4% in 2018. Leisure, recreation, and holidays account for 56% of international tourism, the majority of which is conducted by air travel. International tourist arrivals reached 1.4 billion in 2018, with over half (710 million) can be attributed to Europe (World Tourism Organization, 2019).

The visit of persons to cultural attractions away from their usual place of residence, with the intention to gather new information and experiences to satisfy their cultural needs, is referred to as *cultural tourism* (Palumbo, Dominici, & Basile, 2014). Within that context, the choice of destination is primarily influenced by cultural heritage landmarks, select collections, and specific artifacts (Plaza, 2000). The 'Holiday Barometer' a survey conducted by IPSOS, shows the desire of European and American travelers to visit iconic landmarks like the Wonders of the World and significant cultural heritage sites, like the Eiffel Tower in Paris (France) or the Statue of Liberty in New York (USA). The choices of European travelers under the age of 35 are especially guided by their own prior experiences (24%), the expected weather (22%), available activities (21%), as well as recommendations (18%) by friends and family. They are particularly conscious about their expenses and would increase the frequency of their getaways (36%), the duration of their stay (20%), or the distance to their destination (17%) if their budget was extended (IPSOS, 2019).

The Global Attractions Attendance Report 2018 underlines that the steady year-over-year growth rates published by the UNWTO also can be observed by the largest European recreational facilities like theme parks (4.4%) and water parks (6.7%). Especially the themed entertainment industry, spearheaded by Disney, profits off the global reach of well-recognized franchises, including Marvel Entertainment and Lucas Arts (Hellerman, 2019). These growth rates do not translate to museums. These institutions can only maintain the status quo (0.1%) on a global level. Within Europe, however, which contains nine out of the worldwide top 20 museums and accounts for 48% of global visitors, attendance has grown by 6.1%. The Louvre in Paris leads that increase with a record surge to 10.2 million visitors in 2018. Mobile devices such as smartphones and social media channels, like Facebook-owned Instagram (Shead, 2019), offer the opportunity to share personal involvement and create the demand for unique immersive and digital experiences by visitors in both an entertaining and educational manner (Themed Entertainment Association, 2019).

This desire can also be recognized, by the fact, that at least 15% of travelers are concerned with the quality of the internet access during their trip (IPSOS, 2019) when considering their destination. These social media channels can significantly improve performance, reach, and visibility by aiding institutions to understand their competition and visitor demands (Komarac, Ozretic-Dosen, & Skare, 2017).

Furthermore, trends like eco-tourism shift the focus toward resource efficiency and sustainability. That provides an entirely new set of challenges transforming audiences and their expectations (IPSOS, 2019) (World Tourism Organization, 2019).

2.5 Summary: External Influence and Impacts

When these findings related to the external impulses, summarized in **Figure 2.6** are contextualized, it becomes apparent that creating content and designing experiences to be delivered to a volatile and heterogeneous customer base in a mobile world connected by the internet is a tough endeavor. Additionally, the way in which museums operate increasingly depends on their economic prowess (Conn, 2010), inducing the field of tension surrounding the institutions comprised of digital transformation, mobile technology, and tourism.

Figure 2.6 External Impulses Surrounding Museums

Within the Museum Application Domain—in consequence—both the physical and digital spaces need to be connected to convey additional information to the visitor without disrupting the desired museum and learning experience

(Addis, 2005) (Haesler, et al., 2016). Therefore, it is inappropriate to start digital projects just for the sake of transformation, but to rethink and evaluate where change is mandatory, can help to increase productivity, and to attain sustainability (Baumgaertner & Lehner, 2017.1).

A strategy needs to be implemented to create long-term value. Existing processes, accessible resources, and obtainable know-how need to be taken into consideration (Baumgärtner & Lehner, 2017.2). Those challenges magnify if small and medium-sized institutions, which struggle with the allocation of resources as is, try to compete with the pinnacle of industry innovators (Plaza, 2006) (Skinner, Ekelund Jr., & Jackson, 2009).

3 The Problem Domain

The described socio-cultural developments lead to a situation where museums today are surrounded by a field of environmental tension caused by the three aforementioned external impulses: tourism, mobile technology, and digital transformation. To not be left behind, that situation demands an internal response and strategic alignment. Yet, it is not possible to approach just one of those dimensions independently. Interdependencies related to specific conflicts inherent to the assignments, which define the operating conditions of a cultural heritage institution, dictate certain priorities as well. The core tasks expected to be performed by museums are conservation and communication while being restricted by a tight budget as well as sustaining their non-profit character, as shown in **Figure 3.1**.

Figure 3.1 Operating Conditions Defining the Cultural Heritage Institution

Cultural heritage institutions are most often rooted within a certain temporal or spatial dimension, and their message is directed toward a passive audience. Those circumstances embedded within the general funding situation of many organizations provided a natural economic moat. As a result, traditionally, it has not been necessary to adopt new technologies or practices, and fostering innovation has been selective and rather optional. Today, a holistic view is mandatory to create

T. Baumgärtner, *A Software Framework for Mobile Apps in the Museum Application Domain*, Gabler Theses, https://doi.org/10.1007/978-3-658-44367-2_3

and maintain a sustainable and future-oriented digital strategy. The goal must be to stay relevant for more engaged visitors and to compete with other destination attractions.

This chapter first discusses the museum identity and its mission forged by the societal role as a conservator assigned to museums, comprising the inherent processes and the dedicated role of the museum professional (*Section* 3.1—*Inside View: "The Museum Identity"*). Second, the responsibility of communication is met by discussing the integration of the visitor by cultural heritage institutions. The goal is to emphasize the educational role of museums as well as the use of technology directed toward the visitor (*Section* 3.2—*Outside View: "Visitor Integration"*). Third, these situations and associated challenges are intensified for small institutions in particular (*Section* 3.3—*Challenges for Smaller Institutions*).

3.1 Inside View: "The Museum Identity"

The term *museum* has been defined by the International Council of Museums (ICOMSection 1) as follows: "A museum is a non-profit, permanent institution in the service of society and its development, open to the public, which acquires, conserves, researches, communicates and exhibits the tangible and intangible heritage of humanity and its environment for the purposes of education, study and enjoyment" (ICOM Statutes 2017, Article 3—Section 1.). "Established in 1946, ICOM is a non-profit organization subject to French law (the 1901 Associations Act) and a non-governmental organization that maintains formal relations with the United Nations Educational, Scientific and Cultural Organization (UNESCO) and has a consultative status with the United Nations Economic and Social Council." ((ICOM, 2017)—Statutes 2017, Article 1—Secttion 2.).

Over time, the most central task of conservation has heavily coined today's museum identity. That causes the naturally grown structures and long-existing domain processes to be structured around the collection. Additionally, the role

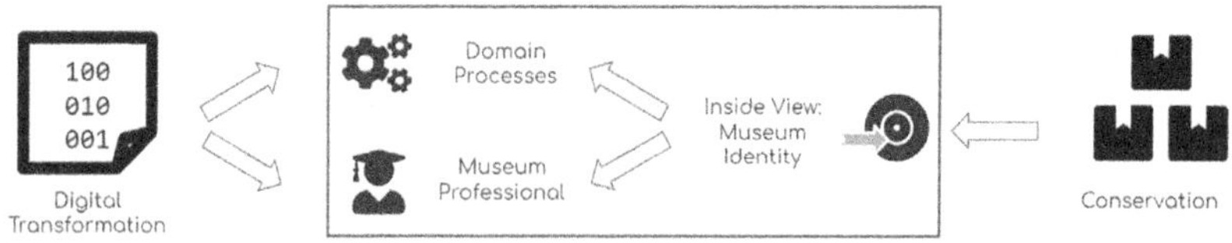

Figure 3.2 Inside View: Conflict between Digital Transformation and Conservation

of the museum professional is to be mostly recognized as a custodian. However, the impact of digital transformation introduces an extraordinary disruption to be accommodated. Those effects are shown in **Figure 3.2**.

The ICOM acknowledges those effects and the general tension affecting the core idea of how museums are perceived by trying to revise that very definition of museums to reflect the current situation and account for the necessary changes. For that purpose, over 250 proposals to help shape an alternative definition have been submitted by stakeholders from around the globe (ICOM, 2019).

Because that attempt was not leading to a conclusive result satisfactory to the members of the council, the decision to finalize any changes has been postponed (Noce, 2019). Nevertheless, it started an international debate about a future strategic alignment (Small, 2019). So much so that the synthesized ICOM suggestion has been pulled from the official website altogether (Kendall Adams, 2019). That first attempt at least revealed the most commonly desired elements among museum professionals. The focus needs to be shifted toward dialogue, open access, diversity, as well as transparency, and overall a clear focus on communication (ICOM, 2019). Therefore, the role of the museum and its identity evolved from a keeper of relics to a provider of information with an ever-growing focus on entertainment.

The traits, necessary to grow into these new expectations and implement the necessary changes, rely strongly on the visibility and accessibility of institutions and exhibitions. The dependencies on interaction opportunities with the demand for innovative products and channels require restructuring established processes and the introduction of new mindsets, turning away from self-centered and monolithic expert-level information silos to more open and approachable access to pieces of information (Alexander & Alexander, 2008) (Conn, 2010).

Some common domain restrictions, however, do affect the leeway of the existing processes in place (*Subsection* 3.1.1—*Inherent Domain Processes*) and the museum professionals who are responsible for executing these important changes (*Subsection* 3.1.2—*Role of the Museum Professional*). Those effects primarily put smaller institutions in an unfortunate predicament (Section 3.3).

3.1.1 Inherent Domain Processes

All companies and organizations in a competitive business environment encounter the impact of digital technologies and have to apply changes to their organizations (CHA, Gregor, & Fernandez, 2008). Over the course of these modifications, new roles have to be defined, hierarchies have to be restructured, and the adoption and usage of new technologies is inevitable to stay relevant, defend market share, and build competitive advantage (Devaraj & Kohli, 2003).

Those requirements and the benefits of a digital strategy are well understood by small and medium-sized enterprises (SMEs) even if they cannot produce the same gains as larger corporations at scale (Ghobakhloo, Benitez-Amado, & Arias-Aranda, 2011). The organizational changes and the involved management decisions in today's data-driven world can be conducted in production and service industries because the processes are often only one-dimensional, and the return on investment justifies the investment (Kwon & Stoneman, 1995).

Galleries, libraries, archives, and other cultural heritage institutions do have a fundamentally different foundation, as described by Alexander and Alexander (2008). The first appearance of such institutions can be found in Alexandria, Egypt, around 300 BC. The complex known as 'Musaeum', which also includes the infamous Library of Alexandria, illustrated in **Figure 3.3**, was founded by Ptolemy I Soter, a companion of Alexander the Great. The central purpose of

Figure 3.3 Artistic Rendering of the Library of Alexandria, based on some archaeological evidence (O. Von Corven, 19th)

the Muesaeum has been the gathering and preservation of cultural artifacts and putting them on permanent display (Lee, 1997). It also acted as a hub for both academic and religious scholars (Erskine, 1995).

Exhibitions were not primarily introduced for recreation or entertainment. Museums then were to act either as a window to inform and educate certain members of society about findings and results of the scholarly work conducted in a university setting or as a private space to express the power and success of authorities by displaying heirlooms, loot, as well as rare specimens of plants and animals (Alexander & Alexander, 2008).

Because of the unstructured interior and the novelty of displayed objects, those were referred to as cabinets of curiosity or 'Wunderkammer'. The depiction in **Figure 3.4** shows the cabinet created by Ferrante Imperato, an apothecary from Naples, Italy, in 1599 (Westerhoff, 2001).

Figure 3.4 Earliest Illustration of a Natural History Cabinet (Ferrante Imperato, 1599)

The first museum, in the sense of today's interpretation, opened in 1671 in Basel as a university museum, still with a strong focus on collecting artifacts. It is directly linked to the Amerbach Cabinet, a collection of 15th and 16th-century art bought by the city of Basel in 1661 (Lourenco, 2003). It was housed in the 'Haus zur Mücke' (**Figure 3.5**), a ballroom near the city's cathedral (Bianchini, 2019) (Sladeczek, 2011).

Figure 3.5 Visitors of the Gallery at 'Haus zur Mücke' (Hieronymus Hess, 1837)

When the idea of public access opened museums up to visitors of the general public and later the industrial revolution, new threats were introduced to those collections, including theft, electrical lighting, and air pollution. Protecting their repositories and the obtainable information about and related to the contained objects, as well as exploring new restoration techniques, had taken the top priority among the institutions in question. During those developments, museum research has been institutionalized. That created the ability to describe accurately and catalogue objects, which often contributed to the immense expansion of existing collections (Alexander & Alexander, 2008).

The lack of a connection of the gathered information to an output format designated to a nonprofessional audience led to a transcendent approach. In Revolutionary France—the late eighteenth century—the Musaeum has thus been reduced to the mere architectural properties of a scholarly showroom (Lee, 1997). That resulted in sanitized exhibitions targeting an expert audience, not dependent on guidance or interpretation. Thus, the dissonance between the intent of museum professionals—presenting their collections and findings—and layperson visitors—often disappointed by what they encounter—has been inevitable (Alexander & Alexander, 2008).

It was not until the 19th century and the arrival of the Neoclassical movement when Swiss and German museums explored the possibilities of applying taxonomies as well as temporal context to their exhibition spaces to enhance their approachability by creating arrangements closely related to the culture and history as well as the time period of the objects on display (Alexander & Alexander, 2008). For example, the Glyptothek in Munich, Germany, built in 1830, houses Greek and Roman sculptures from four different periods. Starting in 700 BC (Archaic period) up until 550 AD (Roman period), those are arranged by their place of origin and chronologically, thus facilitating its layout, as shown in **Figure 3.6**, to guide the visitor throughout the exhibition (Odobasic, 2017) (Staatliche Antikensammlungen und Glyptothek, 2019).

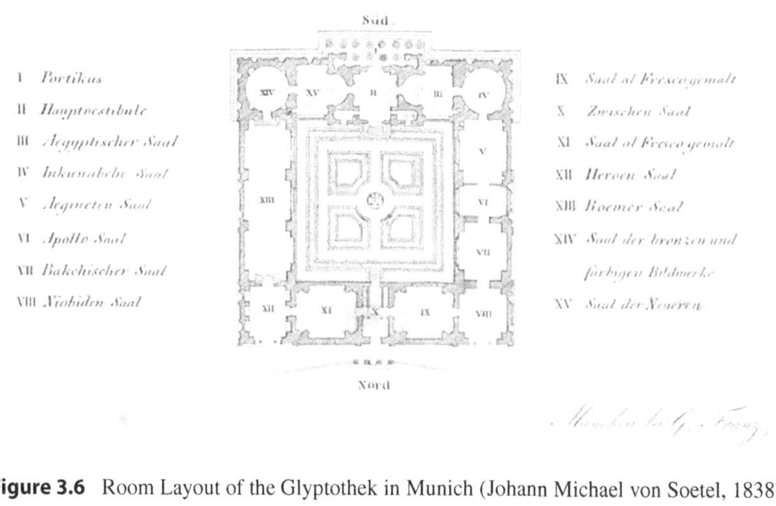

Figure 3.6 Room Layout of the Glyptothek in Munich (Johann Michael von Soetel, 1838)

It still took until the twentieth century before research included museum practices and the contact with the visitor and their perception of exhibitions. Nevertheless, a museum was and still needs to be defined by its collection. An art museum or a historic site without a collection is just a gallery or a local attraction, respectively. What did change over time is the general access to exhibits, how they are arranged by the museum, and the priority, which has been shifted from conservation toward communication, further discussed in subsection 3.2.1. Regardless of those developments, to this day, museums with conservative leadership consider collecting and conserving to be the most imperative task of a museum, neglecting other institutional needs and operational necessities (Alexander & Alexander, 2008).

The importance of efficiency and the general flow of information and internal processes is visible (Jeffers, 2003), but as a result, often marginalized. The lack of operational competition further reduces the general importance of adapting and introducing managerial changes. Public funding incentives discourage external exchange and collaboration (Waibel & Erway, 2009), which additionally dampens the actual necessity of innovation (Zan, 2000) as well as the very ability to innovate (Søndergaard & Veirum, 2012). That causes museums to constitute a black box. Even if all the mandatory tasks are applied to their acquired objects, they are secluded within the institution. Research concerning objects, if conducted, may be incorporated into the curation process. Research, however, rarely includes the collection itself. Findings, while mandatory for the curation and exhibition processes, are infrequently accessible because of the historically protective stance toward knowledge as well as missing outlet opportunities and varying standards (de Clercq & Lourenço, 2004). Content is usually created by describing the objects through providing meaning and context. The resulting information is then delivered to the audience using a specific medium, the historic choice being text panels (Hinrichs, Schmidt, & Carpendale, 2008) or other paper-based means, like

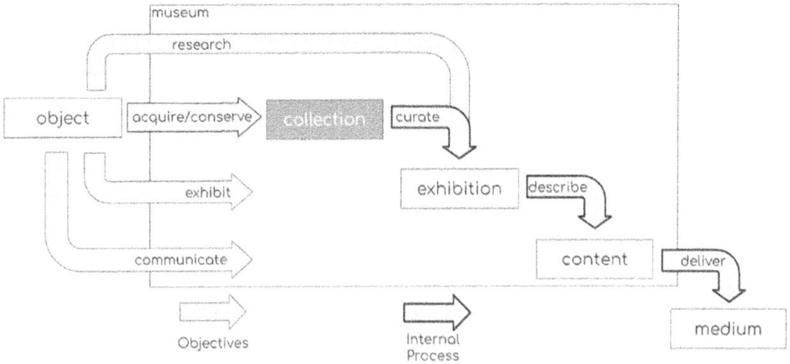

Figure 3.7 The Cascading Process of a Collection-Centric Approach

posters or catalogues. That leads to one-directional, cascading processes that do not allow for feedback and are just a means to an end of fulfilling the minimum mandate of communication. The situation of this 'collection-centric approach' is visualized in **Figure 3.7**.

The main reason is the general lack of quantifiable museum output (Alexander & Alexander, 2008). In conclusion, accountability cannot be attributed to a distinct measure (Manes-Rossi, Allini, Spanò, & Dainelli, 2016). Business administration for cultural heritage institutions and economic questions are not prioritized within the sector nor in related research (Kahlert, 1988) (Johnson & Thomas, 1998) until recent touristic implications (Najda-Janozka & Sawczuk, 2018) as visibility and revenue become more important for the sector. Because of that, digitization does not appear to have an immediate positive impact. Hence, scarce resources are not devoted to digital projects (Jeurgens, 2013) but to the retention or extension of what is already there.

The current situation is similar to the course of events previously observed in the history of museums. Like before, when visitors need to be provided with certain contextual information in a scholarly environment, a particular transition needs to happen going forward. In an increasingly digital environment, dealing with automated information processing, data exchange, and organizational implications is inevitable. While it is possible to operationalize modern technology just to emulate its analog counterpart, it then cannot unfold the full possible potential and interactive capabilities (Hinrichs, Schmidt, & Carpendale, 2008) desired by the individuals involved.

At first, the focus needs to shift from solely being concerned with the collection of artifacts to the available data, as well as their structure and the distribution of available information throughout the institution and beyond.

A digital output medium needs to be able to access an interface fed by available data the museum needs to provide. Information and content generated during the curation and exhibition need to be included in the collection. Only then can those be embedded into the research process. The most important consequence is that research findings are not only used to aid one particular curation process but are generally recorded and manifested within reliable and accessible data structures to also support content creation in the future. The cycles within the 'data-centric approach' are visualized in **Figure 3.8**.

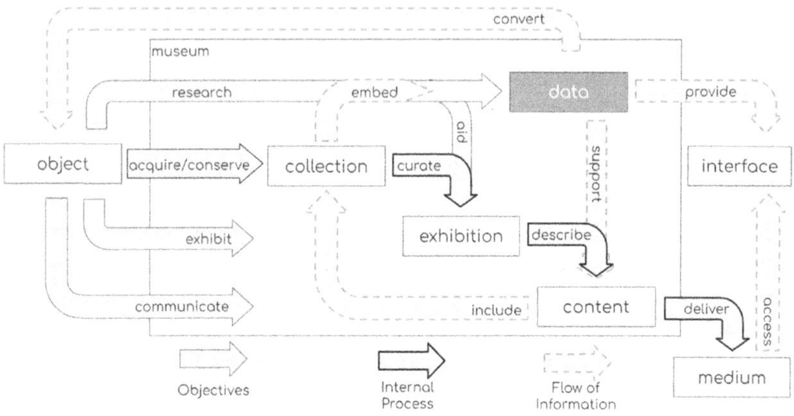

Figure 3.8 The Cyclic Processes of a Data-Centric Approach

Therein rests a further serious issue of this particular domain. Another dimension to the overall problem is added when digitization gets introduced to the overall operation. In many cases, analog information representation and processes can almost entirely be replaced by digital means. Businesses in some industries, therefore, can reduce administrative overhead and quickly adopt innovative business models as well (Müller, Buliga, & Voigt, 2018). Museums and cultural heritage institutions, on the other hand, face the fact that museum objects and documents possess intrinsic value (Conn, 2010).

The pronounced difference can be illustrated by a vivid example provided by John Seely Brown and Paul Duguid (2002) in their book 'The Social Life of Information'. In an exploration of a collection of letters from the eighteenth century in a Portuguese archive, rather than relying on the content, the envelopes were examined to find evidence of the smell of vinegar. That approach, in combination with the dates and locations of the letters, was aimed at tracing the course of a cholera epidemic. Thus, the intrinsic value of the original medium exceeds the mere observable surface level. Accordingly, that applies to most artifacts created in the process of visual arts. Those cannot be easily reduced to their optical representation, as objects are defined by the functional interaction between material, light, and the intent of the presentation and are dependent on the threshold of originality of the physical display (Jeurgens, 2013).

Consequently, digital representations of artifacts collected in museums are not able to replace their existing physical manifestation. Moreover, data describing certain objects and corresponding metadata each represent new objects themselves, which consequently have to be included in the collection. Thus, they are reintroduced into the whole process of conservation. Therefore, digital assets do not replace or reduce efforts within the collection process. Often additional responsibilities emerge (Jeurgens, 2013) because the primordial objects and the connected processes need to be retained regardless of new tasks.

The composition of data, however, if left unsupervised and unstructured, leads to proprietary data structures specific to each individual institution or even smaller internal organizational units. That is bound to fabricate incompatibilities and more problems in the long run. Within cultural heritage institutions, archives and libraries have an advantage over museums in that regard. Because they heavily rely on metadata and predominately deal with documents in the first place, they developed standards allowing them to organize and support the retrieval and exchange process. The range of museum tasks, in general, is more complex because, in addition to collection management, a higher-level interpretation is necessary to understand coherence and heritage (Rengman, 2008), especially when the 'end user' is supposed to be the casual visitor.

Operationalizing the curiosity of that visitor and reducing the impending danger of settling into complacency must be carefully addressed. At the same time, digital solutions must be deployed carefully. The goal should be to find the balance between supporting the visitor to focus on high-interest value creation while lowering search costs (Rounds, 2004).

That step from the passive role of a collector toward adapting to an active engagement with a casual museum audience makes it necessary to investigate channels to engage and identify potential visitors as well as non-visitors and poses the question of how much digital the museum can sustain (Hume & Mills, 2011), without overshadowing the physical museum experience.

3.1.2 Role of the Museum Professional

The influence of technology does not only affect the visitor's point of view or the way in which information is prepared, exchanged, or delivered. The curator, who is responsible for the conceptualization of exhibitions and the creation of associated content, is exposed to an overwhelmingly complex portfolio of possibilities. Trends in digital exhibition extensions go further than just to digitally copying exhibits and printed information outlets (Tu, 2019) (Conn, 2010).

The impact on the overall workflow is tied to an ever-increasing demand for the overall skill set of a museum professional (Rengman, 2008). The typical requirement profile today includes many angles that go beyond the traditional core competencies (Prahalad & Hamel, 1994) in the cultural heritage sector (Perkinson, Bischoff, & Burke, 2003).

Besides, the implications and the influence of intermediary steps on the resulting product quality are not visible immediately. As elucidated above, the historically established linear processes are bound to lead to an incomplete view because each step is secluded in itself. It is fed by the output of the previous stage without acknowledging the further influence of the delivered results on the next one. For that reason, it is important to deploy more holistic concepts in general. It is necessary to cater to different angles simultaneously and to recognize the integrated digital customer experience. At each step of the progression, different interfaces are necessary to fulfill certain tasks, even with a common goal in mind.

It is important that the significance of human–computer interaction be not only tailored toward end user scenarios. The goal must be to generate added value for each user involved, who therefore needs to be the central element of each reflection. That conjunction along the development process has been described as the 'Customer Experience Value Chain' (Baumgärtner & Lehner, 2017.2).

One way to identify the needs of specific groups or individuals is to follow and visualize the flow of information. Looking at a mobile app as an example delivery medium, the customer experience must be propagated over multiple levels. This way, the influence and necessity of each step of the process become immediately noticeable. The end user app may constitute the desired product. However, to deliver anything to be displayed at all, first, the content has to be selected and prepared. To be able to complete that step, certain data needs to be available. Objects have to be thoroughly examined to gather data.

Those steps are all centered around their own process and output. Yet, each of those tasks reflects back to the quality level of the output from the preceding steps. The assessment of the object itself mandates expert domain knowledge to ensure the quality of the respective results. The digitization of derived metadata can be supported via digital interfaces specifically designed for that task. That input data then has to comply with a standardized schema and ontology to ensure its integrity and maintainability in a persistent and comprehensible manner. Only then is the scene set for proper content creation and delivery. Information and data, which is already available, can later be composed and prepared to be consumed by the end user, creating the foundation for engaging the target scope (Baumgärtner & Lehner, 2017.2).

The described coherencies are outlined in **Figure 3.9**. Developing a deep understanding of the requirements of the internal processes and workflows supports the stakeholders involved in keeping the interdependencies in mind. The ability to identify those positions that crave support or the steps that need to be aligned plots the baseline for successfully creating sustainable digital projects.

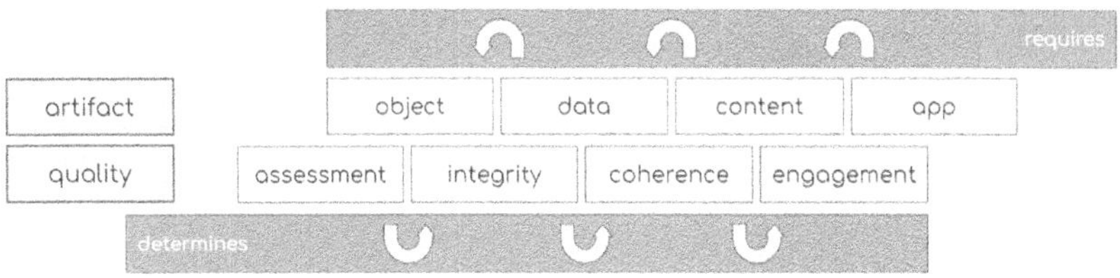

Figure 3.9 The Customer Experience Value Chain (cf. Baumgärtner & Lehner, 2017.2, p. 810)

That shows the main issues are not based on the availability of technology but on its purpose, long-term operationalization, and proper maintenance. The purpose of connecting curators, other museum professionals, and the visitor can be communicated much easier than establishing compatibility between certain technologies, specific operating systems, or databases (Rengman, 2008) in a vacuum without communicating the immediate and lasting value of creating and recording structured data from the very beginning.

3.2 Outside View: "Visitor Integration"

As shown, the museum professional's profile is extending in today's digital era. They not only need to take care of the scientific quality and accuracy of digital resources but also need to develop concepts to integrate specific visitor demographics, to enhance the overall exhibition attractiveness, and communication quality for the heterogeneous audience shaped by tourism. That dictates the selection of channels and media used, as well as the integration of those within their museum's infrastructure. Although traditional options of communication are still important, innovative technological applications, especially concerning mobile technology, are emerging. These can serve to directly interact with the visitor and provide a new level of immersiveness, visualization, and understanding for the learning environment. Those effects are shown in **Figure 3.10**.

While the intentions of most museums are clear, tangible ideas and the visitor's perspective are often underrepresented, which complicates the implementation and meeting usability goals. Depending on the nature of an exhibition Pescarin

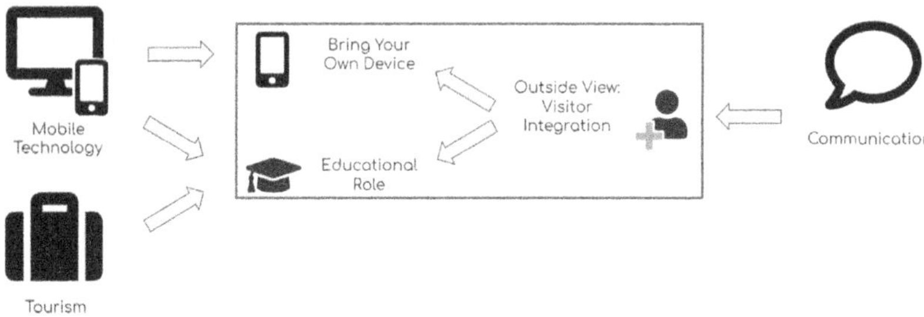

Figure 3.10 Outside View: Conflict between Expectation and Communication

(2014) identified that visitors most often ask a variation of these five basic questions, which should be primarily answered by any form of communication channel related to the artifacts within the exhibition:

- What is that? / What does it represent?
- What would it look like?
- Where does it come from?
- What was it connected to?
- How was it used?

Additionally, most museum visitors are already familiar with the information delivery tools frequently encountered in museums. Those include commonly deployed paper-based means, like printed maps, guides, and text panels; those can be extended by passive multimedia outlets, like stationary audio-terminals or video-screens; and they also cover interactive technology like touchscreen interfaces.

Furthermore, visitors express that it is important for digital museum aides to tell an overarching story, to help them to better process the presented cultural heritage information. To do that, visualization does play a vital role. Visitors are generally interested in details on objects displayed in the museum. However, they want to be in control of the level of depth they do engage with. Closely related to this is the concern of using complicated and abstract language commonly used to disclose information, which may not be suitable for the desired involving and enjoyable experience inside museums, especially the younger generation, would expect.

Overall, it is important that the connection between digital communication and the scope of the physical exhibition is clear and well-integrated with the objects on display, comprehensible, and aesthetically pleasant (Pescarin, 2014). The goal of an app should never be to replace the personal and immersive experience of the museum visit but to complement and extend it.

This perspective does constitute that information needs to be the central object of concern to support the visitor of an exhibition, independently of the digitization of customer service processes like museum shops, ticketing, and other information commonly found on websites or social media outlets. Access to additional information while using mobile guides causes visitors to learn more about artists and exhibits, and most visitors felt that they explored the museum more compared to situations where no such additional information was provided (Kontiza, Loboda, Deladiennee, Castagnos, & Naudet, 2018).

The 'Institut für Museumsforschung' in Germany recently conducted a qualitative study among museums to explore how digital mobile guides are used to extend the analog environment for visitors and if they are suitable to support the educational assignment of cultural heritage institutions. Seven building blocks for mobile visitor applications were identified: 'Games', 'Storytelling', 'Perambulator', 'Multilingual', 'Visualization', 'Video', and 'Inclusion'. Those ideas also may occur in 'Combined Guides'. These elements are recognized in section 6.3 as part of the determination of the scope of the software framework.

Similar to Pescarin (2014), the qualitative advantages of digital guides for educational processes in museums through innovative communication are described to be coined by the interaction of the exhibition concept, the role of the objects, and the visitor within the physical space offered by the institution.

Here it is also suggested that the content to be presented within mobile applications should be selected top-down from the socio-cultural perspective to preserve the intended experience of the exhibition and avoid it from being diluted by the introduction of superfluous and distracting digital elements.

On the object level, a mobile app can encourage the visitor to grapple with related elements and discover new angles, which may encourage asking advanced questions or initiating reflection upon the presented material.

The perspectives uncovered by that expository contact may reveal exciting, playful, or even emotional opportunities for the visitor, to identify themselves with the presented objects within the physical environment.

Only if those conditions are met first, the digital experience then should be extended with the aforementioned digital customer services to provide the visitor additional benefits outside the exhibition. That can include simple information like opening hours or suggestions for further reading regarding certain background information about the exhibition or the institution itself to extend the museum visit for the visitor to both prepare and debrief the visit, independent of time and location (Kuflik, Wecker, Lanir, & Stock, 2014).

Overall, it is stated that even great digital concepts cannot compensate for bad exhibition design. The scholarly distance of museum professionals from their pedagogical responsibilities is part of the struggle that accompanies the introduction of these products, to begin with. That makes it difficult to answer questions related to the core audience, which is necessary to recognize the strategic potential of museum apps for education, participation, and inclusion.

The use of individual devices would also allow for the accurate collection of data on a per-visitor basis to evaluate these strategic decisions and the general exhibition design. However, that is not utilized in most cases, and the information institutions have access to work with does not exceed the number of downloads of their apps. While the inquiry would not pose any technical issues, many institutions do not have access to the resources or the necessary know-how to properly resolve the complexity of data analysis. In addition, certain policy restrictions, like data privacy laws in Germany or the European Union, might add an additional layer of complexity regarding compliance (Noschka-Roos & Kapschulte, 2020).

This section further examines the educational role assigned to cultural heritage institutions (*Subsection* 3.2.1—*Educational Role and Learning Environment*) as well as the technical developments of multimedia and digital aides in the cultural heritage domain (*Subsection* 3.2.2—*Technology and Bring Your Own Device*).

3.2.1 Educational Role and Learning Environment

The relevance of museums as an informal third-place learning environment (Graf & Noschka-Roos, 2009), in contrast to first place (home) and second place (work/school) (Bloom, Cuadra, Fassbender, Weldesn-Smith, & Graham, 2012), for their visitors is steadily increasing (Bamberger & Tal, 2009) (Edinger & Reimer, 2015).

Museums have the ability to create a stimulating environment and facilitate techniques outside institutionalized channels to grant interdisciplinary access to certain segments of cultural heritage in a casual ambiance to a broad audience (Gruber, 2009).

Since the very beginning of public display, museum professionals were therefore put into a didactic dilemma whenever staging exhibitions. Both dimensions of the duality of cultural artifacts, between their role as a historic document and their inherent esthetic virtue, claim a share of available museum space.

In the nineteenth century, growing collection sizes and the physical restriction posed by museum architecture led museums to maximize the artifact count within the available floor- or wall-space, as portrayed in **Figure 3.11**.

Figure 3.11 Visitors at the Exhibition in the Louvre (Martini, 1787)

That caused an imbalance at the cost of restricting singular impressions and interpretations of the historico-philosophical ideals for the visitor. Criticism rose because of the loss of esthetic effects of the art itself within these overflowing exhibition spaces. Some up-and-coming artists brought forth the reproach that museums were degenerating to mausoleums, reducing artifacts to mere statistical units documenting the past. Between 1880 and 1930, the 'Museum of Modern Art' (MoMA) slowly emerged, adopting a new format of presentation focusing on the aesthetic value and the character of artifacts themselves, bringing the experience for the visitor back to life. That concept of isolation, special lighting, and neutral areas has been dubbed 'white cube' (O'doherty, 1986) (Cain, 2017).

However, that concept (**Figure 3.12**) was pressured by serialization and growing collection sizes once more, which led to a historicization of galleries (Parmentier, 2005) (Conn, 2010), again resulting in reduced spacing (**Figure 3.13**).

Today, digital media opens up a new relational space component that enables hybrid learning environments by allowing the rearrangement of the assembly of living entities and social goods (Löw, 2001) (Edinger & Reimer, 2015).

Figure 3.12 View of MoMA's First Exhibition (Juley, 1929)

Figure 3.13 Museum of Fine Arts in Boston, Massachusetts (Detroit Publishing Co., approx. 1920)

To conquer that space, organizing information in a systematic and structured fashion as well as creating intuitive access channels, are key success factors. By applying insights gained from intelligent feedback, the experience within the learning area can be further enhanced. Additionally, visitors can be guided through the exhibition by picking up on their intentions and interests. Repetition and contextualization of critical information over time and space demonstrate the effectiveness of this learning method. The experience can even be extended for pre- and post-visit information delivery (Bruck & Foerster, 2012).

The support of learning environments with electronic and digital tools that enable the delivery of information independent of time and location is described as *eLearning*. This term was coined during a Computer-Based Training (CBT), its conceptual predecessor, conference in 1999. One of the critical aspects of eLearning is not only the consumption of information but also how information is selected (Eghbal-Azar, Merkt, Bahnmueller, & Schwan, 2016) as well as how content is created, delivered (Hubackova, 2015), and presented. In that regard, *M-Learning* describes a subset of eLearning with a clear focus on handheld devices (Robra-Bissantz, 2013). An approach more sensitive to the surrounding environment, utilizing multimodal broadband access for content integration and management, is summarized within the concept of *ambient learning* (Paraskakis, 2005). That list of terms can be extended for each specific tool and purpose, but the core idea always remains the same.

The pursued goals are to increase the motivation of the user to engage with the provided tool as well as the available material and, at the same time, to meet the expectations and the demand for information of the target audience (Bamberger & Tal, 2009) (Khaddage, Lattemann, & Acosta-Díaz, 2014) (Pallud, 2017).

Content must be prepared in small units to be readable and comprehensible without any issues and to prevent information overload (*micro-content*). Depending on the output device, issues due to small fonts and long text passages are often underestimated. Especially in informal just-in-time learning environments, the user is often distracted or engaged in multiple activities at once while also interacting with their physical surroundings (Bruck & Foerster, 2012).

In a similar regard, both the terms edutainment and gamification have been established. The use of simple paper-based pop quiz style questions, which encourages the questionee to interact with the available information outlets, can already dramatically increase the interest in and the thorough and purposeful examination of contextual information like text labels in museums or the exhibits themselves (Bitgood, Patterson, & Benfield, 1992).

That approach can be met with an effort to enhance the visual appeal, using digital multimedia outlets (Haesler, et al., 2016). Furthermore, if the didactic appearance is toned down to align with the informal setting and for the benefit of entertainment, the term *edutainment* is used (Sarkar, Sarker, & Hossain, 2016). The goal once more is to improve the motivation of the user to engage with the presented information (Charsky, 2010) or incentivize them to interact with the subject matter in order to aid the interpretation process (Addis, 2005).

If the informal aspect is pushed even further and fitted with advanced game-based mechanics (van Roy & Zaman, 2017) as well as the possibilities offered by personal mobile devices (Sarkar, Sarker, & Hossain, 2016) the immersiveness of the real-world experience can be significantly molded, shaped, and extended (Khaddage, Lattemann, & Acosta-Díaz, 2014). If the character of the effort is primarily to excite the user in a fun way, using gameplay elements in a context (Su & Cheng, 2015) where they are usually not expected by the user to get them to perform a certain task, the term *gamification* is used (van Roy & Zaman, 2017). That approach, however, may increase the danger of distracting the user when the goal is to enhance the absorption of their real-world surroundings (Sarkar, Sarker, & Hossain, 2016). With more advanced technologies that allow for 3D rendering, training for dangerous or expensive scenarios can be performed by drastically lowering risks if they are performed in a virtual environment (van Roy & Zaman, 2017). In the latter case, with a strict focus on teaching, the term *serious gaming* is often used (Charsky, 2010).

3.2.2 Technology and Bring Your Own Device

The opportunities of information systems for the day-to-day business of cultural heritage institutions were addressed over 50 years ago during the IBM conference in New York City, USA, at the Metropolitan Museum of Art in 1968, where the term 'museum automation' was initially coined (Stam, 1996).

Long before that and throughout time, *paper-based* means and printed text labels were the most common tool to convey information about certain exhibits to the visitor within museum exhibitions. Those, while easily created and understood, are very limited in what they can display and do not always get the full attention of the visitor (Borun & Millep, 1980), as only one out of ten guests does deeply engage in the reading process (Bitgood, Patterson, & Benfield, 1992). That does void the intent of the museum and reduces the retention of available information by the visitor. Reasons for that are the general fit within the surroundings of the exhibition, comprehensive design, time to read, and overall comprehensibility of the information for the target audience (Borun & Millep, 1980) (Bitgood, Patterson, & Benfield, 1992).

Most visitors are casually browsing throughout the exhibition with little focus (Borun & Millep, 1980). Any exhibit that cannot generate interest within ten seconds is usually dismissed or left behind (Hinrichs, Schmidt, & Carpendale, 2008). It has been observed that visitors base their decision to engage certain exhibits on three different criteria. Those are the artifact's spatial position in an exhibition, its conspicuous visual characteristics, and the visitor's familiarity and prior knowledge of the exhibit itself (Eghbal-Azar, Merkt, Bahnmueller, & Schwan, 2016). The latter one, first and foremost, might be based on the 'mere-exposure effect', a form of implicit learning which shapes preferences through repeated contact and general familiarity (Cutting, 2003) (Eghbal-Azar, Merkt, Bahnmueller, & Schwan, 2016). How this affects the overall perception during user-interaction in a digital context is further addressed in section 5.2.1.

Third-place learning environments, and museums in particular, were among the earliest application domains to deploy *multimedia-aides* for their audience based on advanced technology (Christensen, 2011). The first handheld audio guide was introduced in Amsterdam (Netherlands) during an exhibition of the Stedelijk Museum in 1952. The technology back then was based on closed-circuit radio broadcast technology transmitted via a loop aerial, originally intended to aid hearing-impaired visitors of movie theaters (Tallon, 2009).

During that time, the general museum concepts were not only disrupted by the changing pedagogical opinions and exhibition setup as previously described in subsection 3.2.1. In addition, the increasing and widespread availability of photography enabled the reproduction of acknowledged masterpieces and the proliferation of visualization. These advances not only enabled comparability from a scholarly perspective but also facilitated diffusion and accessibility to a broader audience (Malraux, 1954).

As early as 1954, Andre Malraux coined the expression 'museum without walls' to underline the value of the viewing experience of artworks independently of the relative geographical location. The opportunities to perform objective compare-and-contrast operations without solely relying on extensive personal travel or distant memories facilitate the revelation of the world of art on a completely new level (Malraux, 1954) (Nochlin, 2005).

Today, a variety of digital tools allow the creation of channels that can extend, complement, or even completely replace the use of text labels or information panels mounted next to certain exhibits (Conn, 2010). When these tools are operated by the visitor to provide purposeful information in certain spots, they are often referred to as *random-access guides* (Othman, Petrie, & Power, 2011).

Handheld hardware devices, such as audio- or multimedia-guides (Walker, 2008), can provide ways to increase engagement and possibilities of interaction to spark interest and curiosity for additional information (Forbes & Fresa, 2015), not commonly appreciated in a purely analog environment.

That enables the visitor to actively take part in the creation of their own experience rather than just being a passive participant (Hume & Mills, 2011) by engaging and stimulating them to explore objects, collections, and exhibitions (Othman, Petrie, & Power, 2011) in a more meaningful way.

It has been demonstrated that visitors, who use these tools, spend up to 60% more time within the exhibition, also resulting in a more extensive study of individual objects (Eghbal-Azar, Merkt, Bahnmueller, & Schwan, 2016). Additionally, these guides open up the physical trail a visitor might follow (Walker, 2008). They can provide valuable insights for the institution on how the visitor behaves and navigates through the exhibition (Kuflik, et al., 2011) (Pallud, 2017).

For museums, however, the introduction of such guides is not trivial. The initial setup costs occurring during the development contain not only the creation of concepts and content but, in addition, devices have to be acquired in sufficient numbers and provided to the visitor (Othman, Petrie, & Power, 2013). Subsequently, the reoccurring upkeep and maintenance costs increase the entry barriers for non-profit organizations (Lepouras & Vassilakis, 2005). Purchased hardware also locks institutions in a certain subset of available technologies and even prevents long-term innovation (Kelly, Ellis, & Gardler, 2008).

On a similar level, visitors are sometimes hesitant to use these offerings if museum-owned hardware is involved, which often is coupled with a deposit or fee, and the handling might not be familiar or intuitive (Broadbent & Marti, 1997) (Gebbensleben, Dittmann, & Vielhauer, 2006) (Hinrichs, Schmidt, & Carpendale, 2008) (Othman, Petrie, & Power, 2013). Other factors like hygiene and health concerns do interfere with adoption as well (Chen, Chang, & Huang, 2014).

Today, as presented in section 2.3, many members of the target audience possess smart mobile devices (Bitkom, 2019), which are capable of performing most tasks necessary to implement and support functionality essential for in-gallery handheld random-access guides. A Bring Your Own Device (BYOD) strategy utilizes an end user's device to support certain tasks without the need for stationary or otherwise allocated hardware (Wei & Jianping, 2015) (Petrelli & O'Brien, 2018). Obviously, in this scenario, visitors rely on their own hardware to access the available content. Other issues, which arise with that approach and the related technology, are rooted in compliance (Crossler, Long, Loraas, & Trinkle, 2014) and security (Wang, Wei, & Vangury, 2014), if sensitive information is involved.

In the case of visitor-centered services of cultural heritage institutions, these problems do not weigh nearly as high as in other industries or application scenarios. Dedicated content is supposed to be exposed and accessed by the public visitor and, therefore, can easily be prepared, delivered, and accessed using personal mobile devices. That lifts the access restrictions for institutions by a wide margin (Ho & Chua, 2015) (Ng, 2015), and more effort can be devoted to strategic alignment and development as well as content creation and quality.

Furthermore, extra symbiotic benefits can be achieved by incorporating mobile apps within visitor experiences in the Museum Application Domain. Next to the interactive experience, a bidirectional relationship with their visitors beyond the physical borders of the museum can be established. The visitor can gain access to extended contextual information in real-time, before, during, and after, or even completely independent of visiting the physical exhibition (Walker, 2008). Information can be provided more purposefully directed toward intention, interests, and comprehension rate (Afreen, 2014). The museum, on the other hand, can learn from user metrics and other feedback mechanics to improve the overall experience they provide (Moussouri & Roussos, 2014) (Pallud, 2017).

Besides those benefits and the obvious monetary advantages, from the museum professional's perspective, a BYOD strategy may present itself with some challenges. One seemingly fundamental obstacle of such a strategy is to provide the overall desired functionality on the average end user's device, which to some degree may limit the extent of possibilities, such as the discrepancy between necessary and available mobile bandwidth for certain features at the intended location (Jang & Lien, 2014).

The possibilities to curate content do massively exceed the ability to just convert paper-based outlets or basic websites to be accessed via a mobile device. For one because those are often just concerned with information surrounding the museum rather than designated material contributing to the in-gallery experience. The challenges to designate the appropriate resources disposable to the museum in conjunction with the chosen medium are rooted in the lack of experience and the increasing complexity of the medium when innovative and advanced technology is introduced, as shown in **Figure 3.14**.

In the near future, 3D graphics and other innovative peripheral technology like *Augmented and Virtual Reality* (AR/VR) may be readily available for the consumer and offer additional possibilities to improve immersive experiences (Tu, 2019). However, because of the multitude of sensory stimuli in the environment, the museum experience can be overwhelming as is (Kolter & Kolter, 2000). It is

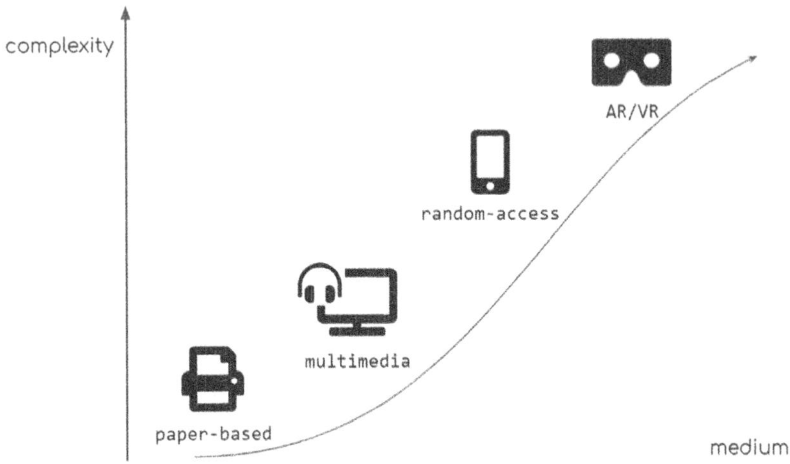

Figure 3.14 Innovation and Complexity of the Presentation Medium

of utmost importance that visitors are not getting lost in the interaction (Petrelli & O'Brien, 2018) with a piece of technology (Othman, Petrie, & Power, 2011). That may lead to a mismatch between the content on the device and the in-gallery experience (Walker, 2008) as the complexity further increases.

The ability to develop entirely new concepts to engage the modern museum audience and find a balance between the subjects of the physical exhibition and the digital space often creates uncertainty to a paralyzing degree. This can only be resolved by providing an entry point to the museum professional to enable knowledge build-up and catalyze the decision-making process in the future.

A key element needs to be the elimination of misconceptions of what exactly constitutes content currently present in the Museum Application Domain. This issue will be addressed in subsection 5.1.2. Furthermore, it is necessary for museums and their staff to develop the ability to accurately describe goals and to assess their own capabilities to support those objectives within a sustainable strategy.

Above all else, the most important elements of such an application must be centered on the end user's requirements, in regard to usability, purpose, and content (Broadbent & Marti, 1997), and not disturb the museum experience for the operating visitor or others. The goals of the museum professionals need to explicitly be aligned with these basic requirements, and thus their expectations must be adjusted accordingly.

The first step to take is to prepare the necessary resources available to museums today and make them readily available within the whole organization. Second, being able to quickly produce results and being capable of delivering a product to the visitor is paramount to understanding the processes involved and building a viable foundation for establishing a digital strategy and the future extension of the digital portfolio.

Additionally, within this process, legal aspects need to be considered, especially concerning copyright and authorship rights on original work. While that problem area dominates all digital media outlets regardless of the application domain, museums struggle with regulation, particularly in Germany and Europe (Reimer, 2016). Because of the vast implications applied by the subsequent circumstances, the legal perspective is to be excluded from this thesis.

3.3 Challenges for Smaller Institutions

The explicit influence of each of the aforementioned factors affects small museums the most (Camarero, Garrido, & Vicente, 2011). These institutions are under severe duress from different aspects, generally stemming from *resource poverty* (Ghobakhloo, Benitez-Amado, & Arias-Aranda, 2011). The available resource allocation within the four major categories in large and small cultural heritage institutions is summarized in **Table 3.1**.

Table 3.1 Resource Allocation in Large and Small Cultural Heritage

Resource	Large Institution	Small Institution
Finance	Grants & Sponsors Steady Visitors	Public Associations Fixed Budget
Time	Project Selection and Runtime depends mostly on long-term Goals	Available Time is spent on short-term Issues
Staff	Staff is specifically selected for dedicated tasks	Staff i contingent to voluntary commitment and availability
Know-How	Knowledge is preserved and transferred on an institutional level	Knowledge is only available on an individual level

Because of the overall complexity of the non-profit ecosystem, it is intricate to generalize income streams. However, roughly 60% of museum revenue is collected via donations, while less than 40% is generated from ticket sales (Hume & Mills, 2011). The dependency on public funding increases dramatically for smaller institutions, especially for those which do not charge any entry fees at all. In addition to this economic footing, it is hardly possible to measure museum output, nor is it necessary, since the services provided are non-directional and go far beyond just counting visitors (Hume & Mills, 2011).

Smaller businesses are usually more flexible and responsive to innovation (Camarero, Garrido, & Vicente, 2011). However, the economic restrictions in addition to the described inherent structures of the Museum Application Domain, cause small and medium-sized institutions to suffer from an effect similar to *cost disease* (Baumol & Bowen, 1966) described in the cultural economics (Blaug, 2001). The general cost basis associated with maintaining a collection and general museum operation increases over time at a faster rate than revenue or productivity can be increased. Bigger institutions can mitigate that by applying *economies of scale* (Stigler, 1958) (Camarero, Garrido, & Vicente, 2011).

Like in other industries, small and medium-sized businesses mostly do face *digital divide* not exclusively because of limited access to technology but rather because of a lack of education and skill within their workforce (Arendt, 2008).

Therefore, museums, in general, are not sufficiently prepared to recognize the mandatory scope to establish a comprehensive strategy within the digital realm, both on an institutional nor an individual level. As previously described in subsection 3.1.2, the average museum professional is exposed to novel tasks in addition to their traditional profile outline. Beyond that, the assignments and expectations discussed throughout Chapter 3, need to be met on an institutional level regardless of their size, as emphasized in **Figure 3.15**.

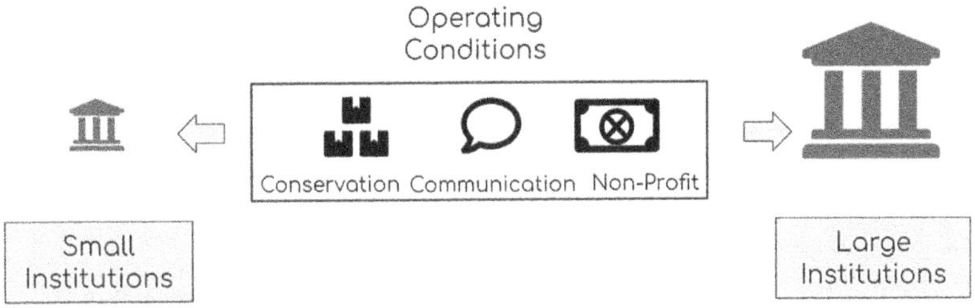

Figure 3.15 Impact of Institutional Size on Dealing with Operating Conditions

At the individual staff level, there is little to no overlap between the core competencies necessary to manage those tasks and the mandatory skill set to offer digital products facing the visitor. Hence, even if access to the necessary tools would be obtainable, they lack the essential knowledge to apply them to their specific situation. The core tasks required to keep up with the existing state of the operation, tasks, and projects preoccupy their full attention; therefore, resources cannot be reallocated toward managerial realignment and long-term, transformational goals.

That leads to an imbalance where prestigious and well-funded museums, such as the Rijksmuseum in Amsterdam (Netherlands) (Gorgels, 2013) or the Cleveland Museum of Arts (USA) (Alexander, Barton, & Goeser, 2013) are able to create and display the possibilities of supporting their visitors with dedicated information systems, resulting in products and services that fit their overall contributions and agenda. These institutions can draft holistic strategies that are aligned with their abiding tasks and fueled by the resources they have at their disposal. With these products, precise experiences can be offered to museum visitors. If they are well crafted, it is feasible to convey select information and purposeful insights, which traditional channels could not do in a captivating fashion.

Therefore, in this case, the visible product is embedded within a long-term strategy directly motivated by the underlying assignments, as presented in **Figure 3.16**.

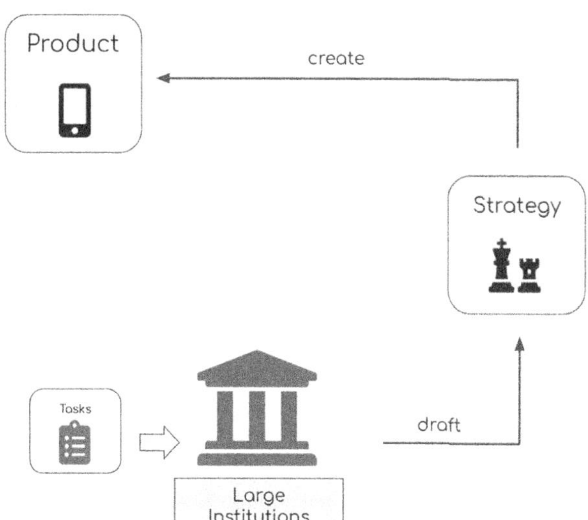

Figure 3.16 Approach of Large Institutions

Simultaneously, the public, as well as small museums, are then merely confronted with the resulting magnificent outcomes. These products attract attention within the media and increase the overall presence of an institution. Furthermore, they may enhance the in-gallery experience for the visitor. Small institutions are then pressured by those desires and expectations to produce similar encounters on their own, in addition to their day-to-day tasks, as shown in **Figure 3.17**.

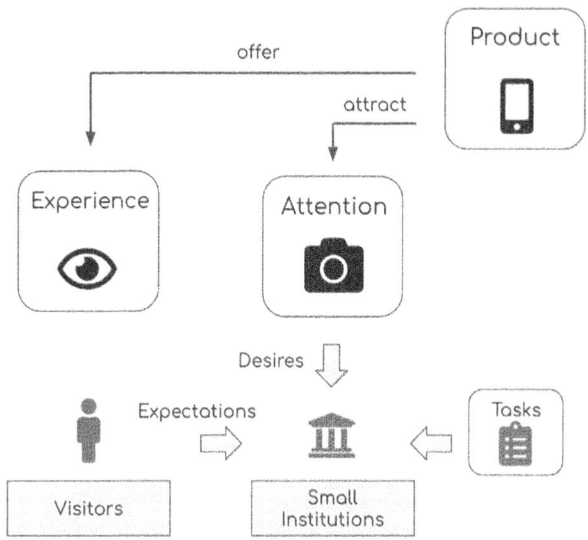

Figure 3.17 Approach of Small Institutions

However, the processes behind the scenes, required to make those products work, are well hidden and usually not visible to or perceived by the public or those who try to replicate them. The true nature of sizable digitization projects is much more complex than just the tangible output and connected products.

Pioneer projects like the 'Gallery One' and 'ArtLens App' which premiered in the Cleveland Museum of Arts in 2013, deliver a breathtaking integration of modern in-gallery interactive technology, digitization, and mobile applications (Alexander, Barton, & Goeser, 2013). However, to do that, several years of development were necessary, and around ten million US dollars were spent (Rodley, 2013). These expenses were necessary to digitalize close to 4 000 pieces of artwork and to digitize the corresponding metadata as well as to prepare them for a seamless presentation for a broad audience (Alexander, Barton, & Goeser, 2013) (Rodley, 2013).

For the Rijksmuseum to start its online gallery named 'Rijksstudio' in 2013, it was necessary to create digital reproductions of more than 125 000 exhibits and artworks. To offer their service to the public free of charge is largely made possible due to funding via the BankGiroLoterij, the national cultural lottery of the Netherlands, with an annual grant of around seven million Euros (BankGiro Lottery, 2019) and other sponsors like kpn, an IT and telecommunications supplier (KPN, 2019). Today that digital collection includes over 380 000 high-resolution works of art, with continuous support and redesign of the interfaces, interaction opportunities, and platforms used (Gorgels, 2018).

Even in the absence of these restrictions, it would be hard to follow suit and implement the necessary steps to achieve similar results. Since there is no designated entry point and most solutions are highly individualized, based on the dedicated scenario, and unique to the particular museum or area.

Products like commercial collection management systems do exist (Wu & Chua, 2008). Those can help to mitigate the effect of fragmentation by providing standardized interfaces for metadata exchange (Kraemer & Kanter, 2015), but do not well enough integrate specialized components necessary to prepare data into a narration or to be accessed by the nonprofessional visitor. The target audience for that kind of digitization of metadata mostly are experts, such as researchers and other museum professionals.

Those conditions not only dampen but mostly circumvent innovation, as digitizing and digitalization projects require dedicated resources to be invested upfront, clearly beyond the obligatory tasks, such as finance, time, staff, and overall know-how. Furthermore, small museums do not usually have access to those consistently.

For that reason, smaller institutions that are more inclined toward the visitor-facing aspects of ICT are avoiding databases, content management, digital knowledge accumulation, and other *bottom-up solutions*. The claim to have long-term benefits for growth, development, and digital strategy sometime down the road is no convincing argument if the goal is just to solve short-term issues.

However, the danger when just the visible result is considered, and the short-term results are prioritized over long-term benefits, is to trip the pitfall of *top-down exploration*. In digital projects, the overhead and ongoing maintenance costs are much higher than those associated with traditional channels and print media, later within its lifecycle (Shenton, 2003). Mindsets in the cultural sciences are often tied to printed publications, and therefore, museum professionals often are inclined to transfer their learned experiences and behaviors to digital products, as suggested in subsection 3.2.2. That often leads to missing semantic relationships of content and reduces the interpretability of digital output in general (Walker, 2008).

The schematic overview of the overall conditions is presented in **Figure 3.18**.

Thus, it is immensely important to introduce integrated innovation through tangible use cases, immediately demonstrating the first-hand benefits of these tools. At the same time, the long-term responsibilities (Baumgaertner & Lehner, 2017.1) are to spark interest and give museum professionals a chance to explore the possibilities at their own speed by gradually extending their capabilities in a continuous manner without losing progress when shifting directions.

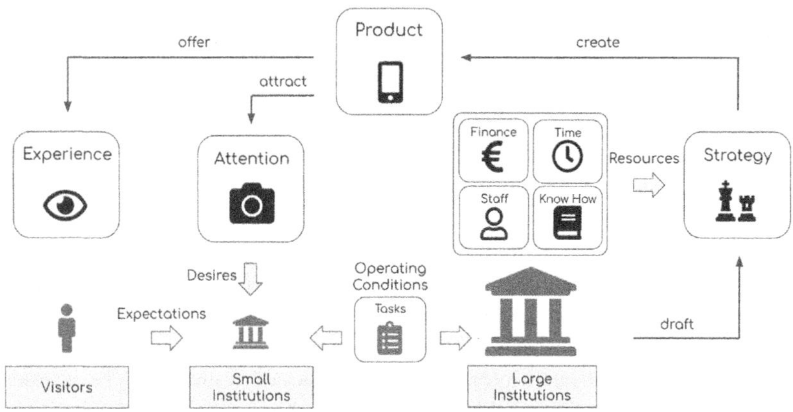

Figure 3.18 Comparison between the Top-Down and Bottom-Up Approaches Encountered in Small and Large Institutions.

In that position, a compromise must be reached to cultivate the museum's integrity, accepting that museums cannot implement every single facet that is technically possible but need to define their own goals and focus on their own abilities to accomplish their own lasting success. It is necessary to provide a path that combines immediate benefits and visualizes results with the possibility of long-term cultivation and strategic development (Kotler & Kotler, 2000).

3.4 Summary: Internal Conflict and Challenges

The unique environment, which unfolds within the Museum Application Domain, requires special attention. Because of the historically grown processes inside the museum, based on the collection of cultural heritage artifacts, those institutions possess a firm temporal and spatial moat, which does not incentivize innovation (Zan, 2000) (Alexander & Alexander, 2008).

Therefore, it is difficult to adopt elements necessary to conform to the newly formed expectations toward providing information in a collection-centered approach. The visitor's expectations are triggered by digital transformation, which also changes the composition of the audience (Baumgaertner & Lehner, 2017.1). The internal perspective and role of the museum professional are immediately affected by that disruption (Baumgärtner & Lehner, 2017.2). The core competencies required to fulfill the new expectations set by other destination attractions and innovators within the field cannot be expected in addition to the skill set necessary to fulfill the original role in the field (Perkinson, Bischoff, & Burke, 2003).

Thus, it is important to enhance the outside view, which includes accommodating the educational role of the museum, embracing the learning environment, and enhancing communication with the museum visitor (Bamberger & Tal, 2009) (Edinger & Reimer, 2015). These goals can be achieved by adopting new technology (Christensen, 2011).

Today, a BYOD strategy can aid in indicating the intent to adopt modern digital technology while simultaneously reducing the entry barriers (Walker, 2008) (Petrelli & O'Brien, 2018). Because of the explosively increasing complexity of media outlets, museums depend on an entry point to gain access and confidence.

These challenges weigh even greater for small museums, which cannot access or rely on resources available to larger institutions. The speed of innovation causes massive spikes in complexity, and the lack of a dedicated entry point toward a comprehensive digital strategy makes it difficult to follow suit (Kotler & Kotler, 2000) (Baumgaertner & Lehner, 2017.1).

4 Research Design and Goals

In the past, the adoption of information and communication technology has not been necessary for the Museum Application Domain, as the core assignments were to collect and preserve artifacts of cultural, historical, and scientific value.

However, the impact of the field of tension surrounding the environment has changed market conditions and shifted the center of attention. Today, museums need to compete with other tourist attractions; therefore, their role increasingly relies on communication and the provision of information. Because of that, small institutions feel compelled to imitate the output of first movers and industry leaders. By doing so, they often fail to recognize the necessary effort associated with such an endeavor, especially because of the historically grown structures, which tend to dampen the progressive mindset and adaptability digital projects require.

Nevertheless, the step from the passive role of a collector toward adopting an active engagement with a casual museum audience makes it necessary to investigate digital channels to engage and analyze visitor needs. A balance to how much 'digital' the museum can sustain (Hume & Mills, 2011), without overshadowing the actual museum experience, needs to be identified.

The structural and technical barriers must be recognized, especially within smaller institutions. It is necessary to determine and provide a dedicated entry point for museum professionals. The first step is reducing the friction associated with data inquiry to be able to introduce innovative products at the point of intersection with the visitor. Concepts like utilizing the benefits of smart mobile devices without the immediate necessity to restructure the existing processes are one way to initially approach that complex subject in a visually compelling manner. Utilizing the visitor's device to provide information during their museum visit in a BYOD strategy can assist museum professionals in engaging in the creation of dedicated content in addition to their existing mandatory tasks.

T. Baumgärtner, *A Software Framework for Mobile Apps in the Museum Application Domain*, Gabler Theses, https://doi.org/10.1007/978-3-658-44367-2_4

This chapter first analyzes the problem areas to highlight the misalignment within cultural heritage institutions and help to identify a foundation for tangible goals (*Section 4.1—Problem Areas*). Next, the relevant research problems to be addressed throughout this thesis are derived (*Section 4.2—Research Problems*). Finally, the research paradigm and methodological approach applied in the pursuit of cultivating a solution are described (*Section 4.3—Research Paradigm*).

4.1 Problem Areas

The general influence of information and communication technology on the Museum Application Domain does spark the interest of many disciplines. Each of those disciplines, however, follows a different path along the problem-solving process. The influence of stakeholders, the emphasis on their perspectives, the implementation process, as well as the evaluation of results all do impact and transform the initial perception of the problem. Thus, adopting a dedicated search process and identifying the objectives accordingly may differ tremendously depending on the socio-technical context and the applied perspective. The potential imbalance between the identification of user and quality requirements and their architectural implications exerting themselves at the stages of software engineering generally creates further challenges (Krempels, Ohler, & Terwelp, 2019), especially in agile development environments (Schön, Winter, Escalona, & Thomaschewski, 2017) that require short-term iterative evaluation cycles to be aligned with a long-term strategy.

Basic requirements engineering does fail to yield the necessary gain of knowledge needed to achieve certain objectives upfront. Especially if the degree of innovation on the structural, strategic, or organizational level exceeds the conceivable outcome, the solution space itself is going to be transformed and disrupted. In combination with IT agnostic environments, that may lead to the misdirection of focus or ambiguous requests because of missing experience. Then, vague desires cannot sufficiently be translated into achievable goals. Thus, obtaining alignment between business problems and fitting IT solutions is often compared to "drawing a line in the sand" (Luftman & Kempaiah, 2007).

Regularly, it is not possible or sufficient to initially capture the status quo to define the problem boundaries because of the evolutionary attributes of the potential solution. However, involving stakeholders and potential users of the resulting product demands strict discipline to not get distracted by minor details while the big picture is diluted or completely lost (Schön, Winter, Escalona, & Thomaschewski, 2017).

Potential solutions are regularly underestimated or omitted entirely if the necessary steps to solve underlying issues cannot be adequately characterized. Commonly, one of two situations will occur. On the one hand, management is overwhelmed by the decision-making process, and IT representatives take over too early (Kaidalova, Seigerroth, & Persson, 2017). The resulting bottom-up solution then often will not satisfy the original desires and thus is not able to solve the original problems. On the other hand, operational demand overshadows desires. Delaying tactics and resource allocations lead to top-down solutions, avoiding changes required to adapt a sensible solution. The absence of structure may cause misaligned responsibilities leading to missing accountability, which invalidates efforts to reach a consensus on an organizational level.

Those issues are magnified even further if incorrect assumptions or wrong perspectives lead to interference in addition to incomplete goals. Thus, in most cases, it is not enough to only improve initial requirement specifications. It is mandatory to enable communication between all parties involved, initially and throughout the entire process. To identify the correct starting point for that conversation, first, the existing gaps within the organizational environment need to be identified (Reinheimer & Robra-Bissantz, 2014).

To do that, the conversation needs to be extended beyond the insulated view of people, technology, and information within a particular domain. A wider degree of comprehension is necessary to separate fads from trends to guide the path of innovation and avoid standstill in an efficient manner. Capturing insights into developments within an array of areas of application is mandatory to build lasting knowledge of certain phenomena (Mertens, 1995). Notably, the deep connection with databases, expert-level information, and catalogues in cultural heritage institutions may overcast particular objectives by fixating on the specific secluded context without considering certain elements vital to innovative objectives.

The discipline of Information Systems tries to approach economic and societal questions by connecting them to their technological solutions, applying rigorous methods, and considering concepts in an all-embracing manner. Supplying users and technical systems with information by incorporating application programming and graphical user interfaces to engage the customer is a vital element (Mertens, et al., 2001) (Stormer, Meier, & Lehner, 2005).

Therefore, that field provides the ideal methodological foundation and a balanced knowledge base for the goal of designing a holistic and sustainable approach to resolving influential issues (Stein, Galliers, & Whitley, 2016).

To manifest the approach suggested within the field of Information Systems, the Gap-Model of the Business-IT-Alignment (BITA) provides a valuable tool to

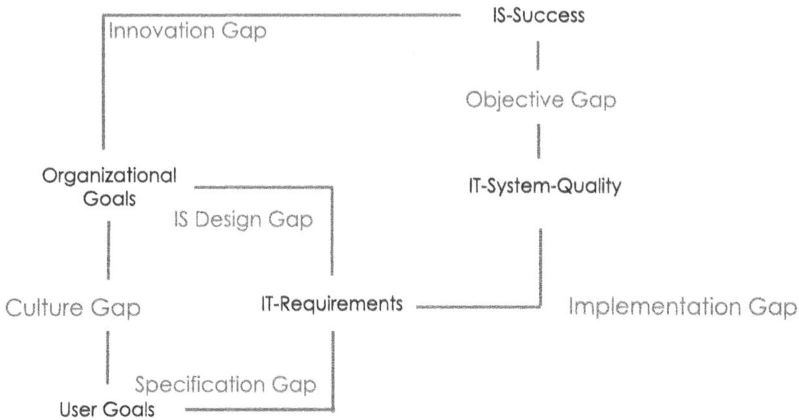

Figure 4.1 The Gap-Model of Business-IT-Alignment (cf. Reinheimer & Robra-Bissantz, 2014, p. 532)

determine deficits and problem areas. This approach should be considered whenever new concepts are discussed, and their impact on the core business is to be evaluated. The model describes six general gaps and their strategic implications that may exist within the context of Business-IT-Alignment, one of the core tasks of Information Systems Research (Reinheimer & Robra-Bissantz, 2014). Those gaps are illustrated in **Figure 4.1**.

In the following paragraphs, each gap is first briefly described and then contextualized within the MAD to highlight the core problem areas encountered within information distribution in cultural heritage institutions. On that basis, the identification of tangible research problems is conducted in the next section.

The **Objective Gap** between 'IS-Success' and 'IT-System-Quality' is described as the discrepancy between the capabilities and the contribution of an information system to the specific problem resolution, independently of the intrinsic system quality. That overarching disparity which may or may not occur, is composed of the remaining five gaps within the model.

The differences between the long-term 'Organizational Goals' and the generally more nearsighted individual 'User Goals', in practice, leads to the **Culture Gap**. These issues are rooted deep within the historically grown structures of the environment surrounding cultural heritage institutions. The tension between keeping consistent internal data structures suitable for long-term archives and providing appealing visualization accessible for the casual visitor is thoroughly described in subsection 3.1.1. Additionally, the missing alignment is reinforced by the hereditary interdisciplinary nature of the research areas Information Systems and Digital Humanities, providing the anatomical knowledge base from the perspective of the researcher. The incentives to conduct research in the general problem area of the Museum Application Domain and the influence of information systems differ greatly between the museum professionals' and the visitors' perspectives. Consequently, the results depending on the specific point of view of the user, are not suitable to fit both viewpoints. However, the combined effort of what it means to provide visitor-facing applications and how these are to be set up, furnished, and maintained is rarely discussed. Yet, in practice, the institutions in question struggle exactly with that responsibility.

The **Specification Gap** exists between 'IT-Requirements' and the particular 'User Goals' within the organization. Taking a close look at the Customer Experience Value Chain, described in subsection 3.1.2, helps to visualize the reliance between individual tasks and intra-organizational communication, as well as the necessity of structured interfaces to avoid loss of quality in the big picture. The **IS Design Gap**, on the other hand, maps the inconsistency between the 'IT-Requirements' and the 'Organizational Goals'. That case is highlighted in section 3.3. Especially smaller institutions struggle to draft consistent propositions suitable for long-term sustainability, as their access to resources is limited. One of the central objectives is the alignment of operational and strategic goals (Forbes, 2009). These issues are also closely related to the **Innovation Gap**. It specifically abates the failure of 'Organizational Goals' to reflect the ongoing technical innovations and the marginal evaluation of shifting market conditions as discussed in Chapter 2 and their strategic reflection, jeopardizing sustainable 'IS-Success'.

The **Implementation Gap** *refers to the divide between the 'IT-System-Quality' and the 'IT-Requirements'.*

That gap can be promptly identified when existing solutions for *visitor applications* and *collection management systems* are observed, as outlined at the beginning of Chapter 6. The core issue emerges from the involvement of different domains and peripheral discipline areas. Multiple levels of perspective need to be reflected throughout design and development stages. The involvement of Computer Science, Psychology, and Software Engineering on both ends of the spectrum of the area of examination makes it imperative to define a purposeful concept directed toward overall feasible and attainable goals.

In **Figure 4.2**, the two protruding gaps are brought face to face with the specific issues encountered in the problem environment within the Museum Application Domain. These problem areas are primarily observed while investigating potential solutions throughout the remainder of this thesis.

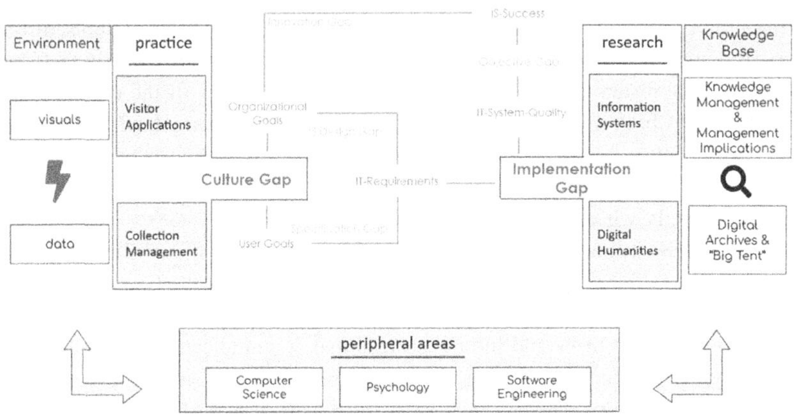

Figure 4.2 Dominant Problem Areas in the Museum Application Domain

Therefore, addressing the *Culture Gap* is an important step. Reducing organizationally induced friction and emphasizing the possibilities of technological innovation can provide a foundation for a conversation. Highlighting the coherence between data inquiry and user application interfaces which target both the consumer and the creator, does prepare a connection necessary to take further steps. This enables the consistent verbalization of requirements as well as realistic expectations toward the resulting implementation in practice.

Consequently, it is important to address the *Implementation Gap* to minimize the divergence between the two core disciplines involved in the overall search process. The resulting information system is supposed to accommodate both perspectives. The needs of collection management are met by maintaining a consistent data model to be searchable and shareable. The app targeting the visitor provides a visual and conceptual anchor by offering visualization options for their specific needs and the museum professionals involved in the content creation process.

4.2 Research Problems

The normative approach of the BITA-Gap-Model does raise awareness and sensitizes the external observer toward the existing problem areas. However, it does not project any potential path to a solution. To summarize, the pivotal issue is the lack of an entry point to the general adoption process of information and communication technology for the MAD, especially for small museums. The disconnect between the necessary creation of structured data by the museum professional and the desired visualization of content directed toward the visitor prevents the adoption of certain solutions and innovation in general. Thus, the Implementation Gap closely intertwined with the Culture Gap inherent to those structural issues of the Museum Application Domain are emphasized throughout the following investigation.

Those circumstances consequently open up an array of questions spanning from the economic implications, of issues stemming from the humanities, to in-depth technical problems. The reflection needs to be balanced between the development aspects, including the significance of real-life application and the human-computer interaction from both the technical and the user-specific perspectives regarding the interpretability of the emerging digital assets. The dominant influence of technology and the possibility to harvest the power of smart mobile devices does offer museums the capability to interact with their audience by providing innovative mobile applications. A BYOD strategy allows even small museums to participate without excessively committing resources.

However, to do that, it is necessary to establish an overall digital strategy to inquire, file, and supply structured data for such products. The concern of how much functionality a contextual random-access guide for the deployment within a museum needs to initially offer has to be addressed. It must appeal to the visitor while simultaneously creating sufficient value for the institution and its members without dissipating scarce resources. Additionally, the uncertainties associated with the initial setup and its long-term operation need to be eliminated. Providing guidance for smaller institutions to recognize the interdependencies between the benefits to their visitors and the related mandatory tasks expected from the museum professional's point of view is imperative.

To overcome that complexity, this dissertation does focus on three pivotal research problems. The first is committed to the fundamental conceptual implications; the second is concerned with the socio-technical perspective and the technical design; and the third is focused on the practical feasibility and academic implications of the resulting software framework. The evaluation of the findings and the IT artifact concludes the study (compare: Chapter 8).

RP1. *"Which fundamental ideas need to be considered to reduce the persistent inconsistencies emerging from the divide between technology, people, and strategy in the MAD?"*

The task with the highest urgency is to closely analyze the general problem of communication between technical and non-technical personnel as well as the creator and consumer of content or client and supplier, respectively. The lack of knowledge to accurately characterize and evaluate the vital points of contact to introduce innovation is rooted within the Culture Gap, leads to the misalignment in digital projects from the very beginning, and causes the Implementation Gap. To reduce these hurdles, it is inevitable to define a 'bridging language' so that expectations can be expressed as fulfillable requirements on both an organizational and an individual level. Nevertheless, to reveal these needs, adequate knowledge of the technical components and terms required to characterize a profound solution has to be obtained (Kruger, 2012).

To create long-term value, museum professionals need to recognize the intangible value of structured data. Providing the context of virtue, the efforts can be visualized through immediate results within an information system, presented in a way that an untrained user can access and operate instantaneously. Such a system, to an extent, needs to reflect basic predefined workflows closely related to their existing daily activities.

RP2. *"From a socio-technical perspective, which components need to be considered in a framework design to cover basic expectations towards mobile applications within the MAD?"*

Some of the main issues, when features of a system are approached in a vacuum, may directly originate from the overwhelming possibilities offered by modern and innovative exhibition design. While the realm of digital channels and individualization opportunities can add depth to the visitor's experience, it quickly can get distracting for the visitor and overwhelm the creator. The goal of providing added value for the visitor is closely affiliated with mandatory changes of internal processes that may benefit and enhance the organization as a whole, reflecting the issues summarized within the Culture Gap.

To do that, the limitations associated with the chosen technologies and the application domain itself need to be acknowledged, especially in the context of small museums. Thus, reasonable constraints need to be introduced as early as during data inquiry. That highlights that the endeavor is not only about technology but also must include the creator's perspective to yield a holistic result. Building knowledge and reasonable expectations for those involved in the content creation process, in addition to the visitor's perspective, within the contextualized environment of the MAD need to be prioritized to approach the Implementation Gap sufficiently.

RP3. *"What architectural choices and data structures are necessary to compose A Framework for Mobile Apps in the MAD to reflect the academic urgency as well as the practical feasibility?"*

The underlying data structure and the necessary technical infrastructure of the framework need to be a subordinated element, not requiring initial hands-on interaction. Nevertheless, the interpretability and extensibility of emerging results must be prioritized, and the rules of the data model must be enforced to enable sufficient application quality. Only then the benefits of intuitive visual user interfaces exposed to both user groups can be asserted. Thus, the goal is to facilitate immediate benefits, avoid technology lock-in effects, as well as enabling the tasks of acquiring, conserving, researching, and communicating exhibits in a sustainable and approachable manner to satisfy the identified gaps.

Subsequent to resolving those arguments, the development of a prototype implementation of the framework is methodologically imperative. An IT artifact for the evaluation of the objective fit of the suggested framework solution does provide proof of concept. It allows identifying problems within the target domain and uncovers further concerns and requests not clearly recognizable without such a tool. **Figure 4.3** summarizes the connection between these three questions and the structure of the remainder of this manuscript.

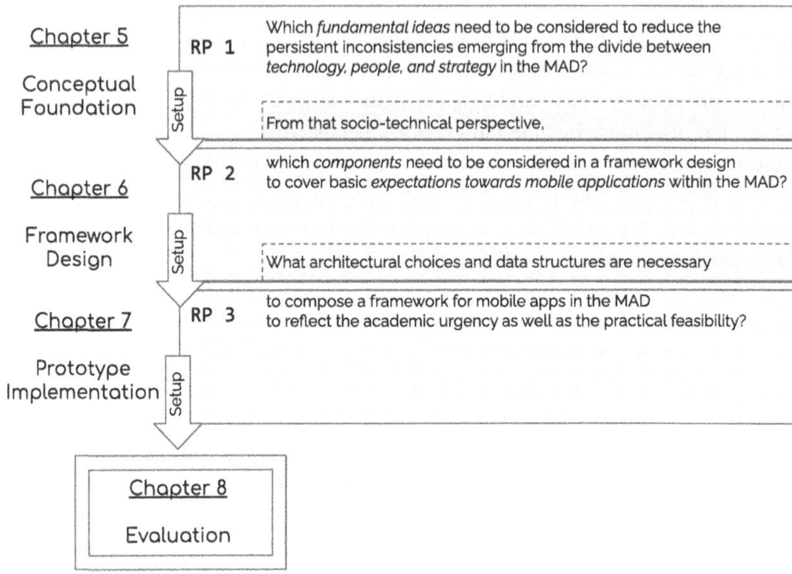

Figure 4.3 Conjunction between the three Research Problems

4.3 Research Paradigm

Especially within the German-speaking IS research community, different paradigmatic orientations are applied when research is conducted. The major distinction in IS research has to be made between behavior science research and design science research. The behavioral approach is more in line with the international understanding of the discipline. The goals include the development and justification of theories that explain human or organizational behavior. These procedures usually concentrate on narrow issues and most often deploy one specialized method to examine a particular or isolated problem. In contrast, the intent of the design approach is to create novel IT artifacts to solve organizational problems. As this technique requires multiple steps to build and evaluate suitable solutions, the majority of propositions require multiple methods to conduct the research appropriately. German-speaking countries have historically been driven by engineering disciplines; thus, the design approach is more dominant here (Friedrich, Schlauderer, Weidinger, & Raab, 2017).

While the research paradigm generally summarizes "the most fundamental set of assumptions adopted by a professional community", a research method itself is defined as "a set of activities that must be undertaken to conduct the research" (Friedrich, Schlauderer, Weidinger, & Raab, 2017).

The solitary argumentative-deductive analysis of the situation within museums may contribute to the identification of the shortcomings of the target environment. Evaluating the present circumstances in the Museum Application Domain, as performed throughout Chapter 3, does primarily contribute to the synthesis of the solution space; yet, on its own, it is not sufficient to subsidize solving the identified underlying issues. The serious practical implications require the ability to tap into a significant amount of knowledge distributed among various other disciplines. Unraveling the potential resolutions concealed within the original complexity of the targeted application domain requires a research approach that allows the examination of concepts beyond the passive observation encapsulated within the preexisting mindset of museum professionals.

Furthermore, the fact that many smaller cultural heritage institutions do not yet deploy any form of information systems that could possibly provide the basis for behavioral observation or collection of data to allow for obtaining knowledge at this point in time, a design-oriented approach is advantageous anyway.

In consequence, because of its hybrid and interdisciplinary nature, as well as the practical implications, information processing within the characterized setting of visitor interaction in museums involves technical, personal, organizational, philosophical, linguistic, and mathematical elements. That is challenging regarding both method selection and continuous interpretation, as well as the eventual evaluation of results. This does present serious boundary conditions, particularly true for innovative information systems, designed to solve novel problems in unique environments, as no two organizations are completely alike (Antill, 1985).

Thus, repeatability may be achieved only in a very abstract and narrow sense but not over the entire system, including organizations and stakeholders. The investigation itself impairs the repeatability of results because it changes the initial situation in which it is to be inserted. In these situations, the experience and observations by the designer have to be applied to the problem rather than being an impartial observer of reality (Antill, 1985).

The components that enable stakeholders to engage in the process of successfully understanding information systems are called IT artifacts and include *constructs* (vocabulary and symbols), *models* (abstractions and representations), *methods* (algorithms and practices), and *instantiations* (implementations and prototype systems) (Hevner, Ram, March, & Park, 2004).

The *design science research paradigm* (DSR), in particular, facilitates practical relevance to the application domain by elevating the pragmatic approach to IT artifact conception. As suggested, these tasks were originally attributed to technical disciplines. The relevance of design science research regarding the effectiveness and utility in the context of real-world business problems was recognized by the IS community in the 1990s (Hevner & Chatterjee, 2010).

To resolve uncertainties associated with that approach, especially in contrast to linear behavioral approaches, a reference frame for design science research has been developed by Hevner et al. (2004). Their approach introduces three circles fundamental to facilitate design science in Information Systems, accompanied by seven guidelines to appropriately conduct the underlying research method. These cycles feature the exchange between the three pillars: 'environment', 'design science research', and the 'knowledge base', as shown in **Figure 4.4**.

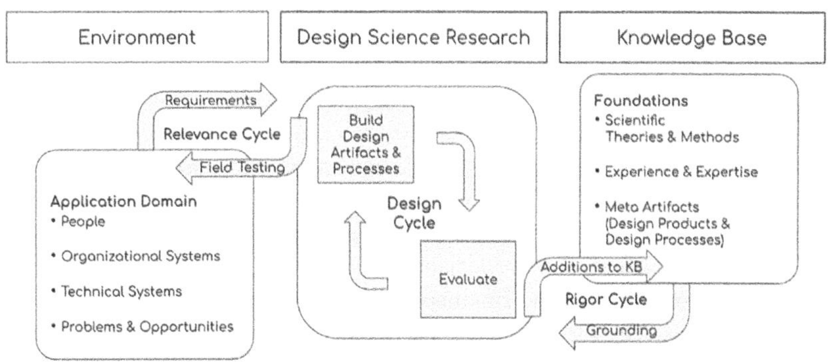

Figure 4.4 Design Science Research (cf. Hevner, Ram, March, & Park, 2004)

The **knowledge base** contains scientific theories and methods that act as the foundation for an accurate DSR execution alongside the specialized experience and expertise of field experts. Additionally, the state of the art and existing artifacts and processes within the application domain (meta-artifacts) are included to enable the grounding of DSR via the 'rigor cycle'. Research results are to be absorbed into those research findings to provide additional knowledge to be then applied by practitioners and included in further research.

In opposition, the **environment** describes the elements of the application domain itself, consisting of people, organizational, and technical systems that interact to work toward a common goal defined by the identified business problems and opportunities. Therefore, the 'relevance cycle' initiates the research process by providing requirements as well as acceptance criteria for the result evaluation of the emerging artifact in the end.

Alongside these described processes, the authors point out seven guideline principles to be followed for the successful conduct, evaluation, and presentation of design science research projects. The most important principle to be followed is the production of a viable artifact (*Guideline 1*). The developed product should address an important and relevant business problem with a technology-based solution (*Guideline 2*). The design artifact then must be evaluated to demonstrate its utility, quality, and efficacy (*Guideline 3*). In addition, effective design science research must provide verifiable contributions in the areas of the design artifact or its foundation (*Guideline 4*). Throughout the process, rigorous methods need to be applied (*Guideline 5*). However, to identify the features of an effective artifact to solve the intrinsic domain problem, the laws of the environment need to prevail in an iterative process (*Guideline 6*). The channels the research is communicated to need to address both technology- and management-oriented audiences (*Guideline 7*).

The general idea these guidelines pursue is to ensure that the initial purpose of the resulting artifact is met and to allow for creative approaches while not elevating the method over the relevance of the target result. Furthermore, the artifact definition is to be relaxed to the extent that it does not expect a fully-grown enterprise-level information system but rather a simplified abstraction to firmly convey the innovative character and its technical capabilities. They also should include well-documented constructs, models, and methods involved in the development process (Hevner, Ram, March, & Park, 2004).

Drechsler and Hevner (2016) themselves closely monitored the developments surrounding that method and tried to account for the dynamic nature of IS artifact design within certain context domains by introducing a fourth cycle to their model, namely the 'change and impact cycle'. It extends the immediate application context by the socio-technical system context to include the second-order impacts of an artifact being adopted within the organization, as well as its long-term effects. That external view also includes the problem trigger, which does set the original cycles in motion, previously not being an explicit part of the model itself. That allows for the resolution to be approached in a more agile fashion and include objectives beyond just the development of a single artifact to contribute toward the extension of the volatile knowledge base.

The view on how the artifact is to be evaluated is also altered. More emphasis is put on the search process, resulting in general fit being valued more than the directly observable utility, which generally is difficult to quantify. That observation is grounded within entrepreneurship literature, moving from a narrow, causation-oriented view to an effectuation-oriented approach taking the long-term organizational and general societal transformations into account (Drechsler & Hevner, 2016).

Next to the conception of design artifacts, their evaluation, in theory, is a key activity to assure the rigor of the research. However, the guidance provided by DSR literature often is insufficient to generate satisfactory feedback for further development and research. That can be attributed to the nature of the procedure, as each instance is unique. As the initial situation is often iteratively distorted as it is necessary to establish and apply certain changes, it is not always evident if improvements were achieved or when, why, or how to evaluate the progress against the status quo. Thus, it is not trivial for the evaluation to be both effective and efficient, especially if time is of the essence. The Framework for Evaluation in Design Science (FEDS) tries to provide guidance to establish a path to proper evaluation strategies. To do that, it suggests two dimensions, the functional purpose of the evaluation (formative vs. summative) and the paradigm of evaluation (artificial vs. naturalistic). Within those dimensions, the process is further broken down in four steps: To set the goal (1), choose the strategies (2), determine the properties to evaluate (3), and design or derive the evaluation episodes (4) (Venable, Pries-Heje, & Baskerville, 2016).

The key aspect of design science research remains to address unsolved problems in a unique and innovative way to grow the knowledge base, which later can be applied by professional designers to known problems (Hevner & Chatterjee, 2010).

Case studies are frequently deployed for gathering feedback on design science research projects and the impact of the artifacts they yield, while prototyping is more uncommon. Less than 10% of research articles pursue instantiations in the first place (Friedrich, Schlauderer, Weidinger, & Raab, 2017).

Introducing apps within the heterogeneous environments encountered in small museums requires prototyping as an integral component. Otherwise, the evaluation and generalization of the desired qualities of the framework's conceptualized model would become impossible if compiled in a vacuum, as the intrinsic value of the software framework is based on the utilization of the resulting mobile applications.

The development of *A Software Framework for Mobile Apps in the Museum Application Domain,* therefore, must not end with the conception of a basic proposal or an abstract model. To offer a relevant solution to the identified problems, the development needs to be pursued to such a state, which can be made available to and tested by those who are actually supposed to benefit from it in the intended setting. The chosen method of DSR to be concluded with a prototype implementation thus provides sufficient flexibility and accommodates iterative progression throughout the scope of this thesis and beyond.

Those interdependencies and certain relationships indicative of the research goals need to be addressed to comply with the intentions set for this dissertation. domain-driven design (Subsection 6.1) provides the tools to facilitate the fundamental foundation for the development process; at the same time, human-centered design (Subsection 5.1.3) ensures the essential feedback loop between the introduced concepts within the environment and encourages a holistic view as it enables coherent communication. Creating a common ground between stakeholders encountered in the Museum Application Domain with different levels of technical comprehension is decisive in achieving their mutual goals.

5 Conceptual Foundation

Up until this point, the necessity of a certain scaffold to capacitate the structural and procedural resources mandatory for the digital venture is exemplified. Along these lines, the core idea of a dedicated software framework has been formed to wrap the identified conceptual abstractions in a tangible way, with the main purpose of creating value for stakeholders and transferring the knowledge created. The resulting IT artifact thus needs to go beyond just the technical representation or any one implementation. Hence, consolidated resources and focused documentation need to be provided to purposefully operate said implementation, apply the conceptual findings, and extend both the theoretical model and the corresponding information systems in practice.

Overall, the deficient conceptual awareness, as well as the inability of museum professionals to express or specify their own goals and desires, are closely connected and can be ascribed to the phenomenon of categorical perception. The basis is provided by the linguistic relativity hypothesis, suggesting that expressed language influences mental processes as well as the perception of the exposed environment. The example most often cited to describe this concept is color cognition. The most relevant aspect in the context of this topic is that between-category discrimination is easier than within-category discrimination; i.e., most people can effortlessly distinguish red and yellow, while it is more difficult to determine the difference between the shades crimson and ruby as they are often grouped within the broader category of red. There are two major takeaways applicable to the problems encountered within this thesis. First, many issues are tracked back to the available vocabulary of an individual or a group. Second, that can be improved through thorough definitions, conditioning, and repeated practice (Özgen & Davies, 2002). Thus, this chapter aims to address the first research

T. Baumgärtner, *A Software Framework for Mobile Apps in the Museum Application Domain*, Gabler Theses, https://doi.org/10.1007/978-3-658-44367-2_5

problem related to the *fundamental ideas* and concepts to form the theoretical foundation for the further steps taken during design and development.

The preliminary implications suggest that the underlying issues cannot be solved by an isolated information system or addressed with a software solution alone, as the prevailing lack of knowledge leads to miscommunication and misconceptions, impeding potential progress. Thus, a domain language, including the terms and concepts mandatory to precisely express ambitions and expectations, is necessary, especially in multidisciplinary areas where similar linguistic concepts express different things between the domain experts involved.

In regard to mobile applications in the MAD, the line of sight needs to be extended beyond the product itself, targeting the end user, or consumer, and include the interactions of the museum professional, or creator, as the intermediary user accountable for the content creation process (Baumgärtner, 2019.2). The obligations and responsibilities connected to those tasks are most often neglected. Thus, the composition of the *socio-technical perspective* is deconstructed to set up the second research problem. To ensure quality for the intended product—in this case, a random-access guide for the museum visitor –the expectations and responsibilities, as well as the technical feasibility, need to be emphasized. Thus, the principal elements of human-centered design need to be inducted and propagated throughout the creation process. The influence of psychological phenomena related to the mental model presents valuable insights for the design and development processes involved as well (Stojmenovic, Pilgrim, & Lindgaard, 2014).

In any way, the expectations of the consumer as the primary user group regarding the interaction with the resulting mobile applications have to be preprocessed in regard to technical feasibility and the capabilities of the designated creators. As the museum professional is going to be responsible for the tasks related to data entry, they depend on structure and context to recognize the reasons and benefits of engaging in the efforts of creating structured data (Baumgärtner, 2019.1).

This chapter sets up the conceptual foundation necessary for the design and development processes to conceive the framework. First, the unavoidable terms and recurring concepts contributing to the comprehension of the museal context and the general proposal are defined. This includes the detrimental distinction of the central purpose of a framework, the influence on the approach of knowledge and content, as well as the concepts often encountered in human-computer interactions (*Section 5.1—Important Terms*). By shining a light on the needs of the primary users and the psychology involved in the general interactions and related to the design of on-screen interactions, the necessity for a software framework to provide proper guidance becomes observable. The expectations of the consumer regarding the content are discussed alongside the different procedures for the potential creator (*Section 5.2—Breakdown and Integration of the 'User'*). Those insights provide the gateway for the development of the framework and demonstrate the disparity between the anonymous base situation and the personalized target situation to fathom the comprehensive procedures that need to occur during the design and development processes (*Section 5.3—Setup for Design and Development*).

5.1 Important Terms

Before the relationship between the creator and the consumer can be addressed successfully, the communication between museum professionals and the researcher or developer respectively has to be asserted. To address those perspectives and to establish a common ground for both the design and development processes, it is important to understand the foundation of what is to be included in the audit and consequently expected as a result. This section is devoted to the definition of the essential terms and concepts to form a universal understanding necessary as a foundation for the following sections and chapters.

Notably, the terms and concepts related to the idea of a *framework* (*Subsection 5.1.1—Framework*) need distinct contextualization, as they act as key elements throughout the following phases of design and development. In addition, the difference in awareness of *data* and *content* between knowledge management and within the museum context needs to be clarified (*Subsection 5.1.2—Data and Content in the Context of Museums*). The core concepts of human-centered design do include usability, user experience, and user interfaces (*Subsection 5.1.3—Human-Centered Design*). Those specific insights affect the general approach to domain issues, the system design, as well as the specific project goals.

5.1.1 Framework

It is necessary to distinguish some terms that are related to and commonly confused with the conceptual idea of a framework. The clarifications follow the explanation of Shukla (2017) and cover the four terms platform, library, toolkit, and framework, as compiled in **Table 5.1** (Baumgärtner, 2019.2).

Table 5.1 Distinction of the Term Framework

Term	Explanation	Example
Platform	Target software for which the application software is built.	Mobile Operating System (iOS, Android) Web Browser (Chrome, Firefox, Safari)
Library	Code that provides singular or bundled functions, to reduce the complexity of generic problems , which can be called by the application software.	Mathematical Functions (logarithm, mean) String Operations (capitalize, splice)
Toolkit	A collection of 'tools' that serve a common goal during the application development.	Android Development Kit
Framework	A generic structure or skeleton architecture that enables the implementation of a specific software solution.	AngularJS (JavaScript Framework for Single Page Applications)

A **platform** describes the target hardware or software for which application software is built. That choice may restrict future access to the application, as it happens to be with mobile operating systems. As previously described in section 2.2, the market share of mobile operating systems is split between two major platforms. Because of the varying specifications of those different systems, *native applications* are built specifically for just one single platform; hence, to supply multiple platforms, each one demands an individual implementation. To circumvent that, the internet can provide a universal platform for so-called *web apps*. While there are different vendors offering web browsers, the way information is retrieved and displayed is standardized, which is further investigated in section 7.2. The World Wide Web (WWW), a service accessible on the internet, is overseen by the Web Hypertext Application Technology Working Group (WHATWG) and the W3C (Jaffe J., 2019). While those standards were not reliably implemented into each browser in the past, the collaboration between the two aforementioned organizations and most of the vendors, a consolidation of the underlying software engines between the existing browser implementations today do offer a more unified platform (Bishop, 2020). Since the latest iteration of Microsoft's browser Edge adopted Chromium, the open source project that fuels the dominating market leader, Google Chrome, together with Safari by Apple, three of the four major browsers are based on the WebKit engine or the forked variation Blink closely related to it. According to NetMarketShare, those three make up over 80% on desktop computers and far over 90% on mobile devices if the Samsung-specific Chromium implementation is included. Mozilla's Firefox is based on the Gecko engine and contributes less than 10% on desktop computers and less than 2% on mobile devices (netmarketshare.com, 2020). Another way to approach the development process is *hybrid apps* that are built using a unified language and later packaged or transformed to fit each desired target platform. The reasons for that are mostly related to knowledge and resources needed specifically for each platform. While the development costs for an app depend heavily on the content and desired functionalities, prices quoted for small to medium-sized cross-platform projects approximately range between $35,000 and $70,000 for full native support, while that cost can be reduced to $20,000 to $40,000 in hybrid approaches (Hu, Wang, Bezemer, & Hassan, 2019).

A **library** in this context acts as a shortcut for application development. It bundles and provides solutions for complex computations or common tasks. Functions provided could be developed and self-engineered, but it is usually more convenient not to do that, like in cases requiring basic and widely available knowledge, i.e., trigonometry or plotting data. Functions provided by libraries are usually accessed via Application Programming Interfaces (API).

The term **toolkit** is not directed toward a specific deployment situation but usually refers to any set of software tools that work well together or follow a consistent goal. The term is the baseline for the term Software Development Kit (SDK) used for toolkits, which evolved around the development for a certain platform. Within such toolkits, Integrated Development Environments (IDE) may provide assistance for programmers during the coding process by offering syntax highlighting, consistent refactoring, compiling, and debugging aides.

Finally, the goal of a **framework** is to highlight common components and reusable patterns for a given problem while not dictating the specific implementation, providing a generic structure or skeleton architecture for solving similar sets of problems (Shukla, 2017).

Since a framework is supposed to provide a reusable logical stack, it is much more complex to design and implement, as it needs to fulfill certain criteria to be effective, six of which are described by Hunt and McManus (1998). A framework needs to be *generic* relative to its application domain so that it can be adopted across multiple organizations and applicable to their problems. Because of many of the same reasons, it needs to be *easy to use* to be approachable by those who are truly supposed to use it. Also, it needs to be *complete* in the sense that it provides everything necessary to construct applications, including documentation and instructions on both how to use it and the skeleton structure underneath. That should not prohibit the framework from being *extensible* but rather include instructions on how to modify the default behavior. While it is required to be *flexible* regarding the initially intended application, it is required to be *robust* from both a conceptual and a technical perspective.

The benefit stemming from the creation of a framework is the common language it provides, which can improve developer and user communication. Components grounded in expert knowledge can promote long-term guidance and provide a structure for change. On the flip side, during the development process, benefits might not be immediately visible as those are validated by hands-on experience rather than abstract testing. That missing methodological support for identifying appropriate objects and abstractions may either lead to an oversimplification or pattern overload. The general guidance for framework development provided by the authors is very similar to the concepts introduced in subsection 6.1, as certain elements overlap with the approaches described in domain-driven design.

To fulfill the aforementioned criteria, the detailed examination of the problem domain (Chapter 3) is important as a foundation for the inquiry of requirements (Chapter 4) as well as the determination of the scope for the initial design. Creating a common ground also mandates the prior abstraction of the domain knowledge and the interpretation of the viewpoints of the stakeholders (Chapter 5). Along those lines, the diagnosis of existing (sub-)systems and gaps within the domain context to identify possible components and interfaces to create the necessary compatibility for future adaptation or at least alignment between systems for possible hooks or for later additions to the framework. Subsequently, the construction of a skeleton for the framework provides the basic abstract infrastructure (Chapter 6). That then serves as the foundation for an iterative refining process for the concept and its default behavior and user interaction. At this point, it is unavoidable to produce a concrete instantiation to test its organizational utility and general environmental fit (Chapter 7). That instantiation needs to be accompanied by comprehensive documentation from a design, implementation, and the user's perspective. For the first contact with the components, guidelines should be provided to the user in a cookbook-style manner for particular operations. Furthermore, it is necessary to convey the expert knowledge that went into the design and development, which often is not covered by the code itself. Software components may transfer code rather than encapsulated knowledge and transport the details of the framework both in design and in use as well as reuse, which should be the ultimate goal of the framework itself. Within the realm of object-oriented programming, the architectural concept of *patterns*, attributed to the architect Christopher Alexander, has been applied to document reusable components to preserve the attributed knowledge. To allow the extension of a framework and to contribute to the reusability of its abstract components, the documentation must provide the purpose of the framework, how to use the framework, and the detailed design of the framework too (Hunt & McManus, 1998).

For the MAD, that implies enabling members of cultural heritage institutions—despite the lack of IT skills—to independently create contributions for their visitors in a professional manner by providing the technical software framework. By doing that, museum professionals do not need to answer the technical questions right out of the gate and can concentrate their efforts on developing and enhancing the output intended for their visitors. Additionally, they are enabled to later engage in further development once the foundation has been established, as hinted in section 2.2. Furthermore, the financial burden is lifted as the underpinnings for the content structure are not to be developed from scratch in the very beginning (Noschka-Roos & Kapschulte, 2020).

5.1.2 Data and Content in the Context of Museums

In knowledge management, as a part of Information System Research, the data-information-knowledge-wisdom (DIKW) pyramid is a common and accepted hierarchical model. The concept has been borrowed from a poem from T.S. Elliot from 1934; however, the model itself is attributed to Ackoff (1989). While the elements themselves are well described in a business process setting (Rowley, 2007), as summarized in **Table 5.2**, one of the issues that the model is confronted with is the lack of proper definitions of the relationships between the basic concepts, which leads to uncertainties within the very model. The bottom-up hierarchy suggests that the lower layers are supposed to add value to the higher ones as they become more human-dependable. Thus, they are less programmable as they require interpretation.

Table 5.2 Terms of the DIKW Pyramid

Term	Explanation
Wisdom	A wider accumulation of knowledge, on a unique and personal level, applicable to new and tricky problems with an emphasis on ethical and practical foresight (know why).
Knowledge	The understanding and capability to enable the transformation of information into instructions (know how),
Information	Data which is given a structure to represent properties of objects, events,or their environments, making it useful and relevant (know what).
Data	Symbols without any meaning or value, because of the lack of context and interpretation (know nothing).

Data and *information,* however, can appear in different granularities depending on their underlying signals and thus pose different demands on the respective structure depending on the use case and the actors interacting with the system regarding their observable properties and the symbolic representation. For that reason, some scholars argue for inverting the pyramid to a top-down approach, as meaning needs to be added to the lower levels by the concepts which are conceived in the higher ones (Rowley, 2007).

Because of recent developments regarding architectural concepts and the implications for database designs in application contexts, as discussed in subsection 6.4.1, the pyramid today is often considered unsatisfactory in a technical or transactional sense. The hierarchical structure is often no longer sustainable in practice, with the concept of document-based storage increasingly gaining popularity. The possibility to structure data in a way that the intended informational context is conveyed so that knowledge can be inferred directly has not existed. Thus, creating knowledge is the key element to enable users to ask the right questions, which can then be applied toward iteratively building wisdom and supporting the decision-making processes moving forward. The intangibility of that concept restricts the possibilities of observation, and thus, research regarding wisdom in that sense is very limited (Rowley, 2007) (Frické, 2019).

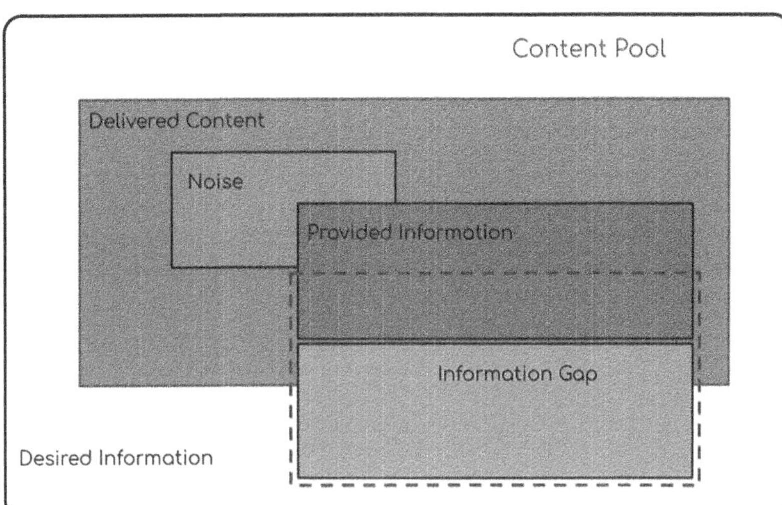

Figure 5.1 Content and Information Interaction (cf. Excolo, 2014)

The fundamental idea is that information is being inferred from data to create value for the consumer. *Content*, similar to information, is a set of data that is supposed to provide a certain value for the recipient. In addition to that, content is required to be loaded with a particular message and address a certain audience. That goes beyond just the specific loaded data and consists of the significant conversational elements of the subject matter, including visual packaging, as well as the behavior and timing of the delivery, which does constitute the *content pool*. Those ascendancies may dilute the intent of the provided information. Therefore, the goal is to reduce the *information gap* by attaining the desired information of the intended audience while avoiding contamination with excess *noise*, as summarized in **Figure 5.1** (Excolo, 2014).

Structuring data in such a way that it is accessible to dedicated users at their convenience is relevant in every field connected to information technology. In any way, shape, or form, data thus is usually the most fundamental element, as information systems are supposed to generate, store, retrieve, and process data (Ackoff, 1989). Capturing data is often perceived as an anonymous and enclosed task that ends in itself. A system, however, consistently needs to transcend the sole lexicographic function of a dictionary. That generates operational problems, especially in environments where information and communication technology is not a key success factor and data is inherently understood as an index where the goal is to ensure searchability, like in a library.

Within the Museum Application Domain, collections need to be administered in the same way. Thus, content management systems for the specific intent to be deployed for the functional purpose of keeping track of the collection are often referred to as *collection management systems*. To an extent, those can include further components necessary for operational efforts, like handling customers and contracts relevant to domain tasks associated with the lending and borrowing of certain objects or digital assets. The base motives, however, are steadily linked to the internal processes and the metadata about certain items necessary to keep track from the curator's point of view.

When the data has an inherent structure to it and is tied to a certain purpose, which is well understood within the domain and by its experts, these records can represent the building blocks for the information to be managed (Tombs, 2004). That can create a more personal relationship for those responsible and does highlight the value of the inquiry, as visualized in **Figure 5.2**.

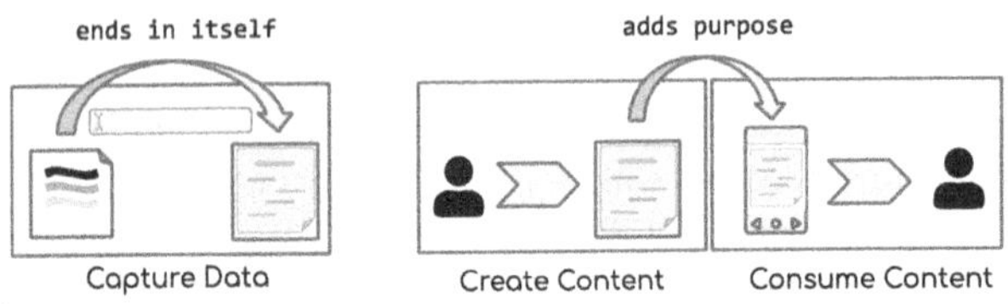

Figure 5.2 Inquiring Data vs. Creating Content

If specific rules are applied to ensure the integrity of the underlying data and to enforce a certain structure, the collection of a set of such rules is referred to as an *ontology*. Today the term knowledge graph, popularized by an initiative started by Google in 2012 as a complement to its string-based search service, is often used as a synonym for a free-form ontology using a graph-structured data model (Paulheim, 2017).

The issue with these rules is the lack of interoperability between institutions, if they do not comply with industry-wide standards, or if those standards are not widely adopted because of their complexity or the lack of implementation (Van Ruymbeke, Hallot, Nys, & Billen, 2018). Thus, it is necessary to look beyond the technical ontology or its implementation and provide a more simplistic reason for structuring data in a certain way if the goal is to provide an association with the designated content. Purposeful data visualization upon the moment of inquiry may ensure consistency and quality within the specific context of providing apps in the MAD.

Ultimately, that is the reason to break down content into its informational components, as well as the layout and presentation layers. That process usually results in the addition of computer-readable attributes and other metadata to create extensibility and compatibility with other information systems, even outside the designated context.

Regardless of the intended purpose, the proper management of that related data always leads to implicit value, but in a situation where the internal structures of an institution do not demand the collection of specific information, no explicit value can be extracted, thus rendering the inquiry dispensable. In these situations, often encountered in small museums, rather than approaching information systems from the museum professional's perspective, the content expected by the visitor as the user within an exhibition setting needs to act as the focal point. This also enhances the understanding of museum professionals, who often dismiss the structural benefits of content and thus are tempted to rely on information, even when the goal is communication with the visitor.

Multiple possibilities are available to process, cluster, and deliver certain information, which populates the initial content pool. The effort associated with each of these options varies tremendously based on the means of production, prior experience, and the ability to transport information without creating disproportional noise. Those complexities associated with the different levels of the content creation process are often overlooked.

The most basic approach is to use text to deliver an intended message. However, the text must meet certain linguistic and structural criteria to conform to the wishes of the designated audience. Within the MAD, even that often poses a challenge if the visitor is addressed since most publications are intended for a professional audience. Therefore, existing material cannot just be repurposed but needs to be specifically modified or personally produced for the intended assignment.

Similarly, this is the case with visualization aides. Using certain figures, graphs, and images may increase the intake of information, while others cannot be fathomed by a casual audience or are not suitable for the exhibition setting or the display on mobile devices.

Games throw a bridge to increasingly intricate compositions. They provide a viable tool to allow for an interactive discord and can combine various forms of content, which also may drastically increase their complexity. As previously pointed out in subsection 3.2.1, even small text-based games can aid the retention of critical information for the museum visitor. At that, the challenge is to identify the appropriate elements as well as the point of balance between the threshold of originality, the ability to carry the desired information, and lasting maintainability for those taking the role of the creator.

That is also applicable to audiovisual content. However, in addition to the requirements of the previously described types of content, the production value is to be considered; i.e., the technical quality of the output, including sound and cinematography, as well as the means and methods applied to accomplish said quality, which often depends on the time and talent devoted to the project. The creation of text or even still images is relatively inexpensive, measured by the necessary tools and expenditures of audiovisual elements. Even short audio recordings require pre-production planning, including composition and scripting, before recording, followed by post-production requirements, like editing (Cartwright, 1996).

Today, standards in film are even more difficult to realize as the required equipment, like 4k cameras or drones, and their operation to meet modern expectations exceed commonly available or accessible appliances.

Those thoughts have to be extended toward digitalization techniques like topographical scans or magnetic resonance tomography (MRT), necessary for the creation of 3D models of exhibits or buildings encountered in the museum. The excessive volume of raw data not only exacerbates pre- and post-production but poses logistical concerns as well. The increasing complexity of content by type is illustrated in **Figure 5.3**.

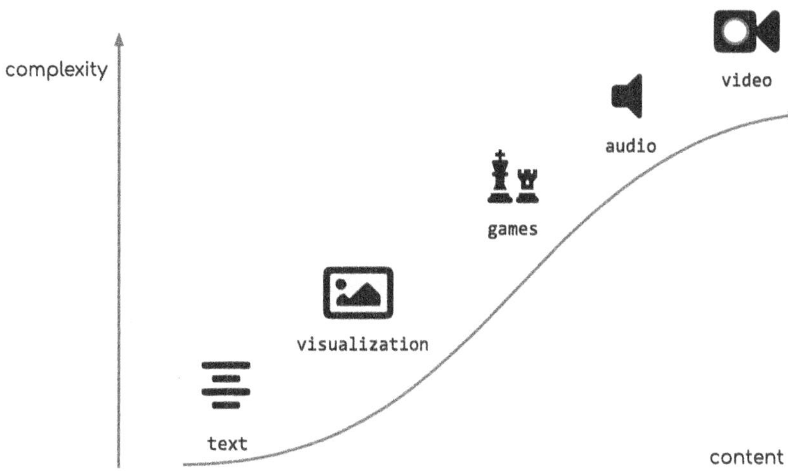

Figure 5.3 Content Complexity

As summarized in section 3.3, well-crafted examples exhausting the whole spectrum of complexity do not necessarily reveal the resources and ingenuity necessary during production and deployment. Depending on the deductive permutations of each of the content types surrounding the portrayal of a certain message, the transportation medium, as well as the physical manifestation of the ambient environment, further adaptations are necessary. Consequently, it is indispensable to understand the differences and connections between data, information, and content to create and share knowledge. However, not only the sourcing of the information but also its processing and presentation requires associated efforts that are not explicitly visible.

5.1.3 Human-Centered Design

"The term 'human-centred design'

is used rather than 'user-centred design'

in order to emphasize [the impact]

on a number of stakeholders,

not just those typically considered as users."

(ISO 9241–210:2010, 2.7)

Many of the identified issues present within the Museum Application Domain transcend the bare business problem at the core, which could be solved by abstract or impersonal design approaches. Thus, the user's perspective needs to be considered throughout the whole problem-solving process to be injected into the aspired solution. Therefore, it does make sense to consider human-centered design. It is characterized as the "approach to system design and development that aims to make interactive systems more usable by focusing on the use of the system; applying human factors, ergonomics and usability knowledge and techniques" (ISO 9241–210:2010). Therefore, this section presents the three most closely related concepts: usability, user experience, and user interfaces. The ISO definitions of these terms are provided in **Table 5.3**.

Table 5.3 Elements of Human-Centered Design

Term	ISO Definition	Core Concept
Usability	Extent to which a system, product or service can be used by specified users to achieve specified goals with effectiveness, efficiency and satisfaction in a specified context of use (ISO 9241-11:2018, 3.2.1).	What is expected from the product?
User Interface	All components of an interactive system (software or hardware) that provide information and controls for the user to accomplish specific tasks with the interactive system (ISO 9241-110:2006).	What is presented to the user on the screen?
User Experience	Person's perceptions and responses that result from the use and/or anticipated use of a system, product or service (ISO 9241-210:2010, 2.15).	How does the user feel during the interaction?

Usability

In the early 1980 s, the term *usability* was conceived with the intention of distinguishing the concept of 'user friendliness'. It was too vague and was convoluted by subjective connotations. In 1991, Bevan et al. discussed three views on which usability should be measured. First, the *product-oriented* view regarding the ergonomic attributes of the product; second, the *user-oriented* view in terms of the mental effort and attitude of the user; and third, the *user performance* view focusing on the interaction of the user and the product. These three views are embedded in the *contextually-oriented* view, taking the environment of the designated user into account (Bevan, Kirakowski, & Maissel, 1991). These considerations are well reflected within the ISO definition.

The purpose of the field of Human-Computer Interaction (HCI) is to bridge the communications gap between the human user and the machine language of an information system. "It is easier to teach a machine how to communicate with people, than it would be to teach everyone in the world to interact with computers" (Winick, 2018). One of the most common design mistakes does occur if that intent is overlooked. Many designers, at some point, are passionate to the degree that 'genius mentality' takes over. That means excluding the target user groups or even the context from the design process and rather relying on the knowledge or previous experiences of the designers themselves. As a result, systems then tend to get more complex, as they exceed their intended features or the abilities of the designated users, which impairs usability (Ray, 2020).

The primary target user group, with the higher number of active transactional interactions with the information system resulting from the desired framework design, is the creator, i.e., the museum professional. Thus, it is imperative that the product can be embedded in their daily routines while at the same time enforcing the structure and context necessary for them to pass on the desired features to the secondary user group, satisfying the desires and expectations of the consumer, i.e., the museum visitor. That puts the museum professional in a tight spot between the developers who want to achieve what is technically feasible, which might exceed their capacities, and the museum visitor, who might not be looking to process historic information on the curator's expert level, as they just want to casually experience the exhibit and thus expect appropriate content.

Additionally, the product is bound by the intended context. If it is necessary to use a device's camera to take pictures of sensitive objects, it must be considered that flash photography may harm certain materials. Those restrictions can be lifted by either adapting to the context, e.g., by installing protective framing, by accommodating the restrictions within the product design, e.g., disabling the camera flash, or by finding an innovative design solution that does not rely on the camera at all.

Moreover, the issue with software is that most processes are run in the background and therefore are not visible to the operator. Thus, almost all usability concerns regarding the users need to be addressed and manifested within the graphical user interface.

User Interface

To facilitate usability, on top of the underlying processes of a computer program, visual cues and elements need to be provided to support the user to interact with a system via a visual interface without them relying on machine language. The historical development of the user interface and the designated input method is presented in **Figure 5.4**.

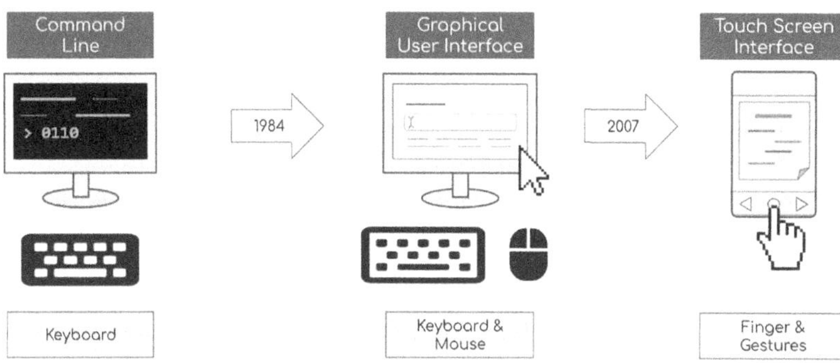

Figure 5.4 User Interfaces and Input Methods

The on-screen representation of intractable elements necessary to manipulate the displayed information at the beginning of personal computers (PC) in 1975 was very limited, as was software in general. The electronic spreadsheet developed by Dan Bricklin in 1978 made the difference, which advanced the capabilities of the PC from an electronic typewriter to a powerful business tool. The input, however, still relied on the 'command line' controlled by only the keyboard (Knight, 2014).

The idea of the 'graphical user interface' (GUI) with a mouse controlling a cursor on the screen to make the computer more appealing for the user had its origin with the Alto by Xerox in 1973. Apple managed to make it available to the masses with their Macintosh computer, released in 1984, primarily by drastically reducing the price. Steve Jobs, the founder of Apple, allegedly announced that the computer he was constructing would "put a dent in the universe". That was substantiated by Microsoft quickly following suit by adopting that look and feel, which does define how most users interact with computers today (Powell, 1997).

The next step was the development of the 'touch screen interface', which allowed the user to perform input interactions directly on their device's screen. The idea has been around since 1968, when it was theorized to be used in air traffic control. The first product to use the name *touch screen* was co-developed by Siemens in 1977. The way we experience touch screens today, in combination with mobile devices, originated in the 1990 s, once again spearheaded by Apple and their handheld Newton PDA, capable of handwriting recognition. While other competitors were able to enter the market with Microsoft releasing the Windows XP Tablet Edition in 2002, those systems were clunky and, at best, could support other input devices or heavily relied on specialized input pens. It took until 2007, for hardware and computing technology to become mature enough to truly support handheld devices requiring nothing more than the user's fingers and their gestures for their input to control the GUI via a touch interface. The release of the iPhone put Apple in the lead once again, making the technology of smartphones available to the public (Bellis, 2018). The further development of the market is discussed in section 2.2, and mobile technologies in section 7.2.

Today, other innovative input methods like voice recognition or conversational interfaces are available but are not considered in the further discussion because of the lack of practical applicability in the specific situation regarding the MAD.

All three of those possibilities to design user interfaces are still viable, while the context of use heavily determines their usability. The command line is often preferred for simple tasks, especially in technical environments; the average user never is inclined to use them and relies on some sort of GUI that guides their interaction. Laptop or desktop computers using the combination of keyboard and mouse are standard in most business environments. Almost all regular users are familiar with the operational mechanics of such a workstation, and necessary inputs can easily be made. Touch interfaces in stationary contexts become increasingly popular in settings where choices and inputs are limited and mostly intuitive for the user as they are familiar with the process, like at ATMs or checkout counters.

A design by itself is not usable or unusable. While the overarching design space may offer nearly unlimited possibilities to display content on a screen, certain constants need to be identified and preserved, especially when system complexity is increasing, as examined in section 3.1. Regarding the creator's knowledge and goals, the interface needs to support them to quickly recognize the available features and guide them through the necessary sequence of actions to fulfill a task upon first appearance. For subsequent tasks, the user should be able to learn from the information provided and apply their knowledge obtained from interacting with the system before on consecutive interactions (Soegaard, 2020).

Some of the greatest decisions concerning user interface design are made because of mechanical restrictions and therefore were not originally designed to be accessible and ergonomic but set to be efficient and feasible. Examples of elements directly translated from the physical realm are telephone keys, media player controls, and keyboards. The user's prior knowledge of interaction in the analog environment unburdened the adoption of the digital counterpart.

The delivery of 'micro-content' (Bruck & Foerster, 2012) on smartphones for the consumer needs to be approached similarly. Content of that nature should not use up more space than one screen can accommodate, comparable to flashcards in the analog world. Thus, avoiding scrolling and information overload (Eppler & Mengis, 2004) does benefit the screen design in the non-stationary context of use of in-gallery guides.

Therefore, the layout needs to fulfill two important criteria. Since the consumer is inclined to use the application in an information-heavy environment, it is crucial that the information offered additionally does not lead to a distraction while still providing added value. Additionally, it should offer continuity; similar information and controls should occupy comparable screen areas, partly grounded in psychology, as discussed in subsection 5.2.1.

Thus, simply addressing product features and interface elements necessary to get the job done in a vacuum without considering the experience of the user while interacting with the finalized system, fulfilling their designated task or goals in the expected environment, may gravely impair usability (Ray, 2020).

User Experience

The resulting perceptions and responses of the interaction with a system comprising the product and the user within the context of use are referred to as *user experience* (UX).

The ISO definition strongly focuses on the resulting outcome, while the origin and the influence from outside the system are not considered. As a result, UX is often reduced to product features, especially the user interface, disregarding the resulting interaction processes fundamentally embedded in the systems and their intangible surroundings. This concept must be approached through a more practical lens with a focus on designing an experience in a broader scope of interest, in an iterative fashion, specifically incorporating the cognitive process of the individual user and their environment (Law, Roto, Hassenzahl, Vermeeren, & Kort, 2009). The components were examined by Arhippainen and Täthi (2003) (Baumgärtner & Lehner, 2017.2).

The baseline is set by the *socio-cultural environment*. An example is the user's language. If it requires special characters or the reading direction is inverted, the scope of design possibilities and their perception of it is affected. Since the software framework is set to be targeted primarily toward creators within Central Europe, this is less of a concern. While tourists do play a significant role on the consumer side in the MAD, and it is possible to accommodate most Germanic languages, considering the necessary skill set of the creator and the context of use, those factors are considered as given. This applies to other cultural influences as well.

How the user experiences the product is primarily determined by the *context of use*. To reiterate, the Museum Application Domain sets clear boundaries for the consumer application. If the area in which it is to be used is remote and has no access to mobile data or Wi-Fi, content associated with that location must not rely on a data connection. It must be pre-loaded onto the user's device beforehand to not be unavailable at the intended location or at an inconvenient point in time.

The *user* then is expected to accomplish a certain task or to fulfill goals within the stipulations set by that context. The means to execute those tasks need to be communicated to the user such that they are clear to understand and evaluate the associated process. The ability to provide product features that can do that sufficiently is the baseline for usability. The optimization of human performance and user satisfaction, both in a pragmatic and hedonic way, is the primary objective of user experience (Bevan, 2009). From the content creator's perspective, that implies being able to recognize the inquiry's purpose and anticipate the results obtained during their system interaction, which in turn are delivered to the consumer.

Just being presented with forms and executing inputs without being connected to the desired structure or the ability to comprehend the necessity of the process impairs their incentive to do so. It clouds the perception of the achievement of pragmatic goals associated with the task's success (Bevan, 2009).

That perception is closely coupled with the ability of the user interface of the *product* to contextualize the anticipated interaction and provide the reflection of the context of use. It causes user experience to be considered especially imparting the evaluation of a product's design (Arhippainen & Tähti, 2003).

The diminishing factors are hidden subtler, resulting from asking for or offering too much information in a narrow time frame (Ray, 2020). These issues are deeply rooted within the user's psychology and tied to fundamental design decisions, which will be mindfully discussed in the next section.

That vast complexity is the reason for the issues in the evaluation of design beyond elements that can be discreetly measured, like the availability of technical resources or loading times. In these cases, expert opinion is deemed the most effective evaluation measure, especially in early-stage development, e.g., during prototype implementation or if experiencing time pressure (Bevan, Kirakowski, & Maissel, 1991).

It is required to adopt a personalized perspective related to each task specifically to recognize the characteristic problems of the user and their issues related to the interaction with a given system.

5.2 Breakdown and Integration of the 'User'

In practice, the ambiguity surrounding the term user is often a problem when complex information systems are discussed. Usually, the expression is supposed to describe a singular entity supposed to interact with a certain interface of a given system. However, as most sophisticated systems are not atomic, often several user groups do collaborate within a larger system environment, each with its own subset of goals, tasks, and responsibilities to be addressed individually at certain times (Baumgärtner, 2019.2). Thus, a holistic outline of the system's composition is unavoidable.

The *infrastructure layer* of a system gets the most attention during the development process as the fundamental component and is not visible to the user. Yet, the rest of the system does heavily depend on the performance of the 'business and validation logic', to ensure that the information, which is put into the system, is processed and translated into valid data, which then can be stored and later used by the 'application logic' to be transformed and delivered.

Within the *interface layer,* the perspective tends to quickly gravitate toward the 'application interface', which is responsible for providing visual access to the existing information and the ability to interact with the system. This does cause issues, especially in system landscapes, including mobile apps, where the consumer's device—a smartphone with a touch-screen interface—is distinctly different from the creator's device to access the backend—usually a stationary computer with separate input peripherals. Consequently, the manner in which the data inquiry is to be performed is often ignored.

That issue naturally perpetuates to the *operator level.* In that sense, the user of an app interacting with the application interface to access the content is regularly considered the exclusive target. The practical implications, however, call for a more ubiquitous approach, extending that 'consumer'-centric view by integrating the perspective of the 'creator' as well. While these two described tasks may be performed by the same entity, the effective goals between data entry and information retrieval are fundamentally different. That is even more difficult within environments where the purpose of recorded information historically is to convey expert-level insights directed toward fellow scholars rather than providing compelling content for external consumers.

These differences thus need to be reflected within the interface layer, which needs to target the purpose and the intent of the designated user. In general, even other systems can be considered users and demand interfaces if they access the data for the purpose of transformation or transportation. Here, however, just the human connotation of the term is considered (ISO 9241-210:2010, 2.7). Machine readability is to be projected by the data structure itself. Thus, it is only relevant to the infrastructure layer at the time of system development rather than the user at the time of interaction.

Figure 5.5 illustrates the typical application architecture of a system composed for information processing for mobile applications. The fact that the technical system is exposed by the interfaces to the users illustrates that the flow of data or information respectively is directional. While the observation typically does

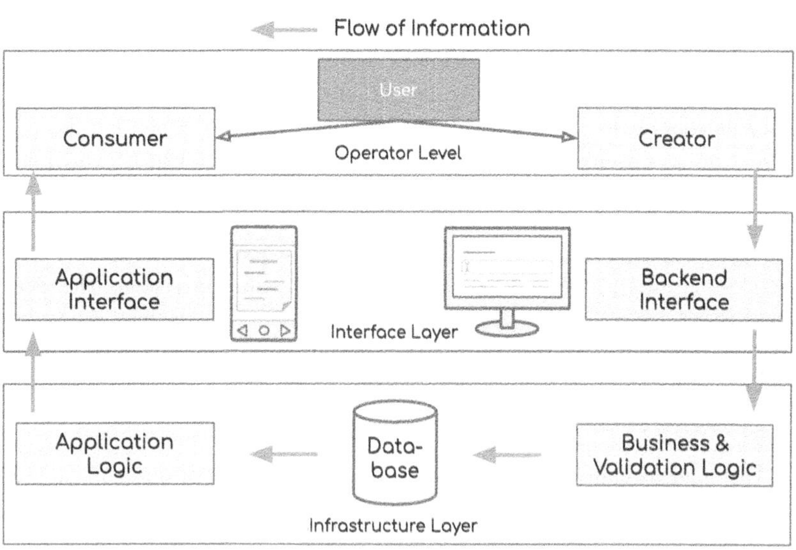

Figure 5.5 Duality of the Term User (cf. Baumgärtner, 2019.2, p. 6)

emphasize the user's perspective, which in itself is often ambiguous, fundamentally, the infrastructure necessary to convey the data model and to provide the interface layer is vital, too (Baumgärtner, 2019.2).

The quality of the presented output at the consumer's end does rely heavily on the upstream system interactions of the creator, as previously described in subsection 3.1.2. Thus, the backend interface required for the data input is at least equally important as the consumer app. Eventually, it is necessary to create a product that appeals to both actors at the operator level. Offering interfaces that enable the creator to produce content accessible to the target consumer audience does require the implementation of human-centered design.

Thus, for a successful design, it is necessary to apply certain principles deeply rooted within the psychology responsible for the perception and processing of information by the user, regardless of them being the consumer or the creator (*Subsection 5.2.1—Psychology in UX Design*). Furthermore, the selection of the content presented to the consumer depends primarily on their specific expectations (*Subsection 5.2.2—'Consumer' Expectation and Content Selection*). To invoke the intended structure for that designated content, the backend interface must facilitate the tasks mandatory for the creator to intentionally approach the data inquiry of the necessary information throughout the process directly related to the physical data input (*Subsection 5.2.3—'Creator' Tasks and Data Entry*).

5.2.1 Psychology in UX Design

To underline the generic contemplation and advance the overall objective, it is mandatory to reiterate the expressions previously introduced. As content is supposed to pursue a defined purpose and is supposed to carry the intent of the creator to reduce the information gap of the consumer, certain criteria need to be met. That linguistic structure itself has multiple layers, which impose a variety of behaviors and outcomes (Mavisakalyan & Weber, 2016). However, to be able to distinguish and apply the applicable concepts, it not only is important to build vocabulary and comprehend the complexity related to their realization. A software framework, as proposed by this thesis, can aid in managing initial expectations, purposefully reduce complexity, guide the user, package logical entities, and showcase real results to facilitate further discussions and aid the selection of which path to follow. Especially for the inexperienced content creator, the depth of possibilities of and the necessities for some decisions involved in the app development process are not clear at first glance. To simplify that decision-making process, good design is necessary to convey the intent of the action required to fulfill certain tasks.

While the ties between psychology and design are quite strong, the goal of this subsection is not to perform a deep dive into the field of psychology itself but rather to illustrate the influence of proven psychological concepts related to some traditional design fundamentals. Some stimuli can be isolated in an experimental setting. However, in the mixed environment of reality, it is more important to not deviate from certain established concepts than to try to control and conform to potential control variables providing only infinitesimal benefits.

The complexity introduced by design and carried by the advances in electronic devices leading up to the 1970 s contained "[a]n impenetrable confusion of forms, colours and noises" (Dieter Rahms). In a quest to counterbalance that trend, the German designer Dieter Rams has laid the foundation for the functionalist school of industrial design. The mentality of 'less is more' and sustainability in design should translate to the form of an object. The goal was to avoid any kind of distraction to the user, thus highlighting the purpose rather than the aesthetics of an object. His designs of the 'Braun T3 Pocket Radio' and the 'ET 66 Calculator' have had a major influence on designers like Jonathan Ive, who was responsible for the design of many Apple products like the iPod and a whole generation of user interface designers (Chadgar, 2015) (Rams, 2019) (Domingo, 2020).

Rams' ideals are compiled in his 'ten principles of good design'. These can also be recognized within the 'ten usability heuristics for user interface design' by Jakob Nielson of the Nielsen Norman Group, developed in 1990 (Nielsen, 1994). These guidelines are brought face to face in **Figure 5.6**, some of which can be directly linked to known psychological phenomena, as is argued below.

Aesthetics, as mentioned in both compilations in points *(3)* and *#8*, can aid in the perception of the product during the intended task from the operational perspective but is a trait open for individual assessment if reduced to just the optical features. Overall, the product is not supposed to be predominately decorative. Thus, it should be neutral and restrained to enable the user's self-expression *(5)*.

Most users, who are supposed to interact with a new system, already have gathered prior experiences and expertise with the aesthetics and the functionality of other systems they previously interacted with. The resulting subjective perception of the representation of an external reality formed by the user is referred to as a *mental model*. These types of cognitive notions allow the user to understand and remember relationships between objects as well as to predict certain events likely to occur during an interaction with a similar product (Stojmenovic, Pilgrim, & Lindgaard, 2014). Deviation from these models can induce cognitive

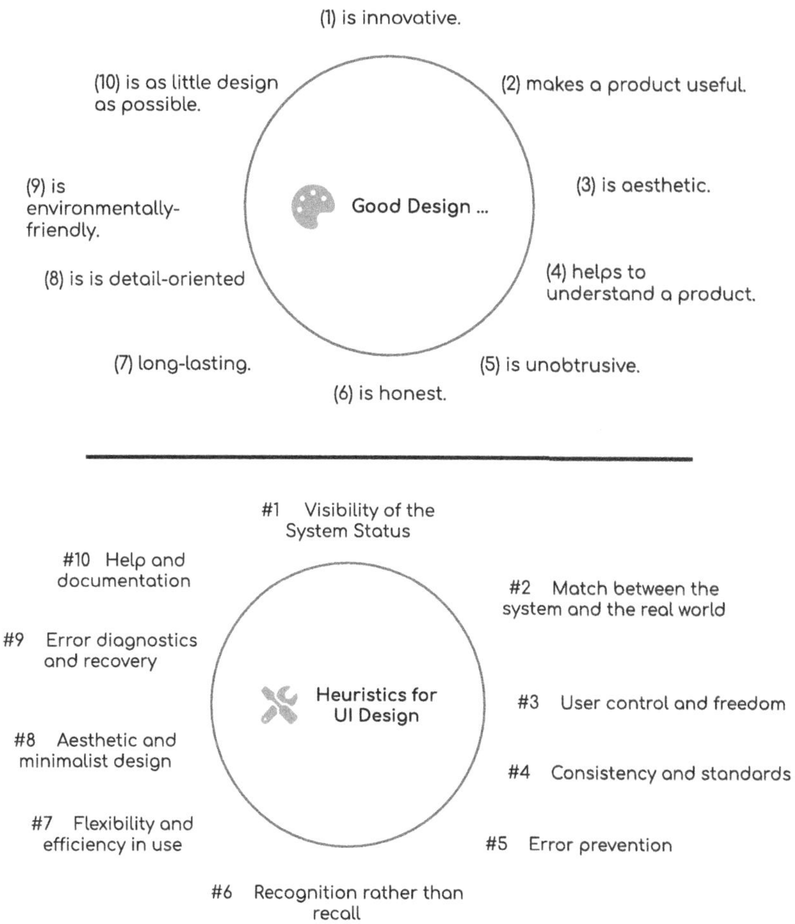

Figure 5.6 Design Principles and Usability Heuristics: The "Ten Design Principles" by Dieter Rams and the "Ten Usability Heuristics for User Interface Design" by Jakob Nielsen

friction and distress, which may impair the usability of the product, as mentioned previously.

Design should put an emphasis on sustainability and longevity, as the product should be able to keep up with its designated task for a long time *(7)*. Users should not have to guess but be able to rely on convention *#4* if at all possible.

The reason why this is important for the success of a product is directly linked to the user's perception. E.g., to gain proficiency, a mental model is necessary for the content creator to master the handling of the interfaces necessary to assemble and deploy visitor applications. For the visitors, it is important to instantly familiarize themselves with the resulting consumer application without any extensive orientation period. To speed up the process, it is crucial to understand that it is very difficult and cognitively exhausting to build that model from scratch in comparison to applying or adapting existing ones to fit the new situation.

Since users spend most of their time interacting with other products, especially in the digital realm, choices in layout and user interface design of popular websites or system interfaces, in general, are a benchmark for many users (Stojmenovic, Pilgrim, & Lindgaard, 2014). That is summarized by the essence of *Jakob's Law.* It states that users will transfer expectations they have built around one familiar product to another that appears similar. If there is a mismatch or inconsistencies between the user's mental model and a specific design choice, mental effort has to be allocated toward the knowledge transfer rather than being spent on the actual task (Nielsen, 2020). That also is closely linked to the mere exposure effect discussed in subsection 3.2.2.

Other than those tangible suggestions, some of the principles are intended as a general reminder of the intention of the design process in the first place. Innovation *(1)* and the emphasis on usefulness *(2)* are integral for design from the very beginning. A product should match the expectations of the user based on the task and fulfill its intended purpose *#2*. There is no reason to manipulate the user with promises that cannot be kept by the product *(6)*.

Directly linked to those concepts is *Conway's Law,* which states that "organizations, which design systems, are constrained to produce designs which are copies of the communication structure of these organizations" (Conway, 1968). That has direct implications for the situation identified within the Museum Application Domain and the impact of their historic roots, discussed in section 3.1. Structures within cultural heritage institutions do not accommodate the visitor's perspective very well. That means the outside perspective revealed by the framework can aid museums in breaking open and reevaluate their own structures while simultaneously reducing the cognitive load necessary to form and reevaluate their existing mental models surrounding existing solutions.

Additionally, the system should give appropriate feedback within a reasonable time *#1*. That can also contribute to reducing the user's memory load by making necessary information and navigational elements only accessible if, when, and where they are required *#6*.

Because of that, it is crucial to be detail-oriented from the start to avoid the inclusion of confusing or unnecessary elements *(8)*. *Hick's Law* postulates that with an increasing number of choices or stimuli, the time the user needs to interpret and determine their appropriate action or reaction drastically increases (Hick & Hyman, 2020).

The focus on the essential elements can emphasize the purpose of the resulting product *(10)*. *Miller's Law* engages the principle that the number of items, which can be processed by an individual at any given time, is around seven, plus or minus two (Miller, 2020). Restricting the relevant on-screen elements to that number as well as grouping related items, does aid novice users in getting accustomed to the product and supports experts in navigating their tasks more efficiently *#7*.

The inputs required from the user should be communicated through the design of the product as much as possible *(4)* and not hidden or obstructed by complex visual elements. Users want to be able to operate the system without having to perform unnecessary actions to quickly reach the desired outcome (Ray, 2020). That has two direct design implications. First, required actions need to be presented in a way that the user can recognize their necessity. Second, results need to be tangible and reasonable in comparison to their perceived complexity.

Mark Rosewater (2011) describes three levels of complexity related to these problems regarding the evaluation of a certain situation and the necessity of the problem-solving ability of the user, which is also commonly encountered in game design. The first stage is *comprehension complexity*. It refers to the ability of the user to intuitively evaluate and comprehend how a certain action is to be performed mechanically.

While the task to fulfill should be as linear as possible, users should have the freedom to take control of the process and mend minor mistakes without losing progress *#3*. Errors, however, should be precisely communicated to the user *#9*, or preemptively avoided by design *#5* (compare: Subsection 5.1.3).

The second level is described as *board complexity* and ties into the sentiment of Miller's Law discussed above. If too many things are to be kept in the user's mind simultaneously to fulfill a certain task, their actions are clouded by the necessity of keeping track of the current state, which can quickly become overwhelming and overshadow the intended outcome.

The third level of *strategic complexity* describes the impact of a single action or choice on the overall task or goal pursued by the user (Rosewater, 2011).

Especially in application software, if the complexity of features needs further description, additional aid in the form of documentation is going to be necessary.

Such additional information needs to be quickly accessible and in itself focused on the user's task *#10* and comprehensibility.

While in physical product design, these choices can help to conserve resources and thus contribute to reducing pollution *(9),* digital products can aid as well, however, from a different angle. For example, reducing the necessity for printed information outlets like flyers does resonate well with an eco-conscious audience, as mentioned in section 2.4.

The impact created by these explicit and implicit influences on the mental model is summarized in **Figure 5.7**. These insights need to be applied to the actual product beyond the graphical user interface during design and development. The visitor's perspective is easier to accommodate since the decision tree is relatively simple, as content consumption is typically a one-dimensional process. The creator, however, faces an overall more complex task, which is defined by both the operational context and structural implications.

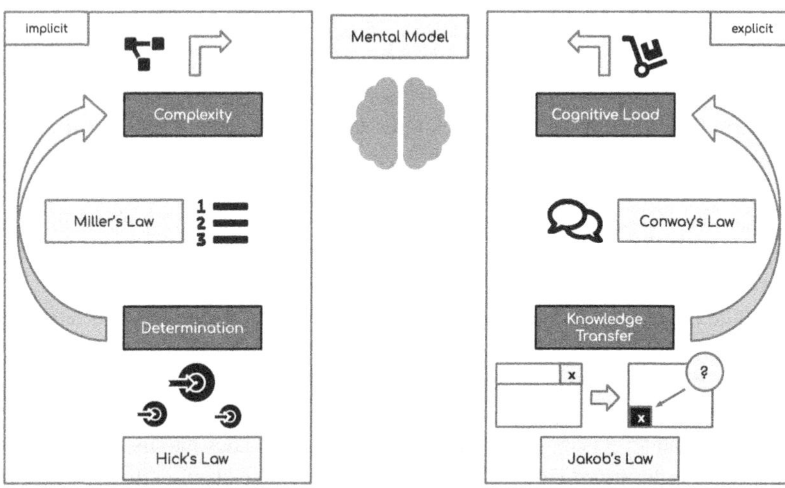

Figure 5.7 Components of the Mental Model

While most of these observations are subject to personal preference and the initial perception of the individual user, these UX design elements rooted in psychology should be applied universally. Overall, that does contribute to increasing the usability of the resulting product regardless of the intended context of use. That may aid in achieving the goals and tasks by enabling relevant structures and processes through accessible user interfaces, primarily by reducing cognitive friction, as summarized in **Figure 5.8**.

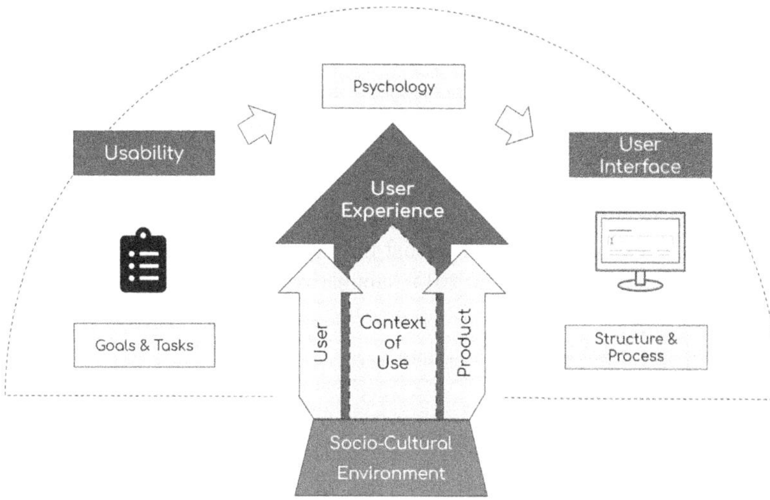

Figure 5.8 Psychology and Human-Centered Design (cf. Baumgärtner & Lehner, 2017.2, p. 818)

Cognitivefriction or *designfriction* refers to the difficulty that may occur while interacting with technology. Responsible for that experience is the gap between the intent of the designer and the expectation of the user (Cox, Cecchinato, Gould, Iacovides, & Renfree, 2016).

It is not possible to eliminate that friction altogether. In some cases, it is even necessary or beneficial to purposefully introduce friction to a certain task or interaction. During the first contact and onboarding phases, the general user experience should be as smooth as possible with atomic actions and few dependencies to ease the user in and aid them in familiarizing themselves with the product or process. Intentional friction, also referred to as 'micro-boundaries', can then be deployed for the purpose of error prevention, to keep the process on track, or to prompt a more mindful interaction (Cox, Cecchinato, Gould, Iacovides, & Renfree, 2016). Deeper into the encounter with the product, elements can be embedded into the process to enable learning opportunities, to increase overall efficiency for future encounters, or to prevent irreversible or time-consuming detours in the moment of interaction (Babich, 2017). This is particularly relevant for the creator's experience, who is responsible for data entry and the compilation of the resulting application.

5.2.2 'Consumer' Expectation and Content Selection

From the museum professional's perspective, it is not trivial to deduct the wants and needs of their visitors, as there usually is no direct exchange in the existing processes, as discussed throughout Chapter 3. While their intrinsic goals may include reaching out to that audience, it is easy to miss the mark when it comes down to the selection of content and the preparation of its presentation. This subsection discusses the expected content from the consumer's perspective based on the findings of Palumbo et al. 2014, summarized in **Table 5.4**.

Table 5.4 Expectations of Museum Visitors

• How to get to the Museum • Opening Hours • Tickets and Admission • Additional Services • Contacts • Timetable of Events and Tours • Real time news on events and products	Museum	Artworks	• Explanatory files of the artworks • Museum Artworks Photo-Gallery • Virtual Tour Bookmarks • Audio Guide • 3D virtual tour
• Museum Map • Suggestions for guided tours	Map	Usability	• Friendly and Efficient UI • Accessible on any Device • Available Offline • Free Download • Multilingual Option

These desires are put directly into contrast with the ability of the designated creator to provide the corresponding information in the expected way and the integrity of the specific item within the target environment that presents itself within small cultural heritage institutions to select the components to be included to the framework's scope, defined in subsection 6.2.4.

The identified desires are grouped into four categories. The **first category** includes basic information about the 'museum' itself. Most of these elements are important for the consumer upon the first contact, often even before the visit occurs. These include the location of the museum and how to get there, the opening hours, as well as information about admission fees and ticketing. From the creator's perspective, these should not pose any challenge to provide, as they are necessary to operate the exhibition anyway.

Online ticketing in itself, while technically feasible, is not to be included necessarily. As disclosed in section 2.1, many of the target institutions in question do not charge an entry fee, and the processing of online payments would just add unnecessary complexity with certain organizational and legal implications.

Visitors appreciate being informed about current aspects and additional services. These include but are not limited to, shops or restaurants associated with the museum and the schedule of events and tours alongside real-time news about the institution and its immediate surroundings. Once again, these are not applicable to the situation of most small institutions. They rarely hold special events nor have the capacity or frequency to maintain a news feed in real-time. That feature would either put stress on the museum professional to come up with content on a regular basis or disappoint the consumer by showing no news at all, or, even worse, outdated or irrelevant information. As discussed in section 3.2, those customer service processes should be decoupled from the in-gallery experience and handled separately downstream only after the central in-gallery components have been established.

The **second category** is concerned with the core elements, the 'artworks' or exhibits on display within the museum. The most important intersection between the abilities of the museum professional and the consumer's desire is explanatory files of the artworks, which should focus on answering the questions of the visitor posed in section 3.2. While these explanations need to fit the environment and the target audience, to maintain sustainability, it is imperative to perform appropriate annotations and semantic indexing of the resulting digital objects to avoid inconsistencies from a technical perspective as well as for both the consumer and the creator as further discussed in the following subsection. For those reasons, supporting and providing the opportunity to the museum professional to create structured data suitable for the predetermined content is going to be the core goal for the framework development.

For the museum professional as well as from the technical perspective occupied by the developer, it is quite easy to provide photos of and related to objects of interest. Issues might arise with regulatory or legal issues of ownership. Especially in Germany, image copyright disputes often cause problems. Thus, the possibility of extending these explanatory files with photos should definitely exist without them being mandatory.

While offering the possibility to save certain information for later consumption, i.e., bookmarking, per se, is a good idea, the issues related to individualization, especially offering user accounts for the consumer, are connected to further legal implications. Because the museum professional might not be equipped to handle these properly on their own, that is not going to be considered during design and development.

As previously stated in subsection 3.1.1, multimedia features bear the danger of developing a distraction to the consumer or other visitors and overshadowing the museum experience. That potential is amplified even more so with audio and video content. Especially within a BYOD strategy, the output cannot be supervised like in dedicated devices for audio guides. Furthermore, the effort and skill set required to reach a satisfactory production quality might not be available within any given institution. With the increasing complexity of the content, even specialized hardware might be required for content production, like 3D or RDI scanners, which cannot be expected within the assumed context.

The **third category** discusses 'maps' and the ways in which visitors navigate the museum. In general, there are two main models for providing added information in an exhibition setting. Some visitors like to *explore* an exhibition on their own. This is especially the case in the extremes of the artifact's density; either exhibits are far and in-between or very close to each other in a narrow space. In these cases, content needs to be provided upon the visitor's demand and does not require any particular connections to the bigger picture. However, that changes if the goal of the museum professional is to provide a linear and structured *guide* for the visitor, where the consumer is to be told a coherent story, including the order in which artifacts on display are supposed to be visited. Then the visitor is required to strictly adhere to the instructions and follow from one exhibit to another selected by the museum professional. The choice between these two options strongly depends on the content as well as the environment it is going to be presented to the visitor in. Thus, that choice should be made individually by the creator, depending on the situation.

The **fourth category** revolves around the general topic of 'usability', which has been thoroughly discussed throughout this chapter. The main goal of the software framework is to conceptually and technologically decouple the information entered by the creator and the user interface presented to the consumer while maintaining a strong visual connection, i.e., the application content. The museum professional needs to be able to be completely focused on the content creation process to understand their own capabilities and improve their ability to communicate. That should not be interfered with the need to worry about the efficiency of the user interface or the availability of their content on the consumer's devices. The technical details related to the consumer application should be of no concern to the creator and should be fully embedded within the framework's prototype implementation.

Anyhow, one of these options, which should reside with the creator, is to include the possibility of creating content in different languages. That feature, however, should not enforce the symmetry of the available information across all available languages, which may not even be applicable or necessary for the intended context. The selection of the elements provided in different languages should be an independent choice, similar to the variation in language complexity for different consumer demographics, i.e., scholars vs. students (Palumbo, Dominici, & Basile, 2014).

5.2.3 'Creator' Tasks and Data Entry

The creator is required to perform appropriate data entry operations to facilitate the desires of the consumer, as discussed in the previous section. These need to be properly structured and contextualized within the operational outcome to be reasonable for the museum professional to appropriately fulfill their role as the creator.

While the content and user interfaces of the consumer product are typically tightly interwoven, the responsibilities are vastly different from the creator's perspective. While the UI is repeatedly provided by the system, the content has to be prepared manually and requires creative activity and extensive domain knowledge. The benefits of digital transformation are directly correlated to that

Table 5.5 Structure and Content of Information Entry

	contextualized	without context
structured	**App Page Form** • entry is restricted by provided data fields • entered data to be used within a mobile application • visual link between data fields and app page	**Entry Form** • entry is restricted by provided data fields • no immediate use case is provided
unstructured	**App Page** • no restrictions apply • entered data to be used within a mobile application	**Plain Text** • no restrictions apply • no immediate use case is provided

separation, best described by the four types of facilitating the data entry process presented in **Table 5.5** (Baumgärtner, 2019.1) (Baumgärtner, 2019.2).

The simplest way to handle digital data entry is **plain text**. That method does require the least amount of effort, skill, or technology. However, it does possess a number of drawbacks. Since no restrictions are applied to the structure, it is hard to maintain consistent output, which makes it more difficult to be accessed and interpreted by others. While digital text can be distributed more easily than an analog representation, the information it contains cannot be processed, and thus, only little value is added. Furthermore, if no context is given for the reason to perform that input, there is no immediate use case for the creator to perform the input operations. That renders the effort almost pointless since there is no incentive to enter nor to retrieve any information other than taking personal notes. Creativity may be stifled by the lack of directed effort of the attempt.

There are solutions for either one of these problems. An **entry form** is the best option for inquiring structured data. Individual input fields can be used to restrict the entered data to certain predefined values or lengths and provide further guidance for the creator's task. That structured approach allows the comparability between different records of the same type. Maintainability and access for other users can be facilitated more easily because data can be indexed, sorted, and searched. That works well if the data to be entered is crucial for the business process in general and has to be recorded as part of a defined process. However, if the input is not explicitly necessary, the lack of incentive remains. An additional drawback is that this approach tends to translate into a fairly abstract and technical understanding of the whole process. Furthermore, the restrictions applied to the input values may not be reasonable for the creator without any given context.

The same argument can be made if only the context is provided for unsupervised data entry. The use case of an **app page** may provide a reason for the data inquiry. However, in a vacuum, the creator may still be overwhelmed by the endless possibilities of the content to be structured and displayed on the screen. Without any restrictions, the comparability to similar documents may suffer, which ultimately compromises the approachability for the designated consumer. Furthermore, that defeats the whole concept of the separation between the content and the UI layout, putting the creator in a situation to be responsible for the usability aspects in addition to the quality of the provided information. Once more, that may repel the creator to contribute to the process. Comparable to the plain text approach, the unstructured content created this way is hardly approachable by any third party and is more difficult to maintain.

That is the exact situation for the software framework's necessity to provide guidance and support for the creator. Data required to be entered into the system needs to be justified by the desired results, and the purpose of the restrictions of the input fields must be directly linked to the layout of the content shown within the final product. That can be achieved by creating a visual link between the data fields and the resulting app page. By limiting the design space with a predefined outcome, product quality can be enhanced drastically for the consumer and the creator alike.

For the creation of digital content, it is mandatory for the necessary information to be entered into, passed through, and processed by some sort of information system, as explained at the beginning of this section. The combination of the entry form and the data visualization from the consumer's perspective, by always mapping the entered information to the corresponding layout of the app page, has an impact on the creator and creates a visual and mental connection to the content.

That can provide an entry point for the museum professional to understand what steps and components are necessary for the app creation process and can teach them to communicate their requirements and own desires for further developments, as discussed in section 2.2. As a result, data is no longer blindly archived into a system for possibly being accessed at a later point in time but is immediately available as an app page for consumers and accessible for creators.

The benefits attributed to the logical decoupling of the output interface and the underlying data structure are not affected. Even if the layout should undergo changes at some point in the future or if the data is to be used in a different context or system, the reference to the available dataset can be altered or replaced without rendering it useless.

Furthermore, all the benefits of structured data demonstrated above can be harnessed within that **app page form** approach, developed in section 6.2.

5.3 Setup for Design and Development

The close contact with museum professionals during the ViSIT project (compare: P*reface*) enabled the detailed observation of the base situation in the environment of the involved cultural heritage institutions. As previously disclosed, analog workflows are prevailing, paper-based publications are the popular choice, and tasks not directly related to the core interest of the preservation or study of the collection are often delegated, sourced out, or ignored entirely. The readiness to facilitate digital technology for individuals within an organization is often overlooked (Parasuraman, 2000). Thus, existing procedures are often instinctively projected onto new problems, which may lead to unrealistic expectations or an overall naïve approach. The conceptional base situation for mobile application development, which is abstract and impersonal, is illustrated in the use case diagram in **Figure 5.9**.

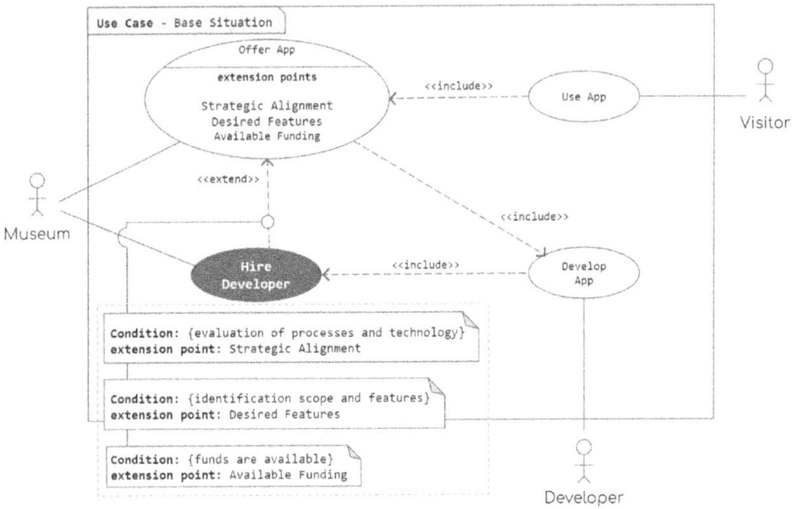

Figure 5.9 Use Case—Abstract Base Situation

As the necessary know-how to effectuate the actual offering of a mobile application to be used by the visitor is not available within the entity of small museums or their staff, external aid is unavoidable. However, multiple conditions, represented by the dashed box in the figure above, need to be fulfilled before it is even possible to strive for these goals.

Prior to any further steps, the individual situation of the institution needs to be evaluated regarding the strategic alignment of the proposed endeavor. To do that, a deep understanding of the involved choices regarding the integration of the current structures and the target technology must be attained to portray both existing workflows and future advancements, for that matter.

Furthermore, the necessary scope of the product and the desired features need to be carefully analyzed. It is indispensable to identify the actual users for the services to be offered. Only then is it possible to accommodate their needs within the associated interfaces and to consider their long-term obligations, the technology itself, as well as the actual content to be inquired and displayed.

The most prohibitive stipulation of that process remains the financial restrictions of the museums in question. As this condition is an extrinsic requirement set outside the area of accountability of most institutions, the situation needs to be absorbed within the decision-making process and thus puts a burden onto every single action within the boundaries. On that account, even if most of the intrinsic concerns could be met, which in itself is challenging enough, the involvement of an external designer or developer depends on several other factors that each reflects back once more on issues previously discussed. However, the issues related to the tasks and processes necessary to offer mobile applications to visitors in the Museum Application Domain can mostly be traced back to the museum being perceived as an anonymous entity. The absence of strategic planning and poor digital involvement causes unclear patterns of responsibilities. This prevents any internal authority from being established or other resources from being allocated to innovative causes. In turn, that does obstruct essential communication and may conceal the transgression of the intended objectives even distinctly before the system development itself can be initiated.

Thus, if the interaction with the developer becomes an anonymous affair and the development process is perceived as an autonomous mechanism, detached from the day-to-day operations, the results are going to reflect just that. Accordingly, to create a sustainable product, the personalization of the stimulus is essential to generate desire and invoke responsibility.

Nevertheless, the effective utilization of resources must be prioritized to achieve a personal connection between the actual needs of the cultural heritage institution and the individual accountability of the museum professional. Still, many organizations fail to accommodate the actual needs or the ability of the designated user (Miaskiewicz & Kozar, 2011).

Constructing *personas,* as suggested by Cooper in 1999, is one way to establish and maintain a firm connection to different user groups throughout development and to apply the guidelines demanded by human-centered design. A Persona is an abstraction of a real user or user group symbolizing an aggregate of common behavioral characteristics, thus manifesting a hypothetical archetype. These are often represented by fictional characters and referenced either by a name or by one of their key features. The primary purpose of that approach is to improve communication between stakeholders, designers, and developers and to maintain the focus on the identified users and their needs without the necessity to constantly involve actual users. That contributes to the reduction of the overall product complexity by preventing self-referential design as it does encourage a more consumer-centered attitude (Miaskiewicz & Kozar, 2011).

On this basis, the dialogue which went along during the ViSIT project encouraged the identification of four distinct personas to represent those museum professionals who are expected to engage in the resulting processes associated with the software framework by devoting their time and effort. The key features of each of those personas are summarized in **Table 5.6** and are characterized in more detail hereafter.

Table 5.6 Creator Personas

Persona	Characterization		Features
Enthusiast	Desires (self-)improvement.		
⇒ Reveal Know-How		+	Has no system in place. Can make decisions rather quickly. Is usually a "Single Museum Operator".
		−	No contact to like-minded individuals. Has limited access to resources. Is not interested in "databases".
Mover	Choses the trend.		
⇒ Reveal Limitations		+	Has affinity for technical gadgets. Is well informed and willing to learn. Is experienced in exhibition planning.
		−	Is not involved in budgeting decisions. Is fixed to certain product or system. Has little experience & low stamina.
Repudiator	Despises change.		
⇒ Reveal Opportunities		+	Is closely engaged with the visitor. Puts emphasis on "the experience". Is primarily interested in preservation.
		−	Has no executive "responsibilities". Does not recognize the potential. Is not interested in technology.
Reserved	Is intrigued, but preoccupied.		
⇒ Reveal Value		+	Has affinity for solutions and results. Is heavily involved in scientific tasks. Is primarily concerned with "curation".
		−	Is picky and resource-oriented. Is not interested in "gimmicks". Has long decision periods.

The "repudiator" is deceptible to despise changes or suggestions that seem to threaten their established comfort zone.

They have been involved with the intrinsic mechanisms for a long time and have been part of the existing structures, which makes them the most conservative force within the museum. They are usually highly knowledgeable about the contents of the existing exhibitions as well as the existing efforts regarding visitor relations. Without being involved in executive decision-making, they emphasize the museum experience, e.g., by guiding tours. Overall, they have an adverse attitude toward technology, induced by the lack of exposure in their own everyday lives. Through their unique profile, they are able to provide valuable insights into visitor interaction and the preparation of information to emphasize essential topics in the exhibition setting. To convince this group to recognize the potential of new concepts like apps, first and foremost, the *opportunities* for improvement of the overall experience for them and for the visitor need to be accentuated.

The "reserved" is mostly preoccupied with administrative or managerial tasks, but often intrigued by the possibilities offered by innovative concepts or technology.
Similar to the repudiator, they share a sense of preserving existing structures. However, they are actively interested in results and are driven by tangible solutions. This positive attitude leads to some side effects. Because of the restrictions introduced by the domain and the scarcity of resources they face in their day-to-day operation, they are particularly picky and refuse novelties and short-dated gimmicks. Furthermore, they are heavily involved in research and other scientific tasks, which may include exhibits currently on display but usually transcend the visitors' level of insight. Their duties not only require sufficient dedication but also prolong their decision periods as the curation of an exhibition usually is established for an extended timescale. To reason with those people is immensely important, as they are primarily in charge of the decision-making process. Thus, the *value* that mobile applications can add to existing processes without absorbing valuable resources needs to be highlighted.

The "mover" is chasing the trend as new and exciting innovations emerge.
This group is remarkably experienced with the inner workings of the administration of exhibitions and the individual exhibits on display. They have access to information beyond the cursory level, as they are often involved with the practical collection management and the compilation of information for the visitor. As they are directly involved in the execution of the exhibition right down to the preparation of the showroom, they are familiar with current trends and available technical gadgets for those purposes. This gives them an unprecedented understanding of the actual needs in the exhibition setting from both perspectives. Overall, they are more accepting of technology and usually willing to continuously expand their horizon. Apart from that, they must adhere to the systems already in place at the institution as well as the superjacent monetary restrictions, which makes it difficult to justify the introduction of proprietary, incompatible, or costly components. These restrictions lead to little experience and low stamina, as they usually chase the trend without being able to ever establish actual innovation. By contrast, they do not need to be persuaded but rather be provided with some guidance and *limitations* to achieve sustainable solutions.

The "enthusiast" is driven by the desire for self-improvement and would like to act by themselves, but is limited by his own experience and level of involvement.
This crowd usually is more deliberate than the mover, as they are to be found mostly in the smallest cultural heritage institutions. They are more aware of the overall situation within their organization because all assignments and responsibilities tend to be concentrated on fewer people or even concern just one individual operator. The role of the 'allrounder' is handy to maintain established structures, but the isolation from other like-minded individuals prevents communication and the transfer of knowledge or best practices. Furthermore, for them, the restrictions present throughout the Museum Application Domain exert themselves even more explicitly. For that reason, and as the scale of operations they face is very narrow and usually directed toward the exhibition, they do not have any demand for standardized systems. Thus, they often rely on improvised and analog solutions for their collection management. They are very critical of solutions like sophisticated databases that would disrupt their routines without any direct positive impact on their operations, which often is based on the impression of their visitors. The greatest advantage they enjoy is the fact that they are able to quickly adopt new elements, as there are practically no intrinsic nor extrinsic dependencies they have to consider. To convince these people, it is crucial to reveal *know-how* and provide them with documentation as well as material to enable self-organization from the very beginning without building up any external dependencies. Most importantly, this fourth identity is predestined to be captivated by a decentralized solution that can be approached without any direct dependencies or long-term obligations.

Despite all those explicit differences, superordinate objectives must be consolidated. To establish an arrangement that is able to cater to the needs of each of those personas, the idea of outsourcing core tasks of the application development process must be abolished as far as possible. It is crucial to focus on the proper mechanisms, to build personal proficiency on the individual level, and to create the ability to prepare information and arrange content with the primary goal of yielding satisfactory results by offering mobile applications to the visitor.

For the visitor, personas or individual expectations may also differ. However, the underlying necessities during their visit are quite similar on the functional level. Whether an app is directed toward student, casual, or expert-level visitors does not necessarily impact the structural components and is most certainly to be addressed by the content itself rather than the development or creator environment intended for the construction of applications. Exceptions may occur if small children or people with certain impairments or disabilities are to be addressed specifically. However, those situations would require an entirely different approach anyhow. Thus, while the precursory notion of the museum professional does gravely impact the approach of any disruptive concept or tool like mobile applications, in contrast to the museum visitor fulfilling the role of the passive consumer does not immediately impact the suggested setup.

On a similar notion, the type of museum may impact the composition of the presented content but not the presentation of certain information. While a gallery may put more emphasis on artwork and artists, a museum of natural history may feature the era or time period of certain physical exhibits. However, the overall goal of information and content delivery remains unchanged. Furthermore, especially small museums often do not differentiate or identify themselves one way or the other.

It has been found that the capability to express the desired features on an institutional level depends primarily on the particular ability of the museum professional to acquire adequate know-how of the necessary tasks responsible for the desired results. Thus, the goal pursued must accommodate an inverse approach relative to the initial situation while disregarding the actual application development and other confounding technical factors but offering a system that can be self-administered with as little external interference as possible.

The target situation described above is presented in **Figure 5.10**. To facilitate that, the core task is to provide a periphery to enable museum professionals to build mobile applications and the museum to offer the resulting app to be used by the visitor, as marked by the dashed box in the figure. Furthermore, to complete the proposition, for the reason of accessibility, the app development process in itself needs to be extended to the visitor, to enable the whole system to fulfill its intended purpose, and later to retain behavior and usage information to contribute to feature evaluation and identification in the future.

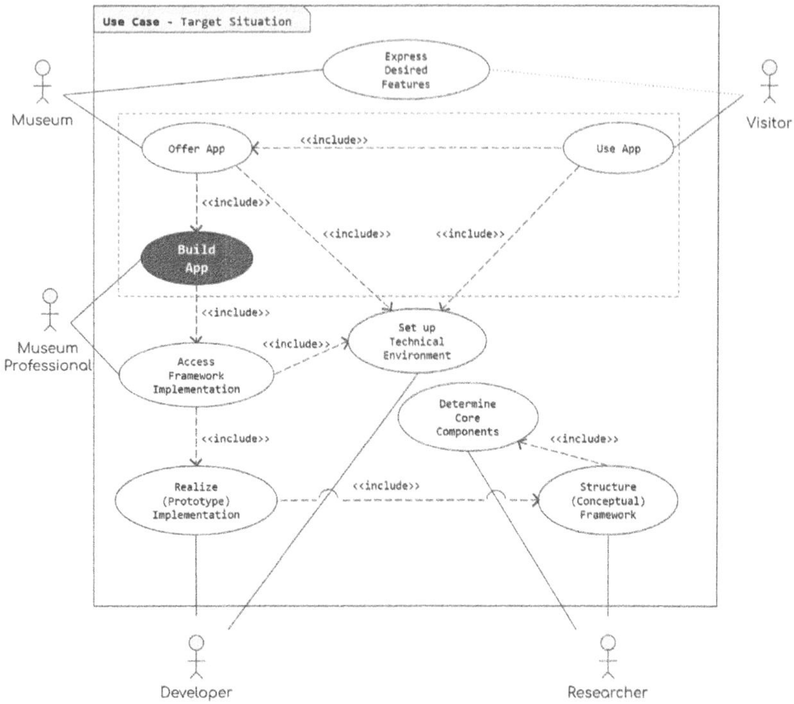

Figure 5.10 Use Case—Personalized Target Situation

Therefore, the research performed throughout this dissertation has been focused on properly structuring the foundation for the conceptual framework. That assignment explicitly does provide the academic grounding for the practical determination of the core components of such a software system regarding both functional and non-functional features and components, as discussed throughout Chapter 6.

Later, the goal during prototype development, presented in Chapter 7, has been to suggest a standalone solution that can be utilized regardless of the experience available on both the institutional and the individual level within the institution. Furthermore, it has been equally important to set up the technical environment in such a way that it can be easily replicated and picked up directly by those users who are supposed to operate it.

6 Framework Design

This thesis initially examines the motivational factors, introduces the specific problem domain, defines the research problems, and sets up the conceptual foundation for the design and development of the framework. The fundamental ideas most influential from the socio-technical perspective on the problem domain are the subject of the previous chapter. Based on those principles, this chapter approaches the second research question. It, therefore, aims to establish the core design choices as well as the essential components of *A Framework for Mobile Apps in the Museum Application Domain.*

Existing reservations and concerns stemming from the contact with technology of certain stakeholders require the focus to be put on the necessary steps and tasks from their own perspective. The goal is to provide an anchor to enable an open and ongoing dialogue between the museum professional and the developer. Only then is it possible to initiate a substantiated decision-making process that enables the implementation as well as distribution of potential features for the benefit of both the creator and the consumer. Nevertheless, all the underlying assets and dependencies should be easily accessible for those who possess the ability to perform design or development tasks themselves, are capable of extending existing structures, or desire to work with the raw data. Framing mobile applications as the starting point to expand and distribute the necessary know-how and to evaluate existing ideas is far more important than putting the focus on technical concerns, restrictions, or strategies, which may not even be amendable by the means available to museum professionals in small cultural heritage institutions.

The motivation for the visitor to use the app during the visit is mostly contingent on the general availability of the application, including accessibility and usability concerns. If certain universal benchmarks can be established and met first, second it is important to primarily create an opportunity for the creator to

T. Baumgärtner, *A Software Framework for Mobile Apps in the Museum Application Domain*, Gabler Theses, https://doi.org/10.1007/978-3-658-44367-2_6

answer the most desirable questions, introduced in section 3.1, and to cater to the local audience by offering relevant languages or otherwise accommodating requests based on the utilization of mobile applications in situ. This includes the type of museum as well as the setup and composition of the exhibition. Detailed ex-ante assessment of the value to be added on an institutional level is next to impossible, as the implementation of certain alignments is only feasible once the system is in place and deployed within the designated environment. However, because the existing issues are often approached from a purely technical perspective, resulting solutions regularly do not satisfy the needs of nor appeal to those supposed to benefit from them. Thus, these never become relevant in practice. To prevent that, a holistic approach that considers the conditions set by the problem environment from each perspective is vital. Furthermore, the framework design explicitly has to accommodate the limitations faced by small museums and reduce the organizational overhead to a minimum.

Beginning with the information system infrastructure, available *application development frameworks* like Django (Python), Spring (Java), and Express (JavaScript) provide aid for the basic structure of web applications on an architectural and technical level (Keyul, 2019), independently of the explicit use case. However, these rely heavily on existing content streams and standardized business problems. Their contribution to the development process quickly offers diminishing returns, as no guidance is provided regarding the strategic approach of a specific domain. Additionally, numerous external dependencies are added to the project, which increases the overall complexity of the development process and overloads the long-term maintainability (Sourour, 2016). These issues are further discussed in section 7.2.

Considering domain-specific implementations, on one side, *museum collection management systems* offer tools and database solutions for inventory and collection management and assist in the curation of exhibitions and associated digital assets. Two examples commonly deployed in Bavaria are 'MuseumPlus' by zetcom (zetcom, 2019) and 'VINO' (Vino Online, 2019). In practice, however, the number of institutions using individual solutions for collection management is far greater than any one of the 16 commercially available products identified. A study among 156 responding German museums found that almost half (63) of those institutions were using individually sourced solutions. Many institutions even stated not to use any structured approach at all. Those rely primarily on office applications like Microsoft Word and Excel to document their objects and exhibits in their collections (Haffner & Schweibenz, 2017). That does elucidate the individual needs regarding data collection, which also differ greatly between organizations.

Within the Museum Application Domain, the ICOM suggests its own Conceptual Reference Model (CRM), "a theoretical and practical tool for information integration in the field of cultural heritage" (ICOM, 2014). It "provides the basic classes and relations devised for the cultural heritage world" based on the reference ontology for the 'interchange of cultural heritage information' as described in ISO 21127:2014 and its specialized modular extensions. Issues are primarily caused by the inconceivable complexity of semantic path modeling. The technical requirements make it necessary to incorporate components like the Resource Description Framework (RDF), a collection of specifications surrounding metadata models, introduced by the World Wide Web Consortium (W3C) primarily designed for computer readability and not for end user consumption (w3schools, 2019). In practice, that leads to only fringe cases adopting that model, such as 'WissKI', a "Scientific Communication Infrastructure for managing scholarly data" (WissKi, 2019), or interpreting these guidelines like the 'Erlangen CRM / OWL' based on ISO 21127:2006, the only attempt at implementing CIDOC CRM. However, those are far too difficult to understand and impossible to be deployed by casual or tech-inept users.

That complexity, in combination with the large number of individual solutions, complicates the effort to standardize available knowledge with database interfaces toward larger systems. The 'bavarikon' portal, for example, tries to funnel publicly available information about Bavarian cultural heritage institutions (bavarikon, 2019). To facilitate such portals and similar efforts, the ICOM Data Harvesting and Interchange Working Group has developed the 'Lightweight Information Describing Objects' (LIDO) harvesting schema based on the eXtensible Markup Language (XML). It defines 14 groups of information to expose, share, and connect data on the web (LIDO, 2019). Approaches like that, however, still are heavily skewed toward the perspective of the traditional museum professional, as they are built as scalable and searchable archives, providing access to in-depth and specialized information, and do not visibly contribute toward the desire to directly appeal to or provide benefits for the casual visitor. Furthermore, to enable data harvesting in the first place, the institutions in question need to recognize the strategic necessity as well as an instrument to generate and provide structured data.

On the other side of the implementation spectrum, the situation is similar with applications supposed to target the consumer. *App building kits*, offering an approach to mobile applications, are often based on the 'What You See Is What You Get' (WYSIWYG) paradigm. The position of content and interface elements on the screen can be arranged freely by the app creator, which offers great flexibility and does not require extensive technical knowledge throughout the development process. Commercial products, like the 'appmakr' by appypie, offer to support the process of creating interfaces for popular mobile platforms and the web (appypie, 2019). The implication of which is, that after the conceptualization, components, and content are geared toward a singular purpose and use case. From there, the information and presentation layers are fused together and may not be accessible in an organized or structured fashion for purposes beyond the on-screen presentation.

Furthermore, elements within the application that are supposed to convey the same or similar information or concepts may not visually represent those coherencies. The reason is that many of these app builders focus on the layout and graphical user interface customization rather than comprehensive content management. That increases the exposure of being tangled up in unreasonable choices unrelated to the actual domain-centered issues, which also are not being addressed in most generic approaches available today.

In an effort to provide better access to such services, contextualized within the cultural heritage domain, ventures like 'fabulAPP' of the 'Landesstelle für nichtstaatliche Museen in Bayern' try to reduce friction between collection and exhibition management described here. However, the overall level of complexity of provided functionality in such approaches makes it necessary to deeply engage creators in the specific process suggested by its developers by attending workshops, which initiates an extensive planning period. In that scenario, the time to publication is estimated to be close to one year (fabulapp, 2019) and mostly does not yield structured data. While the intention is to implement a comprehensive strategy, those requirements do dampen the initial enthusiasm if imposed on small institutions, which are eager to arrive quickly at a tangible resolution. Additionally, it is expected to conceptualize the cornerstones of the intended product.

However, this is usually the very issue, as members of small institutions initially are not able to identify nor communicate their own specific desires and intentions. Matters are complicated further by the fact that access to some of these solutions often is restricted geographically without any noticeable conceptual or technical compatibility with a broader infrastructure (Noschka-Roos & Kapschulte, 2020).

This seemingly shallow reflection is sufficient to dismiss existing approaches and a broad array of other solutions that each lead to a comparable conclusion. Most generic products and tools to support the app development process are either too disorganized or too complex to be suitable for the specific needs of small institutions within the Museum Application Domain. Dedicated models and theories are necessary to engage the specific problems related to collections and exhibitions. However, resulting products often are too narrow and only address a singular issue but neglect the big picture or are not able to solve those issues in the practical context. Thus, to approach the third research problem, which is concerned with the *configuration of the architectural structure*, a holistic approach must be able to express the underlying issues, address the relationship between those challenges, and translate them into the technical setup to synthesize a holistic and approachable solution.

Domain-driven design offers an approach to unify the heterogeneous expectations toward the resulting framework design. The alignment between the scientific requirements expected by design science research and the more practice-oriented stipulations posed by field experts and museum professionals can be conflated within the domain model. Furthermore, the benefits exerted by human-centered design may support the development and create an integrated structure comprehensible from each perspective and to each role involved throughout the design process (*Section 6.1—Domain-Driven Design*).

The three fundamental iterations of the initial top-down design process for the framework approach, which forewent the underlying architectural composition and design implications, are briefly discussed. Those demonstrate the conceptual progress necessary to identify the basic process steps and components mandatory to be included within the overall framework design. Conclusively, the conceptualization of the structural setup for the suggested framework is summarized (*Section 6.2—Fundamental Design Iterations*).

To clarify the particular adjacent objectives resulting from the coherent exchange throughout those major iterations, ten particular goals to be met by the framework are derived. That scope does entail the intended implementation and summarizes the preceding findings embedded within the conceptual preparation (*Section 6.3—Detailed Framework Scope*).

Next to those conceptual implications, the architectural boundaries for the project are summarized. Those invoke the relevant technical considerations of the environmental influences and elements contained. Furthermore, the core technological concepts are introduced to facilitate the specific characteristics of the Museum Application Domain. Additionally, the relevant design patterns in the context of mobile application development are discussed. Especially the composition suggested by the Model-View-ViewModel (MVVM) pattern provides a technology-agnostic reference point for the cognate components essential for the construction, assembly, and layout related to the key domain model (*Section 6.4—Technological Scaffold*).

On that foundation, the particular framework design and its components contingent upon *A Software Framework for Mobile Apps in the Museum Application Domain* are devised (*Section 6.5—Engineering of the Framework Components*).

6.1 Domain-Driven Design

The pace of emerging trends and general technological advances occur rapidly. Therefore, an incidental exchange between the environment and the knowledge base often occurs unmediated, which frequently offsets the scope. Facilitating the insights offered by *Domain-Driven Design* (DDD), as described by Eric Evans (2003), can offer support to the research proposition and set a track to follow. This approach is primarily based on the premise of cultivating a common 'domain language' throughout a digital project to connect field experts of the problem domain and IT professionals. In addition, building blocks and architectural guidelines are suggested to enable direct communication along each step of the implementation process. In **Figure 6.1**, the elements introduced by DDD are put into the methodological context previously outlined.

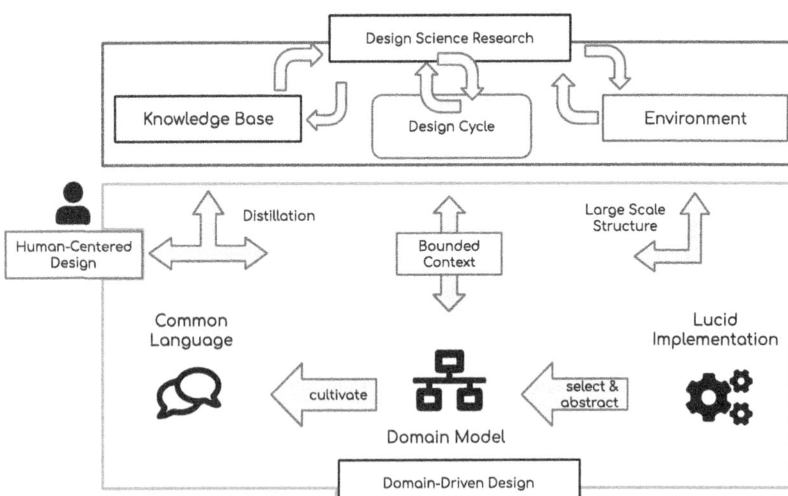

Figure 6.1 Integration of Domain-Driven Design

The main reason to adopt those suggestions is the importance of the iterative nature of modern software development. That same concept also is crucially represented within the guidelines of design science research. Complex designs need to be avoided to maintain the primary focus of software creation on the domain itself and to keep the domain logic accessible for all of its members. Based on an open and extensible model. The outcome of software projects depends heavily on a controlled set of predefined priorities. A clear array of rules should be established as early as possible and diligently adjusted depending on emerging issues and feedback along the way. Thus, the underlying problems and the immediate environment for the solution need to be well understood throughout the process. Maintaining the integrity of the project necessitates the contextualization of the problem, which requires a practical and personalized perspective. Usually, that goes beyond just plain design in a vacuum, as presented throughout Chapter 5.

To generate the proper focus and reduce unnecessary and distracting clutter, the concept of 'distillation' is applied. The goal is to block out peripheral domain issues as well as external liabilities to focus on a solution within the actual context's core scope. The processes and value-adding aspects of the system need to then be prominent within the domain model. On the other hand, the endeavor must be approached with an overarching theme to not end up with incompatible or confusing micro-solutions not applicable within the bounded context defined by the environment. Therefore, supporting roles as well as system-wide design elements and patterns are necessary to ensure a 'large-scale structure'. DDD thus acts as a moderator between the environment of the application domain and the fundamentals provided by the knowledge base by enabling communication of the stakeholders within the 'bounded context'.

In that sense, the 'domain model' is not just a particular diagram nor an intangible idea but the general concept of describing and organizing the expert's domain knowledge in a rigorous and comprehensible way. It should be presented in a logical manner, accessible and conceivable to each party involved. The goal of the model is not to replicate reality as closely as possible but to represent the components necessary to set up an informed approach toward the issue. It is supposed to entail guidelines to provide orientation and should avoid contradictory or overlapping definitions to yield a consistent foundation for the domain language.

The main purpose of the resulting software solution is to solve the domain-related problem for its effective users. Therein lies the greatest challenge, requiring technical skill and intense effort. All other features are to be constructed to support this central agenda, regardless of how vital other components may be for the overall system. To do so successfully, the developer needs to build up extensive knowledge of the domain and its environment to be able to construct a valid model to establish basic communication, which then can lead to a 'lucid implementation'. That then provides the grounds for selection and abstraction to improve the domain model and future implementations further, narrowing down the expected solution.

Gathering the necessary knowledge is an effort complicated by the fact that information is usually fragmented and not available from a central source. Thus, obtaining, prioritizing, and crunching scattered bits and pieces often disguises the fact of what information is actually missing, which may lead to false assumptions and consequently to the dismissal of the suggested solution.

That does translate directly to the construction of the *model*. The terms and relationships, which exist in the heads of particular domain experts, need to be thoroughly examined, assembled, and condensed to accurately reflect domain insights. Those determine the semantics of the necessary language abstraction, which needs to be precise to such a degree to provide a reliable foundation for the technical development. Furthermore, the vocabulary in use must be present throughout the whole process, from the program code itself, ranging all the way to the user interaction to avoid as much translation or disruption as possible. However, it needs to transcend the mere technical modeling and possibly include informal techniques so that it can represent the names and patterns existing within the holistic model, respectively.

That model then also needs to be maintained within any possible *implementation* of the application to avoid a situation where transactional integrity is contradicted by convoluted associations. Otherwise, during development, the domain model may be invalidated. Taking shortcuts to design units, which may comply with the technical prerequisites just to ensure short-term success, can invalidate the existing model. That then directly affects the utility of the resulting software and obstructs further iterations or prevents feedback entirely. That is why the mental model of the user and the conceptual model formed by the designer need to be brought in alignment to be later reflected and exposed within the resulting system. The concept of "*Letting the Bones Show*" not only ensures long-term model integrity but can aid those with lesser technical know-how to take part in the downstream design process by reducing the overall system complexity and dependencies by enforcing isolation and encapsulation. It also promotes certain usability benefits, as described in subsection 5.1.3.

To further ensure the quality of the code produced during implementation, suggestions are made to avoid interrelationships and diffusion of domain-related code and establish clear layers to ensure a certain degree of abstraction and separation of concerns regarding the following four layers, with the overall goal to establish simplicity within each of them. This composition mirrors the representation introduced in section 5.2 with the exception that it does specifically include the model itself. The *presentation layer* is concerned with the graphical user interface. The responsibilities include showing information on a screen and interpreting the user's input commands. It is often tightly coupled with the *application layer*, containing support code necessary to coordinate tasks and delegate requests to the layer underneath. The state of the application is kept here to reflect the progress of the current task for both the program and the user. The *model layer* represents the heart of business software. It is where the domain model is actively represented, and the included concepts find their technical realization. The technical execution and logistical tasks are delegated once more to the level below. At last, the *infrastructure layer* consists of utility functions regarding technical capabilities to support the higher layers. It takes responsibility for managing the interaction originating from the interface elements down to the processing and execution of database queries and each interaction in between.

Dependencies within the system can be drastically reduced by establishing one-way binding only. To support that layered architecture, the following building blocks are defined. First, the distinction between 'entities' and 'value objects' needs to be made. Some objects are not primarily defined by their attributes but rather by their identity. The focus, therefore, needs to be directed toward the most intrinsic characteristics to enable general continuity and predictable behavior. Thus, an identifying attribute that ensures the entity's uniqueness across the entire system is mandatory. That identifier may be combined with a symbol to ensure uniqueness within a certain class; however, that symbol needs to be immutable over the entire lifecycle of the system. Thus, most domain objects need to be assigned an identity. However, if that concept were applied to every element of a given system, it would inflate the overall complexity. Thus, objects necessary to facilitate the execution or aid the fulfillment of certain tasks or the system itself, with the focus primarily on their value, do not have to be assigned an identity, enabling those resources to be shared across multiple tasks. That does reduce the number of necessary resources by providing a single point of access but demands immutability to protect against inconsistencies and to avoid data corruption.

Furthermore, pragmatic design requires utility components that do not conceptually belong to any object. Those should not be forced to fit any existing class but rather exist as an explicitly independent 'service' within the model. Those situations are common regarding tasks related to navigation and data processing but should not be overextended to avoid procedural constructs. Services should not encapsulate the state and provide a clear interface to be called by the dependent client components. Multiple components should be bundled into 'modules' to encapsulate logical unity and cohesion while maintaining low coupling to other modules. Those modules are supposed to be part of the model for conceptual consistency and should not follow patterns primarily motivated by the underlying infrastructure. That allows the necessary connection to be made for the individual and prevents important details from getting lost in the aggregation.

Suggestions regarding the structural assembly of those building blocks are often made in the form of the hexagonal architecture. That approach, however, is meant primarily for enterprise-level implementation and does not scale down well enough to reasonably be used for this particular application. Thus, for the reference implementation, the Model-View-ViewModel pattern is applied, which ensures the most important principles of the described layers but allows for a leaner implementation, as explained in subsection 6.4.2 below. Overall, it is a better fit for this project, as it does reduce coupling, requires less refactoring, and offers better coherence between the concept and the implementation.

6.2 Fundamental Design Iterations

Beginning with the procedural large-scale structure at the point of interaction, a formative ex-ante evaluation of the feasible approaches has been conducted. This search process to manifest the initial configuration is supposed to follow a naïve approach to constitute the contiguity between the information inquiry expected from the creator and the structural integrity of the appropriate mobile application experience for the consumer. As the inner workings and the transactional processing can be defined only after the factual process flow has been established and outlined to a satisfactory degree, they do not matter at this initial stage of the (framework) design. More importantly, the distillation of the findings related to the concepts of human-centered design presented throughout Chapter 5 must be implemented at this conceptual level to enable eligibility and practical feasibility for the user or, more specifically, the creator. **Figure 6.2** does illustrate the access points on both ends, which need to be addressed by the framework implementation to support the overall development process.

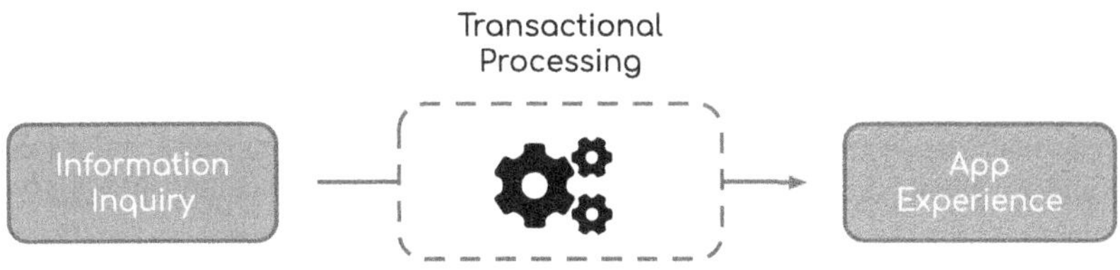

Figure 6.2 Top-Down Design Process

Over the course of the ViSIT project, different ideas on how to approach the design for the application framework were given a trial. Three major approaches were conceived, each with a distinct focus on how to support the task of generating structured data for the creator while preserving the focus on the proper visualization of the task with an emphasis on the resulting consumer application to anchor the creator's interaction throughout the process.

The design iterations discussed within this section (*Subsections 6.2.1–6.2.3*) traverse the composition between structure and context presented in Subsection 5.2.3. Afterward, the conceptual structure and the components relevant to the bottom-up development are properly specified (*Subsection 6.2.4*). Foremost, the identified issues and expectations within the problem domain obtain priority.

6.2.1 Text Selection

The first draft of the framework design has been based on the preliminary assumptions derived from the initial assessment of the problem domain, as well as the unified goals of the different units involved in the ViSIT project.

The main objective of the chosen procedure does make a pass at transforming unstructured text into structured datasets by adding semantic markers as well as extrapolating connections and relevant relationships. The utility of the resulting design and the involved data-entry process were primarily considered for the internal tasks that occupy the museum professional on a day-to-day basis. Consequently, in this scenario, mobile applications were not considered as the primary feature. Apps were supposed to be supplied by a unified database later.

The approach utilizes manual text markup to annotate elements of an existing text document to provide meaning and structure in a way that produces machine-readable metadata. Since an available text is the point of reference, it would not be necessary to provide a traditional entry form. In a setting similar to a text editor, the user would apply the cursor to *select snippets* within the text provided to the system. Then, they would have the opportunity to *classify the selected snippet* by adding attributes or relationships that would apply. Additionally, the opportunity to *annotate the selected snippet* by adding a comment or reference would be provided. Those steps are supposed to be repeated until each relevant element within the text has received that treatment. This process manifests itself as shown in the workflow described in **Figure 6.3**.

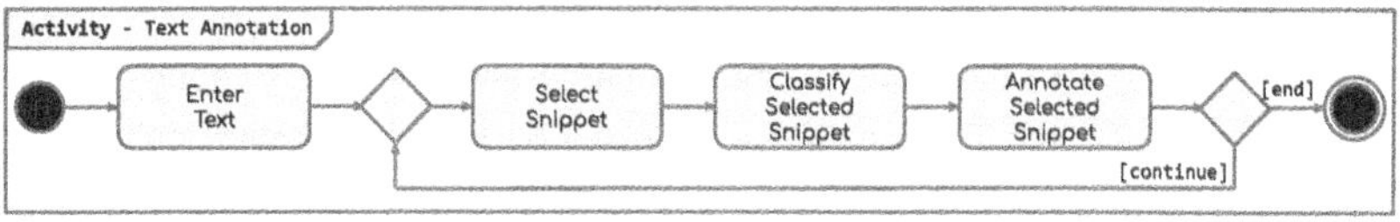

Figure 6.3 Text Annotation Workflow

In the dialogue with the museum professionals involved in the project, two major issues related to the suppositions this approach has been based on could be pinpointed. First, the expectation of encountering existing digital material, in general, to serve as a starting point for this approach has proven to be a challenge throughout the environment, especially in smaller institutions.

Therefore, the very foundation of this design does not resonate with the established situation within cultural heritage institutions. Second, even if the text were made available on an institutional level, i.e., by digitizing analog material, the transformational steps which would be necessary to produce data suitable to provide content for apps or other applications facing the visitor would pose a completely different challenge on its own. The absolute disconnect between the data inquiry and the requirements for apps prevents harmonizing the different alignments between the structured data necessary for an expert database and the visitor's expectations. This would imply additional efforts while simultaneously reducing the quality of both outcomes.

Even if the relevant goals could be achieved by the suggested approach, the steps necessary to perform the entry are too abstract for the level of IT proficiency of the average museum professional. The primary functionality of the suggested text selection mechanism is visible in the mockup provided in **Figure 6.4**.

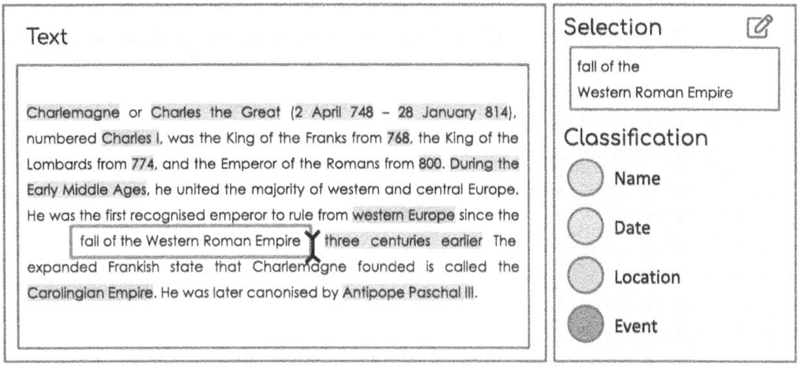

Figure 6.4 Mockup Text Annotation

As the resulting datasets are still visually tied to the original text, the benefits provided by structured data are not backed by any "physical" manifestation, which would support the suggested advantages. While this approach would address the data inquiry in an elegant way, it does not provide the necessary bridge between the performed task and the utilization of the created data.

Thus, this idea has been swiftly dismissed before attempting extensive testing beyond the initial interaction because of the obvious erroneous assumptions clarified by the closer examination of the environment. In turn, those insights would not have been easily obtainable without this first attempt.

6.2.2 WYSIWYG Components

The second design attempt took into account the findings of the previous conceptual trial. First and foremost, the intent of the preceding design to provide apps for the visitor has not been sufficiently apparent, which does not resonate well with the specific goals set for the framework to begin with.

Therefore, the objective of a unified database, which would simultaneously cover the needs of the museum professional as well as the requirements regarding the usability of mobile apps, has been relaxed within the context of the ViSIT project. Then, the declared goal for the framework was to directly connect the data-oriented inquiry procedure with the resulting visual appearance of the visitor's application interface. Thus, the museum professional is confronted with the expected outcome and a reason for their efforts as soon as possible.

The starting point in this scenario would be a blank canvas representing one screen to be displayed within the mobile app. Furthermore, this approach utilizes a "What You See Is What You Get" (WYSIWYG) editor, which offers commonly recurring visual components typically encountered within mobile applications, like headlines, multimedia panels, or articles. This does provide a frame of reference for the information expected or required to be provided in the context of mobile applications. Additionally, content or information for the topic to be described does not have to already exist. The creator would first *choose a UI element* to add to the app screen and *appoint a screen position* for the selected component. Then, to *add information* they deem appropriate to represent the intended argument and which does fit the category of the chosen UI element. Depending on the screen allocation and in relation to other components that may have been chosen for the page, the creator has to *adjust the UI elements* to fit the desired layout. Those steps can be repeated until the page is considered finished. The described workflow is represented in **Figure 6.5**.

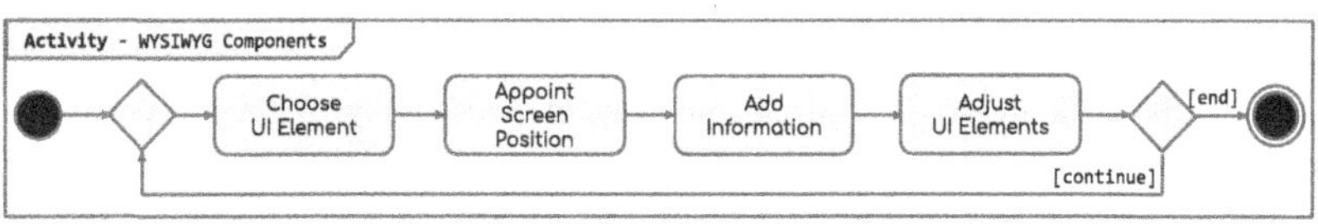

Figure 6.5 WYSIWYG Components Workflow

This approach offers multiple degrees of freedom for the creator. In consequence, it does become almost impossible to provide proper guidance for the content creation process. While a clear context for the data entry is provided, no proper boundaries between information and its visualization are established. Certain aspects can be mediated through the visual components suggested by the editor. However, the amount of decisions the creator has to consider quickly becomes overwhelming and might intimidate inexperienced users. Additionally, the mental model to be conceived by the creator might not be complete, as it is hard to maintain continuity between the content of different pages within the resulting application. This does impair both the resulting content and the required communication with the consumer. The mockup to summarize the primary creator task is displayed in **Figure 6.6**.

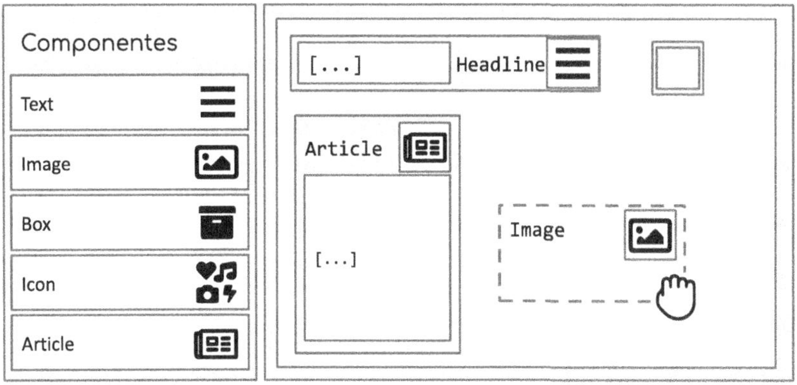

Figure 6.6 Mockup WYSIWYG Components

Furthermore, asserting a persistent appearance throughout the institution is not the only issue. Reflecting coherences within the resulting app pages and the related datasets would create further problems regarding the shareability and maintainability of the underlying data and any dependent system. Without enforcing a reliable architecture to establish semantic meaning or relationships between certain entities, the framework cannot be conveyed.

The overall proposal would certainly be able to accomplish the short-term goal of offering the ability for museum professionals to create mobile applications. Yet, it would fail to inject long-term value and a coherent strategy into those institutions the framework is supposed to be exposed to. Thus, the usability on both ends of the process would suffer tremendously. To focus on the next iteration, the concept has been dismissed in the early prototyping stage because of its incompatibility with both the domain itself and the desired problem solution.

6.2.3 App Pages

The third major iteration—to serendipitously yield the concept which is pursued throughout the remainder of this thesis—strives to find a solid middle ground between properly structuring datasets and the visual connection between the data inquiry and the resulting consumer application.

The lessons learned throughout the previous iterations as well as the knowledge accumulated by interacting with domain experts, allowed the conceptualization of this final approach to satisfy the expectations for both the creator and the consumer use cases to be addressed. In general, within the ecosystem occupied by mobile applications, the majority of choices that would determine the appearance of content on the consumer's device are already well established. Without any good reason, those should not be reinvented to maintain the existing mental model of the consumer regarding mobile applications, as suggested in section 5.2. Furthermore, the Museum Application Domain provides a quite narrow context with a small number of predetermined and recurring elements to be characterized within the exhibition setting.

Those factors can be materialized by essentially inverting the previous approach and traversing certain restrictions on the app pages based on known parameters. The objective in this case then is twofold; first, a predetermined fixed structure for expected input values has to be established, which expresses the semantic conjunctions related to the resulting datasets; second, since then the information to be available is known, it is possible to map certain inputs directly to the visual representation of the resulting app pages to achieve consumable content from the very beginning.

Through this approach, the amount of free decisions and interactions the creator has to perform during data inquiry becomes drastically reduced. Furthermore, the setup enables easily repeatable patterns and processes while leaving open the door to alter and extend certain configurations within both the suggested data model and the user interface.

Consequently, this does require some upstream effort to define certain page types, including the underlying data model and the layout to render the expected content of the resulting app pages. The benefits of those pages being self-contained include lucidity, consistency, and predictability. Furthermore, the complexity associated with data entry, filing, and retrieval is drastically improved, which in turn facilitates the process for the creator.

At this point, they simply have to *choose a page type* relevant to the information to be entered and *select a template* to represent the information within the mobile application. Since the parameters to be entered are determined by those choices, a form can be provided, including a field for each necessary data element. The creator then has to provide the information *to fill in the content form*. The core responsibilities of this approach are shown in the workflow in **Figure 6.7**.

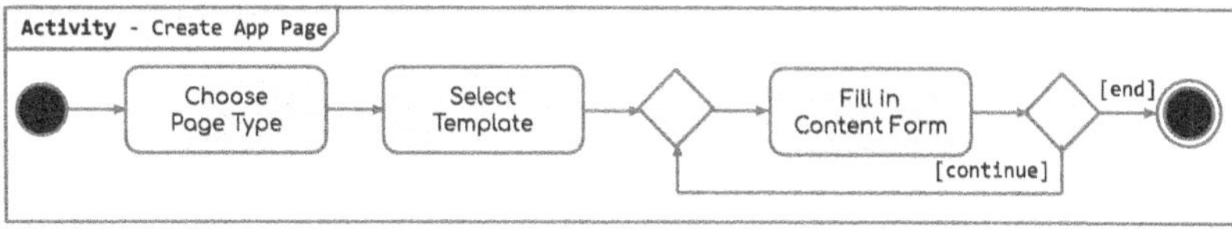

Figure 6.7 App Pages Workflow

Coincidentally, if the inquiry is form-based, it does implicate the contributions of structured data that enable data validation, integrity, as well as shareability and searchability. Considered in isolation, this usage of a form would not offer any advantages toward typical database prompts, which would interfere with the actual goals of the framework. However, since a template has been prepared and selected prior to the inquiry, it becomes possible to represent the context and demonstrate the immediate utility of the performed task. A preview of the resulting content for the app page can be provided in real-time by displaying the template and filling in the values entered by the creator to showcase the content to be received by the consumer. Providing the visual cues to convey the coherence between the semantic connotations of the data model and the content elements on the screen is going to increase the celerity of introducing non-expert to the task. Additionally, it increases comprehensibility and creates awareness for the purpose of the obligatory burden represented by the inquiry without being exposed to the underlying complexity of the interaction itself. The composition is represented in **Figure 6.8**.

Furthermore, the introduction of predefined page types incidentally has the added benefit of gathering experience throughout the progress and providing guidance for the composition of the final consumer app. The necessity to assemble the consumer application is an intrinsic goal of the framework. The determination of the order—or the orchestration of the sequencing, respectively—of the available pages to be accessed by the consumer via the app can be easily conducted in a subsequent process, as shown in **Figure 6.9**. As the visual connection has already been established during data inquiry and is maintained by the underlying data model, the creator can go ahead by *choosing a page type*. At this point, all the pages of the chosen type can be displayed for the creator to select and *add a certain app page* of that type to the consumer application.

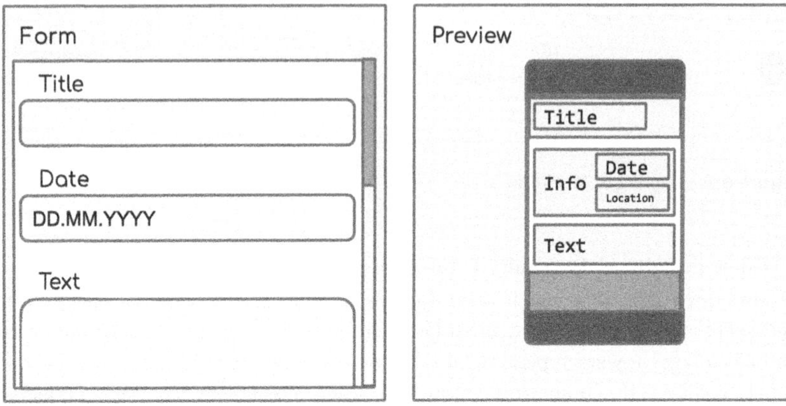

Figure 6.8 Mockup App Pages

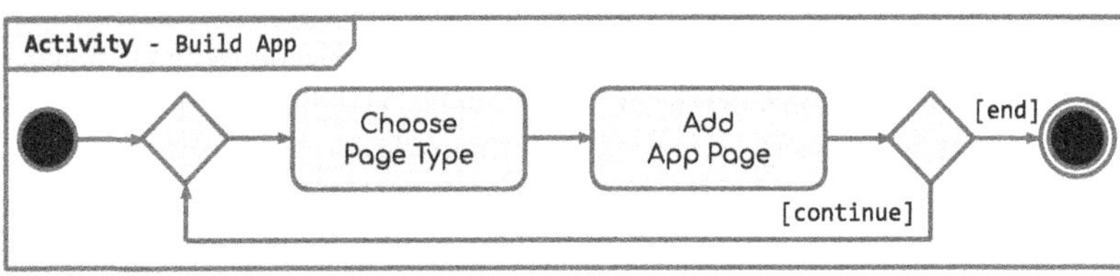

Figure 6.9 App Assembly Workflow

The overall exercise to create a mobile application is thereby split into separate tasks. That differentiation between the two workflows does take advantage of a logical breakpoint, which does not interrupt any one of the necessary responsibilities and allows the creator to focus and take one step at a time.

6.2.4 Conceptual Core of the Framework

That third iteration does show that by limiting the essential choices of the creator for their initial interaction, the resulting product quality can be drastically enhanced. However, on the conceptual level, four distinct tasks associated with the involved assignments need to be addressed by the framework to cultivate a holistic approach. Furthermore, a vital characteristic to be enforced throughout design and implementation is to keep those components self-contained such that each task can be approached independently while serving the common goals of the framework. These four tasks can be divided either *(one)* into two layers to cover both the operational perspective, which is primarily perceptible to the users, and the formational aspects, fundamental to the allocation of the required services; or *(two)* into two columns to separate the components into the visual approach as well as the data-centered responsibilities. For the sake of argument, the first viewpoint, primarily observing the two layers, is chosen to follow the logic organically occupied by the progression described above.

Within the first layer, the operational tasks the creator and consumer need to perform are addressed. By providing the domain context and thus exclusively requesting indisputable inputs, the identified procedure for the *mandatory task* allows for a structure emulating distinct breakpoints that logically connects to each of the other adjacent components. To fulfill the goals and to reflect the necessary responsibilities within the framework with a clear focus on the outcome, i.e., the consumer application, *context visualization* is essential.

On top of that, the second layer tends to those assignments which do facilitate the interactions previously described but do not directly require the creator's involvement. First, the *creative possibilities* associated with the look and feel of the content to be delivered to the consumer as well as the observable structure of the creator application must be asserted. In that regard, especially the insights into human-computer interaction discussed in subsection 5.1.3 need to be incorporated. Furthermore, it is necessary to supervise the inputs effectuated by the creator and to establish robust datasets associated with the inclined content pages by enforcing strict *data validation.*

Overall, both the data inquiry process, to be performed by the creator, and the presentation of the content, to be approached by the consumer, are closely tied to those app pages. They are the foundation directly embedded within the domain model at the core of the framework. The one-dimensional nature of the single-page app paradigm creates clarity during the page creation process but causes certain undesirable restrictions later. As transpired during the early stages of testing, while overall beneficial, from the creator's perspective, it has not been possible to express certain connections and affiliations between those pages during app assembly if pages were only to be chained together in a linear fashion (compare: Section 8.1). One common way to arrange those connections between different content elements are hyperlinks. Hyperlinks are digital references to other content, resources, or data to be accessed by the user, and are the backbone of the World Wide Web (compare: Section 7.2). However, in the context of the application framework, deep link-chains would invalidate the integrity of the underlying concept of collecting coherent and isolated data documents and also would disrupt any linear process for both user groups, equally essential for the data creation and presentation.

The *Composition Ubiquity Building Element* (**CUBE**) concept has been developed to maintain the framework's desired capabilities at the data document level and enable the portrayal of certain dependencies. That concept associates certain content elements with sides from the surface of a cube—hence the backronym—and utilizes the consumer navigation elements in the app to grant access to associated content pages.

That CUBE concept, shown in **Figure 6.10**, therefore, enables more volume for creators to express their intent to create and deliver better content. It allows for injecting the properties necessary for the navigation and appearance of the resulting consumer application directly within the data model at the architectural level. That allows to maintain the linear approach and reduces overall complexity, while offering a way to enable a compelling means for portraying content, storytelling, and engagement. The CUBE is further described throughout the prototype development in Chapter 7.

Figure 6.10 The CUBE Concept

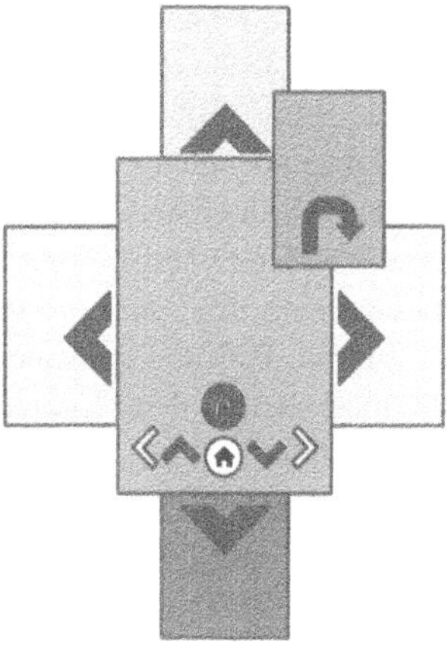

Finally, the acronym **PCCR**, short for *Page CUBE Content Representation*, is chosen to outline the four essential tasks to represent the conceptual core of the framework, as summarized in **Figure 6.11**.

Figure 6.11 The Conceptual Core of the PCCR App Framework

To achieve a deeper understanding of those components and to suggest concrete guidance for the following steps necessary to design and develop the framework itself, the inner sequencing of these components needs to be accentuated.

The creative possibilities encapsulate the *design workflow*, which does include the selection of the required data elements as well as the arrangement of those elements on the screen of the consumer's device. This step can be approached bidirectionally, either by examining a model derived from an existing database and *creating a template [1a]* to include and arrange the relevant data elements or by *building a data model [1b]* first to introduce a new model altogether, which in turn can provide the blueprint for a template.

The significance of the mandatory task representing the *creator workflow* and the necessary connection to the context visualization represented by the *consumer view* has been previously underlined throughout each of the three featured design iterations. Thus, the *data input [A]* itself does rely on the model previously conceived. The model for a certain page type does provide the foundation for *data processing* and validation, as it contains the information to *generate a form [i]* for the inquiry of the required data. Thus, the inputs performed by the creator can be compared to the expected values by *validating the input [ii]* against the said model. This procedure does enable two major operations. First, it allows auditing the integrity of the resulting datasets and to *persist the data [iii]* to the connected database. Second, as the model is bound to a template by design to *display the data [B]* as it is supposed to be approached by the consumer, the resulting dataset can be inserted without any unnecessary transformation.

The internal flow of the interaction and the role of each component within the PCCR framework are projected in **Figure 6.12**.

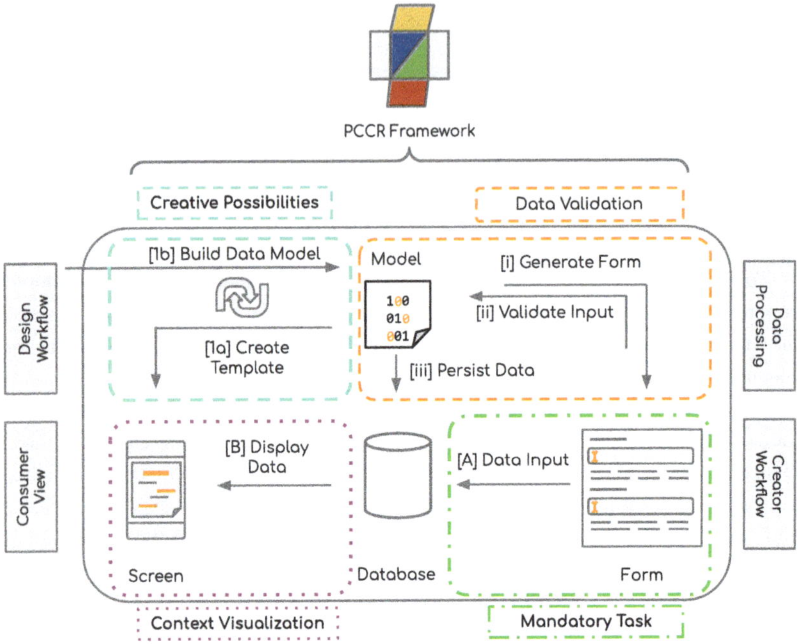

Figure 6.12 The Components provided by the PCCR App Framework

6.3 Detailed Framework Scope

The presentation layer for the consumer acts as the conceptual anchor for the creator. However, depending on the *content* to be prepared for the resulting mobile application, different levels of *complexity* emerge. The orthogonal alignment of those two dimensions directly results in the possible configuration of content preparation, delivery, and interaction opportunities, as shown in **Figure 6.13**.

First, it is important to state that the output of the framework is not meant to replace solutions already existing within the exhibition, like labels or in-person tours, nor systems facilitating the administration of the collection. The goal is to complement and extend the overall portfolio, especially for small institutions, to facilitate the first steps toward a digital strategy. Thus, the intent is to provide an

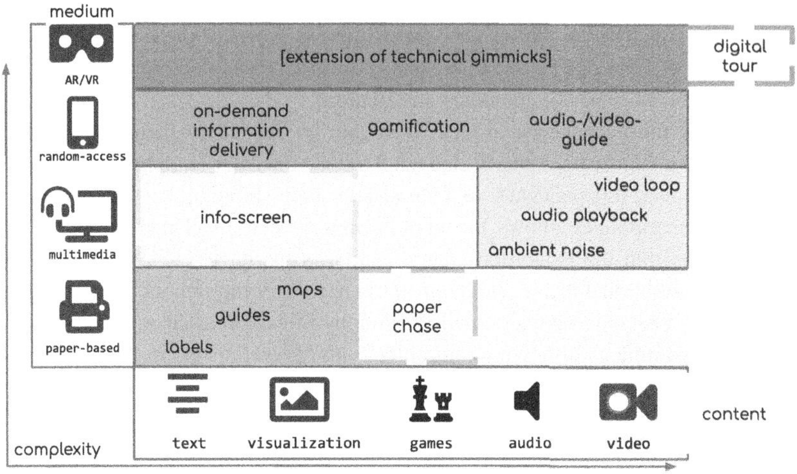

Figure 6.13 Resulting Output Realization

entry point for museum professionals for creating digital content and providing access to information for the visitor. That also allows providing digital information in spaces that could not have been supported by traditional means (e.g., outdoors).

It is decisive to understand the cohesion of the vertical extension of established and well-understood *paper-based* formats to their technical, more complex manifestation. This perspective aides in identifying certain blind spots and channeling desires and expectations. Nevertheless, actual needs must be aligned with the intended purpose and the capabilities within the organization before horizontal integration can be reasonably pursued to avoid misguided experiments which cannot be sustained long-term.

Herein lies the significant issue of most passive *multimedia* installations. Info-screens can supplement traditional information outlets, like printed labels, guides, or maps, reasonably well. Yet, the actual benefits of screens occur at an increased content complexity, consisting almost exclusively of audiovisual elements. As previously stated, the adequate production of that content cannot be carried out successfully by the institution. The inevitability of outside assistance does not encourage knowledge transfer and leads to long-term dependencies. Furthermore, the gap in the interaction opportunities, which to a certain degree can be created within the paper-based realm, i.e., paper chases, prevents the consumer from being put into the center of attention. This is further interrupted by the limitations and accessibility issues of stationary installations.

Many of those obstacles can be overcome by the deployment of *random-access guides*. Information can be delivered to the consumer on demand in a more targeted manner, independently of time and location. In addition, the interactive nature of smartphones allows the gamification of certain elements to support immersion within the exhibition environment. As the device of the recipient is utilized, no additional technical equipment is necessary throughout the exhibition space. This especially enables small institutions to explore their options without upstream investments or downstream obligations, as well as to cover larger areas that cannot be supported by stationary infrastructure.

To further reduce external dependencies for the museum itself and to encourage organic knowledge transfer, the same attention usually received only by the consumer needs to be paid forward to the creator. The setting of using mobile applications within the exhibition space creates a symbiotic context, recognizable and beneficial for both user groups. This holistic approach highlights the restrictions presented by the domain and the technology while supporting the composition of objective guidelines to yield reliable results.

Since the production and presentation beyond static text and images are difficult to support without prior knowledge, specialized training, expensive equipment, or a combination of those resources, the content creation processes embedded within the suggested framework are going to be organized accordingly. Yet, the framework should provide suitable interfaces to allow for extensibility in the future, both within the data and presentation layers. Thus, content relying on complex digitalization of exhibits, like 3D models, or specifically designed for delivery systems that require technology more advanced than offered by commercially available smartphones will not be considered going forward. That does include *Augmented and Virtual Reality* and, by extension, digital tours, as well as other technical gimmicks of subjacent content layers.

This leads to ten specific *(1–10)* stipulations for the requirements of *A Framework for Mobile Apps in the Museum Application Domain*, which are summarized in **Figure 6.14** and then outlined throughout the following pages.

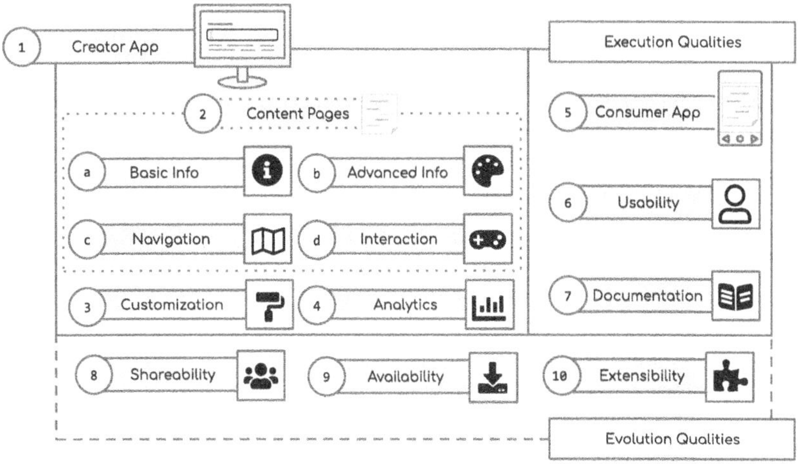

Figure 6.14 Requirements of the Framework for Mobile Apps in the Museum Application Domain

The clear differentiation of the tangible requirements from the structural components is imperative to solidify the intent and create a frame of reference to test the resulting IT artifact. The primary objective consists of four functional requirements consequential to the creator's perspective (*1–4*). On top of that, six non-functional requirements are to be drafted to complete the operational capability of the framework, as well as to reflect and unite the demands of both the consumer and the creator (*5–10*). Those demands can be further divided into three execution qualities which are going to be observable during operation (*5–7*), and three evolution qualities directly embedded into the system's structure (*8–10*) to enable growth and approachability.

Additionally, the resulting system is supposed to meet the meta-requirements derived from the building blocks for mobile visitor applications presented in section 3.2 to fulfill its purpose within the Museum Application Domain. Of those seven criteria, 'Visualization' (*2c*) and 'Games' (*2d*) are directly subsumed within the primary goals above. Furthermore, the ability to weave fragmental information together to achieve compelling 'Storytelling' within the consumer application (*5*) must be available from within the creator application (*1*) and is resolved by the CUBE architecture. Support for 'Multilingual' distribution is represented within the goal of shareability (*8*), and catering to the 'Perambulator' is part of the general considerations for the availability of the application regarding the visitor (*9*). The two elements consciously omitted from that suggested list are 'Video' for the issues related to its production and 'Inclusion', for the obvious challenges that arise within the complexity of adjusting content for visual or otherwise impaired individuals. However, the possibility of including those elements during a later iteration should not be overlooked (*10*).

(1) The Creator App

The application of the creator is the linchpin of the whole framework realization. Without a proper way to comprehend and execute the steps necessary to input and preprocess information, it cannot be transformed, stored, or accessed by anyone.

The disclosure and discovery of existing demands and possibilities connected to mobile applications in small museums can only be successful by acknowledging the context and the inherent issues. Furthermore, those issues cannot be solved exclusively on a conceptual level nor in theory alone. The two dimensions of complexity summarized in **Figure 6.13** indicate the necessity of the fundamental goal to enable museum professionals to take the steps up from their known medium and to utilize the possibilities of the random-access guide to their advantage.

The practical implications need to be considered, and hands-on experiences are encouraged to directly enable museum professionals with no prior knowledge and minimal resources to get started with digital projects and engage in the application creation procedure. Thus, the whole process needs to be broken down into steps that are easy to understand, to learn, and to perform.

Beyond that, it is not quite enough to create only the opportunity. To realize the unmitigated value of structured data, creators must be provided with an intuitive interface to guide them through the process of creating information pages for mobile applications. The assembly of actual apps, ready to be deployed, and to be instantly accessible by visitors without the need to involve developers, is supposed to provide the main incentive for the data input.

Regardless of the input mechanism, content must be directed toward a dedicated audience. The setting within the Museum Application Domain requires answering the most urgent questions of the visitor, introduced in section 3.2:

- What is that? / What does it represent?
- What would it look like?
- Where does it come from?
- What was it connected to?
- How was it used?

(2) Content Pages

To answer those questions and to prepare content suitable for the consumer in general, a certain shift in perspective is required, compared to the usual tasks related to data input museum professionals are confronted with.

There are different ways in which the data input can be approached within the historico-cultural context. The three fundamental design iterations on how to engage that process for the creator are described in the previous section. To achieve the desired outcome—a way to guide and incentivize the creator to contribute—content pages that represent the consumer's perspective throughout the whole process have been embraced. Ergo, the content page is the architectural backbone of the framework as it represents the connection of the requirements, which descend from design and data-structure specifications and directly enables the CUBE architecture introduced above. The underlying free-form ontology, responsible for mapping the content to the data model and its template, is described in subsection 6.5.1.

The framework is meant to enable cultural heritage institutions to represent themselves in the digital realm for a casual audience. Thus, information about the museum itself, as well as their exhibitions and exhibits, needs to be included. The information must be collected and presented in such a way that the consumer can easily access and comprehend it while being flexible enough to meet the requirements of the creator and the institution itself. The content necessary to fulfill those demands for the framework is divided into the four categories 'basic info', 'advanced info', 'navigation', and 'interaction' (*a–d*) as described below.

(a) Basic Info

Firstly, museum professionals need the opportunity to compose essential 'basic info' including "information" about the museum itself, "opening hours", and "admission fees".

On the one hand, this is a suitable opportunity to get familiar with the ergonomics of the framework implementation from the creator's perspective as this information is readily accessible to them, and usually, its structure is quite obvious; on the other hand, this information is essential to complete the expected experience for the consumer.

(b) Advanced Info

Secondly, the data, metadata, and description of certain entities related to the exhibits encountered within the dedicated exhibition space or related to the collection of the museum must be recorded. The assortment of page types represented in the 'advanced information' category includes the entities "objects", "persons", "events", "places", as well as generic "text" to elaborate on certain material about those entities.

The selection of those select entities to be included within the framework and its prototype implementation has been based on standards encountered within the Museum Application Domain and the needs of the participating museum professionals and institutions in the ViSIT project.

(c) Navigation

Additionally, next to the information directly related to the museum and its exhibits, consumers need to be supported in navigating the premises they encounter. The creator must be able to address the layout of the museum or the exhibition space, as well as the location of the exhibits to be explored by the consumer. For the framework, it is important to facilitate this without any additional hardware requirements for the operation of the app itself.

The so-called 'blue dot' navigation is the pinnacle for indoor spaces, which would require triangulating the consumer's device to identify its location relative to the observable area at any point in time. However, that would require the distribution of Wi-Fi Routers, Bluetooth, or Radio Frequency Identification (RFID) beacons throughout those spaces. In consequence, the addition of such a feature would add complexity, increase costs, and is often impractical. Thus, it does not contribute to the solution of the actual issues to be discussed (Khruahong, Kong, Sandrasegaran, & Liu, 2017).

Nevertheless, way-finding, orientation, and 'navigation' still need to be addressed but in a more simplistic manner. To be sustainable in the proposed scenario, the suggestions are derived from well-perceived paper-based mapping solutions.

(d) Interaction

Lastly, the possibilities provided by touchscreens in random-access guides compared to passive multimedia devices and installations facilitate user engagement by adding simple interactive and gamified elements.

While these opportunities are almost limitless, in the spirit of the suggested framework, any included component must be simple to curate and easy to interact with. Furthermore, not all forms of digital games are suitable for the Museum Application Domain and the environment encountered throughout the exhibition setting.

Nevertheless, simple pop-quiz style questions can be utilized with almost no restrictions or downside and contribute to a more desirable consumer experience, as suggested in subsection 3.2.1.

(3) Customization

As briefly acknowledged before in subsection 5.2.3, most museum professionals are concerned with the adaptation of controllable visual cues well known from paper-based information outlets to adjust certain elements of the appearance of the resulting application. This helps to promote and integrate the resulting app into the existing environment. This goal explicitly applies only to the influence which can be exerted onto and applied within the consumer application by the creator. The creator application itself is excluded in that regard, as it is only accessible by members of the institution and not visible to third-party individuals.

Customization may also help to enhance the user experience for the consumer to a certain extent. Particular conditions must be met for those effects to unfold. To provide such a personalized experience for the consumer, often the concept of recommendation engines is applied (Kontiza, Loboda, Deladiennee, Castagnos, & Naudet, 2018). In the context of museums, that does require a certain number of comparable objects to generate accurate predictions and create satisfactory individualized subsets. However, small museums are usually furnished with limited inventory. Thus, the exhibition environment itself also predetermines some key criteria. The time spent by the consumer within an exhibition is usually limited, and the exhibits are arranged in a linear manner. Thus, recommendations that violate the natural order would generate additional friction, which in turn leads to a disruption of the overall experience for the consumer. Additionally, the legal issues associated with customer tracking and account management are difficult to communicate. Therefore, content customization for the consumer is not pursued by the framework and the corresponding prototype implementation suggested by this thesis.

That does not imply that there are no possibilities for individualization which can be addressed from the creator's perspective beyond adapting the app's appearance alone. If anything, it is most desirable to allow them to communicate their intent and individual goals to encourage their engagement in the content and app creation processes. To control and steer those possibilities, it is helpful to offer some key parameters that reflect the intent and purpose of the application, including the expected audience for the content contained within the resulting app.

Furthermore, the CUBE architecture allows the creator to group and combine existing app pages as well as to add images and interaction opportunities to construct and customize the experience for the consumer.

(4) Analytics

One of the central elements of any information system is the ability to measure its impact on the environment it is going to be deployed to. However, in the spirit of the framework, it is not quite enough to just collect certain data. The goal is to produce a useful tool for members of the institutions within the Museum Application Domain to get an idea of their audience and to improve their offerings over time.

Ongoing analysis of the visitor's behavior is not commonly pursued by many institutions, as discovered in subsection 3.2.2. This can be primarily attributed to the limited opportunities for museums and exhibitions to track and gather relevant data. To avoid the possible legal issues associated with tracking user information, it is important to do so in a secure and anonymized way.

While it is not compelling nor useful to track every step of the consumer's way throughout the exhibition, some crucial insights on time spent within the exhibition and on the priority of the examined exhibits can help to sharpen the self-awareness of the museum and its offerings. To let the creator gain those fundamental insights based on the usage of the consumer application, both automated logging and proper presentation of those insights are necessary.

(5) Consumer App

The framework must also offer a mechanism for the institution to deliver the processed information to its visitors. The 'consumer app' grants access to the content pages created by the museum professional. This is supposed to occur in a manner that consumers who want to visit a museum and learn about or interact with the exhibition can access this information on their own devices without operating proprietary technology. The benefits of BYOD have been discussed in subsection 3.2.2. Furthermore, the necessary data to enable the functionality described within (*4 'Analytics'*) must be collected within the app and channeled back to the institution.

While mobile applications, in general, have some functional implications on their own, within the context of the framework, the mere conceptual existence of the consumer app acts as an anchor for the whole content creation process.

(6) Usability

For the implementation of both the creator and the consumer application embedded within the framework, it is important to follow the insights for human-centered design summarized in subsection 5.1.3 and apply the design principles introduced in subsection 5.2.1. These concepts identified and the state of the art surrounding modern web- and mobile-technology need to be reflected so that the individual user of each system can engage in a suitable experience that satisfies their expectations.

The greatest difference in screen design of mobile applications is device orientation, distinguished between portrait and landscape mode. *Portrait* does refer to the long edge of the device held vertically, while *landscape* assumes a horizontal alignment of that edge. While certain designs use landscape mode to accommodate controls and menus, especially in the realm of mobile games, the default for most mobile interactions is portrait mode. Thus, the layouts for the consumer app in the prototype implementation of the framework use portrait mode exclusively. In contrast, the default for desktop applications is landscape, as most screen setups are oriented in that fashion (Bandi & Fellah, 2017).

The creator application is focused on the tasks of data entry and the app assembly process, which both heavily influence the experience of the consumer. Thus, it is important to consider the learning curve and guide the creator from simple data entries to more complex assignments, including the aforementioned technical storytelling capabilities. The quality of the resulting consumer application also relies on long-term engagement. Therefore, the functional design of the application and the fundamental architecture must be anticipatory in those regards.

The consumer app, on the other hand, is supposed to be operated by the visitor within the exhibition. Thus, it is important not to pose any distraction for the duration of the museum visit while offering additional information where it is warranted. Therefore, the user must be able to quickly grasp the on-screen information, as well as the elements, interaction opportunities, and assignments presented by the application. For both, the sparse utilization of scrolling and clear visual cues are factors to ensure a satisfactory user experience.

(7) Documentation

While, at the application level, it is important to provide user interfaces that are self-explanatory and easy to use, to support the adoption process offering an in-depth manual is essential.

Depending on the context and the prior knowledge of the expected user, different levels of support need to be prepared and offered. The consumer application should not require any accompanying documents for the consumer at runtime and should work 'out of the box' to preserve the user experience throughout the entire encounter. At the creator level, this is different. First, it is important to present the possible features of the consumer application in detail to create a sense of the possibilities offered by the framework implementation. Second, the features of the creator application and how to fulfill certain tasks need to be accurately exemplified. Even more support is necessary at the design and development stages, as well as documenting the interfaces provided by the framework.

For future developers, it is imperative to understand the structural components, data models and classes, as well as the functions and namespaces, which directly constitute themselves within the listings of the framework implementation. Comments need to be readily available at the lowest level of code, and critical information on the application interfaces must be elevated within comprehensive technical documentation.

Furthermore, the recurring user interface elements utilized by the framework implementation should be standardized and recognizable throughout the system. Especially, the templates for the app pages within the consumer app should follow an inner logic and thus need to be conceptually and visually preprocessed.

Those three critical levels of documentation ('user manual', 'technical documentation', and a 'styleguide') are vital components of the framework.

(8) Shareability

The documents discussed just before contribute to the accessibility and shareability of the framework itself. Providing these resources is essential to bestowing the difficulties of bottom-up design while enabling a smooth top-down experience that can produce viable results to be deployed instantly. The comprehensive knowledge to getting started is supposed to be easily accessible for the members of those institutions who want to engage in the creation process and deploy mobile applications for their visitors.

The explicit goal is not to provide a highly specialized product that rivals the state of the art of high-level individual institutions but a generalized product that can be deployed in the broad proximity of the Museum Application Domain to offer approachability from every perspective. It is supposed to spark curiosity and provide a learning opportunity for the creator to expand their understanding of the technical possibilities, as well as to provide and share information with their visitors.

Beyond the comprehensive entry point for the creator at the surface of the framework and the fundamental opportunity to share content with the visitor, the core architecture must directly enable and encourage collaboration. Especially within the context of the ViSIT project and the immediate involvement of many small individual institutions, it is important to enable them to connect, grow communities, and form relationships to cultivate and establish a network. As the underlying data model is supposed to ensure compatibility of the app pages created within any given institution anyway, the framework can act as a platform to share templates, app pages, and finished apps across institutions as well. That enables communication and allows museum professionals to pass on and share the knowledge they accumulate without introducing permanent attachments or long-term obligations. Also, that presents opportunities to make the visitor aware of existing connections between certain participating museums.

(9) Availability

Those arguments are also applicable to the availability of the framework, its implementation, and the allocated content. If the inquired information is only stored in a remote database without the opportunity to be accessed by the intended audiences, the whole purpose of the database is defeated. Thus, to guarantee availability for both user groups, it is important to select reasonable technology to implement the creator and consumer applications. The input devices for the creator, i.e., desktop or laptop computers, can be supervised by reasonable actions. However, the range of possible consumer devices and their associated software is vastly different and hardly comprehensible.

The wide array of mobile devices available today and the spread of their capabilities often lead to problems with accessing certain software solutions and constrain certain engagement opportunities. Web technologies do offer a convenient approach to circumvent the compatibility issues associated with native apps. As the latter are being bound to certain devices or distributors, web apps are supported by any appropriate device independent of the underlying platform. Also, that way, it is possible to ensure long-term resilience while preventing being locked in a temporary technology fad. An additional benefit of web applications is that they do circumvent the necessity to install software, granting instant access to the desired features, which does not only benefit the consumer but the creator as well. Nevertheless, one key feature that should be provided by the consumer application is to access relevant data, even if the device is offline, as it is often not possible to guarantee connection throughout the entire exhibition space.

To accommodate the necessities of the intended user, localization, i.e., offering the applications in multiple languages, is necessary not only for the consumer app but for the creator application as well.

Furthermore, availability is not just restricted to providing the proper software to the user. The framework and its associated applications need to consider the requirements discussed in (*6 'Usability'*) and (*7 'Shareability'*) as well as their operational area. Similar to the problems discussed in (*2c 'Navigation'*), consumer features that would rely on internal or external sensors do create subjection to which devices may not be capable of running the application in the intended environment or would increase the content complexity from the creator's perspective. Thus, it is desirable to not rely on using the sensors of the device, if at all possible.

These reflections concerning availability explicitly must apply not only to the deployability and approachability of the resulting system and its user interfaces but also to its documentation and other associated resources and components.

(10) Extensibility

The primary intent of the Framework for Mobile Apps in the MAD is to offer an entry point for inexperienced end users who need guidance to perform the associated tasks within an enclosed system. However, its architecture and structural components must not present themselves as an isolated black box. The system itself needs to be receptible for adaptations, changes, and extensions. That required extensibility does aid potential users by requiring simplicity and comprehensibility throughout the design, development, and implementation at any layer of the resulting information system. Thus, it is important to avoid complexity through to the very core of the framework.

To avoid structural limitations and to allow the flexibility to adapt to new devices and interfaces in the future, an independent and flexible model is necessary. That construct is supposed to be technology-agnostic and must avoid external dependencies. That should not block the acknowledgment of existing structures but encourage the definition of proper interfaces and invite collaboration wherever possible to not eliminate any compatibility possibilities. Because of that, the conscious decision has been made against adhering to the complexity associated with the strict adoption of a domain-specific ontology (i.e., CIDOC CRM) or an existing data modeling technology (i.e., WebML). Those might not fit the unique perspective of the problem domain, nor the identified set of issues, and may restrict innovation and comprehensibility for the tangible goals moving forward.

In the sense of distillation, the model itself needs to be available to anyone who is capable of executing the development process independently and must remain recognizable within any resulting implementation. In addition to the demand for the extensibility capabilities of the framework, it is important to offer the user to partake in design and governance to further reduce the barriers of entry by adjusting the complexity accordingly.

6.4 Technological Scaffold

Some of the defined goals can only be met at the time of implementation as they manifest at the runtime of the given application or are directly connected to the interaction between the user and certain applications. The prototype development thus is an integral element of this thesis and the evaluation process, and as such, is addressed in Chapter 7.

An implementation, however, does not create value on its own if considered in isolation. As any instantiation only provides a limited snapshot of the available possibilities. The resulting software, thus, is not supposed to solve the problems which should be addressed by the framework, as it does encounter a finite serviceable life, but to provide an environment to demonstrate and assess the suggested solutions.

Thus, a proper architectural foundation that can be replicated, validated, and extended has to be constructed first. Moreover, if those preparations become established, an implementation can further substantiate the concept based on the core issues within the domain and as a starting point for future examinations (*Subsection 6.4.1—Architectural Concepts*).

Therefore, before any implementation attempt should commence in a meaningful way, the conceptual core, as well as the functional scope, have to be translated into a concrete set of architectural instructions. This is also necessary to satisfy the underlying requirements of the app framework. To engineer such a skeleton architecture, the top-down design primarily based on the visualization of the target application must be met with a solid structural foundation to support proper bottom-up development with a set of appropriate technologies.

Especially the three evolutionary qualities suggested above need to be addressed at the architectural core of the framework. Therefore, this section proposes a comprehensible blueprint to contain and satisfy the architectural requirements posed likewise by the two methodological approaches, DSR and DDD (*Subsection 6.4.2—The MV* Design Pattern*).

6.4.1 Architectural Concepts

With the rapidly advancing possibilities of information systems, over time, their internal complexity also did escalate, and it became increasingly difficult to maintain monolithic architectures and to administer specific responsibilities properly. Design patterns have emerged to facilitate systematic designs and manifest proven solutions to problems commonly expected to be encountered in software engineering projects. Those patterns aim to address the reusability of certain components by bridging many levels of abstraction and addressing both the functional and non-functional properties of the resulting IT artifact. Especially in dynamic environments, it is essential to provide close alignment to the fundamental structure of the problem domain. That allows structural coupling to the identified problems without requiring a complete model of all associated operations, which does create the flexibility necessary for modification and to accommodate evolution in the future (Winn & Calder, 2002).

In object-oriented software projects, in particular, suggested by domain-driven design, a variant of the hexagonal architecture introduced in 2005 by Alistair Cockburn is utilized (Evans, 2003) (Cockburn, 2005). The primary purpose of that approach has been to avoid structural entanglements and undesired dependencies within certain systems, especially those following a layered structure, as discussed in section 5.2. The primary concern is the contamination of the user interface code with business logic. Additionally, if external data services are involved, the migration of crucial data operations may impair the executability of the core application (Cockburn, 2005).

This does apply especially to environments and data-driven systems closely related to embedded preprogramming. Those strongly subscribe to the idea of pipelines, consisting of *pipes and filters*. As these approaches inherently do require loose coupling to the degree that it becomes difficult to introduce more complex layers onto the top (Sandoval, 2020). The main purpose of pipelines is to transport data from the data source to the data target. Thus, they best support linear processes (Hasan, 2019). The transportation via pipes is supposed to guarantee efficiency for precise and narrow applications like compilers. Operations performed within the filters may exhibit high levels of transformative complexity that even may be hidden inside black boxes and therefore masking previous operations or the data source itself. Thus, this approach struggles to keep up with the requirements of more substantiated or dynamic implementations. Requiring deep point-to-point integration in larger systems, which also require human interaction, would introduce profound dependencies and thus hinder comprehensibility and maintainability.

The hexagonal architecture, therefore, suggests the deployment of *ports and adapters* to process events triggered from outside the system and to preserve the boundaries of the use case represented within the application core. Other than the name would suggest the setup does not require six components. The hexagon is merely a visual aid to accommodate sufficient ports and their connected adapters. By defining clear interfaces (ports) for each service connected to the application, they can be exchanged at will, as each is addressed independently without eroding the application core, as long as the exposed API rules are observed. These ports are then able to provide specialized components (adapters), which apply the appropriate gateway to process requests to the application or to provide the applicable outcome (Cockburn, 2005). The inner business logic within the application core thus can operate independently and uninterrupted, as the communication is facilitated by supplying the defined ports. The connections to the database and the presentation mechanisms can be managed separately under consideration of the resources allocated by the application core. That distinct disjunction also does contribute to a clear line of communication as the core features are isolated. Issues this approach does experience are related to fragmentation and scalability, which may impair the overall performance in large systems. Especially in networked and enterprise architectures, it is crucial to keep certain services available or distribute resources across multiple locations.

One notable suggestion that attempts to organize the architectural setup of business applications in a network is known as Service-Oriented Architecture (SOA). The initial goal of the approach that was proposed in 1998 by the Network Applications Consortium is to break down the inevitable complexity of larger enterprise systems into logical units closely related to the core business processes and tasks encountered within a company (Laskey & Laskey, 2009).

These service components are supposed to be self-contained in the system. The individual connection to the affiliated data storage is to be encapsulated within the service provider level. Thus, each service constitutes an independent black box to not expose the inner complexity to the service consumer layer. However, to enable the primordial business use case, the interoperability and exchange between those services must be established and safeguarded. That communication is supposed to be managed within the *enterprise service bus*, a brokerage system layer requiring discrete governance and security measures to manage the availability of critical information to the services attached. The added layer of complexity decreases the approachability of the provided application environment for inexperienced or non-specialist associates. The inherent asymmetry does introduce the necessity for scalable structures and performance issues, especially in smaller application environments (Bianco, Kotermansk, & Merson, 2007) (Sarwar, 2020). Additionally, the bus is susceptible to shadow structures or inner arbitrage, inducing convoluted permission structures and overhead. The requirement for services to facilitate the bus causes a vicious circle, resurfacing the issues previously experienced with the layered architecture.

Therefore, the scope of SOA is not limited to one individual application but rather an enterprise-wide concept. To recognize these issues and to acknowledge individualized interpretations, the SOA Source Book published in 2009 by the Open Group chose an almost arbitrary definition. To emphasize the service orientation beyond self-contained systems, it addresses distributed software systems that rely on external resources or services outside the manageable scope connected via the internet (The Open Group, 2009) (Goebelbecker, 2019). In that regard, SOA is commonly confused with 'web services'. While SOA represents an architectural concept, the term 'web services' refers to a collection of technologies able but not restricted to facilitating the implementation of SOA (Bianco, Kotermansk, & Merson, 2007). That confusion primarily originates from the similarity between the SOA acronym and the Simple Object Access Protocol (SOAP). SOAP is a standard protocol based on the eXtensible Markup Language (XML) designed for communication and compliance between applications built on different platforms or languages within a distributed environment, i.e., web services (Box, et al., 2000).

The main reason to emphasize that differentiation is the growing popularity of microservices. The microservice architecture is based on the combination of the three aforementioned architectural considerations. While Netflix—a popular video streaming provider—is often referred to as the innovator, the exact origin is disputed. In general, the approach has been popularized primarily by agile and innovative companies to govern service granularity based on the organizational context to accommodate rapid enterprise growth (Thönes, 2015). In that sense, microservices can be understood as a dilation of SOA with the goal to avoid the reemerging of silo structures and to enable more flexibility. That is supposed to avoid the overhead and structural issues related to the centralized construct represented by the enterprise service bus.

Furthermore, the necessity to compartmentalize services into actual business use cases is abandoned in favor of modularity and lucidity, as well as to avoid integration issues by eliminating shadow structures and black boxes. Each service would be perceived as an individual application, constructed comparable to a hexagon, which can be developed, tested, deployed, scaled, and maintained independently (Hasselbring & Steinacke, 2017). Ideally, each of these applications is supervised by a dedicated team. To realize reliable communication and achieve loose coupling in a designated application environment, multiple of those (micro-) services would then be connected via dedicated pipelines. That requires reliable data flow and transparent information transfer, as a considerable amount of complexity is deferred to the networking layer. A popular approach to guarantee accuracy for internet-scale applications is the basic concept of 'smart endpoints' in a 'dumb network' (Thönes, 2015).

To enable a homogenous process for the transfer of resources between client and server, Uniform Resource Identifiers (URI) are deployed. These identifiers consist of a compact sequence of characters unique to an abstract or physical resource. Thus, ideally, these identifiers are unique, at least within the application environment or even beyond, to ensure a homogenous interface landscape. The exposed server port must provide the requested resource to a precise client-request within the application environment accordingly (Berners-Lee, Fielding, & Masinter, 1998).

Thus, filters are not to be applied within the pipeline but administered directly by the responding service, according to the inbound request. Additionally, these precise interfaces are supposed to ensure stateless client-server communication. In other words, the requesting (client) system is self-contained and does not have to expose the state of its session to other services at runtime. The transferred resources are ideally represented by the domain model of the bounded context within the application environment and, thus, transferred in a standardized form. These resources can be cached to be steadily observed, eliminating certain recurring transformations or redundant client-server interactions, especially to aid the scalability of layered systems. That also does reiterate the emphasis on domain-driven design. APIs that adhere to these guidelines are also referred to as RESTful, referring to the embedded Representational State Transfer (REST) (Fielding & Taylor, 2002) (Rodriguez, 2008).

Since both the unique identifier and the transferred resources are supposed to be standardized within the scope of the application environment, the requirements concerning the transportation itself are minimal. Thus, it is sufficient to resort to the HyperText Transfer Protocol (HTTP), originally designed for the communication between web-server and browser but utilized for many internet-based services (Rodriguez, 2008). To ensure compatibility between different systems, the resource is preferably transposed via JavaScript Object Notation (JSON), which despite its name, is a lightweight text-based format independent of platforms and languages while preserving human readability (Peng, Cao, & Xu, 2011). JSON is preferred as a data exchange format in comparison to XML as it offers a text-based approach to model objects and arrays, as shown in **Figure 6.15**.

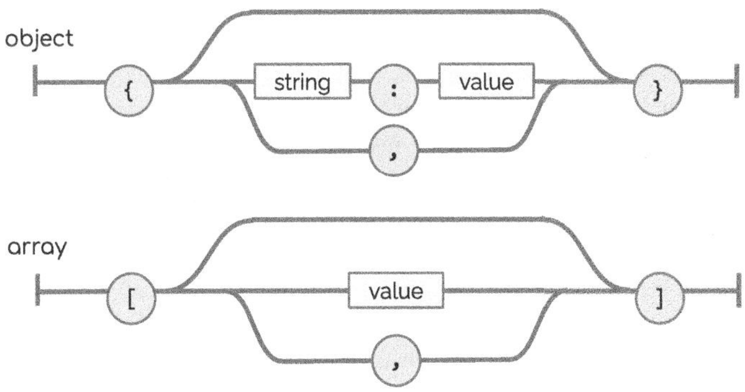

Figure 6.15 JSON: Object and Array Notation

Those structures can be easily translated to their representations within many programming languages, thus increasing readability while reducing overhead and maintaining interoperability (Crockford, 2006). Therefore, a RESTful is more resourceful and carries less overhead than SOAP as it does not patronize transaction compliance (Rodriguez, 2008).

The client-side counterpart of REST would be Asynchronous JavaScript and XML (AJAX). Again, other than what the name would suggest, the technology is not tied to XML and is mostly deployed with JSON for the reasons explained above. The goal is to make the interaction of users with web applications feel more organic, like traditional desktop applications. To do that, requests from the client application would be sent to RESTful APIs via HTTP, and the data received in response can be received and processed using JavaScript without the need to reload the entire page, hence asynchronous. That does eliminate the necessity to request additional resources necessary to display the data and allows the state of the page to be preserved without tracking it throughout the interaction cycle (Paulson, 2005). Additionally, that approach does reduce traffic, which is especially relevant in mobile use cases. This deployment approach for a website is also referred to as *headless architecture*, where the standalone frontend-components communicate with the (distributed) database backend only via a (RESTful) API which is operated independently (Dee, 2022) (not to be confused with headless computing, which refers to disregarding GUI for certain systems—compare: Section 7.3).

One of the most important drivers of such distributed systems is the growing popularity of cloud computing and containerization, immensely reducing hardware dependencies. It becomes possible for software applications to be deployed within a serverless architecture—in that context, architecture refers to the hardware level—a cloud computing execution model may utilize subscription-based billing to allocate hardware event-based or on-demand as required rather than reserving dedicated machines for specific tasks. That commoditization eliminates the need for planning hardware resources or utilization thereof in advance, enabling seamless scaling and virtually no up-front investment for the application developer (McGrath & Brenner, 2017).

These four architectural concepts, visualized in **Figure 6.16**, tend to provide guidelines on how to assemble and compose complex enterprise application landscapes. Thus, it is possible to efficiently avoid certain problems and provide a blueprint for the bigger picture. However, they are unsuitable to provide the necessary insights for outside observers, as the resulting application environment quickly becomes reduced to a black box once again. The imposed requirements often produce massive overhead to govern the expected service mash, as well as the integration of critical service paths between internal dependencies. That may be necessary to preserve interoperability within a larger system environment; however, it does restrict the verbosity of any particular system embedded within. Nonetheless, the recent advances in web technologies rely on the significant and defining core principles explored above and, therefore, can be observed in most modern web applications.

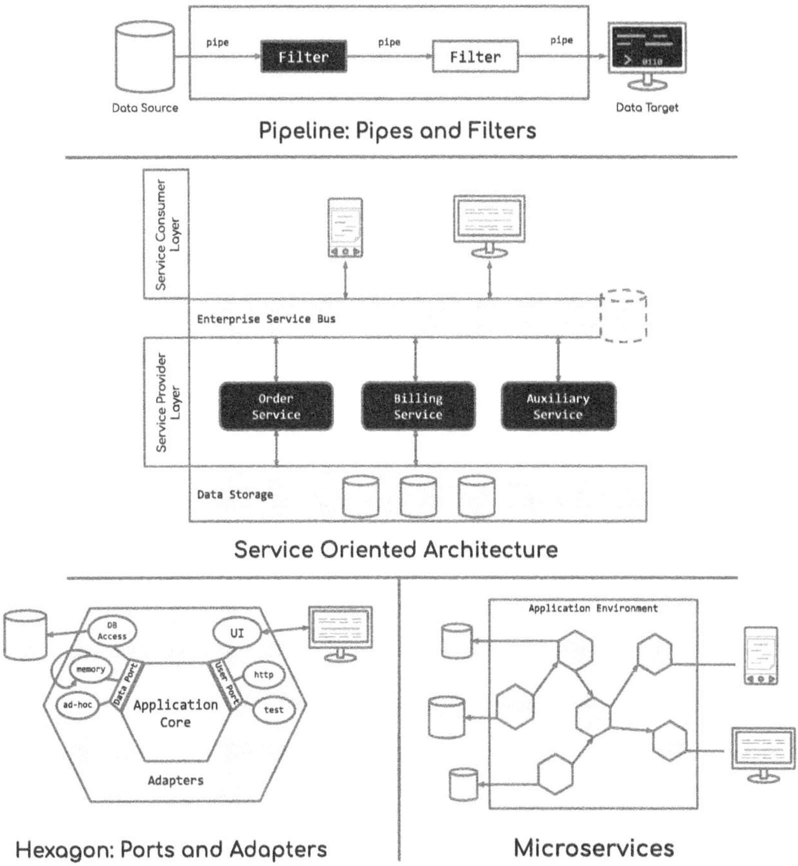

Figure 6.16 Architectural Concepts

Between these cardinal approaches, the general development of the architectural landscape over time becomes apparent. The steadily decreasing hardware dependencies within the backend infrastructure allowed the development of purposeful interfaces to break down monolithic server structures. They enabled the creation and connection of specific dedicated consumer applications. Thus, some parameters concerning the infrastructural landscape underwent significant changes, while common superincumbent ideas did outlast the evolution of the peripheral computational system environment. Furthermore, in practice, the described approaches are not deployed purely dogmatic, and the boundaries between different concepts may not be clearly distinguishable depending on the perspective and even can change throughout the lifetime of any observed system.

6.4.2 The MV* Design Pattern

In the context of the app framework, both data storage and visualization are pursued. Thus, the previous concerns related to the transportation layer are fundamentally valid and should not be disregarded. The resulting applications are supposed to be delivered via the web to facilitate the ubiquitous BYOD strategy for the consumer and easy access for the creator. To facilitate data inquiry and storage, offering a simple entry point for the creator without rigid hardware requirements is essential. However, looking closely at the intended operational area of the Museum Application Domain—especially within small institutions—it is unreasonable to assume the ability nor the necessity to appoint multiple development teams, and neither should the degree of complexity demand a classic enterprise approach.

Nevertheless, it is important to preserve key structural properties of the framework during design and development to ensure the sustainability, maintainability, and extensibility of the resulting artifact. However, these criteria need to be applied primarily at the application core to highlight and preserve the relationships between the domain model and the intent represented within the framework rather than to prioritize externally exposed or potentially transformative channels to existing systems. Moreover, if the first is executed in a suitable manner, the opportunity to exchange and present resulting and existing datasets is consequential, provided that a complete API documentation and comprehensive user manuals do exist.

Therefore, primarily the observable connection between the data structure and the user interfaces has to be embraced throughout the emerging system. That affiliation needs to be transferred directly to the architectural level. One of the most utilized design patterns in the context of interactive web applications to embrace that relationship is the Model-View-Controller (MVC) pattern. While it was conceptually conceived as early as 1979 by Trygve Reenskaug, its origin is attributed to the SmallTalk programming language, which was created in 1980. Yet, it took until 1988 for the pattern to be introduced as a general paradigm for building user interfaces. Over time, its utilization has then been gradually expanded beyond just composing interfaces to orchestrate the cumulative development of more complex software projects. Its mainstream adoption occurred in the early 2000s when many web application frameworks did adopt the concept to cover the growing demand for online presence and customer interaction (Fowler, 2006) (Grove & Ozkan, 2011) (Hunt & McManus, 1998).

As stated above, the primordial purpose of MVC as well as some related concepts, is to maintain the separation between the (G)UI and the corresponding business logic responsible for processing the data for its presentation and validating the input according to the domain model. Therein the focus is to retain modularity within and between the involved components defined by the three namesake abstractions: The Model, the View, and the Controller, as presented in **Figure 6.17**.

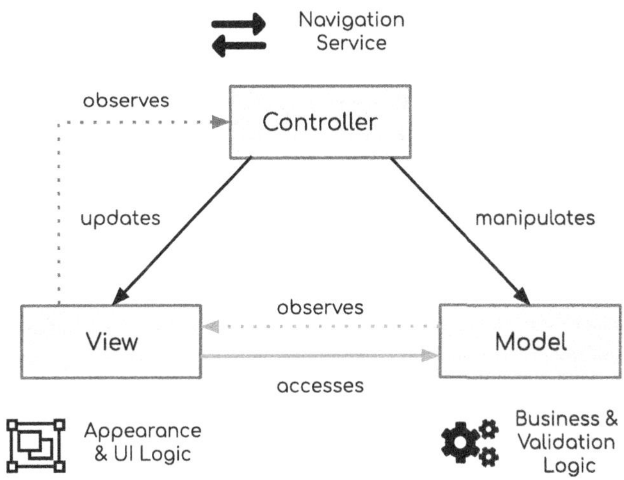

Figure 6.17 The Components of MVC

The *Model* does provide an independent abstraction, which is supposed to encapsulate the state of the relevant data as well as the procedures necessary to manipulate that state enclosed within the architecture's domain, similar to the requirements described for the domain model introduced by DDD. The application to access the Model is then mediated by independent View-Controller pairs for different layout components.

The *View* encapsulates the visual structure as a gateway of the application to interact with, ordinarily, the GUI components exposed to the (human) user. It is usually connected to a template engine to provide a consistent interface to be accessed by its associated Controller.

The *Controller* acts as the mediator between the two previous components. It does administer the interaction between the Model and the View by converting requests introduced by the user via an input device into logical commands and updates the state of the application accordingly. To do that, it may validate user input, manipulate the Model, and match the View accordingly. The state of the View is observed by the Controller to receive dynamic updates based on the user input or requests, even if the Model is not directly accessed or modified. However, that includes the responsibility to actively notify other Views and Controllers of occurring changes. That is referred to as *flow synchronization* and is applied primarily for simple and linear navigation styles. More complex implementations with multiple connected clients or complex interfaces need to allow the View to directly observe the Model, which in turn is supposed to represent the current domain state, thus referred to as *observer synchronization*. That does enable multiple consistent Views of the same underlying data object without having the individual Controllers to synchronize nor to be aware of each other or occurring model transformations. That extended observability is also known as *two-way binding,* as changes in the Model cause the View to update without being triggered or processed by the Controller and vice versa (Grove & Ozkan, 2011) (Hunt & McManus, 1998) (Fowler, 2006).

However, one significant flaw of the MVC pattern is the internal complexity directly introduced by the requirement posed by that interactive two-way binding, which often leads to tightly coupled components. That may cause modules to agglutinate to monolithic structures, which are difficult to develop, test, scale, and maintain, as the application code does not represent the application's implicit behavior (Fowler, 2006). Additionally, if the processing and manipulation of the data are almost exclusively managed server-side, the efficiency expected from single-page web applications becomes obstructed by the requirement for a continuous connection to the network (Harms, Rogowski, & Iacono, 2017).

Another issue is caused by attributing for the responsibilities implied by the domain language, which cannot be realized by the Model itself as it might affect the presentation state at runtime, also referred to as code-behind (i.e., applying a different color to a screen element depending on a certain threshold for the value it does contain) (Fowler, 2006). Shifting the responsibilities, as well as the resulting interactions between components, would disguise the inner workings of the application and the associated data and process flow even further. That can be tolerated if the user is supposed to only interact with the information system to fulfill a certain task. However, If the task itself does require the user to proficiently understand the inner workings of the database or domain model itself, a certain level of verbosity is required, a property also referred to as *observability* (Hunt & McManus, 1998) (Harms, Rogowski, & Iacono, 2017) (Tamburri, Bersani, Mirandola, & Pea, 2018).

In web applications and modern service-based designs in general, that stipulation is difficult to uphold and often obsolete, even for thin-client approaches. Especially if RESTful data sources and setups are considered, continuously supervising the current state of the client application on the server-side, would introduce unnecessary latency and obstruct their observability (Harms, Rogowski, & Iacono, 2017). Particularly Dev-Ops, an enterprise-cultural paradigm to embrace the challenges of fast-paced projects involving agile approaches, demands observability as there is a certain uncertainty regarding the requirements for and the behavior of a product during development and production (Harms, Rogowski, & Iacono, 2017) (Tamburri, Bersani, Mirandola, & Pea, 2018).

Thus, as its popularity increased, the MVC pattern underwent certain changes and interpretations because the focus shifted away from the tight relationship between the View and the Controller. The user interaction was increasingly handled within the View-components, and only impactful events would be propagated through the Controller. In that scenario, if the tight coupling between the Model and the View is to be embraced as a one-to-one relationship, the pattern would be referred to as Model-View-Presenter (MVP). Overall, a multitude of frameworks has been inspired by the underlying architectural approach, and different interpretations of MVC were created to suit modern application development environments and client-side applications scenarios. To embrace the ambulatory role attributed to the mediatory component, related architectural styles are referred to as MV* (Model-View-Star) (Tamburri, Bersani, Mirandola, & Pea, 2018). Furthermore, it is very important to note that these approaches are specifically focused on the presentation and the underlying data while not being concerned with any parsing, routing, or networking issues that may be involved. Thus, the communication would be addressed independently of those architectural styles by the surrounding framework or client-server architecture, as discussed in subsection 6.4.1.

Because of the two previously described considerations (latency and observability), the architecture chosen for the framework does follow one pivotal variation of the MV* family. With an increased emphasis on the frontend applications in mind, which are intended to be interacted with by the consumer on a mobile device, namely the Model-View-ViewModel (MVVM) pattern approaches the orchestration in a more linear fashion. The intention is to intensify the separation of the GUI layout from the business logic and the related development efforts while maintaining an independent data model capable of unambiguously representing the core domain model. MVVM was created by John Gossman, Ken Cooper, and Ted Peters for the.NET (read: dot net) graphics system of the Windows Presentation Foundation in 2005. The primary argument was to address the coupling issues caused by code-behind. With the proper separation of UI components and the business logic, UX designers could focus on maintaining and modifying UI elements without being obstructed by business development decisions. It gained increasing popularity as the necessity for mobile application frontends grew in the early 2010s. The embedded data-binding approach of MVVM may increase memory consumption, and the overhead created within the ViewModel would complicate smaller standalone projects. However, it does prove helpful, especially for headless and event-driven application designs, within broader contexts, as it greatly reduces interaction between layers and does enable unit-tests throughout the whole application without concealing state-based obstructions (Pedamkar, 2018) (Tamburri, Bersani, Mirandola, & Pea, 2018). The composition of the MVVM pattern is shown in **Figure 6.18**.

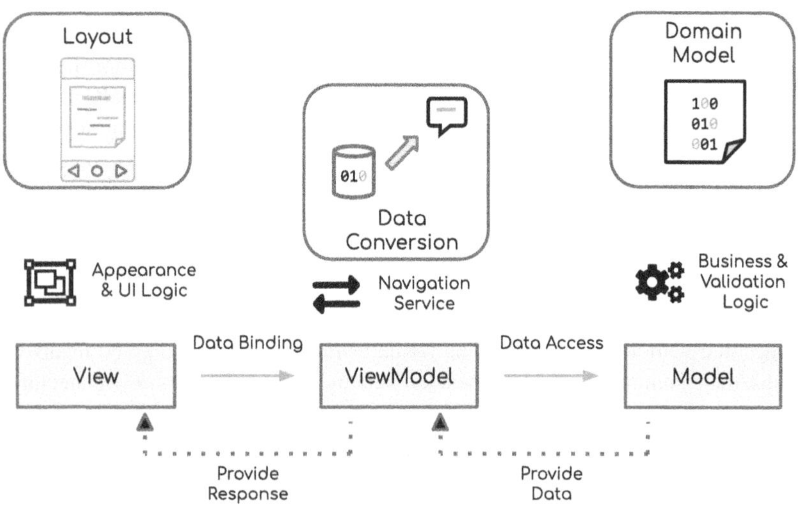

Figure 6.18 The Model-View-ViewModel Design Pattern

At its core, MVVM does preserve the essential ideas of the MVC pattern without submitting to the overhead introduced by the responsibility put on the Controller to keep track of its connected View(s). Overall, that does achieve a more verbose system while also addressing the growing concern of platform compatibility by further eliminating responsibilities attributed to the visual components.

Therefore, the *View* does encapsulate the layout and appearance of the UI via a markup language and administers the UI logic via GUI code to represent the actual use cases to be offered by the application interface. The user interaction is transferred to the ViewModel based on the events triggered by the input device, i.e., clicks, keystrokes, or, in the case of touch-screen interfaces, gestures. The response is automated and directly provided to the View's embedded fields (e.g., predetermined placeholders) within its layout via data-binding to certain objects provided by the ViewModel.

The *ViewModel* is expected to expose the corresponding data objects from the Model in a lean and approachable way, thus acting as an abstraction of the View. By insulating the data conversion, it is possible to preserve an agnostic Model which is independent of the state of the application. Furthermore, other than the Controller in MVC, the ViewModel is not aware of the View(s) connected to it. Thus, the entity is reduced to the navigation service—the responsibility to locate the proper resources within the Model and access the appropriate data—and to perform the data conversion necessary to fulfill the request by the View. That enables independent changes to the software, as it tightly encapsulates the respective responsibilities and eliminates unnecessary dependencies by delegating communication to the binding mechanism.

That binder, assumed to be an implicit element within MVVM, is responsible for synchronizing the exposed public properties provided by the ViewModel and the fields required by the View to display the requested content. For that reason, the approach is sometimes referred to as Model-View-Binder outside the.NET ecosystem. As per usual more boilerplate code is required to implement the expected synchronization automation.

The understanding of the *Model* remains essentially unchanged compared to other MV* interpretations. It either embodies the content provided through the data access layer within data-centric concepts or exemplifies the actual state-based domain model within object-oriented approaches. It contains the necessary business and validation logic to process the queries sent to an exposed API—usually imposed by the ViewModel (Pedamkar, 2019).

6.5 Engineering of the Framework Components

The logical structure of the app framework design does follow the structural composition derived from the MVVM design pattern. To accommodate the scope previously stipulated, in this section, the architecture of the necessary components is described. Therefore, the three elements—Model, View, ViewModel—act as an excellent scaffold to present the pathway of the buildup ahead. First, the Model is discussed. The ability to maintain its independence from the superjacent technologies surrounding it in practice and during production is prioritized. That intent does unfold its impact on the resulting design of the free-form ontology chosen for the framework (*Subsection 6.5.1—The Model*). Second, the View elements provide the visual anchor for the user (*Subsection 6.5.2—The View*). Third, the ViewModel does act as the link to translate certain data objects between storage and presentation (*Subsection 6.5.3—The ViewModel*).

6.5.1 The Model

Even if it is not apparent at the surface level of modern applications, the data model at their core is decisive for a coherent experience for developers and users alike. In the past, static applications were built primarily to administer transactional data, which in turn had to be structured according to its associated processes to function reliably. Thus, it has been necessary to create data models in a highly efficient, yet equally inflexible manner, which often generates abstract and complex structures. That does lead to reduced interpretability or causes elaborate associations and relationships. Incidentally, the transactional origin organically invoked data models, which did closely resemble the actual domain model, i.e., it closely follows the behavior and the operational setup of the environment addressed by the information system (Lawler, 2017).

The technical development to facilitate these structures is linked to the inception of the Structured Query Language (SQL) by IBM in 1974. SQL provided the foundation for *relational databases,* becoming the prime standard for storing data. The precise ruleset enforced by the language paradigm contributed to its superiority and utilization across most use cases encountered at that point in time and beyond (Melton, 1996).

Relational databases consist of datasets organized as tuples, which are stored in static tables. A table consists of columns, each describing a predefined data field. Each row constitutes an instance of a dataset, consisting of up to one of each of those data fields. Each tuple within a table must be identifiable by a primary key, which is supposed to be unique within that table. Relationships to other tables can be established by referencing that primary key in different tables as a foreign key. That precise composition is helpful if the structure of the underlying Model is certain and remains static. Since each row consists of uniform data, queries yield high payloads with minimal overhead. This is ideal for complex analytical use cases, like the implementation within OnLine Analytical Processing (OLAP) intended to process multi-dimensional analytical queries on hypercubes (Moniruzzaman & Hossain, 2013)

The characteristics that do distinguish relational database management systems (DBMS) are Atomicity, Consistency, Isolation, and Durability, or ACID for short. That transactional paradigm enforces *consistency*, i.e., the validity of the transactional data before, during, and after every transaction, by executing each transaction entirely or not at all (*atomicity*). Thus, each transaction needs to be coherent in itself to not affect other concurrent transactions in case any issue requires the rollback of any one transaction (*isolation*). That does ensure the valid state of the database and it being resilient to subsequent failures at any point in time (*durability*) (Moniruzzaman & Hossain, 2013) (Mapanga & Kadebu, 2013).

In modern use cases, however, especially imposed by distributed systems and ubiquitous just-in-time applications, that strict ruleset does lead to certain issues. Those are primarily related to restricting the accessibility of data and thus interfering with scalability. Additionally, based on the increase in complexity of applications and their behavior, it became more important for the data to reflect the intended use case and to be readily available rather than to be represented and stored as efficiently as possible. Thus, the presence of that intent to be found within the domain model must be evident, especially at the API level. The primary objective is to provide access to stateless and serializable data to be delivered at runtime without being constrained to execute complex and resource-consuming queries to assemble or exchange the necessary data composition for certain time-sensitive tasks (Stonebraker, 2010). These developments are closely related to the architectural progression of the exchange layer, discussed in subsection 6.4.1.

To this effect, the dissimilarity between how data can be modeled and accessed within the relational approach and how it is supposed to be deployed to meet domain-specific needs does stifle innovative development. As the data model must be defined first, the design possibilities of applications built on top of it are immediately limited by the initial data model (Lawler, 2017). The necessary shift within priorities from efficiency to availability is summarized within the BASE paradigm, short for Base Availability, Soft state, and Eventually consistent. As expected, this approach favors the accessibility of the data over uniformity. Distributed systems necessitate a high degree of replication to guarantee a stable system even if certain nodes become unavailable or overloaded (*base availability*). For that reason, it is unrealistic to keep each node in sync at every point in time or, more specifically, with every transaction performed throughout a larger ecosystem. This is resolved by the promise for each node to reach a consistent state at some point in the future (*eventual consistency*). Thus, the system is kept in a *soft state*, even if no transactions are performed, due to the recursive effort to establish uniformity between existing nodes (Moniruzzaman & Hossain, 2013) (Mapanga & Kadebu, 2013).

To underline that clear distinction to systems that follow the ACID paradigm, database management systems that deploy the BASE paradigm are referred to as *noSQL*. Rather than a complex query language, these usually rely on record-at-a-time interfaces. The prime examples are key-value stores and document-based data stores. Additionally, graph data stores are often subsumed under the umbrella of noSQL. However, their primary objective is to explore semantic relationships between certain datasets by describing triples, each consisting of a subject, a predicate, and an object. Thus, the corresponding database management system may follow the BASE paradigm while also relying on more complex interface languages to account for the semantic path modeling (Moniruzzaman & Hossain, 2013) (Chauhan & Bansal, 2017). The records within key-value stores consist of pairs of descriptive identifier-keys and payload-values, resembling distributed hash tables. Document-based stores are composed of collections of documents. Those documents often rely on key-value pairs plus an additional meta-related payload. That additional overhead reduces the payload ratio efficiency compared to relational data stores while granting more flexibility, especially for update- and lookup-intensive OnLine Transaction Processing (OLTP) workloads. (Stonebraker, 2010).

To support more complex operations and query-intensive workloads, it is not uncommon to establish a relational persistence layer outside the scope of the application domain. Those central repositories, also commonly referred to as data warehouses, are responsible for storing or accessing data self-sufficiently and independent of a specific use case. Furthermore, modern database management systems in the realm of noSQL also support joins and queries to offer similar abilities previously only available in the space of relational databases (Stonebraker, 2010) (Mapanga & Kadebu, 2013). In the case in which the context itself relies on information from outside the specific domain model, a conversion mechanism or interface needs to be deployed to establish a reliable connection between the data model and the domain model. As the focus of this dissertation is put on small and medium-sized institutions within the MAD that usually do not yet operate databases or interact with structured data, to begin with, opportunities to integrate external data sources are not being investigated further. Nevertheless, this space could be analyzed by exploring the technologies previously discussed at the beginning of this chapter. An example for each of these two options—the table-based relational data model and the document-based noSQL data model—is illustrated in **Figure 6.19**.

Regardless of the conceptual emphasis of these two opposing paradigms, the manipulation of datasets does require the four basic operations Create, Read, Update, and Delete, often delineated as CRUD.

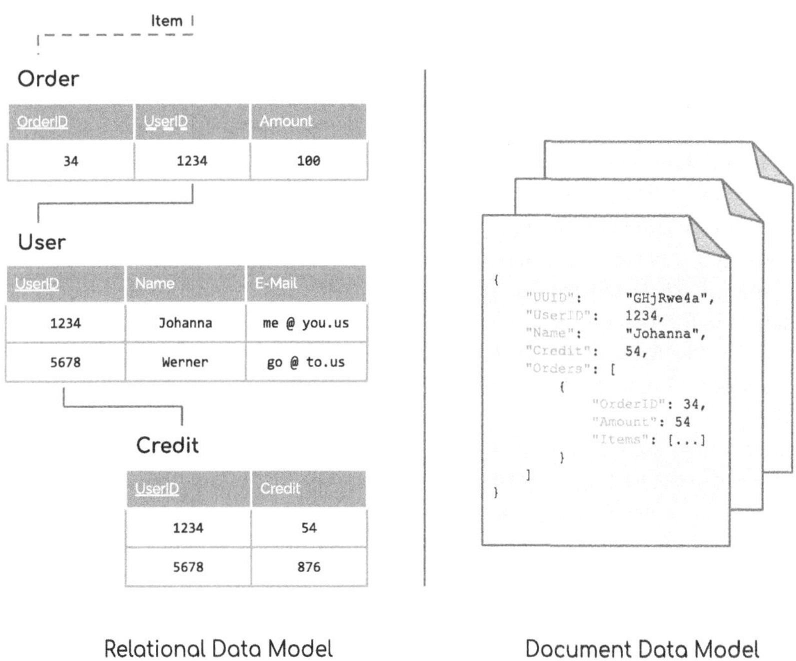

Figure 6.19 Relational vs. Document Data Models

Because of the described benefits and its verbose exposition, a document-based data model provides a fitting basis to be deployed within the application-centric target domain encountered in the MAD. Yet, even starting without a reference database, it is difficult to explore any specific solutions without being heavily invested or locked into a certain technology, which can rapidly change as innovation does occur. Therefore, it is most important to retain human-readability in addition to serving the structural integrity for the purposes of deployability. The intended application framework is supposed to ensure long-term viability by promoting the evolutionary quality of shareability (Baumgärtner, 2019.2).

This could be accomplished by utilizing an abstraction for the data description layer or a projection of a proprietary formation. However, then the implied capabilities cannot be translated to an operational prototype implementation without a margin of interpretation. By utilizing the JSON format—created by the developer Douglas Crockford in 2001 for the Cartoon Network– it is possible to represent and store array- and object-structures in a text-based document-style format. It follows the ECMA-262 standard, which is the foundation for the JavaScript programming language, meant to provide an abstraction layer to ensure the interoperability of web pages across different web browsers. Thus, it does project the exact composition that would be utilized by the application at runtime without the necessity to transform the input string. Therefore, it does drastically reduce the costs associated with parsing and interpreting the data source, which would be inevitable if relying on SQL response tuples or XML documents. While JSON is associated with the JavaScript language by name, it is not limited to that scripting language and is technology-agnostic by design. Thus, in practice, many noSQL DBMS directly rely on JSON or a superset thereof (Chauhan & Bansal, 2017). Additionally, JSON is suitable for transfer of the data as well, as discussed in subsection 6.4.1 (Crockford, 2006) (Peng, Cao, & Xu, 2011). Thus, the technological availability of the resulting data can be established as well.

Even if the buildup of document-based data models is more dynamic than their relational counterparts, sensible structural integrity must still be enforced throughout the system from the beginning. Otherwise, it would be hard for applications to reliably store and access necessary datasets and their corresponding properties (Klettke, Störl, & Scherzinger, 2015). Furthermore, certain constraints can be directly enforced by the Model. Thus, the burden of defensive programming patterns can be avoided at the application level as the input data becomes predictable. JSONSchema is the defacto schema language standard to reliably describe the expected document structure (Fruth, et al., 2020).

As discussed in subsection 5.2.1, it is meaningful for the system interaction to address the cognitive efforts and aid the individual user in comprehending the Model. Purposeful visualization can aid the necessary transformative cycles which are necessary to assimilate the required mental model to effectively interact with the resulting system (Pederson, 1997). The primary objective of the Model is to describe *abstract data*—per se, it is supposed to exist independently of any visual representation and does not accommodate a straightforward mapping to any particular geometry. However, that may impair the interpretability of certain datasets (Däßler, 1999). Therefore, especially in this use case, it does make sense to attribute certain metadata to assert aspects of the expected visualization. As long as that correlation is not determined but only implied at the data level, the overlaying representative application interface can be adapted and replaced at will without changing the underlying descriptive data model.

To satisfy those requirements and to accommodate adequate allowance during development without compromising its integrity, an extensible free-form ontology has been developed. It does provide an envelope that entails the necessary metadata as well as the specific properties related to the entities encountered in the Museum Application Domain suggested in section 6.3. As the resulting Model does make no claims of completeness, while each entity is self-contained, the general extensibility is not compromised by structural constraints. As intended, the data model revolves around the domain-specific structure of a single app screen content page. That is reflected by the resulting document for each instance of an entity is represented by. The visual expectations and the resulting implications are explicitly discussed in the introduction of the View in subsection 6.5.2.

The skeleton data document contains three key-value pairs on the base object level to characterize the necessary instructive metadata, three key-value pairs to satisfy the JSONSchema specification, plus the properties object assigned to the "properties" key. The abstract structure of that setup is outlined in **Figure 6.20**.

The particular schema based on that Model is introduced throughout the following pages. The components contained by the suggested generic schema file are defined in **Table 6.1**. The resulting JSONSchema document is set up in **Listing 6.1**, while the corresponding document, i.e., a representative instantiation of the generic entity, can be found in **Listing 6.2.**

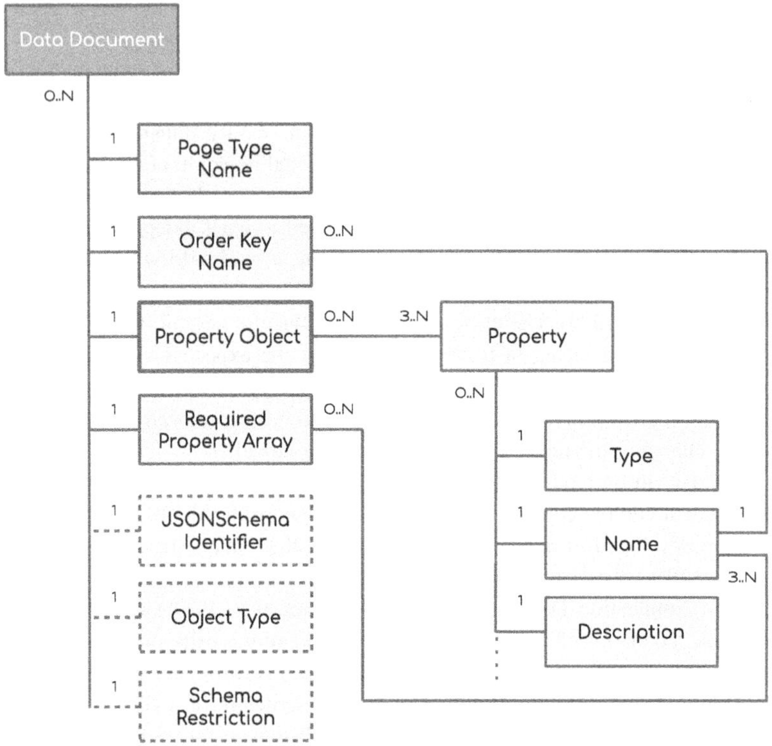

Figure 6.20 Structure of the Data Document

The "$schema" key holds the reference URL to the deployed schema version, which is required by the JSONSchema specification to identify the draft to correctly identify the schema and validate the resulting documents. This schema representation is based on JSONSchema Draft-06.

The value of the "type" key does represent the data type to be described by the schema. JSON supports the abstract type "object" and "array" as well as the primitive types "string", "number", "boolean" and the null value. As the base object is supposed to describe the properties object, it has to be set to "object".

The value of the "name" key describes the entity the schema is supposed to represent; thus, it has to correspond with one of the available entities defined by the framework, e.g., "admission", "person", or "event".

Table 6.1 Key-Value Mapping for the 'schema.json' Document

Key	Datatype	Description	Values
$schema	string	The reference URL to the JSON Schema version.	http://json-schema.org/draft-06/ -> V6 is recommended.
type	string	The schema type.	"string", "number", "boolean", null, as well as "object", or "array" -> must equal "object".
name	string	The schema entity name.	e.g. "admission", "person", or "event".
sortBy	string	The property-key the page instances should be sorted by.	"name", "caption", or "date" -> must be contained within the properties object.
properties	object	This object contains the properties, i.e. available data elements, of the page type and the associated layout.	This object is described separately in the main section of each page type in the 'App Screens' section.
Additional Properties	boolean	This marker makes sure that only defined properties are allowed.	true or false -> false is recommended.
required	array	This array may contain property keys which must be included in the object at the minimum.	i.e. ["layout", "name", "text"] -> must contain each element from the "properties" object supposed to be displayed in the "basic" layout.

Finally, the "properties" key references the object, which does contain the catalog of properties specific to the defined entity. These properties can consist of the six aforementioned types supported by JSON. However, often it is necessary to describe the desired value more precisely. Thus, JSONSchema does offer different possibilities to further restrict these possible type values to a range appropriate for specific properties. The most obvious are "minValue" and "maxValue" for numeric properties, "minLength" and "maxLength" for character-based properties, as well as "minProperties" and "maxProperties" or "minItems" and "maxItems" for abstract properties. Additionally, strings can be restricted to a certain set of values by an array that does contain the available choices assigned to the "enum" key. It is even possible to add and evaluate conditional properties using the "if" and "then" keys. As objects and arrays can be stacked and combined in multiple ways, it is possible to define arbitrarily complex properties. In that endeavor, the priority of maintaining human readability should not be overlooked.

As document stores identify their elements by (randomly) generated UUIDs rather than explicitly specified values, the value assigned to the "sortBy" key does suggest one property name resulting documents should be ordered by, within a standard query. Thus, the value must be a key of a property contained within the properties object.

By default, any JSONSchema validates the property values only for keys described within its property object but does omit checking values of keys not contained entirely. To restrict the document content to property keys explicitly defined within the schema, the value of "additionalProperties" must be set to false. This also does apply to child-objects contained within the properties object and must be applied accordingly.

The "required" key again does refer to the keys contained in the properties object. It does expect to be assigned an array containing those keys expected to be included in each document instance derived from the schema. To provide a reliable frame of reference, by default, each schema should contain the following three keys, independent of the entity it is supposed to describe.

As of the JSONSchema specification, each individual property object does need to specify its "type", chosen from the available JSON types and a "name", in this instance, corresponding to its own key. Furthermore, any necessary value-restricting elements may be added. For specific reasons outlined below, each property object also must be assigned the "description" key holding a reference key-string for its string value.

Listing 6.1 Generic JSON Schema Document

```
generic.schema.json
{
"$schema": "http://json-schema.org/draft-06/schema#",
"type": "object",
"name": "GENERIC",
"sortBy": "caption",
"properties": {

   "language": {
      "type": "string",
      "name": "language",
      "description": "page_language_description",
      "enum": ["en", "de"]
   },

   "caption": {
      "type": "string",
      "name": "caption",
      "description": "caption_description",
      "minLength": 5,
      "maxLength": 25
   },

    "//": "insert entity properties HERE",

   "layout": {
      "type": "string",
      "enum": ["basic", <more layout options go HERE>]
   }
},
"additionalProperties": false,
"required":["language", "caption", "layout", <more properties>]
}
```

Overall, three property keywords are always expected to be included in the properties object. The first property key is "language" to indicate the language of the instantiated document. Its string value is supposed to correspond with the international country code for the expected language, e.g., "en" for English or "de" for German.

The second mandatory property key is "layout". It is to be assigned a string value to indicate the corresponding layout suggestions for each of the instantiated documents corresponding to its entity type. Each enum contained in the schema must at least provide the "basic" value, supposed to be associated with the View, to visualize these elements included within the "required" array of the schema.

In addition to those two elements, at least one element is necessary, which does represent actual information associated with the defined entity. That element key also acts as the identifying key to be assigned to the "sortBy" key of the schema file. The key chosen for the example provided in **Listing 6.1** is "caption". Beyond that, any number of additional properties may be assigned to the schema as long as the criteria described above are met. Those properties may also be added to the "required" array.

Following that logic, each page type included in the framework prototype implementation has its own JSONSchema file, which defines the necessary properties of each resulting data document. Those schemas explicitly designed for the framework prototype are summarized within subsection 7.3.1.

A correct data document to fulfill the requirements of the generic example above would be stored inside the collection that corresponds with its entity name ("GENERIC") using its unique identifier ("1234") assigned upon creating the document within the document store. Accordingly, the document provided in **Listing 6.2** contains the three key-value pairs, as defined in the schema above.

Listing 6.2 Generic JSON Document Instance Example

```
GENERIC/1234.json
{
    "language": "en",
    "layout": "basic",
    "caption": "My Page"
}
```

6.5.2 The View

The View tends to the visual interface presented to the user. More precisely, that conveys instructions for the arrangement of certain graphical elements on the screen of the target device, how to appropriately integrate a particular representation of the Model, as well as guidance and interaction opportunities for the user.

In the context of the framework, the primary purpose of the View is to offer a blueprint to visualize the abstract information contained within the properties object of each data document, defined by the corresponding JSONSchema file. Accordingly, the basis for each View is a single app page screen. It is important to establish an explicit connection between the Model and the View to form a uniform perception, especially in shared information spaces. The ability to tap into the existing mental model of the user and project certain expectations does reduce the complexity of information retrieval, processing, and navigation to free up the cognitive load and enhance creative thinking (Pederson, 1997) (Rosewater, 2011) (Stojmenovic, Pilgrim, & Lindgaard, 2014).

The areas, the user would expect to be occupied by certain elements on a mobile device, are usually coined by prior stimuli and experiences, as discussed in subsection 5.2.1. The resulting visual representation of data and navigation elements, therefore, is supposed to encapsulate these established connections by invoking spatial elements to contextualize the (text-based) data representation. To do that, it is obligatory to define an information space by providing dimensional instructions to represent those objects and their relationships (Däßler, 1999).

Thus, before any visual components can be conceptually connected to the Model itself, it is essential to characterize the relationships and components involved in that mechanism. Initially, the implications of specific terms have to be introduced. The most general form to describe the rules for the observable scaffolding is the *template*. Templates represent the relationships between the elements to be displayed, their hierarchical structure, and define the spatial areas supposed to contain certain data. Additional rules are necessary to describe the exact appearance and proportions of those elements. The *layout* combines that structural directive from the template with particular instructions concerned with actual positions, size, and further information necessary for the proper presentation. While it is possible for the layout to contain those expositional directives as a whole, it often does make sense to decouple certain cosmetic information that is not tied to the immediate structural preparation, e.g., color, font style, or size, into a *theme*. Themes can then be applied to a broader group of layouts or the entire visual application interface to unify its appearance, which can be exchanged quickly without replacing layouts entirely. Finally, the combination of the combined instructions from the template, layout, as well as the data provided by the Model or other external resources, e.g., icons or images, results in the *instantiation* of the View. That then is subject to the rendering process on the target device to match its individual dimensions and device-specific properties (Albert, Charaf, & Lengyel, 2013) (Rodrigues, et al., 2017) (Laine, Nakajima, Dayama, & Oulasvirta, 2020) (Holman, Reynolds-Haertle, Griffin, & Dunham Kroes, 2022). **Figure 6.21** does illustrate those three conceptual stages.

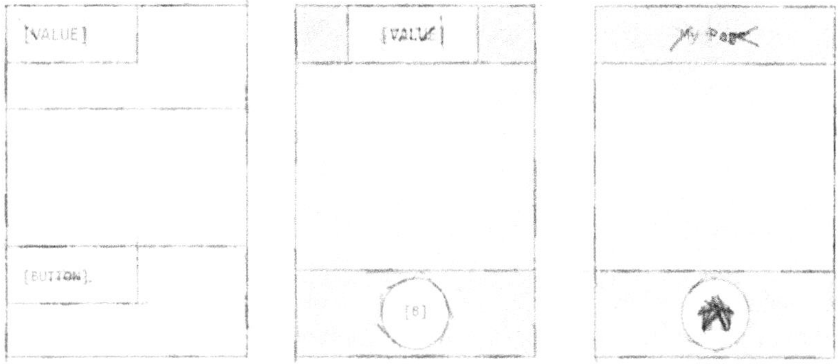

Figure 6.21 Visual Representation of the Template, the Layout, and the Instantiation

These elements translate well into the composition of the Screen element suggested by the framework, shown in **Figure 6.22**. Each instantiation is represented by one "Screen" element acting as the visual representation for one "Data Document", which is described by the corresponding Model and by applying the "Layout" specified within the "Property Object" of the "Data Document". The data to be displayed by the "Screen" is determined by "Template" representing the "Page Type"—specified in the "Data Document"—and the mapped "Properties" available. How the elements and data fields are arranged is then enforced by the "Style" and the applied "Theme", if applicable.

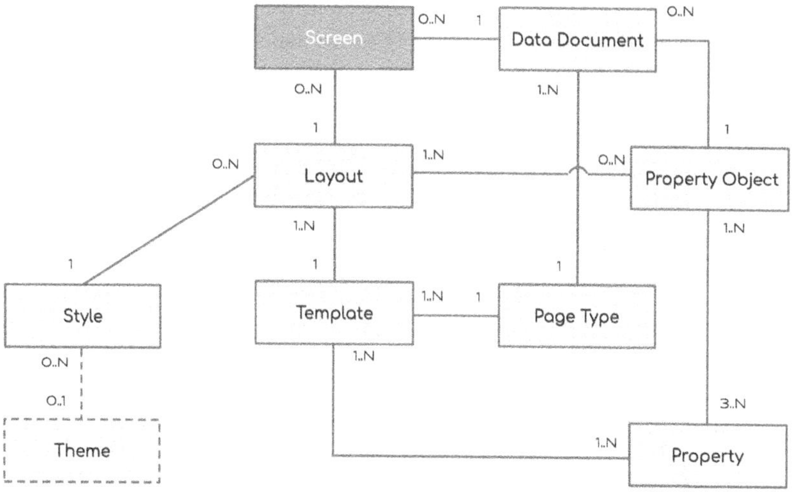

Figure 6.22 The Composition of the 'Screen' Element

Similar to the structural construction of the Model, multiple means are available to represent the elements to characterize the necessary UI components and to describe platform-independent specifications for the View. Naturally, the most feasible approach is going with the straightforward visualization of the desired structure in the form of a sketch or providing a simple visual outline. That is especially useful during the early design process, as it does showcase an instant impression of the desired outcome while requiring few resources. Also, early evaluation is encouraged, as those visualizations are easily approachable, even for non-technical stakeholders. This can be helpful to quickly assess initial requirements. Those high-level visual representations are often referred to as wireframes or *mockups*. Especially in software engineering, the term mockup is used relatively broadly, starting from basic design elements but may include (semi-) functional elements as well (Rivero, et al., 2014).

A mockup for the Screen element would exist somewhere between the layout and the template, as it does describe the structural markup while also hinting at the expected depiction. While this approach is invaluable during design, for an actual implementation, the blank canvas approach and the inevitable inaccuracies are problematic. To create a reliable foundation that can be deployed and displayed throughout multiple devices, those uncertainties need to be eliminated by translating the mockup representation into a structural blueprint expressed by a high-level, editor-friendly description language.

The descriptive technologies commonly used in web development, particularly HTML and CSS (compare: Section 7.2), have the ability to simplify the following steps concerned with implementing and testing the prototype. Additionally, it is possible to quickly generate a visual representation that is close to the results end users are going to encounter in the final product, including interaction events, such as hover or click responses. While browser-based websites are generally platform independent, implementations involving certain native application programming approaches, foremost Android and iOS, would need to translate those descriptions into their respective representation. However, these universally recognized web technologies do not have any disadvantages against technology-agnostic approaches in that regard. On the contrary, the resulting files can be inspected and rendered directly in any browser while also being reasonably well-legible by the human user. Thus, the required documents to describe the desired styles and templates of the framework are described below.

The HTML file shown in **Listing 6.3** constitutes the structure of the template for the generic page type introduced by the Model. While HTML does provide certain elements that would semantically correspond with the suggested hierarchy, the neutral div element has been chosen throughout, such that the file is more generically approachable. Every single element consists of a start tag (<div>) and an end tag (</div>) surrounded by arrow brackets. Each element may be assigned multiple attributes, a key-value pair joined by an equals sign, with the value being surrounded by quotation marks (key="value"). The hierarchical structure can be achieved by including child elements within the tags of any given parent element. The template follows the general guidelines for the app screen. Thus, the surrounding container (id="phone") is assigned the type and layout attributes containing the reference to the page type name (type="GENERIC") and the associated layout (layout="basic"). It is divided into the three sections, the "header", the "body", and the "footer" identified by the respective class attribute. As the caption is supposed to be displayed within the header, the corresponding element is inserted into that hierarchy level (id="caption"). The data binding is indicated by a placeholder indicated by double curly braces surrounding the reference to the available field within the properties object {{PROPERTIES.caption}}. Using this method, all available—or at least the required data fields—can be placed within the template. Other elements, like the button within the footer (class = "home"), also can directly be included within the template. However, for some elements or groups thereof, it does make sense to bundle them together and insert them into each page of the app rather than including them in each template separately, e.g., the general page navigation elements.

Listing 6.3 HTML Template for the Generic Schema

```
GENERIC/basic.template.html
<div id = "phone" type = "GENERIC" layout = "basic">
    <div class = "header">
        <div id = "caption"> {{PROPERTIES.caption}} </div>
    </div>
    <div class = "body"></div>
    <div class = "footer">
       <button class = "home"> [B] </button>
    </div>
</div>
```

A certain style is to be applied to the described template elements—based on the value assigned to the layout attribute of the template—resulting in the appearance of the layout. These instructions are demonstrated in the CSS file included in **Listing 6.4**. A style document does contain those instructions which are applied to each referenced element of the template to accurately qualify the desired appearance of the layout. A reference can be established by citing the id (#id-value) or class (.class-value) attribute value assigned to particular elements. The instructive values are grouped and assigned to the reference using curly braces. Comparable to JSON, CSS utilizes key-value pairs to parameterize the values representing certain characteristics. Each of these pairs is delineated by a semicolon (key: value;).

Listing 6.4 Style Instructions to Define the Visual Appearance of a Screen Element

```
GENERIC/basic.style.css
#phone {
  height: 100%;
  width: 100%;

  display: grid;
  align-items: center;
  justify-items: center;
}

.header {
  height: 15%;
  width: 100%;
  background-color: var(--header-color);
}

.body {
  height: 65%;
  width: 100%;
  background-color: var(--body-color);
}

.footer {
  height: 20%;
  width: 100%;
  background-color: var(--footer-color);
}

#caption {
  font-family: Verdana, sans-serif;
}
```

The parent container (#phone) referenced in the basic-style.css file is supposed to fill the entire available vertical and horizontal space on the screen of the device (height: 100%; & width: 100%;). Its child elements are to be arranged along the vertical space (display: grid;) and centered along both the horizontal and vertical axis (align-items: center; & justify-items: center;).

The three child elements of the root container (.header,.body, &.footer) each shall occupy the entire horizontal space (width: 100%;) but different vertical expansions by the values assigned to the height of each of those elements.

As pointed out above, while all characteristics describing the appearance can be directly included inside with the rest of those styling instructions, it does make sense to parameterize certain values to separate the structural instructions from the appearance-defining characteristics. Most commonly, that does apply to the color, to enforce a uniform cosmetic appearance throughout different pages of the same application. Thus, the background-color of the three visible elements is each assigned a variable pointing to the value (var(<color-reference>);) resolved by the theme file described in **Listing 6.5**. That file can then easily be altered or replaced to change the appearance of each page without editing every single style document individually.

Listing 6.5 CSS Theme to Encapsulate Cosmetic Information

```
APP/theme.style.css
:root {
  --header-color: darkgray;
  --body-color: lightyellow;
  --footer-color: darkgray;
}
```

In addition to that basic blueprint, certain presentation logic is to be included in the View, e.g., specific indicators to propagate guidance indicators to the user, which are not represented by the Model itself but are necessary for the application to convey its state at runtime.

As argued above, using descriptive web languages to express these instructions, the rendering of the resulting combination of the presented template and the corresponding style can be instantly provided by any browser. For the data to be available to the View, the required Properties Object does need to be provided by the ViewModel, which does apply any necessary transformation to the raw model.

Figure 6.23 does contain the actual rendering of the layout as a direct result of the presented files, providing a reliable reference compared to the 'hand-drawn' representation included in **Figure 6.21** above. An additional advantage of this approach, different screen sizes, themes, and aspect ratios can be directly reviewed and evaluated without relying on any additional tools.

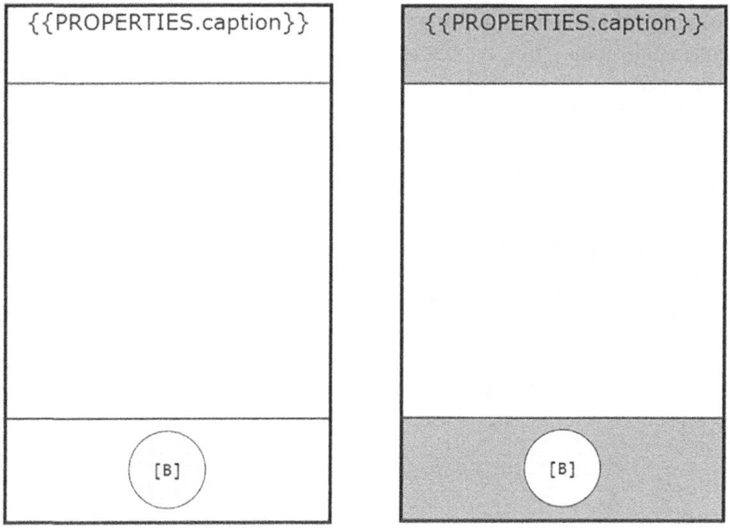

Figure 6.23 Rendering of the Screen Layout without and with the Theme

The reflections above are primarily centered around the consumer View because most elements truly stem from the initial mental model, which is directly connected to the mobile application interface. Through that context visualization, as presented in **Figure 6.12**, the desired outcome can be perceived and communicated rather intuitively. The creative possibilities necessary to initiate the template and layout and engage in the task of building the associated data model also are closely related to that representation. This is where most descriptions of the View come to their natural conclusion.

Thus—as demonstrated—the creator's perspective is mostly overlooked. The input process is unavoidable to generate the data documents essential to assemble the Screen and present the applicable content to the consumer. While it is possible to isolate that mandatory task into an abstract database interaction for the creator, it is hard to justify that effort if the association to the potential output cannot be established. That, however, is an integral step to grasp the scope of the potential possibilities offered by structured data and the feasibility of mobile applications. Highlighting that connection, therefore, is one of the primary concerns of this thesis. The actual creator processes must be presented on an abstraction layer aligned with the responsibilities to be encountered within the specific domain context of the MAD. Simultaneously, the abstract knowledge communicated on that level must enable the association within the big picture and generalize the problem awareness (Pederson, 1997).

To demonstrate that cohesion within the View—beyond the philosophical and psychological implications—a form containing input elements reflecting the properties defined within the schema document in the Model—thus exactly matching the content of the screen element—is supposed to facilitate the suitable means. Each input field is based on the type requirement as well as the defined property description and restrictions. Thus, an input element template must be provided for each available data type.

The structural buildup of the "Input" is identical to the Screen, as the "Layout" results from the combination of "Template" and "Style" documents, with an optional "Theme". Besides that, it does require the "Labels" key-value store, including three pairs representing the placeholders for the text appearing to the creator. The "Name" does represent the property name, the "Description" does offer a textual explanation of the expected input, and the "Constraints" do verbalize the specific restrictions defined for the property.

These placeholder keys, as well as their corresponding values, are enclosed within a separate JSON document (**Listing 6.7–6.11 below**) and must be provided by the ViewModel analogously to the data document for the Screen. That process is discussed in the following subsection.

Listing 6.6 does represent the template for the "String Input" element, following the example of the generic schema, including the "caption" property. The container element (class = "stringBox") does enclose one element for each of the three labels with the corresponding class attribute names, as well as the actual <input> element. The universal composition for the Input element can be found in **Figure 6.24**.

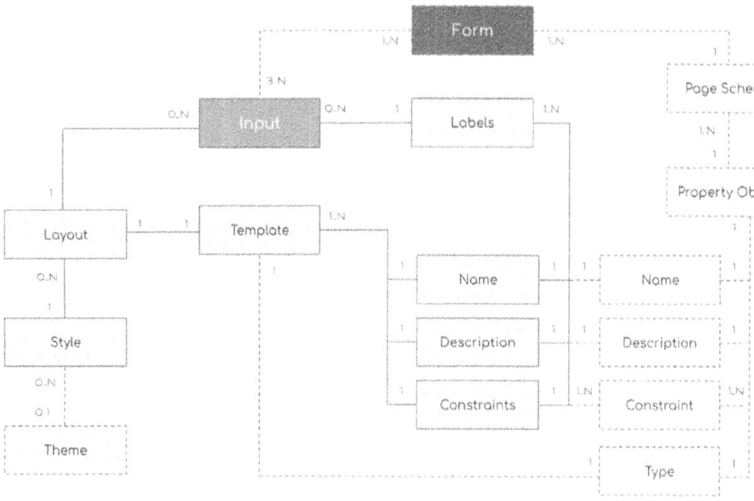

Figure 6.24 The Composition of the 'Input' Element

The placeholder for each of the three labels does reference the applicable key within the labels key-value store (LABELS), either by directly referring to the relevant property within the properties object of the relevant schema file (PROPERTIES.caption.name & PROPERTIES.caption.description) or by directly applying the data type (string_constraint) in case of the constraints processing the corresponding values provided by the specific schema property. While these values could be directly included into the schema file, it is best to separate them from the structural instructions and access them separately. Similar to the theme, those values can then be maintained within a centralized dictionary and swapped out, e.g., to offer the opportunity to include different languages without changing the actual schema file.

The information required by the input element itself does depend on the data type of the required input value. First, it is assigned the class attribute value applicable to the input type, "stringInput" in this example, the name of the property to be inquired (PROPERTIES.caption.name), as well as the restrictions also defined in the underlying schema (PROPERTIES.caption.minLength & PROPERTIES.caption.maxLength).

Listing 6.6 HTML Template for the String Input Element

```html
INPUT/string.template.html
<div class = "stringBox">
    <div class = "name">
        {{LABELS[PROPERTIES.caption.name]}}
    </div>

    <input
      class = "stringInput"
      name = {{PROPERTIES.caption.name}}
      minlength = {{PROPERTIES.caption.minLength}}
      maxlength = {{PROPERTIES.caption.maxLength}}>

    <div class = "description">
        {{LABELS[PROPERTIES.caption.description]}}
    </div>

    <div class = "constraints">
        {{LABELS[string_constraint]}}
    </div>
</div>
```

In general, for the creator interface, it is most important to convey the data inquiry task and the relationship to the resulting Screen element. Thus, the structural integrity and legibility of the input are prioritized, while the actual appearance is to be determined by the implementation and the surrounding container element. This is because, unlike the Screen, the input element is not going to appear unaccompanied but is consistent to be integrated into a form container consisting of one input element for each property of the chosen page type layout.

CSS does offer the grid-template key to describe the arrangement of the expected child elements, deferring further instructions about those elements to the surrounding structural markup. The accompanying value is split into numbered rows, with the [row<X>-start] and [row<X>-end] keywords in square brackets. Inside each row, the class names as defined in the template file can be referenced. The number of elements in each row determines the column count and should be equal across each row. One element can be repeated to occupy more space. If fewer elements are supposed to be included in a row, a dot (.) can act as a placeholder to maintain the general structure.

Listing 6.7 describes the style for the string input. The name is to be placed left-bound in the top row. The stringInput field should occupy the entire second row, while the description and the constraints occupy the space available in the third row below that.

Listing 6.7 CSS Style Instructions to Define Arrangement of the Input Element

```
INPUT/string.style.css
.stringBox {
  display: grid;
  grid-template:
  [row1-start] "name . ." [row1-end]
  [row2-start] "stringInput stringInput stringInput" [row2-end]
  [row3-start]     "description . constraints"     [row3-end];
}
```

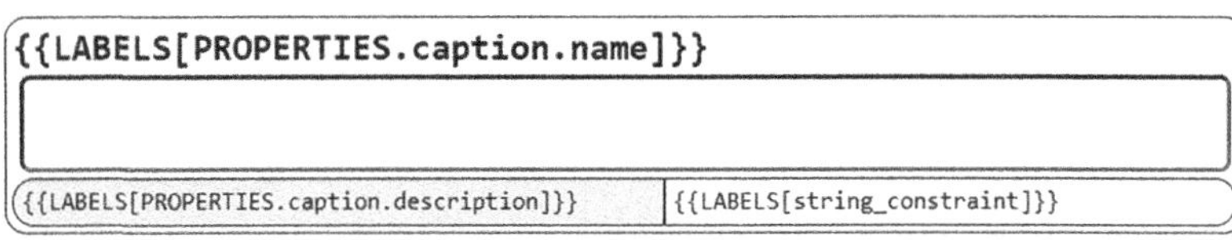

Figure 6.25 Rendering of the String Input Layout

Figure 6.25 does show the rendering of the resulting Layout of the input element as it would occur within a form container, which would provide the proper height and width instructions and an accompanying theme applied. The element remains isolated to itself, independent of possible sibling elements on the same hierarchy level, as it does follow the element hierarchy described in its template file. These elements are then arranged following the instructions in the style file.

6.5.3 The ViewModel

The ViewModel is the programmatic abstraction of the View. It is responsible for maintaining the desired application state and performing the conversion of the Model, as well as for exposing its relevant properties to the View accordingly.

The access of the View is automated via the Binder. Thus, synchronization is compulsory and inherently enforced by the pattern. Most importantly, the benefit of this approach is to avoid code behind. Therefore, the ViewModel is not allowed to access or reference any GUI element, as this would violate the benefits generated by the loose coupling and defeat the purpose of data binding in general. If such code was necessary, it would exist directly inside the scope of the View and create a new binding to access certain data.

The ViewModel is the most vital part of the resulting implementation; its character does directly influence core design decisions. It does primarily facilitate the connections between the View and the Model. Therefore, this subsection does not discuss the details of the ViewModel itself but rather its role in the resulting system environment and the required steps to perform the data retrieval and conversion at the basis of the binding process. The ability to retrieve the data from the data store and to manipulate the resulting documents are presupposed without assuming a particular programming language.

The initial transformation is almost trivial and happens to the data document upon retrieval. For all subsequent steps to access all the necessary information at any time, the id and the page type name are added to the document properties to keep track of the information provided by the ViewModel to the current View. These are not included in the Model as it would introduce duplication and add avoidable redundancy. The exposed ViewModel properties object is contained in **Listing 6.8**.

Listing 6.8 Exposed Properties Object JSON

```
GENERIC/1234.ViewModel.json
{
  "PROPERTIES": {
    "id": "1234",
    "type": "GENERIC",
    "language": "en",
    "layout": "basic",
    "caption": "My Page"
  }
}
```

For most simple data types, like numbers and strings, the View can then access those properties on the ViewModel without performing any further transformational operations. However, more complex data fields and data structures included within the free-form ontology of the framework may invoke certain conversions on properties to achieve an efficient representation of objects and arrays directly on the Model. Even if those are represented by simple types within the Model for storage and evaluation purposes, substantial transformations may be required to achieve the specific representation required by the View.

One of the most tangible examples throughout development does involve dates and times. One well-known format encountered in many systems is the UNIX Timestamp. It is expressed as an integer representing the seconds passed since 01.01.1970 as counted by Coordinated Universal Time (UTC), the current time in Greenwich, London, UK. While it is a very efficient representation at the system level, it is not easily interpretable for the human user and thus has to be transformed before being displayed. Furthermore, most applications do require more contextual information to properly function, like time zones or daylight savings adjustments. In addition to that meta information, the appearance of the date-time format may depend on the localization. The North American system would suggest displaying a date following the MM/DD/YYYY (month/day/year) representation, while the European system does prefer the date to appear as DD.MM.YYYY (day.month.year) with additional variation in the time being displayed. Time is designated either by the 12- or 24-hour schema and may refer to the applicable time zone. The 12-hour schema requires the a.m. (ante meridiem)/p.m. (ante meridiem) qualifier to denote the time of day relative to noon. To have a common point of reference, the standard ISO 8601 was published in 1988 which today is recognized globally. It specifies the date and time to be listed in the order from large to small units, such as YYYY-MM-DD (year-month-day) and HH:MM:SS (hour:minute:second). Both can be joined by using the T character. By default, time is based on UTC, but time zones may be indicated by adjoining the deviation, e.g., + 2:00 for Munich, Germany, or −5:00 for New York, USA, the latter also referred to as Eastern Time (ET) (Cox S. J., 2016) (Richly, 2021). One point in time recorded in one specific time zone thus needs to be represented differently in the other. **Figure 6.26** does illustrate the given example.

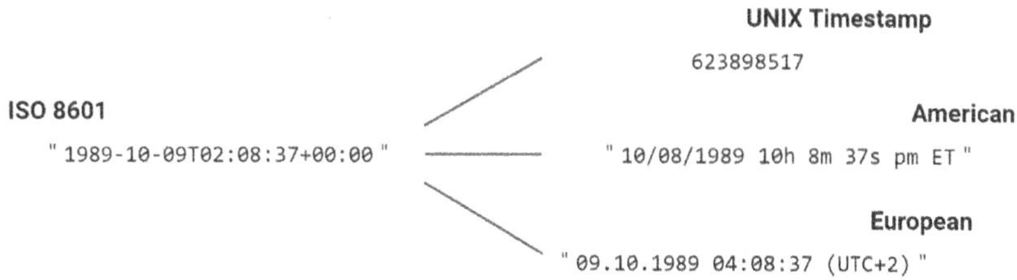

Figure 6.26 Different Date Time Representations

Especially in the context of the MAD, a variety of additional problems compound on these observations. Certain dates often cannot be determined as precisely or involve time spans that may not have a representation within the Gregorian Calendar, as they had been skipped or prolonged. Furthermore, an additional label is required to indicate the era of the Gregorian Calendar, traditionally based on the date defined by the assumed birth of Jesus Christ (1 AD). A date would thus be accompanied either by the letters BC (Before Christ) or AD (Anno Domini) (Rothwangl, 2002).

Nevertheless, the ViewModel is to be aware of the chosen representation in the Model to be able to perform the appropriate transformation to expose it to the View. In general, it does make sense to choose a representation within the Model that allows the resulting document to maintain human readability even without the transformation applied. Furthermore, it is advisable to consider necessary transformations to reduce computing resources at runtime. If at all possible, it also does make sense to rely on standards widely recognized in the field or domain and apply them to the ontology in the Model.

That aspect of the ViewModel also affects the task of resolving placeholders for labels by using references and dictionaries. That is especially important to enable multilingual interfaces but also facilitates reusability and accessibility of the resources involved.

Listing 6.9 Placeholder Allocation for the Caption Input

```
caption.labels.json
{
        "caption": "PH_caption",
        "caption_description": "PH_caption_description",
        "string_constraint": "PH_string_constraint"
}
```

Listing 6.10 English Text Representation for the Caption Input

```
en.labels.json
{
        "PH_caption_placeholder": " Caption",
        "PH_caption_description":
                "The headline to appear on top of the page.",
        "PH_string_constraint":
                "Input a string with
                 a minimum of %i characters,
                 and a maximum of %i characters!"
}
```

Listing 6.11 German Text Representation for the Caption Input

```
de.labels.json
{
        "PH_caption_placeholder": "Überschrift",
        "PH_caption_description":
               "Die Überschrift, die am Anfang der Seite angezeigt wird.",
        "PH_string_constraint":
               "Geben Sie eine Zeichenkette
                zwischen %i und %i Zeichen ein."
}
```

In general, labels are text-based elements that are not a unique part of the corresponding instance of one specific Model but may recur at different places throughout the application. While those could be directly included in those Views they would need to appear in, some problems comparable to the Theme within the View would be provoked. If certain labels appear on different Views and need to undergo changes, each View involved would have to be altered. Additionally, in a multilingual context, each View would need to be instantiated for each language, leading to even more duplication. To avoid that, each View does access the necessary entry on the exposed LABELS object provided by the ViewModel. The keys involved then are resolved using dictionaries or lookup tables that contain those strings, supposed to be presented to the user. **Listing 6.9** contains the key placeholder allocation for the string input element introduced within **Listing 6.6**. Those placeholders correspond with the keys in the dictionary holding the actual string value representations. Thus, the View can be rendered either using the German (**Listing 6.11**) or the English (**Listing 6.10**) labels without being actively affected. As demonstrated by the value for the string constraint ("PH_string_constraint"), those strings can include additional placeholders to expect certain (numeric) values to be inserted into the textual representation, like the character restriction values. **Listing 6.12** contains the exposed labels object for the English version of the labels for the caption input element View.

Listing 6.12 Exposed Labels Object JSON

```
labels.ViewModel.json
{
    "LABELS": {
        "PH_caption_placeholder": "Caption",
        "PH_caption_description":
                    "The text to appear on top of the page.",
        "PH_string_constraint":
                    "Input a string with
                     a minimum of 5 characters,
                     and a maximum of 25 characters!"
    }
}
```

Besides data conversion, the navigation service—also referred to as routing—e.g., properly resolving the events binding and responding to the interaction invoked by the user activating certain UI elements also must be resolved by the ViewModel. Because most applications consist of multiple Views, as the service name would suggest, it is responsible for navigating between the current View and another. Thus, the ViewModel needs to expose the required events to be consumed by the View. Based on the request, the ViewModel has to then collect and expose the necessary resources from the Model or receive and process certain parameters from the previous ViewModel.

Assuming an application consisting of a collection of three Screen elements with ids 1 through 3 as presented in **Listing 6.13**. The corresponding data documents need to be available in the document store, and the necessary files for the layout must be accessible.

Listing 6.13 Application Screen Array JSON

```
screens.json
{
        "screens": ["1", "2", "3"]
}
```

The View then needs a way to communicate the ability to switch between these available Screens to the user. This is usually done by deploying interactable UI elements called buttons. Certain events can then be bound to those buttons. These events need to be exposed by the ViewModel and trigger the expected response when activated. **Listing 6.14** does describe a template for a footer element that would include those buttons and the necessary events (EVENTS.nextPage & EVENTS.prevPage) to be included in any Screen element.

Listing 6.14 Footer Controls Template HTML

```
footer.template.html
<div class = "footer">
    <button class = "prev" onclick = "EVENTS.previousPage"> </div>
    <button class = "next" onclick = "EVENTS.nextPage"> </div>
</div>
```

Those events are received by the ViewModel and are processed accordingly. That usually does involve retrieving the necessary resources and deploying the requested View (navigateTo()). Furthermore, the ViewModel is responsible for keeping track of and exposing the necessary parameters that may be required by other UI elements of the View. The appearance and UI logic included within the View then is able to access these parameters and adopt its characteristics accordingly. Examples of that behavior include deactivating the next button on the last Screen or showing a visual indicator representing the number of the current Screen. Those objectives would require the total number of Screens as well as the number of the current Screen to be exposed to the View, as shown in **Listing 6.15**. The latter would need to change based on the events triggered by the View and processed by the implementation of the ViewModel.

Listing 6.15 Application ViewModel JSON

```
app.ViewModel.json
{
        "screens": ["1", "2", "3"],
        "number_of_screens": 3,
        "current_screen": 1,
        "EVENTS": {
                "previousPage": "navigateTo(%currentPage - 1)",
                "nextPage": "navigateTo(%currentPage + 1)",
                "home": "navigateTo(home)"
        }
}
```

The minimal viable prototype (MVP) of the resulting consumer application thus consists of an appropriate Model—including the Schema to validate the data entry and the document store for the resulting Data Documents—and a View –possessing at least one Template and one Style file as described above—for each available page type. Finally, the ViewModel is responsible for retrieving the required documents from the store as well as for the data conversion to provide the particular values demanded by the View to the Binder. In addition to that, a Navigation Service—in combination with appropriate UI elements—is necessary to enable the user to switch between the available Screen elements.

Those MVVM components introduced in **Figure 6.18** are exemplified in **Figure 6.27** for the exemplary consumer app defined in **Listing 6.15**.

The components of the creator app are structured similarly, as determined by the holistic framework system design. The necessary form can be created by deriving the input element for each property of the Schema for the desired page type (createForm(schema)). As each page type does possess a corresponding

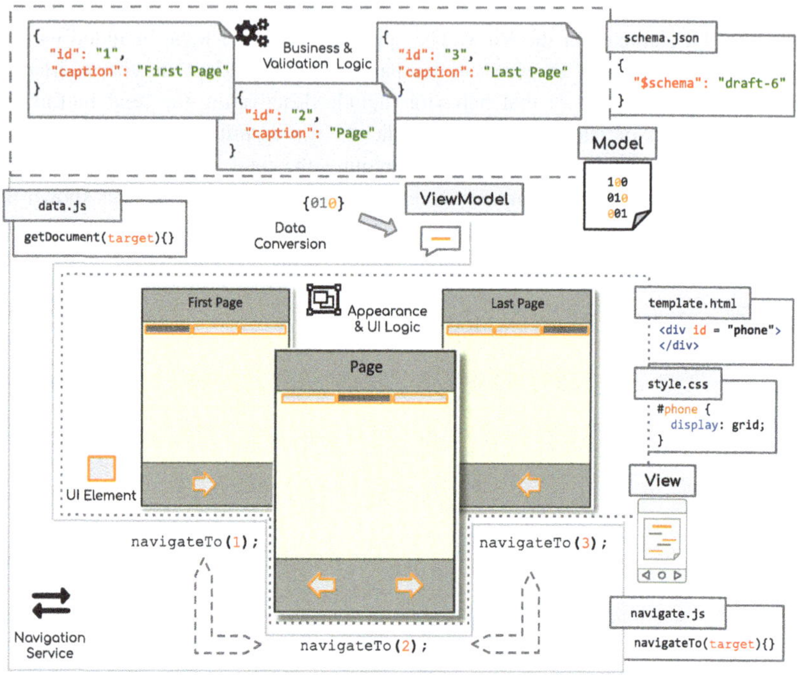

Figure 6.27 MVVM Structure and Files for the Consumer App

Screen element, documents can be rendered and presented to the creator to visualize the connection between the Model and the View (renderScreen(schema)). If any change is performed within the form provided, the ViewModel can be updated for that value and, thus, the Screen element can receive the new value via the Binder (updateVM(element, value)). Lastly, if each input field has been filled to satisfy both the user and the schema requirements, the inquired data can be committed (commitData(data)). That means that the data document is created and stored in the corresponding document store if the validation of the Model can be observed (validateDocument(data)).

The events necessary to be described for the form are included in **Listing 6.16**.

Listing 6.16 Form ViewModel

```
form.ViewModel.json
{
        "EVENTS": {
                "createForm": "createForm(schema)",
                "renderScreen": "renderScreen(schema)",

                "formChange": "updateVM(element, value)",
                "commit": "commitData(data)"
        }
}
```

Thus, the MVP for the creator application makes use of the features described above, plus the necessary documents for each required input element to be embedded in the form structure. Additionally, the files required to render the consumer View need to be available, which have to be prepared anyway to fulfill the requirements of the consumer app. Just the interaction with the ViewModel and the consumer View is not necessary here, as far as it only does demonstrate the applicability and purpose of the data input task. Finally, the ViewModel must provide the labels document for the form elements. The components of the creator app are represented in **Figure 6.28**. If the creator app becomes more advanced, in addition to the described elements, a navigation service becomes necessary to offer the ability to access or change certain pages or to assemble consumer applications.

To summarize, each page type does have at least one template element determined by the layouts suggested within its schema resulting in the Screen element, i.e., the View for the consumer application. The very same schema provides the basis for the Input elements grouped together into a form, i.e., the View for the creator application. Thus, both Views are based on the same Model, which does demonstrate that connection by rendering the Screen in such a way that the creator can experience the resulting app page instantly at the time of data inquiry. The two questions "How is the data stored?" and "How is the data displayed?" are directly and simultaneously answered by the Model and View, respectively. The ViewModel is responsible for retrieving and transforming the data documents from the Model to provide the required properties as well as the events invoked by the View via the Binder.

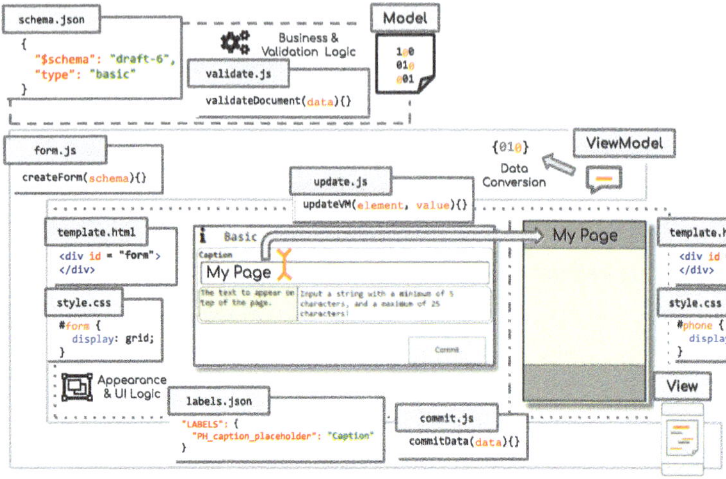

Figure 6.28 MVVM Structure and Files for the Creator App

A tangible reference implementation is required to demonstrate the practical relevance of the conceptual benefits offered by the proposed solution of the framework architecture. That prototype implementation of the framework is supposed to demonstrate its practicability despite the inherent restrictions deeply embedded in the MAD. The primary purpose of which is to show that the complexity and structure introduced by the Model do not necessarily impair the usability and even can aid the approachability of the technology as a whole.

In a similar way, one does not need to be a trained mechanic to learn how to drive a car. Preparing data for mobile applications does not require comprehensive computer engineering skills. Nevertheless, a better understanding of the underlying Model does improve the ability to create content for existing page types as well as to articulate the requirements for new features to be supported by the framework prototype implementation.

7 Prototype Development

The detailed design resulting in the conceptual foundation of the framework, as discussed in the previous chapter, usually concludes the extent of most comparable studies. The identified problem is thoroughly analyzed and solved on a sound theoretical basis, supported by a set of profound technical instructions. In this instance, with the close connections to the Museum Application Domain supplied by the ViSIT project and the academic and practical implications which allocate the problem demand, a genuine instantiation is required. Otherwise, it would be impossible to gain insights and canvas the validity of the suggested software framework or its ability to deliver the expected scope. Thus, a prototype implementation is mandatory to provide that essential grounding.

Furthermore, to enable proper evaluation of the framework on the level suggested by DSR, it is essential to showcase the practical capabilities of the framework by actually engaging the museum professional in the creation process. As acknowledged before, it is compulsory to avoid entry barriers, especially from a non-technical perspective. That does include the practical execution of the data entry process, as well as the necessary infrastructure to deploy the overall system. Especially for the target audience of small and medium-sized institutions, it is unreasonable to commit sparse resources for the introduction of collection management systems or other (software) solutions that would introduce more overhead than benefit from a small-scale perspective.

The opportunities introduced between web-based applications and advances in cloud computing enable a serverless architecture for the prototype implementation to be available as a web service. As examined in subsection 6.4.1, serverless does not indicate the absence of remote infrastructure but rather the capability to refrain from running server-side application logic. The requirement of a web server to distribute the application files and other resources, as well as a database

T. Baumgärtner, *A Software Framework for Mobile Apps in the Museum Application Domain*, Gabler Theses, https://doi.org/10.1007/978-3-658-44367-2_7

server to provide the application with the endpoints to access the required data documents via an API, remains unaffected.

To showcase the abilities of current web technologies as well as to minimize possible third-party dependencies, the implementation of the creator and consumer applications relies entirely on the standards provided between HTML, CSS, and JavaScript. Therefore, it does not rely on any external dependencies at runtime (also referred to as the *vanilla stack*). One drawback of JavaScript during production is usually the weakly typed nature of the programming language. However, especially in the context of a prototype implementation, that can enable shorter development cycles and retain dynamic adaptations by allowing quick changes throughout development that do not provoke the frequent refactoring of the codebase. While type-errors are not automatically prevented at runtime, certain checks have to be present at the API-level and are invoked within the Model by design. External resources are mostly limited to enhancing visual cues, like icons, and are directly included in the application's repository.

The implementation of the consumer application does highlight the capabilities offered by Progressive Web Apps (PWA), invoking the web standards itemized above and utilizing the state of the art of web technologies as well as modern browsers. Thus, access to the creator's content can be provided for most consumers directly on their smart mobile devices without additional barriers that may be introduced by requiring some installation process.

This chapter first does take a comprehensive look at the roles involved in the app development process. The benefits the software framework is supposed to provide to the intended audience manifest themselves by eliminating the manual task of coding, development, and data management. This unique approach enables the creator to simultaneously offer mobile applications and realize the benefits of structured data (*Section 7.1—Tasks and Roles during App Development*). The development of the industry related to web and app technologies is analyzed to realize the circumstantial conditions for the PCCR framework prototype (*Section 7.2—Web and App Technologies*). Lastly, the actual prototype development is summarized in detail (*Section 7.3—Implementation of the Prototype*).

7.1 Tasks and Roles in App Development

The educational element to be fulfilled by the application framework is not only limited to the data inquiry process but also aims to build the know-how to construct and describe Models and Views by observing those elements interact. To be able to request individual features and generate associated insights, museum professionals need to acquire at least a rudimentary understanding of how and why to create and maintain the underlying structured data and evaluate the processes and the technology involved.

However, in practice and especially in small and medium-sized institutions, the benefits of engaging in those activities are outweighed by the friction caused by not generating any immediate benefit if only the data-centric narrative is being promoted. Enabling the museum professional to become a creator directly associated with a use case that immediately does generate utility does aid in supporting their understanding of the underlying structures and dependencies. The goal is to attain a level of proficiency where the existing structures of the institution can be harnessed and aligned with future attempts to achieve sustainable digital goals. This level of engagement is also mandatory for being able to articulate those goals and desired features toward outside developers and to establish a general language for intra- and inter-organizational communication. That can drastically improve the initial expectations as well as the outcome of pursued projects in the Museum Application Domain.

Those general issues encountered by engaging in the development process have been summarized in conjunction with **Figure 5.9** available in section 5.3. In alignment with the objective of the app framework, it is possible to further break down the roles involved and separate the use cases into manageable units. The procedural elements of the framework discussed in section 5.3 can be captured and attributed accordingly. The use case diagram in **Figure 7.1** does emphasize the different roles and the workflows they are associated with to represent the framework environment. It does include the app creation tasks and does facilitate the interfaces to engage in the development process.

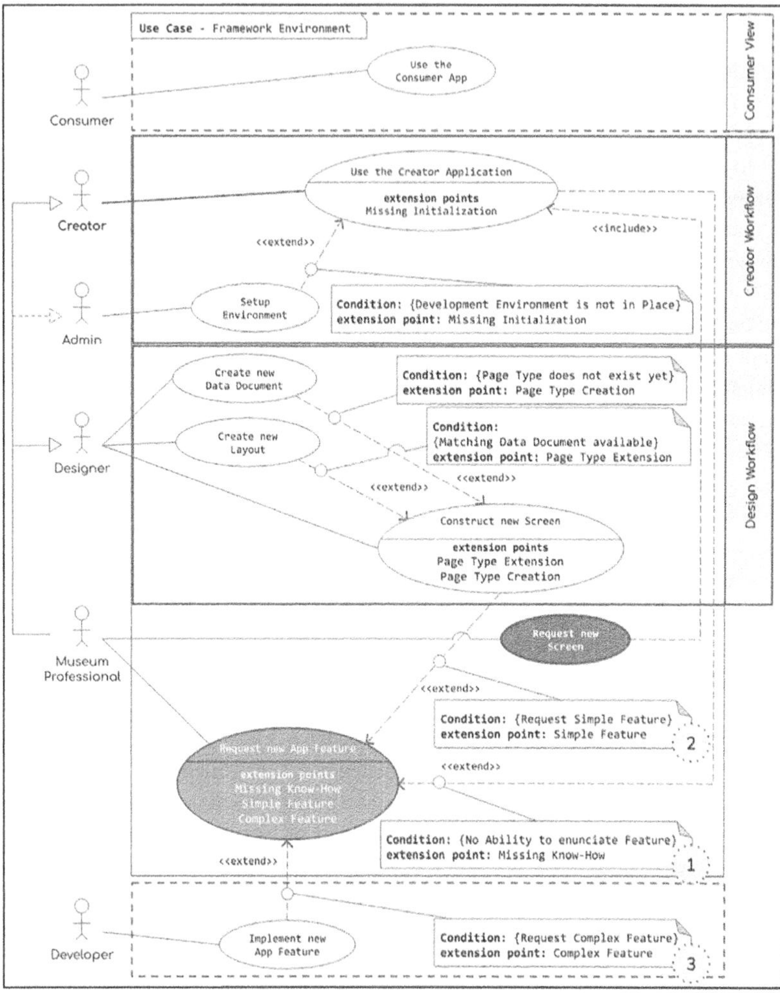

Figure 7.1 Use Case—Environment for the App Creation Process

While the roles of the external stakeholders, especially those of consumers and developers, need to be recognized, the focus is concentrated on the intended main audience of the framework—the museum professional. First, acknowledging the involvement of the museum professional as an individual rather than assuming the impersonal involvement of the museum as an institution does personalize the entire interaction. Second, allocating roles for specific tasks introduces intentionality to each of those tasks and the associated workflow.

Overall, the main goal and entry point is to enable the museum professional to adopt the role of the creator. Assuming the availability of an implementation of the creator application, the setup and initialization of the system environment, such that the creator can access the tool, has to be performed by an administrator. While that may deter potential users from engaging with the tool entirely, this particular barrier of entry can be eliminated by offering the creator application as a hosted service, as is described in section 7.2, which does eliminate that foregoing necessity. Nevertheless, the initialization is an essential task of the system and thus must not be overlooked.

Getting familiar with the concepts and structures suggested by the framework regarding Screens and their composition is supposed to qualify the museum professional to assess the capabilities regarding the digital domain of their own institution more accurately (1). Thus, requirements for the subsequent random-access guide can be articulated more precisely. By comprehending the contiguity between the View and the Model, screen elements can be described, and new features can be enunciated by experiencing the effort necessary to cultivate each corresponding task.

Additionally, the framework does facilitate the option for the museum professional to even go a step further. They can directly engage in the design workflow for simple features, i.e., Screens that rely on a Data Document and Layout in order to create and deliver content, as long as those are based on the available data types (2). In order to create a new Screen based on an existing Data Document, a new Layout can be added to emphasize certain information or select a different subset of the available properties. To create a new Screen entirely, the properties to be displayed have to be defined, either by pursuing the desired Layout or by directly composing a Data Document and then including the respective matching component. Adopting the role of the designer within the framework may require a certain degree of technical dexterity but would allow customization without interacting with the core implementation. Thus, those design tasks can be performed with no to little external aid.

That does capacitate the museum professional to phrase and request new app features but also to immediately apply the acquired knowledge by embracing the role of the designer or at least articulate their requirements more precisely. However, implementing more complex features, which would extend beyond the design workflow, does not only require the ability to describe their characteristics. Technical know-how may be necessary, which often is not available within the institution itself (3). Thus, an external developer would be required to access the core of the framework implementation to contribute the required resources necessary to approach the system as well as to translate the requirements of the museum professional. Those features may involve matters directly related to the framework itself, e.g., creating new data types, the consumer application, e.g., modifying screen access, as well as the surrounding technical environment, e.g., creating interfaces to integrate databases available to the institution. Nevertheless, in any case, it is necessary for the museum professional to be able to communicate their desires.

As discussed in subsection 5.2.3, while it would be possible to also define different user groups and personas for the consumer, the basic technical functionality of the random-access guide and the way it would be approached would not drastically change. Adapting the content for specific audiences is primarily a problem to be addressed during content creation. The resulting Views for the consumer application are a byproduct of the framework by design and do not require further effort, as an app technically is a special page type consisting of a collection of different Screens. However, it is equally important to eliminate the technical hurdles to ensure easy access to the resulting consumer application.

7.2 Web and App Technologies

The general appeal and the influence of mobile technologies are examined in section 2.3, and their benefits within the Museum Application Domain as a gateway to offer random-access guides are discussed in subsection 3.2.2. The possibilities of distributing mobile applications were introduced cursory in subsection 5.1.1. The architectural concepts applied in modern application environments and their development are presented in subsection 6.4.1 and directly embedded in the conceptual core of the framework. As these are present in almost any modern development environment, they do not considerably affect the following examination. Even more so, in the beginning of smart mobile devices in the late 2000s, the platform provided by the operating system did have a major influence, especially concerning the accessibility and distribution of mobile applications.

While Nokia, Microsoft, and Blackberry once possessed considerable market shares, each with their own mobile operating system, these platforms have been rendered obsolete compared to the two remaining competitors, Apple and Google. In the beginning, each of these two major OS vendors remaining today offered one dedicated programming language to develop apps for their respective platforms (Statcounter, 2019).

Apple did continue to utilize Objective-C, a language originally developed at the NeXT company for the NeXTSTEP operating system in 1984, a project also launched by Steve Jobs, the founder of Apple. The language has been used since 2001 to write applications for macOS (now OS X), their main operating system for desktop machines, after NeXT was acquired by Apple. By offering the Cocoa Touch interface to also support development for iOS, Apple's mobile operating system introduced at the time of the launch of the iPhone in 2007, their entire ecosystem had a cohesive point of access for developers (DeVoe, 2011) (Garling, 2012) (González García, Espada, Pelayo G-Bustelo, & Cueva Lovelle, 2015).

In 2008 Google released Android, their mobile operating system (Morrill, 2008). They did not have any prior platform-specific programming interfaces outside their web-centric business models and also went with a different distribution model for their operating system entirely. While Apple has full control over the hardware their systems are exclusively deployed on, Android was meant to run on various devices of multiple manufacturers. Thus, Java, invented in 1995, has been chosen because of its platform-independent features, as well as its popularity in the developer community (Bott, 2011) (Patrick, 2017) (Debnath, 2022).

While both of those two major operating systems are UNIX based, the proprietary modification of each kernel does not allow for the interoperability of native applications dedicated to each base system. Furthermore, over time, the complexity of the distinct platform application frameworks applied to the development process did increase because of hardware advances and new features specific to mobile devices and client-server communication, and other services. This led to certain issues with the chosen languages not being able to project the necessary concepts very well, which often led to convoluted sequencing of functions or complicated workarounds for certain situations not well-supported by the languages. Thus, in 2017 Google officially included the Kotlin language, released by JetBrains in 2011, to develop applications for Android. Kotlin was meant to extend the Android application framework by supporting developers with flexible native platform support while maintaining full Java compatibility (Martinez & Mateus, 2021). Similarly, in 2014 Apple released the Swift language to replace Objective-C, which at the time did lack many features expected from modern languages as it even did precede Java by ten years and had many problems related to its ancestry to the C language. As software in the Apple ecosystem runs exclusively on their own devices, it was also possible to specifically optimize software performance (González García, Espada, Pelayo G-Bustelo, & Cueva Lovelle, 2015).

Today, while each of the four languages is currently supported for app development, in each case, the newer language is recommended (Karczewski, 2020) (Nix, 2021). The bigger issue for app developers is platform compatibility. Over time, certain framework features become deprecated or replaced by newer concepts requiring heavy code refactoring, or the app will become incompatible with its target operating system (Que, Guo, & Zhu, 2016).

The native app platforms and their programming language environments are summarized in **Figure 7.2**.

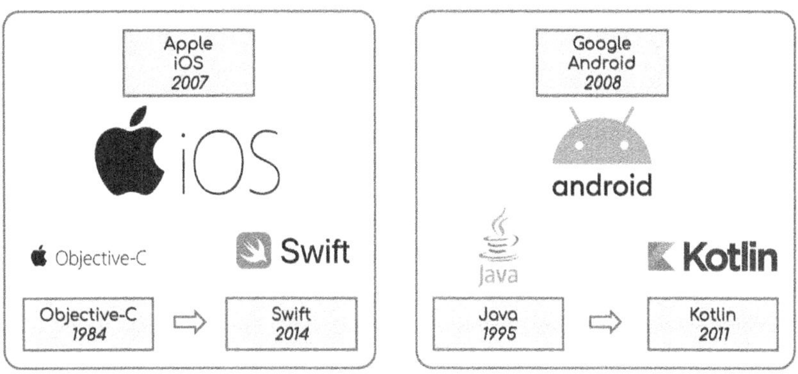

Figure 7.2 Mobile Operating Systems and their App Programming Languages

Especially if the goal is to maintain one app for both platforms, that poses a great challenge. For that reason, certain approaches try to establish a meta-platform to create a single codebase to serve both platforms and, often additionally, the web. One of these is the Flutter software development kit, released in 2017. It does apply the Dart programming language conceived in 2011 during development and then utilizes interfaces to the platform-specific SDKs to compile one uniform codebase to run on the different platforms. That way, native apps can be distributed, and cross-platform support can be achieved (Boukhary & Colmenares, 2019). The biggest issue here is the double lock-in effect originating from the interaction between the proprietary meta-platform and the native systems. However, if changes are introduced to one platform that are not immediately absorbed by the meta-platform, issues similar to the native approach emerge. Taking Flutter as an example, it does best interact with the Android platform as it also is developed by Google. Thus, it can factor in future changes to the Android platform, while changes to the iOS platform have to be integrated only as they do get published (Amadeo, 2018).

In any case, these considerations only address the consumer app. The greatest benefit of native applications is the ability to be distributed through the platform-specific marketplace to be easily discovered by the consumer. This is also the reason why the creator workflow is often ignored as the whole attention is put onto creating the app. Any additional software, tool, or GUI would result in another construct with its own codebase to maintain similar platform restrictions and lock-in effects depending on the intended runtime environment and audience.

A way to circumvent those lock-in effects—predominately tied to select native platforms—is to take a step further away from the operating system and rely on web technologies entirely. The biggest benefit of doing so is a high degree of standardization, which is supervised by independent global committees, enabling true platform independence (Jaffe J., 2019).

The World Wide Web is a service on the internet and has initially been created by Tim Berners-Lee in 1989 to share documents concerned with the documentation at the European Organization for Nuclear Research (CERN) in Switzerland. It was opened to other research facilities in 1991 and spread quickly to many academic and scientific institutions. It was released to the public in 1994 and is the world's most assertive software platform today. Those shared documents consist of hypertext, meaning they may be interconnected via hyperlinks, i.e., references to other resources, to establish a continuous information space. Hypertext documents are usually structured by using the HyperText Markup Language (HTML), are displayed by using a program referred to as a browser, and their appearance may be modified using Cascading Style Sheets (CSS). A static collection of similar or related documents is called a website. That early era of the web is also referred to as Web 1.0 (Mehdi, 2007) (Jacksi & Abass, 2019).

As the popularity grew, the demand for interactive elements emerged and was satisfied by introducing the JavaScript (JS) programming language. It was originally designed for the browser by Netscape in 1995 to enable more complex user interaction with the dominantly static content of websites (Champeon, 2001). As these interactions became more elaborate, it became possible to implement full-scale software programs to run in the browser, which became known as web applications accordingly. As these features became more mature from 2003 onward, the era of the web would be referred to as Web 2.0 (Jacksi & Abass, 2019).

Mobile websites are specifically optimized to be displayed on small devices and interacted with on a touch screen. Dynamic websites adopt their appearance depending on the device they are displayed on. Because of their visual similarities to native mobile apps, mobile websites are often referred to as web apps in general, regardless of their interactive capabilities (Mehdi, 2007) (Cascaval, Ortego, Robatmili, & Gracia, 2015) (MacPherson, 2019).

Responsible for the rendering of the layout on the user's device is the browser engine, a vital software component of every browser—the program used to view websites (Cascaval, Ortego, Robatmili, & Gracia, 2015). In the past, each browser had its own proprietary engine implementation, which led to similar difficulties as demonstrated by the native platforms, although not as pronounced. While the underlying technology is standardized, each implementation had some degree of deviation or features not supported by their competitors. Therefore, developers could resort to the dedicated web standards but had to test and establish browser compatibility of their websites individually anyway (Hoffmann J., 2020).

The earliest implementation was the Gecko rendering engine in 1997 by Netscape for the Netscape Navigator, the most dominant browser at the time (Dickerson, 2018). That engine is still in use by its successor, Mozilla's Firefox browser, released in 2002. The Trident engine was also released in 1997 by Microsoft for the Internet Explorer browser. Because of certain specific implementation details, it was also referred to as MSHTML. That also used to be the most problematic engine for developers because it had the biggest gap compared to the web standards and included more proprietary technology to conform with the Microsoft Windows operating system. The Webkit rendering engine, developed by Apple in 1998, has been used in their Safari browser since 2002. To support their web-centric business model, Google released the Chrome browser in 2008 by combining technology provided by Firefox and the Webkit rendering engine. After a long period of collaboration, Google did fork Webkit into the Blink rendering engine in 2013 to allow more flexibility. However, both implementations remain very similar (Hoffmann J., 2020). Microsoft did eventually replace Internet Explorer with the Edge browser in 2015 and announced, that it would also rely on Blink from 2020 forward (Rajaa, 2020). The primary reason for these consolidations is related to the transformation of the policy committees to become apparent in the descriptions contained in the next paragraphs and has been encouraged by Tim Berners-Lee himself (Hoffmann J., 2020).

Thus, the web as a platform does supersede the operating system in interoperability and reach since browsers are available on virtually all traditional personal computers and mobile devices. Therefore, they offer a homogenous application platform. That feature-rich environment enables the concept referred to as Web 3.0 (Jacksi & Abass, 2019). The current distribution of browsers and their browser engines is shown in **Figure 7.3**.

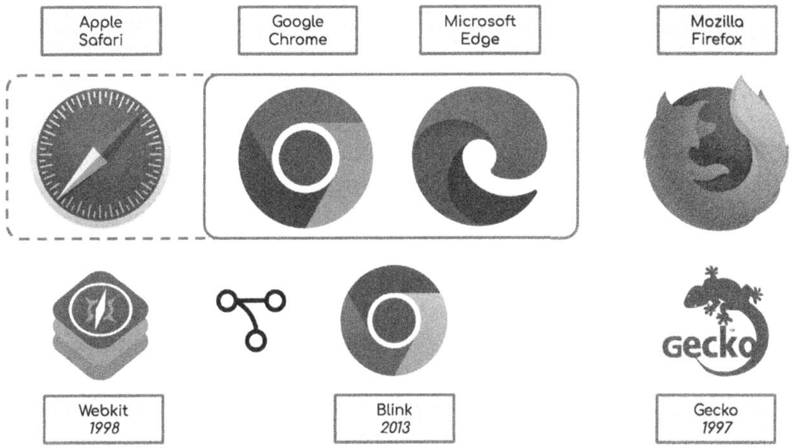

Figure 7.3 Browsers and Browser Engines

Originally the web standards introduced above were supervised by the World Wide Web Consortium (W3C), founded by Tim Berners-Lee in 1994 after he left CERN (Jaffe J., 2019). The W3C was established at the Massachusetts Institute of Technology (MIT) and is concerned with the standardization of technologies to maintain the Open Web Platform to achieve the "web for all" and "web on everything" principles. The administration today is performed by the four international host institutions because of the academic background of the WWW: The Computer Science and Artificial Intelligence Laboratory (CSAIL) at MIT in the USA, the European Research Consortium for Informatics and Mathematics (ERCIM), Keio University in Japan, and Beihang University in China (Jaffe J., 2013). The pursued standards do include those to sustain the central architectural concepts, including URIs and HTTP. Beyond that, the W3C maintains the general accessibility of the web regardless of hardware, connection, or device and input mode. In the context of applications, they are primarily concerned with the traditional static web, i.e., defining document standards for CSS and XML under the Open Standard Principles (Champeon, 2001) (Jaffe J., 2015). Additionally, they support the vision of the "semantic web" based on advancing linked data and the related technologies RDF, SPARQL, and OWL (Jacksi & Abass, 2019). Their standard formation process is structured in four stages, starting with a working draft and resulting in a W3C recommendation to then be implemented and deployed (Jaffe J., 2018).

In the past, the W3C also has been responsible for supervising HTML. However, in 2004 they suggested entirely replacing HTML with XML-based technologies, referred to as XHTML, to further advance their idea of the semantic web. As this would have caused major compatibility issues with the prior HTML standard, some browser vendors have voiced their concerns and announced that they would continue to maintain HTML themselves (WHATWG, 2017). HTML 5 (formally: the HTML living standard) and Document Object Model (DOM) were then simultaneously taken care of by the resulting community named Web Hypertext Application Technology Working Group (WHATWG) and the W3C. A prior conflict involving patent policy with the W3C was resolved mutually in 2019, and HTML was fully placed under the control of the WHATWG, consisting of Apple, Google, Microsoft, and Mozilla (W3C, 2021). For that reason, previous issues regarding the implementation of the rendering engines were almost eliminated, as each company could exert its influence prior to implementation.

After its conception in 1995, JavaScript development has been almost dormant even after the first specification of the standard was submitted to ecma international in 1997 (Champeon, 2001). The committee is the successor of the European Computer Manufacturers Association (ECMA), which renamed itself to ecma international in 1994 and dropped its acronym to express its global reach and activities beyond just Europe (ecma, 1994). Their members are foremost global technology-oriented companies in pursuit of certain standards concerned with file systems, character encoding, and programming languages. Again, Apple, Google, Microsoft, and Mozilla are part of ecma international (ecma, Members, 2021). Since Mozilla joined ecma international in 2005, the committee did prioritize to advance the JavaScript standard and, by extension, the JSON exchange format (Eich, 2005). The standard itself is named ECMAScript, since, technically, the trademark for JavaScript is owned by Oracle; however, most implementations and industry references still identify the language as JavaScript (Sanders, 2018). Simultaneously, Jesse James Garrett, a member of the open-source community not affiliated with ecma international, conceptualized the Asynchronous JavaScript and XML (AJAX) paradigm (Garrett, 2005). That set of technologies—heavily resting upon JavaScript—facilitated single-page applications (Kaluza, Troskot, & Vukelic, 2018). Being able to communicate with the server and request resources without reloading the page and running other operations in the background created the foundation of the modern web platform (Steiner, 2018). One major performance issue of JavaScript was eliminated by the release of the V8 JavaScript engine with Google Chrome in 2008, which allowed just-in-time compilation. Imminent browser compatibility issues were eliminated by an agreement reached between browser vendors in 2009, resulting in the ECMAScrit 5 standard (Kienle, 2010). Today ECMAScript is a living standard that does not track version numbers but individual feature maturity, similar to the W3C approach regarding HTML described above.

As it presents itself, these committees and communities may not be as impartial as one would expect; however, they are bound to open standards and—unlike their native platforms—contribute toward the common goal of developing and maintaining an open platform backed by a large global community. The composition and the influence of these three committees are summarized in **Figure 7.4**.

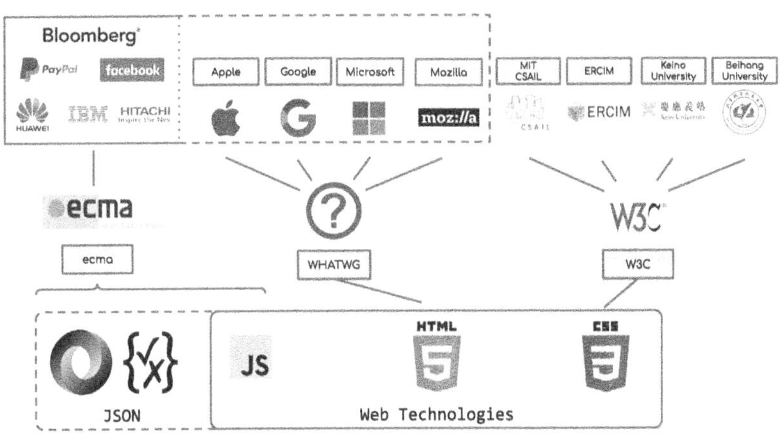

Figure 7.4 Standard Technologies in Web Development

Besides the browser, another way to distribute those web apps is the concept of *hybrid apps* (Hu, Wang, Bezemer, & Hassan, 2019). That approach utilizes a shell application for each native platform, which contains a web-view based on the default browser engine of the platform, which is limited to displaying only the desired website (Steiner, 2018). This does simplify the access to the platforms for the developer, and the native capabilities can address certain issues of web apps, like offline access, which in the past has been difficult to effectuate by the browser directly. App development and testing can be centralized, comparable to the meta-platform approach discussed above, while distribution to each desired platform remains unchanged (Que, Guo, & Zhu, 2016).

A modern way to approach the disparity between the platform-specific native apps and web apps is the concept of Progressive Web App (PWA), a term initially coined by the Google developer Alex Russell in 2015 (Russell, 2015) (Steiner, 2018) (Nuanez & Myers, 2022). The essential idea is to invert the concept of the hybrid app, to extend the capabilities of the web, and to utilize its reach rather than embracing the seamless integration within the native ecosystems. Modern web technologies, design elements, and platform-browser integration, i.e., accessing device components through the browser, are capable of mimicking the proficiency and reliability of native apps. The general scope and functionality have been described by Mozilla in a position paper after joining the W3C in 2004 (W3C, 2004). Along those lines, the initial concept to distribute apps to mobile devices was the web, as described by Steve Jobs himself during the introduction of the first iPhone in 2007. However, missing standardization and performance issues led to the development of those native platforms described above. Today PWAs are supported by all modern browsers on desktop and mobile devices, with the exception of Firefox—which is not as relevant in the mobile sector anyway (Scandi, 2019). To ensure the interoperability with most devices, it is important to adhere to the eight key properties for progressive web apps summarized in **Figure 7.5**. As PWAs are not part of a web standard yet, these proprietary guidelines are mutually maintained and published by Mozilla and Google (Osmani, 2015) (Nuanez & Myers, 2022).

In general, the most important aspect is being capable of fulfilling the general expectations attributed to an app. Apps need to be *discoverable.* In a narrow sense, that does refer to the general ability of the user to approach and identify them as an app; in broader terms, the app itself should be offered to the user within the intended context to fulfill relevant tasks. Those apps, therefore, need to be *network independent* and should reliably provide at least basic functionality regardless of the connectivity of the device. To do that, they must be *installable*, both from a technical perspective, i.e., to preload and save critical resources on the consumer's device; as well as from the user's perspective, e.g., being quickly accessible via a shortcut on the home screen. Regardless, the app should not have to rely on its installation or a container—like the hybrid app approach—to function and must remain *linkable* to be invoked on demand and shared through the browser using a URL. Additionally, the app needs to work reliably for most users. Foremost, PWAs should operate best on recent browsers and devices best suited for the context and task but are supposed to be *progressively enhanced* to

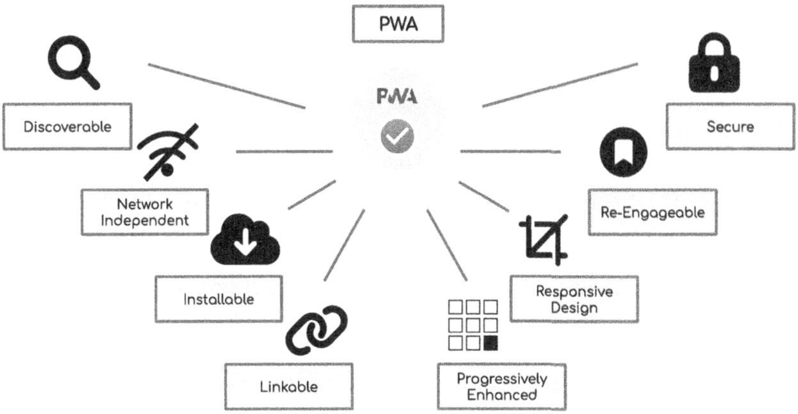

Figure 7.5 Properties of Progressive Web Apps

also support older browsers or different devices over time. The central concept of providing support for multiple devices is *responsive design*, i.e., enabling the app to utilize the available screen size of the device while maintaining operability and legibility. Whenever relevant, the app should be *re-engageable* by updating its content and notifying the user appropriately. Finally, the user data to be processed client-side, the access control of the exposed APIs server-side, as well as the communication in-between must be *secured* against third-party access (Osmani, 2015) (Richard & LePage, 2020) (Nuanez & Myers, 2022).

Following the evolution of JavaScript, numerous technical frameworks and libraries have been released to aid in different stages of the development process and implement the required properties (Ollila, Makitalo, & Mikkonen, 2022) (Aborujilah, Adamu, Shariff, & Long, 2022). The biggest distinction is to be made between the application code and the corresponding UI to be delivered to and executed client-side on the consumer device, referred to as frontend; and the server-side code, to obtain certain resources, the database, and the server, referred to as backend (Abdullah & Zeki, 2014). The general goal is to add more dynamic capabilities to the inherently static web technologies and to reduce the involved effort by bundling repeating concepts and boilerplate code to provide accessible and convenient APIs. That does enable clear communication paths and decouples both components by establishing clear responsibilities for maintaining the integrity of the connections and inquiries exchanged between client and server.

For the frontend, those tools do foremost aim to enforce one of the MV* variants, introduced in subsection 6.4.2.

As the underlying technology is based on open standards, the lock-in effect is not as pronounced as on the OS level, but as the most popular tools are also owned by mostly the same big companies, a certain influence cannot be denied. The most popular solutions are the Angular framework by Google, the React library by Facebook, and Vue.js, a framework maintained by an independent open-source community (Kaluza, Troskot, & Vukelic, 2018) (Ollila, Makitalo, & Mikkonen, 2022). By design, the browser is only capable of executing JavaScript. Thus, all of these utilize the language, or the superset TypeScript maintained by Microsoft, to solve common issues encountered during web development (Kaluza, Troskot, & Vukelic, 2018). The development process, thus, is bound to the concepts emphasized by the framework intended to support the motivation of the owner, which can be problematic as it may limit the capabilities of the resulting application, especially in narrow or specialized use cases.

Additionally, if those tools are deployed, the development overhead and external dependencies do increase the complexity of the project, and consequently, the extensibility and maintainability suffer (Kaluza, Troskot, & Vukelic, 2018). Using the vanilla technology, i.e., relying directly on the default technology as close to the specification as possible, has the advantage of a leaner system and more flexible capabilities. Especially if the goal is to solve a novel problem that requires more degrees of freedom, even if common features and utility functions need to be resolved and implemented manually.

For server-side code, that is a considerably different story. HTTP was meant for the exchange of static resources. While modern JavaScript allows the introduction of dynamic elements in the browser as the standardized client-side outlet, especially with the capabilities provided by AJAX, there is not a single standardized solution for the backend. However, if requests to the server are supposed to yield dynamic responses, it is necessary for these requests and the corresponding response to be pre-processed to generate the desired resources (Kaluza, Troskot, & Vukelic, 2018). In the early stages of the web, the PHP programming language, short for the recursive abbreviation PHP: Hypertext Preprocessor, was the only viable option to execute server-side code in the context of web applications. This was primarily necessary to preserve bandwidth and to allow for dynamic content, which relied on information stored in databases or other remote locations. PHP does extend the HTML file with instructions executed upon the time the file is requested to fill in the information according to the request (Samimi, et al., 2012) (PHP, 2015). This made it possible to perform certain requests with a higher payload not meant to be visible nor to be delivered to the user, with the goal to only select and transfer the intended content associated with the request. The language was released in 1995 and remains the most used server-side programming language today (PHP, 2004) (W3Tech, 2022). However, with the increasing capabilities of frontend technologies and the ability to dynamically request resources, the demands for server-side capabilities and operations transformed. AJAX made it possible to deliver partial pages and request certain resources on demand or only if necessary, as well as to complete processing client-side without reloading the entire page (Kaluza, Troskot, & Vukelic, 2018). This is supported by ReSTful API-endpoints to decouple frontend and back-end code as far as possible, which is especially useful if complicated backend operations are necessary throughout the interaction.

That paradigm shift enabled the possibility for numerous programming languages to fulfill those server-side responsibilities as it was no longer necessary to yield the finalized HTML but rather JSON or XML files to be asynchronously delivered to the client. Thus, the server-side responsibilities mostly include authentication, validation, and database operations, as would be required by any other software system. Server-side rendering may still be reasonable in certain performance-sensitive scenarios but is no longer necessary (Kaluza, Troskot, & Vukelic, 2018). Individual frameworks may emphasize different aspects; however, their purpose is mostly independent of the requirements posed by the client-side use cases. Additionally, they do not require any GUI or other visual components. The most popular frameworks and their corresponding programming languages are summarized in **Figure 7.6** (Ollila, Makitalo, & Mikkonen, 2022) (Aborujilah, Adamu, Shariff, & Long, 2022).

Figure 7.6 Popular Frameworks and Tools for Web Development

One of the most impactful innovations has been the conception of node.js in 2009 and the express.js framework the year after, which does allow for JavaScript code to be deployed on the server-side as well. That does eliminate the previously inevitable bilingual approach in web development and further standardizes the communication if both front- and backend can use the same language principles (O'Dell, 2012) (Kaluza, Troskot, & Vukelic, 2018).

As the next section does describe, in the case of the prototype implementation of the framework, no server-side code is necessary at all. That does reduce the overhead to a minimum and enables developers and administrators to quickly pick up the system implementation. If the database management system is capable of directly providing the necessary APIs, requests can be sent directly to the document store, and responses are asynchronously processed client-side.

7.3 Implementation of the Prototype

This section does provide a brief summary of the key steps involved in the development process resulting in the prototype implementation of the proposed Framework for Mobile Apps in the Museum Application Domain. As emphasized in the previous section, web technologies are a suitable choice to provide an ideal setting to distribute applications to a broad audience on a variety of devices and reach a broad audience.

The components to be implemented by the prototype are threefold, as summarized in **Figure 7.7**. **First**, the viability of free-form ontology to capture the Model and the resulting data structure for the document store is to be demonstrated. Both the ability to represent a model for page archetypes corresponding to common entities encountered in the Museum Application Domain and the capability to conform to mobile-accessible Views are essential. **Second**, the reliability of the distribution and the accessibility, as well as the extensibility and maintainability of the core applications and their Views—including the modularity of the graphical user interfaces—have to be validated. The creator application is supposed to enable the museum professional to interact with and instantiate the allocated Models. The primary goal of the framework implementation is to engage museum professionals in the data inquiry to get familiar with the process, as well as to demonstrate the immediate benefits. Here, the consumer application primarily serves to support those creator tasks, as it is compulsory to observe the desired outcome. Nevertheless, it is supposed to fulfill its expected purpose of being delivered to consumer devices. **Third**, the API responsible for establishing the connection between the document store and those connected applications, as well as the ViewModel responsible for transforming the provided data, must be efficient and well-documented. That does aid developers in extending those existing features as well as the implementation of new components to the system. In general, the conceptual core, including the Model and its implementation, is completely decoupled from the implementation of the connected applications. Thus, its own GUI is not necessary (headless system) (Schmid, 2020).

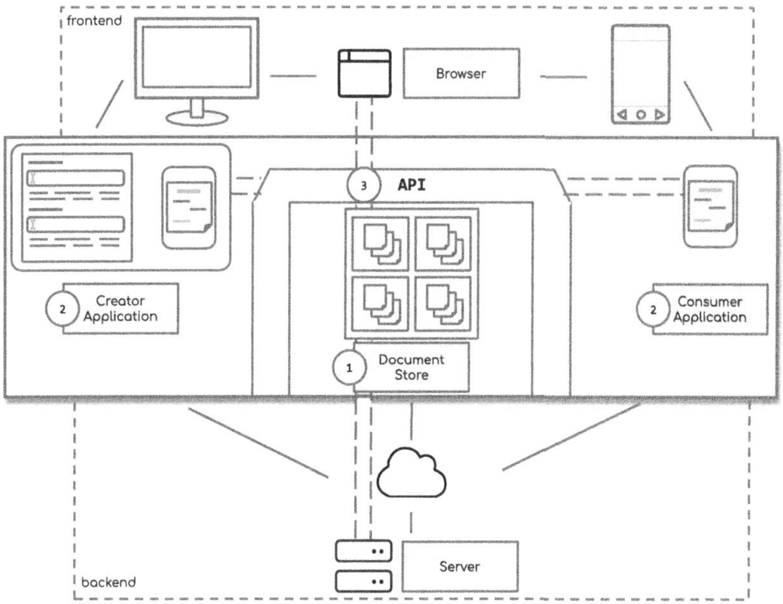

Figure 7.7 Framework Components and Application Environment

Considerations regarding the physical infrastructure in general, e.g., the devices required to access the applications and the physical server to host the document store, as well as the static components of the connected applications, are outside the scope of this prototype implementation. Furthermore, the backend software solution will not be operationalized at all. Consequently, the web-based implementation of the applications is going to rely exclusively on the inherent capabilities of the browser (edge computing) (Accenture, 2022) to execute the applications to achieve independence of specific devices and proprietary technologies (serverless architecture). Communication between the server and the browser is achieved through standardized means via HTTP and relying on the related technologies ReST and AJAX to exchange the required resources via the system's API. To host the resulting prototype system to be accessible remotely for testing and evaluation purposes, it is going to be deployed via a commoditized service solution or Backend-as-a-Service (BaaS). That also does enable institutions and developers to quickly set up their own independent system environment without the necessity of additional on-premise hardware or software requirements beyond those immediately obligatory to be able to access the actual applications, i.e., a machine running a current browser.

In general, comparable to the conceptualization of the framework established in section 6.2, the prototype development has traversed multiple iterations. However, these iterations are often minor and related to technical issues rather than major functional changes or improvements. Thus, only important or noticeable changes are highlighted throughout this section. The rest of this section is structured as follows. Initially, the specific tools and services deployed during the framework development are introduced, including the chosen BaaS solution (*Section* 7.3.1—*Tools and Services*). Then, the structural implications regarding the workflow and user interactions are presented (*Subsection* 7.3.2—*App Structure, Workflow, and Interaction*). The remainder of the section is divided into three components according to the structure suggested by MVVM. The data structures derived from the free-form ontology enabled by the Model are introduced and exemplified by highlighting the primary challenges encountered during implementation (*Subsection* 7.3.3—*Models and Data Structure*). As the very design pattern demands, the Graphical User Interface is structured analogous to the Model. The corresponding Views for the consumer applications aid the creator in performing the data inquiry process. Additionally, the GUI of the creator application attempts to resolve certain obstacles posed by the technical mechanisms of the Model (*Subsection* 7.3.4—*Views and Graphical User Interface*). The implementation of the ViewModel is supposed to mitigate remaining issues by creating and transforming the data documents to be able to properly store them and expose the required information to the View. As there is no native support by web technologies for the chosen—or, for that matter, any other—architectural design, certain utility functions and boilerplate code are required to facilitate the realization of the framework functionality and the associated interpretation of the MVVM pattern. Therefore, additional details concerned with the implementation are subsumed and introduced in this subsection to provide a holistic overview (*Subsection* 7.3.5—*ViewModel and Data Transformation*).

7.3.1 Tools and Services

To facilitate continuous and goal-oriented development, it is necessary to choose reliable tools and services adjacent to the main objective. It is important that the general setup for the project can be easily replicated to enable future engagement with the resulting product. Therefore, individual components need to be accessible and their purpose comprehensible. The goal must be to reduce costs associated with their setup, especially in regard to time and monetary restraints, and to achieve a balance between sufficiently supporting the key process without generating undesirable distractions nor unnecessary dependencies.

For this prototype implementation, the highest priority was to reduce external dependencies to a minimum while keeping the project maintainable by choosing tools that are open source, freely available for the scope required by the project, as well as established in the development community. Additionally, it is important that those tools, which may aid during development, do not diminish the capabilities of the deployed system, i.e., requiring the installation of additional or unrelated software for the end user of the respective application.

The chosen tools and services are summarized in Table 7.1 and briefly described in the following paragraphs.

Chrome

The Chrome browser has been chosen as the primary appliance to run and test the resulting applications. Because of its popularity between desktop and mobile devices, most users and developers are going to access the application using exactly this tool. Minor irregularities which may occur on different or especially older versions of browsers are expected under the progressive paradigm of PWAs. Beyond the primary purpose of displaying the applications, Chrome also does offer many additional tools to support the development process itself. Those include a console to prompt warnings and errors, the ability to inspect local storage, databases, and other resources, as well as an emulator for mobile devices and network connectivity.

While the browser generally is capable of loading and rendering static resources directly from local directories, it is advised to perform tests in an environment comparable to the final production setting, independent of the exact machine used by the developer. Thus, in addition to the Chrome browser, the extension **Web Server for Chrome** allows emulating a local web server to host static resources during development. This does prevent certain errors associated with Cross-Origin-Resource-Sharing (CORS) from occurring while using the localhost and AJAX in Chrome because of security concerns (Ianbi, 2010). Other possibilities to properly test the application within a designated remote server would require a standalone solution to emulate a server environment or actually deploying to a remote server. However, in most cases, that would require the files to be transferred between different physical or virtual machines. During development, that is a huge inconvenience, especially if minor changes occur at a high frequency.

In addition to just creating a functional solution, it is important to conform to certain industry standards. **Lighthouse** is a tool to audit websites and apps on a variety of parameters. It has been created as an extension for the Chrome browser but is now directly integrated into the developer tools natively shipped with the browser. It offers the ability to generate reports within the four categories 'performance', 'best practices', 'accessibility', and 'search engine optimization' (SEO). Furthermore, it offers the possibility to check the conformity of PWAs as discussed above and regarding technical implications.

Atom

While program code can be written and inspected by almost any text editor, a specialized tool can drastically enhance the experience for the developer. Benefits like syntax highlighting, code completion, and linting allow the developer to concentrate on solving the actual problems rather than meta-issues caused by the programming language or coding itself. Standards and code conventions introduced by industry leaders like Meta and Alphabet can be enforced to streamline the general development process and create code that is legible and comprehensible. Atom is a platform independent open-source editor offering all of these features. Furthermore, it is used by a large community that provides a multitude of plug-ins to fully customize the development experience.

Fontawesome

Many user interactions require textual labels and descriptions to clarify their goals and intentions. However, the aid of visual components reduces friction in human-computer interaction and aides in establishing the desired behavior and creating a coherent experience matching the expectations of the user. Fontawesome is a free collection of icons that, in most applications, can be provided via a font-based injection. This presents a uniform appearance for the user throughout the encounter with the application and rationalizes the selection process, as users can rely on an established mental model. Those icons were also utilized for the illustrations within this manuscript.

Nightwatch.js

Unit testing, as the most technical task within the evaluation process, can be tedious and time-consuming, especially if a process requires a combination of different screens and API interactions. Nightwatch is a tool to support integrated and automated end-to-end testing. That gets accomplished by rendering the app utilizing different browser engines to assert certain tests based on the elements visible on the screen and the ViewModel. For each test, a report is generated, including the status and point of failure. Additionally, the output can include screenshots of the UI state when the recorded behavior deviates from the expected outcome. Thus, the main on-screen navigation, as well as the expected API interactions, can be tested efficiently for most standard use cases.

GitHub

Throughout a software project, many files and resources are generated and undergo frequent changes. Git is a tool to track and manage the changes of a set of files within a repository over time and to maintain its integrity. This is important to systematically approach certain features and separate the development environment from the system accessible to the users into different branches; even more so if multiple developers would collaborate on the same project in a non-linear fashion. GitHub is a hosted service that primarily allows to remotely manage repositories in the cloud. The main benefits are the continuous backup mechanism to achieve independence of the local machine, as well as maintaining a current reference state of the source code accessible to other developers. Additionally, GitHub offers certain tools to support general project support by managing the backlog, tracking issues, and continuous integration.

GitBash

While most modern editors and development tools offer a graphical interface to execute the commands related to Git and other important tools, using the command line interface (CLI) is essential for many tasks involved in the development process. As different vendors ship significantly different tools for their operating systems, it can be difficult to switch between those solutions, each requiring proprietary syntax to represent commands and directory paths. As most lightweight server environments run Linux-based systems without a graphical user interface, many developers are familiar with that approach. GitBash provides a uniform Linux-style command line tool for Windows-based systems with integrated Git and GitHub access.

Firebase

The benefits of BAAS were discussed above. Firebase is a hosted service which does manage plenty of technical tasks not directly related to the domain problems to be solved by the framework and its implementation. Primarily those include the hosting and deployment as well as the required database management system and document store to make the applications available via the internet. Furthermore, the user management for the creator application and certain security features are integrated within that platform. While each of these components could be provided independently, the setup of the framework as well as its accessibility, would suffer immensely, primarily invoked by requiring the hardware and know-how as well as the associated costs necessary to host the system. As Firebase is free of charge for small-scale products, it perfectly fits the scope of the PCCR framework prototype implementation.

7.3.2 App Structure, Workflow, and Interaction

Before the actual insights from the implementation are discussed, this subsection introduces the structural composition and the workflow encountered while interacting with the resulting applications. The consumer application does serve as the anchor for the data entry process to be performed by the creator, and at the same time must be easily navigable for the consumer on their own device. The creator application must accomplish more complex interactions; however, its potential utility depends on its ability to be engaged by the creator and thus must provide an intuitive workflow for each task.

Table 7.1 Tools and Services

Logo	Name	Task	Info
	Chrome	Web Browser	Proprietary freeware, based on Chromium (BSD licenses) Source: `SRC/chromium.googlesource.com`
	Web Server for Chrome	Local Test Server Environment	Open Source License: MIT Source: `GIT/kzahel/web-server-chrome`
	Lighthouse	Audit & Performance	Open Source License: Apache 2.0 Source: `GIT/GoogleChrome/lighthouse/`
	Atom	Source Code Editor	Open Source License: MIT Source: `GIT/atom/atom`
	Fontawesome	Icon Collection	Open Source License: CC BY 4.0, SIL OFL 1.1, MIT Source: `GIT/FortAwesome/Font-Awesome`
	Nightwatch.js	End-to-End Testing	Code: Open Source License: MIT `GIT/nightwatchjs/nightwatch`
	GitHub	Source Code Repository & Version Control	Git: Open Source Licence: GPLv2, LGPLv2.1 Website: `github.com`
	GitBash	UNIX Shell /w integrated git for Windows	Open Source Licence: GPLv2 `GIT/git-for-windows/git`
	Firebase	Database & Webhosting	Mobile Backend as a Service Website: `firebase.com`

Consumer App

The reduced complexity within the structure of the consumer app, illustrated in **Figure 7.8**, reflects its primary purpose. The App Landing Page, i.e., the first point of contact for the consumer, provides a visual summary of the app metadata and grants access to all components of the application. The buttons in the footer allow the consumer to navigate the three basic pages (info, hours, and admission), of which the app may be assigned up to one of each. Depending on the content delivery modus chosen by the creator, the corresponding interface module is displayed. In the case of a guide app, it is possible to start (or resume) the tour via a button, which will present the assigned app pages in a sequential order. Here, the buttons in the footer allow navigating between those pages (previous and next) and returning to the app landing page (home). In the case of an explore app, the opportunity to enter a number is offered. If the input is confirmed via a button, the associated page is going to be displayed. The footer then only provides a button to return to the app landing page (home).

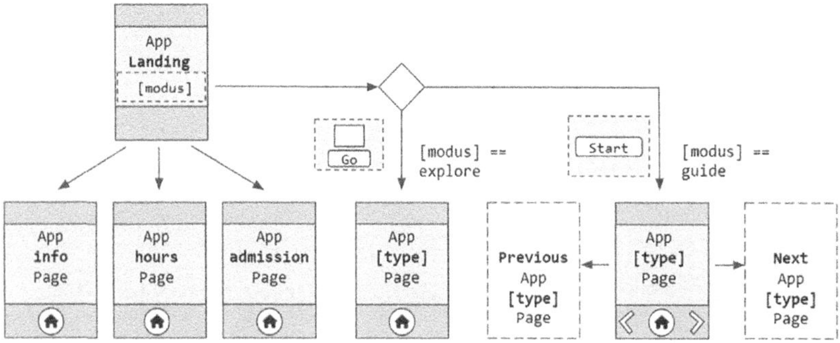

Figure 7.8 Structure of the Consumer App

The creator requires proper guidance to break down the complexity which occurs during the generation and maintenance of the available app pages, as well as the assembly of those pages to build an app. Those activities to be performed within the creator application are outlined in **Figure 7.9**. While the general scope of each activity is described here, elements concerned with those activities highlighted in gray include more complex operations, in part discussed throughout the remainder of this section, and to be best understood by consulting the user manual or technical documentation, respectively.

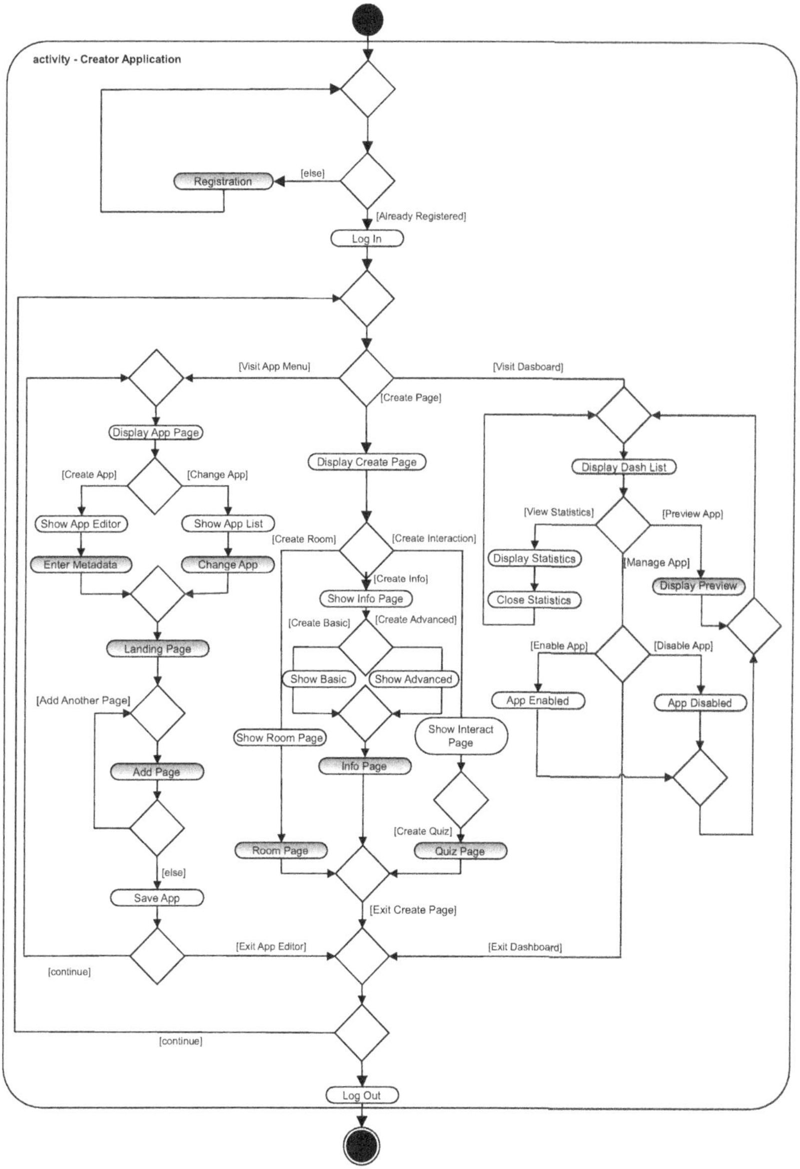

Figure 7.9 Workflow of the Creator Application

For the creator, a dedicated user account is necessary since each creator must be able to access and interact with the pages and apps they created because the corresponding documents are to be stored at a remote document store. Thus, registration must be completed once before access to the application can be granted. The creator then is able to log into their account using their credentials (email and password). The remaining activities after the creator has been successfully registered and logged in follow closely the on-screen navigation available to the creator. To navigate between screens, the user can either select to move to the next screen using one of the designated buttons or use the Back Button to return to the previous screen relative to the current one. The application landing page, i.e., the starting point for the actual creator workflows, shows one button for each of the three main tasks: the engagement with app pages (Create Page), the assembly of apps (App Menu), and the app administration via the Dashboard.

The Create Page Selection again gives the option between three choices: to navigate to the Info Page, Room Page, or Interaction Page screens. On the Info Page screen, it is possible to either select Basic Pages or Advance Pages to create, edit, or delete info pages corresponding to the associated page types via an automatically generated page form. In the Room Selection, the creator can choose between indoor or outdoor exhibition spaces and then is shown the Room Editor to create a room page. The Interaction Selection allows the creator to access the Quiz Editor. Here, it is possible to create and edit question pages and assemble those to a quiz. After those pages have been created, they are instantly available within the App Editor to be added to an app.

The App Menu screen provides two options to either Create an App or to Change an existing App. To create a new app, the creator must first provide certain metadata to be provided via a form. That selection defines the app and may not be changed later. Second, the App Editor allows adding up to one page of each basic page type to the Landing Page. Third, in the editor, advanced and additional (room and quiz) pages, as well as CUBE pages, may be added to the app. In case the creator selected the app to be a guide app, they may change the order in which the pages are supposed to appear in the consumer app. Otherwise, if an explore app has been created, the creator must assign a number to each page added to the app, by which the consumer may access them. After these tasks are completed, the app must be saved, which does create an additional document containing the affiliate page references. To edit an existing app, the creator must select the app to be changed from a list of all existing apps associated with the creator. Then they are shown the App Editor starting from the landing page. From here, they are able to follow the same steps as if they would create a new app. However, the editor will show all pages previously assigned to the app, and the creator is able to add or remove pages and to change their order or assigned number, whichever is applicable.

The Dashboard offers different measures to manage and maintain those consumer apps assembled by the creator. A list is shown containing an entry for each app consisting of the meta information for easy identification and a button for each of the following assignments. Foremost, each app may be Enabled to be publicly available for consumers or Disabled to revoke that availability. The creator also can view certain Statistics, including access times and page views, gathered during the usage of each app. Lastly, it is possible to access a Preview of each app to check the page order or general appearance of the final app.

At the end of each task, the creator may return to the landing page to Continue with another task or Log Out of the application to conclude the interaction.

7.3.3 Models and Data Structure

The core data structure and its derived Models can be defined independently of the resulting document store, its APIs, and the connected applications. Document stores, in general, record data in documents, with those documents being organized in collections. As both of these arrangements can be nested indefinitely in alternating order, document stores are highly flexible. The generic page schema and corresponding Model file have already been introduced in section 6.5.1. As the validation of documents can be ensured through the schema, no additional code is required for the Model to function. This subsection, therefore, focuses on the structure and organization of the documents for the page types which occur in the prototype implementation of the framework, as highlighted in **Figure 7.10**.

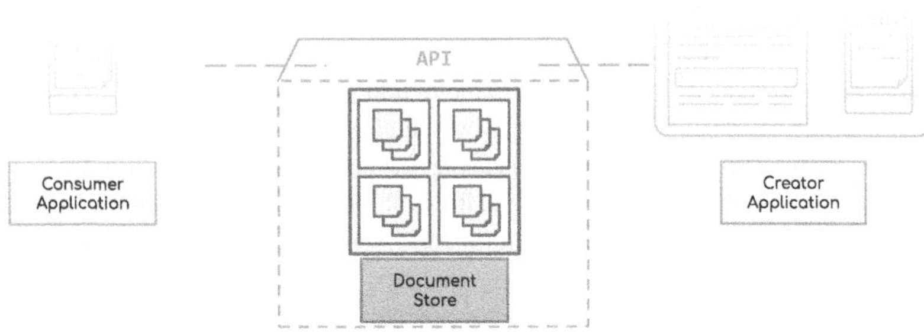

Figure 7.10 Core Data Structure and Document Store

The main storage is partitioned by the creator (creator_ID). Each creator must provide certain information upon registration, which is recorded in the user-info document. Each page created by that creator while interacting with the application is stored in the collection corresponding to that page type, while each of these collections is stored within the pages document associated with that creator. The structural composition of the document store is shown in **Figure 7.11**.

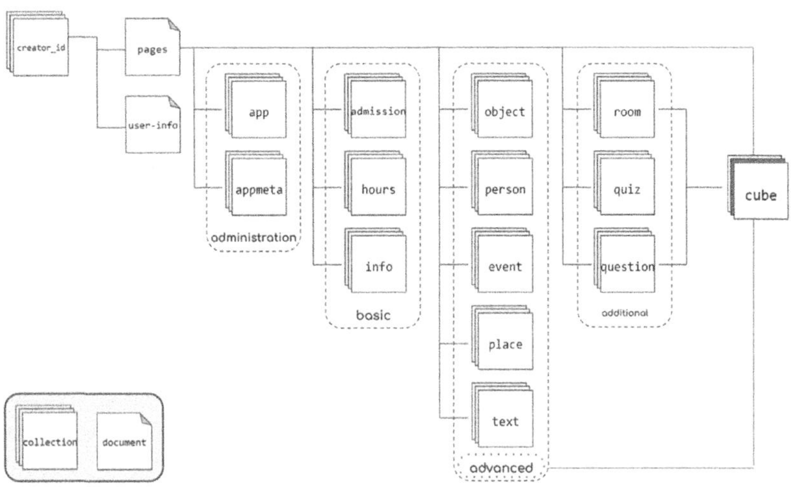

Figure 7.11 Structural Composition of the Document Store

The schema files for the page documents presented below are carefully selected from the four page type groups administration, basic, advanced, and additional. Those are supposed to highlight the most important details of engaging the Model. To further enhance legibility, essential keys are colored green, while keys and elements not intrinsically relevant to the presented file are grayed out. Values to contain only URIs or other basic strings are collapsed and represented by just three dots. The specific values related to the layout key are discussed in the next subsection, as those provide the reference to the specific Views available for each page type. Based on the foundation created by the base model and the information provided below, schemata for each available page type can be derived following the suggested free-form ontology.

Administration Pages

Both administration page types are aggregates that are implicitly created during the assembly of an application and not directly approached nor edited by the creator. The appmeta page document contains meta-information about the application inquired at the beginning of the app creation process, while the app page document mostly contains references to those pages selected throughout the app creation process.

Listing 7.1 contains the app page schema JSON document. The references included in the resulting document do direct to the designated building blocks required for the application. Those include the ID string of the creator responsible for the application, the corresponding appmeta page, up to one page ID string for each of the three basic page types (admission, hours, and info), and the selected pages associated with the app. That pages object contains key-value pairs consisting of either numbered keys in ascending order to maintain the sequence chosen by the creator, in the case of a guide app, or apply the assigned numbers as keys, in the case of an explore app. In any case, the page ID string is assigned as the value to those keys.

Listing 7.1 App Page Schema JSON

```
app.schema.json
{
  "$schema" : "http://json-schema.org/draft-06/schema#",
  "type" : "object",
  "name" : "app",
  "sortBy" : "_id",
  "properties" : {
    "creator" : { ... },
    "appmeta" : { ... },
    "basic" : {
      "type" : "object",
      "name" : "basic",
      "properties" : {
        "admission" : { ... },
        "hours" : { ... },
        "info" : { ... }
      },
      "additionalProperties" : false
    },
    "pages" : {
      "type" : "object",
      "name" : "pages"
    },
    "layout" : { ... }
  },
  "additionalProperties" : false,
  "required" : ["creator", "appmeta", "basic", "pages", "layout"]
}
```

Documents that conform to the appmeta page schema, contained in **Listing 7.2**, include information selected by the creator at the beginning of the app assembly task. The primary intent is to describe the purpose, accessibility, and appearance of the application. The caption represents the name to be used for the purpose of identification and to be displayed by the application. An image is supposed to visualize the objective of the app or its association. Images, like other multimedia resources, are stored and accessed from outside the document store. Thus, the corresponding resource path and name have to be provided to enable the application to locate them within their directory. The string value for the audience key indicates the type of expected subjects presented by the pages included within the application. It can be selected only from the options included in the complementary enum array (general, adults, students, and children). The chosen string value for the content key does have functional implications for the resulting application. As described by the scope for the application framework in section 6.3 and explained in the subsection above, there are two options to access the pages assigned to the application. If the guide value is selected for the content key, pages are presented to the consumer in the order specified by the creator. If the explore value is chosen, the creator can assign a positive integer number to each page, which must be entered by the consumer to access that specific page. In this case, it is also necessary to communicate those numbers to the consumer in the exhibition space. Furthermore, institutions may have certain requirements for the appearance of the resulting app. Especially color can be accommodated independently of the layout and page design, as explained in subsection 6.5.2. The prototype implementation of the framework does offer four stylizing options expressed by the value assigned to the colour key (gray, orange, green, and blue).

Listing 7.2 Appmeta Schema JSON

```
appmeta.schema.json
{
  "$schema" : "http://json-schema.org/draft-06/schema#",
  "type" : "object",
  "name" : "appmeta",
  "sortBy" : "caption",
  "properties" : {
    "language" : { ... },
    "caption" : { ... },
```

```
    "image" : {
      "type" : "object",
      "name" : "image",
      "properties" :{
        "image_path" : { ... },
        "image_name" : { ... }
    },
    "audience" : {
      "type" : "string",
      "name" : "audience",
      "description" : "appmeta_audience_description",
      "enum" : ["general", "adults", "students", "children"]
    },
    "content" : {
      "type" : "string",
      "name" : "content",
      "description" : "appmeta_content_description",
      "enum" : ["guide", "explore"]
    },
    "colour" : {
      "type" : "string",
      "name" : "colour",
      "description" : "appmeta_colour_description",
      "enum" : ["gray", "orange", "green", "blue"]
    },
    "layout" : { ... }
  },
  "additionalProperties" : false,
  "required" : ["caption", "layout"]
}
```

Basic Pages

The purpose of basic pages is to communicate certain meta-information about the institution, the museum, or its exhibition explicitly relevant to the consumer. The framework implementation provides three page type documents for this category: admission, hours, and info.

The admission page can be added to the application to communicate information regarding the entry fees for the exhibition the app is associated with. The schema document (**Listing 7.3**) contains the caption key to be assigned a string value and the rate array. That array may contain any number of objects consisting of three properties each. A name string to describe the target audience the rate applies to, a number to represent the required amount to be paid, and the currency string to be selected from the relevant currency abbreviation (€, $, Kč, and £).

Listing 7.3 Admission Schema JSON

```
admission.schema.json
{
  "$schema" : "http://json-schema.org/draft-06/schema#",
  "type" : "object",
  "name" : "admission",
  "sortBy" : "caption",
  "properties" : {
    "language" : { ... },
    "caption" : { ... },
    "rate" : {
      "type" : "array",
      "name" : "rate",
      "items": {
        "type" : "object",
        "name" : "rate",
        "properties" : {
          "name" : {
            "type" : "string",
            "name" : "name",
            "minLength" : 5,
            "maxLength" : 25,
            "description" : "rate_name_description"
          },
          "amount" : {
            "type" : "number",
            "name" : "amount",
```

```
                "minimum" : 0.00,
                "maximum" : 10000,
                "description" : "rate_amount_description"
              },
              "currency" : {
                "type" : "string",
                "name" : "currency",
                "enum" : ["€", "$", "Kč", "£"],
                "description" : "rate_currency_description"
              }
            }
          }
        },
        "layout" : { ... }
      },
      "additionalProperties" : false,
      "required" : ["caption", "layout"]
    }
```

If applicable, the hours page document contains information about the opening hours of the exhibition the app is associated with. Similar to the admission page, its schema contains an array; however, it consists of seven fixed entries, one for each day of the week. Each entry may either indicate the exhibition being closed, represented by the closed key to be assigned a Boolean value (true), or an object containing the specific opening time and closing time for that day.

The info page document is supposed to provide further information about the institution itself. It possesses a caption string and a text string to add a descriptive string paragraph. In addition, it holds two multimedia reference objects to link a logo and an image related to the institution. Furthermore, it contains a location object, which consists of two numeric values representing the latitude and longitude to indicate the museum's location (compare: lines 9–25 in **Listing 7.5**).

Advanced Pages

Advanced pages are directly related to the exhibition itself and represent relevant entities commonly encountered in the historico-cultural environment. The prototype implementation does offer page type documents for the following entities to be generated by the creator: object, person, event, place, and text.

Within that context, the object page document is the most essential page type. Its schema (**Listing 7.4**) contains a name string to identify the object, an image file reference to showcase its primary features, and a text to describe the object. In addition, certain key meta-information about the object can be recorded. Those include the artist who created the object, the creation date object (not to be confused with the object itself) comprised of the string representation of the date—which is explained in association with the entry method in the next subsection—and the optional calendar era reference (ad or bc), the era string to describe the epoch attributed to the object, and the size object containing the measure number and the unit abbreviation string of that measurement (mm, cm, m, and in).

Listing 7.4 Object Schema JSON

```
object.schema.json
{
  "$schema" : "http://json-schema.org/draft-06/schema#",
  "type" : "object",
  "name" : "object",
  "sortBy" : "name",
  "properties" : {
    "language" : { ... },
    "name" : { ... },
    "image" : { ... },
    "artist" : { ... },
    "creation_date" : {
      "type" : "object",
      "name" : "creation_date",
      "properties" : {
        "date" : {
          "type" : "string",
          "name" : "date",
          "description" : "date_description"
```

```
                },
                "anno" : {
                    "type" : "string",
                    "name" : "anno",
                    "enum" : ["AD", "BC", "EMPTY"],
                    "description" : "anno_description"
                            }
            }
        },
        "era" : { ... },
        "size" : {
            "type" : "object",
            "name" : "size",
            "properties" : {
                "measure" : {
                    "type" : "number",
                    "name" : "measure",
                    "minimum" : 1,
                    "maximum" : 10000,
                    "description" : "measure_description"
                },
                "unit" : {
                    "type" : "string",
                    "name" : "unit",
                    "enum" : ["mm", "cm", "m", "in"],
                    "description" : "unit_description"
                }
            }
        },
        "text" : { ... },
        "layout" : { ... }
    },
    "additionalProperties" : false,
    "required" : ["name", "layout"]
}
```

Similarly, the person and event pages offer attributes to represent the typical features expected to be able to describe those entities.

The place page document has a name and text string. The location object of the schema (**Listing 7.5**) contains the longitude and latitude string that aid in locating the place on a map. The entry and display methods of those values are described in the next subsection.

Listing 7.5 Place Schema JSON

place.schema.json

```
{
  "$schema" : "http://json-schema.org/draft-06/schema#",
  "type" : "object",
  "name" : "place",
  "sortBy" : "name",
  "properties" : {
    "language" : { ... },
    "name" : { ... },
    "location" : {
      "type" : "object",
      "name" : "location",
      "description" : "place_location_description",
      "properties" : {
        "latitude" : {
          "type" : "number",
          "name" : "latitude",
          "description" : "latitude_description"
        },
        "longitude" : {
          "type" : "number",
          "name" : "longitude",
          "description" : "longitude_description"
        }
      }
    },
    "text" : { ... },
    "layout" : { ... }
  },
  "additionalProperties" : false,
  "required" : ["name", "layout"]
}
```

The chosen paradigm deliberately restricts the amount of descriptive text to avoid scrolling and cognitive overload for the consumer. However, certain situations may require extra textual descriptions to aid further comprehension, especially in the context of the CUBE page, which is described below. Thus, the text page has been introduced as an auxiliary page type that only contains a caption string and a text string to offer the flexibility to extend certain descriptions.

Additional Pages

The additional pages are supposed to demonstrate the versatility of the base model and the framework setup in general. Compared to the basic and advanced pages, these are more closely related to their visual representation or imply functional behavior.

The question and quiz document schemata are very similar to the documents described above, as they mostly represent structured data. The question document does contain a question string and four possible answer strings (right, false_1, false_2, false_3) and an optional image media reference. The quiz document is an aggregate, which consists of a name string and the questions array. That array contains page ID strings of those question documents associated with the quiz.

The room page document is more abstract and relies heavily on its visual manifestation. The goal is to enable the creator to construct a simplified representation of expedition spaces to aid the consumer in identifying the location of certain exhibits and points of interest. To do that, the size number indicates the number of blocks (between 5 and 10) to be displayed within each column and row of a square matrix, as indicated in **Figure 7.12**.

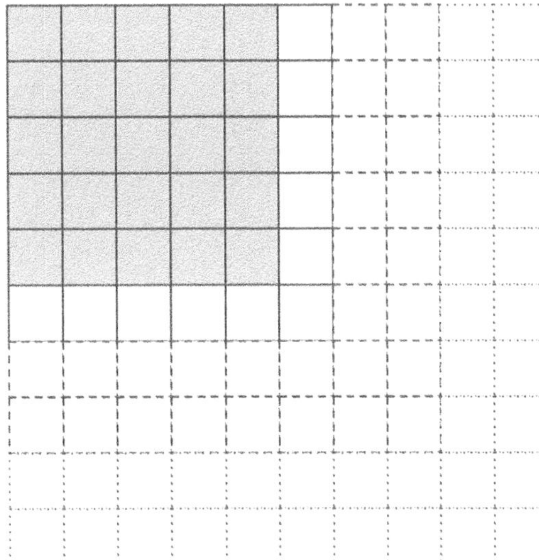

Figure 7.12 Block Structure of the Room Representation

Each block may be altered by the creator to represent a certain element (object, wall, path, or door), which is going to be explained together with the entry method in the next subsection. The blocks object of the schema file (**Listing 7.6**) then contains the ID of each altered block as a key, which is assigned a specific string value representing the chosen block element type.

Listing 7.6 Room Schema JSON

```
room.schema.json
{
  "$schema" : "http://json-schema.org/draft-06/schema#",
  "type" : "object",
  "name" : "room",
  "sortBy" : "name",
```

```
    "properties" : {
      "name" : { ... },
      "size" : {
        "type" : "number",
        "name" : "size",
        "minimum" : 5,
        "maximum" : 10
      },
      "blocks" : {
        "type" : "object",
        "name" : "blocks"
      },
      "layout" : { ... }
    },
    "additionalProperties" : false,
    "required" : ["name", "size", "layout"]
}
```

CUBE Page

The CUBE page document is a compilation of different other pages, comparable to the app document. The goal is to allow the creator to group certain pages without increasing the complexity for the consumer and maintain a linear process during the app creation process. First, within the schema (**Listing 7.7**), the basePage is selected from among the available advanced pages. The CUBE page may then be assigned up to one question page (interact). The media array may contain multiple image references, and the relatedPages array may contain references to other advanced pages available to the creator.

Listing 7.7 CUBE Schema JSON

```
cube.schema.json
{
  "$schema" : "http://json-schema.org/draft-06/schema#",
  "type" : "object",
  "name" : "cube",
  "sortBy" : "_id",
  "properties" : {
    "basePage" : { ... },
    "interact" : { ... },
    "media" : {
      "type": "array"
      ...
    },
    "relatedPages" : {
      "type": "array",
      "items": {
        "type" : "string"
      }
    }
  },
  "additionalProperties": false,
  "required": ["basePage"]
}
```

7.3.4 Views and Graphical User Interface

As the View of the consumer app is the anchor for the creator to engage with the framework, each page type must be accompanied by at least one layout to visually present the corresponding data documents on the screen, as described in subsection 6.5.2. Furthermore, the View of the creator application has to accommodate the functional requirements—primarily associated with the data input based on the schema documents presented above—and needs to visually link them to the resulting app page expected by the consumer throughout the process. These components are highlighted in **Figure 7.13**.

To provide a uniform appearance throughout that creator workflow, four recurring GUI elements represented in **Figure 7.14** (Screen, Card, Input, and Editor) are going to be introduced. The Screen to be displayed on the consumer device

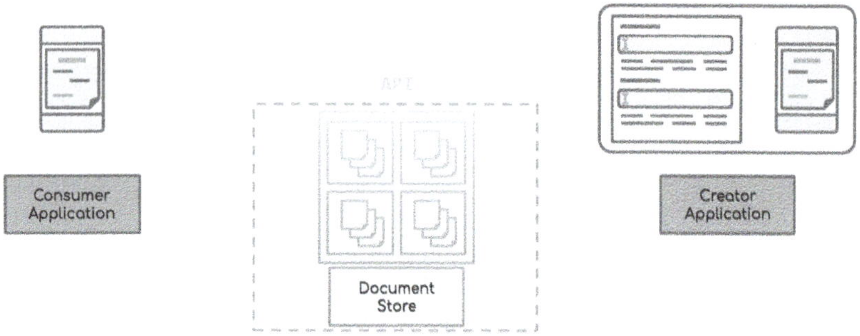

Figure 7.13 Graphical User Interface of the Framework Applications

should be closely replicated and displayed throughout the creator workflow whenever interaction with a page document occurs. The Card acts as an extension of a button. It can simply contain more information or visual aides. It can be interactable on its own or contain a group of more specific choices. Each property type does possess a corresponding Input element, such that for each page schema document, a form can be generated to facilitate the submission of a valid document. More complex page types or the app assembly process that cannot be accommodated within the form approach resort to the Editor element. Analogous to the previous subsection, the primary element composition is introduced and briefly described for each component.

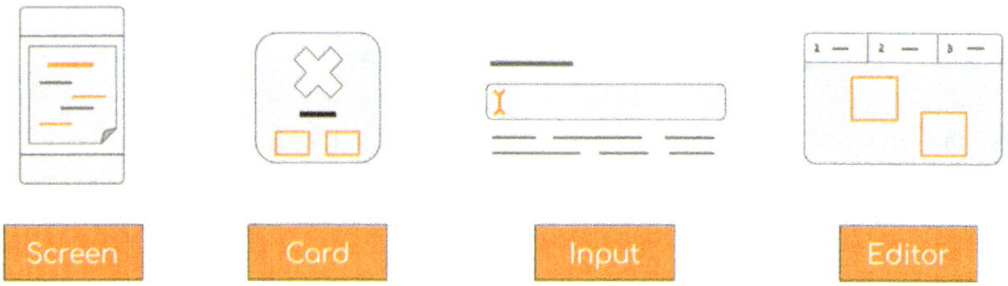

Figure 7.14 Recurring GUI Elements

Those building blocks are embedded within the scaffold provided by the workspace container pictured in **Figure 7.15**. The header contains certain control elements. The button in the top left corner returns the creator to the previous screen relative to the current one, and the three buttons on the top right show the creator's account information, enable full-screen mode, and log out the current user, respectively. The purpose of the footer is primarily for esthetic symmetry, but it also contains project adjacent logos and grants access to the user manual via the link in the center. The gray-colored area in between is designated for the actual workflow interaction.

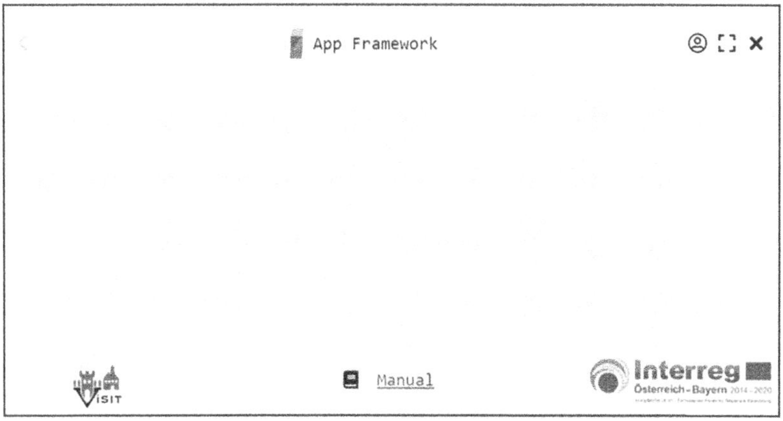

Figure 7.15 Interface Container for the Creator Application

Screen

The Screen element is the basic building block for the consumer application and an integral tool for data visualization within the creator workflow. The generic markup for that element is presented in **Listing 6.3** from subsection 6.5.2. **Figure 7.16** contains a selection of different Screen elements. As stated before, the generic *App Screen* consists of a header, a footer, and the main body. Within the consumer app, the footer contains the navigation elements to trigger the events depending on the content modus exposed by the ViewModel (compare: **Listing 6.15**—previous, next, and/or home), the navigation elements listed in the following descriptions of the Appmeta or CUBE Screens.

The basic layout of the *Appmeta Screen* is supposed to present the data described by documents that validate against the appmeta schema presented in **Listing 7.2**. Its header accommodates the required caption (properties.caption). In the footer, up to one of each of the three navigation elements is displayed to access the *Info Screen*, *Hours Screen*, or *Admission Screen*. The main body contains the image

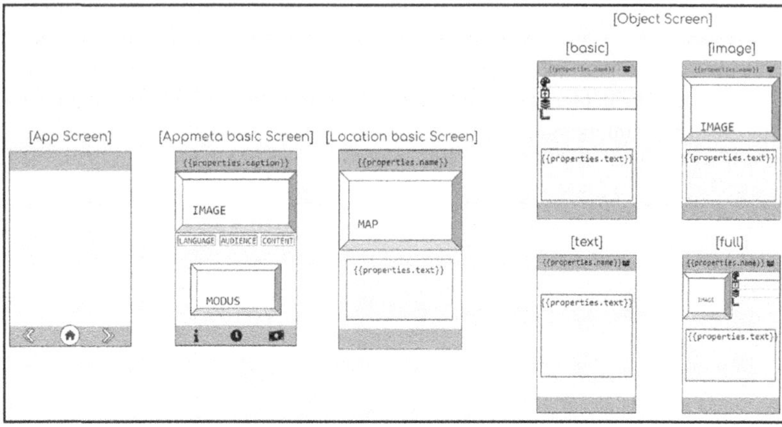

Figure 7.16 Screen Composition for the Consumer App

corresponding to the image reference to be resolved by the ViewModel, the three tags for language (en or de), audience (general, adults, students, or children), and content (guide or explore), as well as the modus controls corresponding to the chosen content type (compare: **Figure 7.8**).

The basic layout of the *Place Screen,* like each advanced page, contains an icon on the right side within the header to indicate the page type. Additionally, the name string (properties.name) from the properties object of the corresponding data document (**Listing 7.5**) is displayed. The coordinates (properties.latitude and properties.longitude) are used to display an interactive map element within the body above the text box (properties.text).

As described in **Listing 7.4**, the *Object Screen* does possess multiple layouts (text, basic, image, and full). Each of these four layouts contains the name string of the properties object within their header (properties.name). The body of the *basic* layout contains the text (properties.text) below a table to display the values corresponding to the artist, creation date, era, and size properties. That table does present an icon for each of these properties. However, the values from within the data document may need to undergo certain transformations within the ViewModel to be properly displayed (compare: **Figure 6.26**). While the *text* layout only shows the text within the body, the *image* layout is supposed to display an image according to the reference from within the properties object. The *full* layout does add the image in addition to the other properties from the basic layout.

To display a *CUBE Screen* (compare: **Listing 7.7**), three additional control elements are displayed on its base page, which is chosen from the pool of advanced pages. The up-arrow provides access to the *Interact Screen*, the down-arrow to the *Related Pages Screen*, and the reverse-arrow to the *Media Screen*. As those three Screens are supposed to be linked to the base page, each only displays the inverted arrow to return to the base page, as shown in **Figure 7.17**.

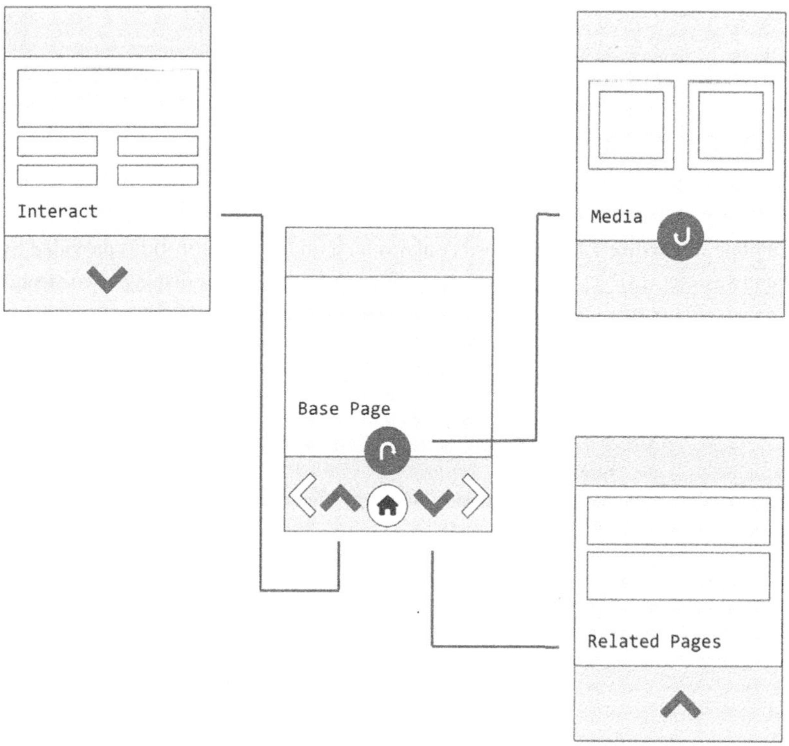

Figure 7.17 Composition of the CUBE Page

Card

To perform any data entry, the creator must first follow the navigation path until they either are presented with a form or editor. **Figure 7.18** exemplifies the path to take to arrive at the basic page selection. Navigation Cards enable the creator to maneuver through the interface pages to access the desired task according to the workflow presented in **Figure 7.9** above.

Figure 7.18 Navigation Path to the Basic Page Selection

Those cards act like buttons (__nav_target) and are structured according to the template in **Listing 7.8**. Each card contains an icon (card__icon-box) provided by Fontawesome (fa) via CSS injection (fa-file). Additionally, it displays two strings for their title (card__title) and a short descriptive text (card__text).

Listing 7.8 Navigation Card Template HTML

```
nav_card.template.html
<div class = "template">
  <button class = "btn card card--square __nav_target">
    <div class = "card__icon-box">
      <i class = "fa-file"></i>
    </div>
    <div id = "navInfoTitle" class = "card__title __string"> </div>
    <div id = "navInfoDesc" class = "card__text __string"> </div>
  </button>
</div>
```

As the basic page selection demonstrates in **Figure 7.19**, each page type is represented by its own page card. These cards are more complex than the previous ones, as can be seen in **Listing 7.9**. While they also contain an icon (card__icon-box) and a title (pageSelect-title), they allow for conveying more information about their intent by presenting a subtitle (pageSelect-subtitle) and text (pageSelect-text) string. While these cards are not interactable themselves, it is possible to either create a new page by selecting the Add button (create-button) or the More... button (more-button) reveals the options to change or delete existing pages of that type.

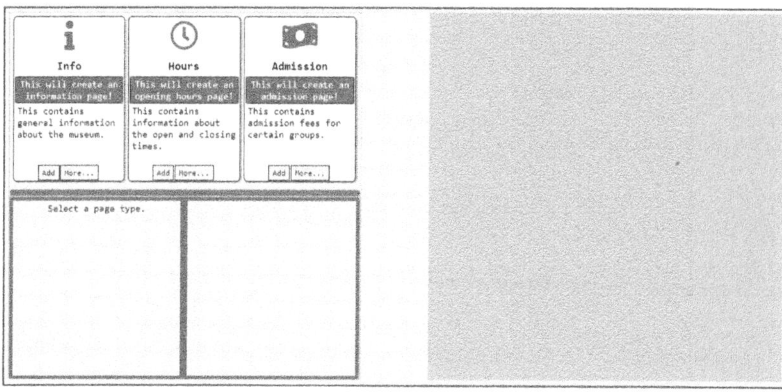

Figure 7.19 Basic Page Selection

Listing 7.9 Page Card Template HTML

```
page_card.template.html
<div class = "template">
  <div class = "page-select">
    <div class = "card__icon-box">
      <i class = "fa-3x"></i>
    </div>
    <div class = "pageSelectContent">
      <div class = "pageSelect-title"> </div>
      <div class = "pageSelect-subtitle"> </div>
      <div class = "pageSelect-text"> </div>
    </div>

    <div class = "buttons">
      <button class = "btn button pageSelect-target create-button">
        [ADD]
      </button>
      <button class = "btn button pageSelect-target more-button">
        [MORE...]
      </button>
    </div>
  </div>
</div>
```

As discussed in the previous subsection, each page schema document does define the layout property key, which is assigned an array listing the names of the available layouts, exemplified once more in **Listing 7.10**.

Listing 7.10 Page Layout JSON

```
layout.json
"layout" : {
      "type": "string",
      "enum": [ "basic", "layout2", "layout3", ... ]
   }
```

Each page type must be assigned at least one layout, which in this context is named basic. However, it is possible to create different layouts for the same page type (compare: *Object Screen* above). Those layouts may utilize a subset of the properties suggested in the page type schema document. Furthermore, for each layout, the corresponding style and template files have to be provided accordingly. If a certain page type is assigned only the basic layout by the schema, the input form is displayed directly, as for the prototype implementation is the case in each of the three basic page types. If additional layouts are available, as is the case in most advanced page types, the layout selection has to be made before the appropriate form is generated, as shown in **Figure 7.20**. To do that, the available Screen layouts are presented as cards that suggest the resulting Screen element and can be selected via the Create button in their footer.

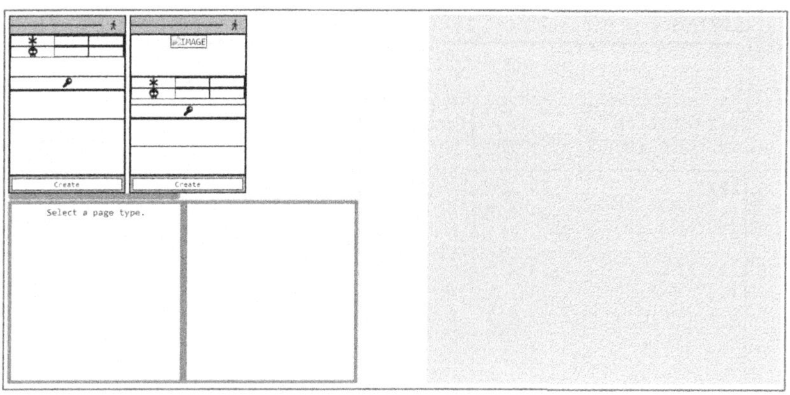

Figure 7.20 Layout Selection for the 'Person' Page Type

Input

Each form is constructed from multiple Input elements. Which elements need to be added to the form is derived from the desired page type and (if applicable) the chosen Screen layout for that page type. For each property key available in the schema document that has a corresponding placeholder element within the (chosen) layout, an Input element is generated for the form. Thus, for each value type among properties, a complementary input field element must be provided by the framework implementation. As introduced in subsection 6.5.2 Input elements consist of the property name, the designated input field for the requested value, as well as the description and constraints for the desired value, which are defined by the references within each page type schema document.

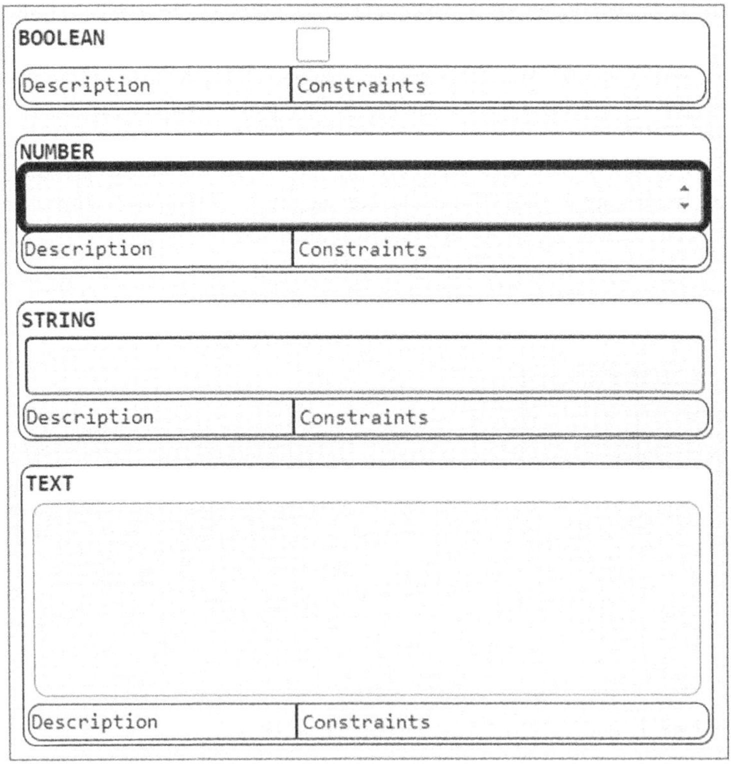

Figure 7.21 Simple Input Elements

For the standard value types natively supported by JSON, like Boolean, Number, and String, it is quite simple to accomplish that. The *Boolean* input field is represented by a checkbox, which can either be selected (true) or left blank (false) to record the value. The *Number* input is a single line where the number value can be entered via the keyboard or via the dial arrows provided at the end of the line. Similarly, *String* values are entered into a single line via the keyboard. For both Numbers and Strings, the possible entry can be restricted to certain predetermined values. In that case, the input field is replaced by a dropdown menu containing the available values. In addition, as it would be inconvenient to be restricted to one input line if the *Text* value becomes longer, the input area is provided if the upper restriction for the value exceeds the characters that would fit a single line. These simple Input elements can be seen in **Figure 7.21**.

Figure 7.22 exemplifies the form generated for the text page, the simplest page type, consisting of the language string selection dropdown menu, a name string input line, and a text string input area, each with their placeholders replaced by the predefined values. Each form is presented on the left side of the creator's workspace and is accompanied by the preview phone containing the resulting Screen element on the right. This preview is updated in real-time each time the user interacts with an Input element to demonstrate the resulting Screen. Once the data document has been created, the creator can switch between the visual preview (PHONE) and the JSON representation of the resulting page document (RAW) via the tabs below the preview area.

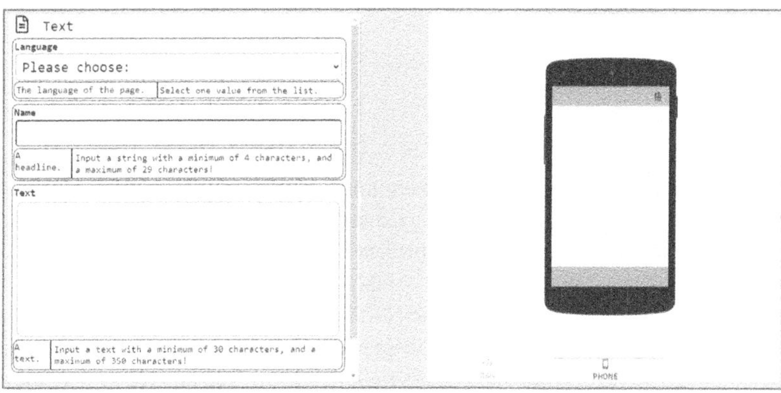

Figure 7.22 Input Form for the 'Text' Page Type

This works well as long as the input mechanism corresponds precisely with the expected result. While most values are stored, represented by strings or numbers at the data document level, it cannot be expected that the creator is able to enter certain values manually. Either the internal structure of these values may not manifest its expected use, or the value itself is too abstract to be produced without proper guidance. This can best be demonstrated by inspecting the three Input elements for time, location, and date below.

The time Input element takes advantage of the limitations naturally posed by the expected result for using the 24-hour clock system according to ISO 8601 (compare: **Figure 6.26**). The hour (00–23) and minutes (00–59) are each represented by two digits, while those two blocks are separated by a colon. Thus, the input can be represented by a dropdown containing these ranges, as shown in **Figure 7.23**. In this case, these limitations are simple enough to be communicated to the creator using the Constraints field of the input element. The dropdown approach also avoids input errors or confusion often caused by the 12-hour clock system.

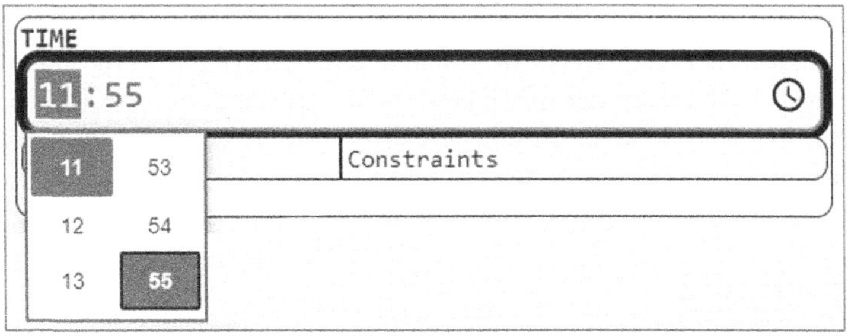

Figure 7.23 The 'Time' Input Element

In contrast, the location Input element must accommodate the standard representation of geographic point location by coordinates according to ISO 6709. That requires two numeric values, which represent latitude and longitude. Each of these consists of an integer and a fractional component separated by a dot preceded by an algebraic sign (+ or −) to denote the Northern or Southern Hemisphere and the east or west longitude, respectively. The integer component consists of two digits for latitude (−90 to +90) and three digits for longitude (−180 to +180 or 0 to 360). The fractional component consists of up to 15 digits, depending on the desired accuracy. In most use cases, seven digits are sufficient as they guarantee accuracy to the centimeter.

Evidently, other than the components of the time value, these numbers are difficult to grasp without proper visual aides. One way to solve that is to provide a rendered map where a pin can be dropped at the desired location to determine the numeric values to be stored in the document. The Google Maps API provides such an interactive map to select any point on the globe and to provide the corresponding latitude and longitude values. **Figure 7.24** shows the location Input element.

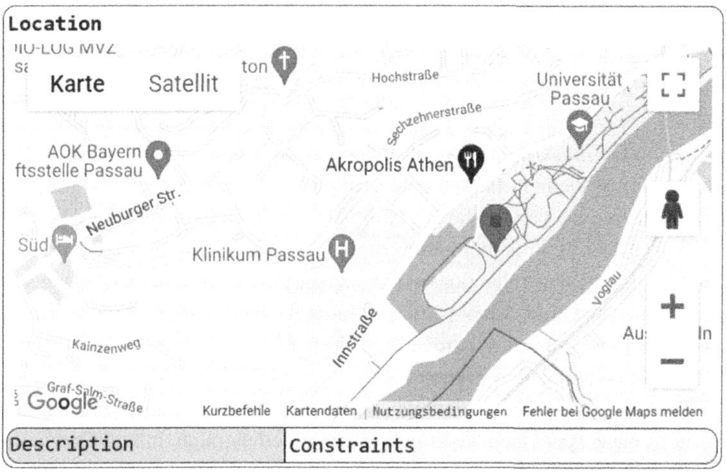

Figure 7.24 The 'Location' Input Element

Conceptually, the date Input element has been the most problematic, not because of the stored value, nor its interpretability, but the expectations of the domain experts. ISO 8601 also does specify a precise calendar date format (YYYY-MM-DD) to represent the year (0001–9999), month (01–12), and day (01–31) following the Gregorian Calendar. That can also be represented by a dropdown menu comparable to the time Input element based on the ranges allowed for dates. However, within the historico-cultural context, dates often cannot be determined this accurately. Thus, they are represented with a variety of qualifiers often manifested by a descriptive text, e.g., "the third quarter of the 12th century", or proprietary abbreviations, e.g.,

"3q + 12". While it is possible—and in some cases even necessary—to just record such a representation as a string value, it then becomes difficult to catalogue and query those values in a standardized manner. In an effort to provide a uniform interface that produces reliable data for most cases encountered and described by the involved museum professionals, a specialized form element has been created. A number can be entered to represent the year. Then, one of the selectors can be chosen to determine a specific quarter, third, or half of that year. Additionally, it is possible to select a modifier if either only the year should be recorded without a selector (Year Only), or rather than a specific year, only the century is to be recorded (Century). The three possibilities provided by the framework to record an exact date (Exact), the Range, or a free-form string value (Free) are included in **Figure 7.25**. In addition, for each date, the creator must select if the year is either Before Christ (BC) or Anno Domini (AD) from a string dropdown menu.

The last Input element facilitates the upload of files from the local machine of the creator. While the path to the target directory to locate the file could be entered manually like a string, it is more convenient to provide a button (CHOOSE A FILE) to open the file explorer. That does serve two purposes. First, the native file system of the creator's machine is more familiar to them than a proprietary solution, and second, errors and conventions regarding the path name can be avoided. The file Input element is included in **Figure 7.26**.

Because these eight Input elements are provided by the framework implementation, new page types and layouts can be added without interacting with the underlying application code, which enables great flexibility to extend the existing portfolio offered by the framework in the future. Nevertheless, the relevant Model and View files have to be added to the appropriate application directory. The template and style files for each Input layout introduced here and delivered with the prototype implementation are included within the styleguide.

Editor

Most information-based and data-driven documents can be generated by the form approach, using the schema document and the layout to generate the page documents. However, more structurally complex or visually challenging page types, which require processes involving multiple steps, cannot. To support that in a streamlined and extensible manner, the Editor element has been introduced. It does consist of the control panel in the top row indicating the order of the process steps (1, 2, 3), a PANE to perform the data entry, and an optional PREVIEW area. That basic structure is illustrated in **Figure 7.27**.

Figure 7.25 The 'Date' Input Element

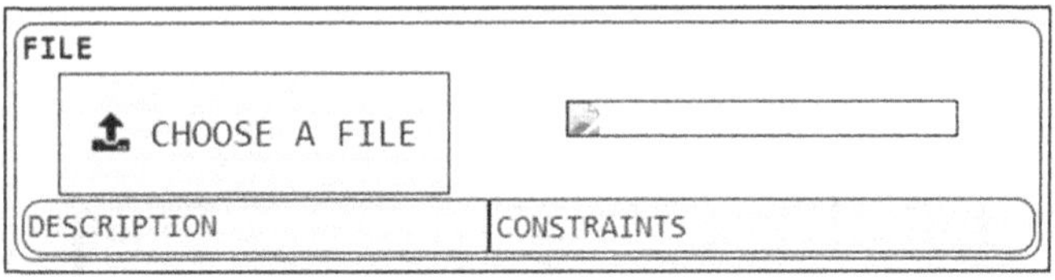

Figure 7.26 The 'File' Input Element

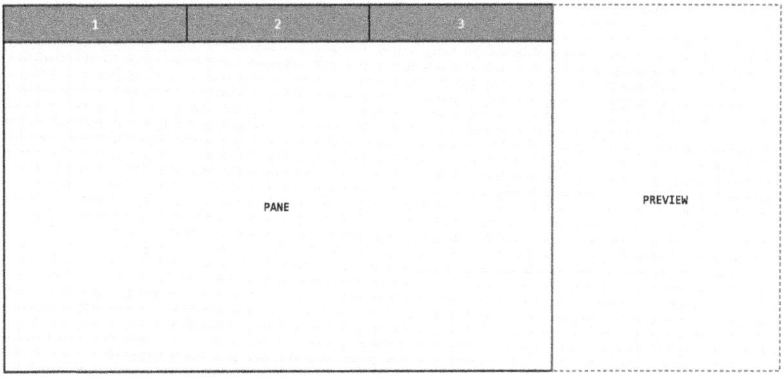

Figure 7.27 Basic Editor Structure

The more complex page types provided by the framework—particularly quiz and room pages—deploy that editor-based data entry. In contrast to the form-based data entry, it is not possible to standardize the behavior, and the respective business logic needs to be implemented individually. The Quiz Editor element, displayed in **Figure 7.28**, guides the creator through three steps.

First, they must select to either create a new text or image question or choose a question previously created. The data entry for questions is form-based, and thus the corresponding form is displayed within the input pane to create an individual question document. As a quiz is supposed to contain multiple questions, that step can be repeated indefinitely. Each question added to the quiz is added to the preview area on the right. In the second step, after all questions have been added to the quiz, the creator must name the quiz using the corresponding input field in the control panel. In the third step, the creator must use the button to create the quiz document,

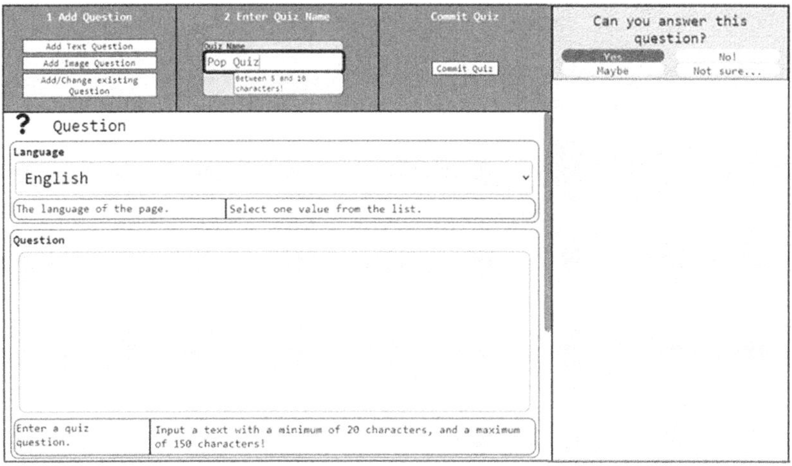

Figure 7.28 The 'Quiz' Editor Element

which does contain references to those question page documents created or added within the first process step.

The Room Editor element, displayed in **Figure 7.29**, does possess four steps. First, the creator has to determine the grid size (compare: **Figure 7.12**). Second, the room page must be named. In the third step, the creator can choose between three simple elements representing walls, doors, or objects. After one of these elements has been chosen, the creator may select any number of blocks within the grid to assign the element type to that block. By repeating that step, the creator is able to construct an approximate representation of the exhibition space. Blocks being marked as an object are numbered automatically. The last step does create and persist the document to the document store by using the Save Room button. Since the desired outcome is directly conceived within the interaction pane, no preview area is necessary for this page type.

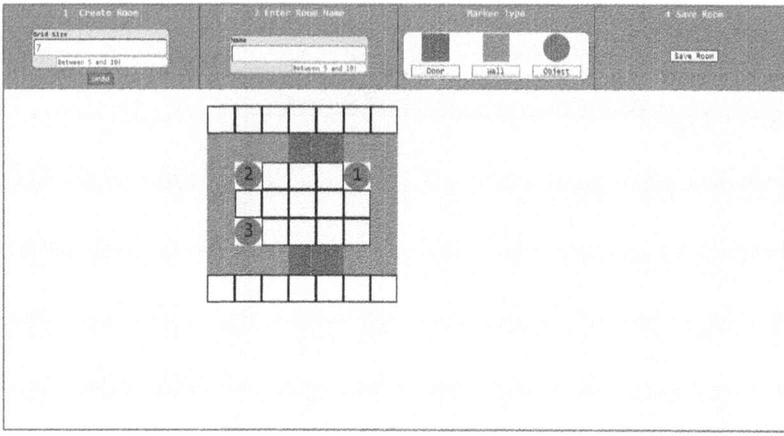

Figure 7.29 The 'Room' Editor Element

The Editor element also is deployed for the app assembly process. As shown in **Figure 7.30**, the control panel contains three process steps. First, the metadata is collected via a form. Second, the relevant basic pages are added to the app by selecting them from among info, hours, and admission pages. Third, app pages can be added from among advanced (Single Page), room (Room Page), and quiz pages (Interaction Page). CUBE pages (Cube Page) can be created here as well. To assess and review available pages from each category, they can be inspected in the preview area before being added to the app. Since either the order of pages does matter, or pages must be assigned a number depending on the chosen mode within the first step, all chosen pages are displayed in a list within the interaction pane (App Page Order). To conclude the process, the app can be saved to the document store by the Commit App button in the bottom left.

Within the third step of the app creation process, the CUBE Editor element can be accessed by the creator via the corresponding button and is displayed within the interaction pane of the App Editor to create CUBE pages. In that process, first, a base page is selected from among available advanced pages. That base page is displayed for the creator with specific buttons to add additional pages (arrow down), a question (arrow up), and images (circular arrow). Once selected, those elements are displayed in their designated preview area, as shown in **Figure 7.31**, to indicate they were added to the CUBE page. Last, the Save Cube button does add the CUBE page to the app, and it does appear in the list element of the App Editor, and the

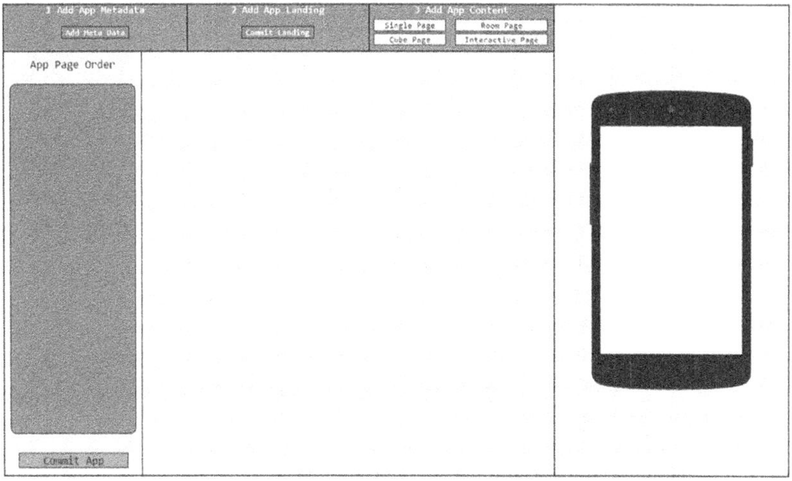

Figure 7.30 The 'App' Editor Element

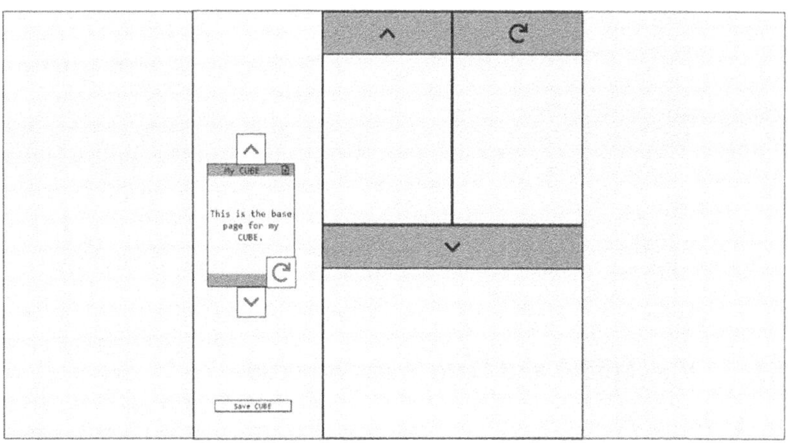

Figure 7.31 The 'CUBE' Editor Element

CUBE Editor is closed. The creator then is able to resume and add further pages or finish the app creation process.

In addition to the static files describing the appearance of the View, certain elements may be dynamically created based on certain data or the state provided by the ViewModel (compare: **Listing 6.15**). For example, guide apps facilitate the available information between the current Screen and the total number of available pages of the app to communicate the progress to the consumer via a progress bar (compare: **Figure 6.27**). The associated appearance and UI logic (**Listing 7.11**) is often subsumed within the View itself.

Listing 7.11 Progress Bar

createProgressBar.js

```
//==Create HTML div-Element
let progressBar = document.createElement('div');
progressBar.classList.add('progress-bar');
//==Add bar segment for each page available.
for (let i = 0; i < Object.entries(appData.pages).length; i++) {
  let bar = document.createElement('div');
  bar.classList.add('bar');
  progressBar.appendChild(bar);
  //--Indicate current page in the progress bar.
  if (i === currentPage) {
    bar.classList.add('current');
  }
}
//--Add the progress bar to the BODY element.
document.querySelector('body').appendChild(progressBar);
```

7.3.5 ViewModel and Data Transformation

The ViewModel in the data-centric approach of the framework implementation primarily represents the data access layer. As such, it is responsible for retrieving and transforming the data from the Model and expose it to the View or processing inputs and invoke those queries necessary to update the Model respectively. In enterprise-level applications, those transformations are often centralized in an additional conversion layer.

Furthermore, it contains the code behind for the navigation service, subject to processing the user input to switch between Views. Here, the single-page paradigm contributes to avoiding load times between these page transitions by closely recreating the haptic and optic properties of native applications (Kaluza, Troskot, & Vukelic, 2018).

Through asynchronous operations, the View can remain responsive while processing operations or accessing the APIs of the remote server, document store, or multimedia storage bucket, as outlined in **Figure 7.32**. This subsection presents an excerpt of the most important concepts and elements also highlighted in **Figure 7.9**.

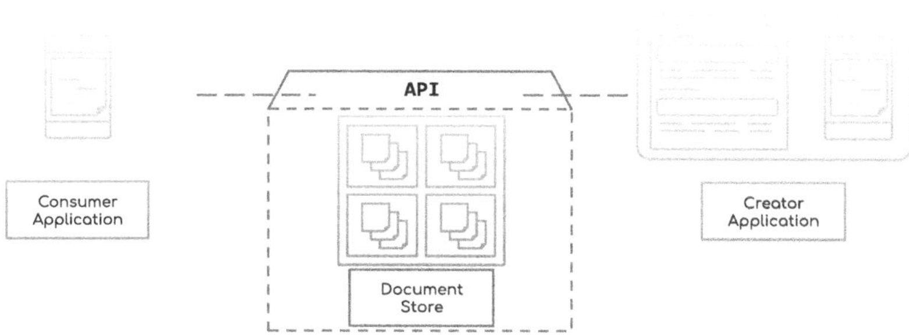

Figure 7.32 Framework API

User Authentication

One aspect not directly addressed by the scope of the framework is user management. While this is not applicable to the consumer application, multi-client capability for the creator application, e.g., being able to have multiple creators use the same instantiation of the framework implementation concurrently, is required to accurately attribute pages to their creator and to properly organize the document store. As Firebase—the BaaS solution to facilitate the document store and web hosting for the prototype implementation—also provides an API for user authentication that has been deployed for this purpose. Describing these procedures allows the introduction of certain concepts important throughout the implementation. **Listing 7.12** represents the auth() method of the firebase API object, which returns the Auth service object. That service grants access to certain functions related to the user authentication. The createUserWithEmailandPassword() method expects a unique email and a password string for parameters and returns a Promise. A Promise object represents the eventual completion (success or failure) of an asynchronous operation and its associated value. In the success case, a return value can be processed by the then() method for other asynchronous actions. In the failure case, the reason can be processed by the catch() method or is thrown to be caught elsewhere. Here, if successful, a new user account with those credentials (email & password) is created by storing that email and a hash value of the password in the document store. Furthermore, the user is going to be signed in to the application, i.e., the access token returned by the Promise is stored in the local storage of the browser, and the onAuthStateChanged() function is invoked.

Listing 7.12 Firebase User Registration

```
register.js
firebase.auth().createUserWithEmailAndPassword(email, password);
```

Similarly, if the user already does possess an account, the creator can sign in by using those credentials (**Listing 7.13**). To facilitate that, the Auth service provides the method signInWithEmailAndPassword(). Analogous, if successful, the Promise returns with an access token to be stored in the local storage of the browser, and the onAuthStateChanged() function is invoked.

Listing 7.13 Login with Firebase

```
login.js
firebase.auth().signInWithEmailAndPassword(email, password);
```

The onAuthStateChanged() method also is provided by the Auth service and is called whenever the access token changes, being passed the user object (**Listing 7.14**). If that object exists, the application can be initialized for the authenticated user; if not, the user is either not logged in, or the access token has expired. In the first case (lines 2–9), the reference to the documentStore is initialized by calling the method firestore() of the firebase API object. From here, all resources and documents required for the initial application state can be retrieved, e.g., the document for the labels in the language chosen by the creator upon registration or the necessary template and style files. As at that point, the View might not be interactable yet, to ensure a convenient user experience, the process of initialization should be communicated to the user, e.g., by showing a progress bar or a spinner until all resources are available. All further operations of the creator require the sign-in to be performed successfully. In the second case (lines 10–16), as the user trying to access the application is not yet signed in, they are redirected to the login page (login.html). The try{}...catch{} statement prevents errors from being propagated to the user at runtime. For simplicity, errors caught during the interaction are outlined as print statements, which can be read by the developer from the browser's console.

Listing 7.14 Check User Authentication Status

```
resolveLoginState.js
1  firebase.auth().onAuthStateChanged((user) => {
2    if (user) {
3      //==Create the document store reference.
4      let documentStore = firebase.firestore();
5      try {
6        //--Prepare initial app state.
7      } catch (err) {
8        console.log('Error retrieving documents: ', err);
9      }
10   } else {
11     console.log('User is not logged in!');
12     //--Return to login.
13     window.location = '../login.html';
14   }
15 });
```

The sign-out works the other way around. By removing the access token from the local storage, again, the onAuthStateChanged() is invoked, which then redirects the user to the login page.

File Retrieval

For the application to be fully operational, it is required to request static files and resources from the hosting server, specifically *.html, *.css, and *.json. **Listing 7.15** demonstrates an AJAX request to fulfill that task asynchronously for .html and .json files. Because of the lightweight nature of CSS and certain cascading interference between various *.css files, the style files are preloaded entirely and not requested on demand.

Listing 7.15 AJAX Request to Retrieve File from Server

getFile.js

```
let getFile =
function(path, name, type) {
  //==Return the promise to deliver a file.
  return new Promise((resolve, reject) => {
    //--Create the http request.
    var httpRequest = new XMLHttpRequest();
    //--Resolve HTTP request.
    httpRequest.onreadystatechange = function() {
      if (httpRequest.readyState === 4) {
        if (httpRequest.status === 200) {
          //-Initialize 'response' variable.
          let response = null;
          //-Handle JSON file.
          if (type === 'json') {
            //-Parse response to JSON object.
            response = JSON.parse(httpRequest.responseText);
          }
          //-Handle HTML file.
          if (type === 'html') {
            let parser = new DOMParser();
            //-Parse response to HTML DOM and get the template element.
            response =
              Parser.parseFromString(httpRequest.responseText, 'text/html')
              .querySelectorAll('.template');
          }
          //-Resolve the given promise.
          resolve(response);
        }
      }
    };
    //--Build 'target' string from parameters.
    let target = path + name + '.' + type;
    //--Send HTTP request.
    httpRequest.open('GET', target);
    httpRequest.send();
  });
};
```

The getFile() function expects the resource's path, name, and type strings and returns a Promise. The Promise constructor takes two functions as parameters, resolve to be called for successful completion (to be processed by then()) and reject in the case of failure (to be caught by catch()) (line 4). Here, the Promise processes the completion of the httpRequest for a file. First, the httpRequest object is created (line 6). Second, the onreadystaechage() method, which is invoked whenever the state of the request changes, is initialized (line 8). Here, two checks are performed. The repose is ready if the readyState equals 4 ('DONE') and the status equals 200 ('OK') (lines 9–10). As mentioned before, the weakly typed nature of JavaScript can be an issue. To avoid ambiguity, the triple-equal (===) is used. While a regular comparison (==) only checks for both values to be equal and, if necessary, will invoke type conversion to match both arguments, the triple-equal also checks for their types to be equal. In case of a successful request, the response variable is initialized. Then, in the case of a requested JOSN file, the responseText of the httpRequest is parsed into a JOSN object and assigned to the response (lines 14–17). In the case of an HTML file, the responseText is parsed into HTML DOM to extract the template elements (querySelctorAll()) to be assigned to the response (lines 19–25). After, the resolve function is called with the response to fulfill the Promise successfully.

To create the httpRequest, first, the target URL string of the resource path has to be built (line 31). Then, the open() method initializes the request. The first parameter is the method of the request (usually 'GET' or 'POST'), and the second parameter is the URL the request is sent to. Finally, the send() method starts the server communication to be later resolved by the Promise.

CRUD Operations

Beyond retrieving static files, the ability to perform the CRUD operations on the document store is essential. In each case, first, the documentStore reference is created by calling the method firesore() on the firebase API object. It provides the tools to access the document store and perform the desired queries.

The commitPageData() function (**Listing 7.16**) expects a dataDocument object and its pageType string. To add that document to the document store, its collections, and documents are traversed in alternating order. First, the collection associated with the current user is identified via the auth() method (line 6) to select the pages document (line 7). Second, the collection to store the document in is chosen based on the page type (line 8). Third, the add() method, which returns a Promise for the document to be created, is called (line 9). That Promise returns with the documentReference from the document store.

Listing 7.16 Create Data Document

```
commitPageData.js
1  let commitPageData =
2    function(pageType, dataDocument) {
3        let documentStore = firebase.firestore();
4        //==Add page data document to firestore.
5        documentStore
6          .collection(firebase.auth().currentUser.uid)
7          .doc('pages')
8          .collection(pageType)
9          .add(dataDocument)
10         .then(function(documentReference) {
11           //--Document successfully written!
12   };
```

Similar operations have to be performed to retrieve a document from the document store. However, to be able to process the return value, the execution of the subsequent program code has to yield until the value is available. The async keyword declares that a function deploys asynchronous operations and allows for the await keyword to be used within the function. This achieves cleaner code without chaining multiple Promises or then() statements, which is also important to allow user interaction. The async getPageData() function (**Listing 7.17**) requires the pageType and documentReference strings describing the document to be retrieved. Again, the document store is traversed, selecting the collection of the required pageType and choosing the document with the desired documentReference (lines 7–11). Finally, the get() method is called, which issues a Promise to return the document. Because of the async keyword, it is possible to await the Promise and directly assign the document object to the result variable. That result can then be returned by the function.

Listing 7.17 Read Single Data Document

```
getPageData.js
1  let getPageData =
2    async function(pageType, documentReference) {
3      let documentStore = firebase.firestore();
4      //==Get data document with 'pageID' from firestore.
5      try {
6        let result = await documentStore
7          .collection(firebase.auth().currentUser.uid)
8          .doc('pages')
9          .collection(pageType)
10         .doc(documentReference)
11         .get();
12
13       return result;
14
15     }catch (error) {
16       console.log('Error getting documents: ', error);
17     }
18   };
```

To update a document, the operations are the same, except the new document is required as an additional parameter. Rather than get(), the update() method is called, expecting the new document as a parameter. Analogous, to delete a document, the delete() method can be called on a selected document, without expecting any parameters.

Certain operations require the entire collection of data documents of a certain pageType to be available. The async getPageTypeData() (**Listing 7.18**) function demonstrates that the get() method also can be called on the collection (line 10), which does return an array of all documents available in that collection.

Listing 7.18 Read All Data Documents for Page Type

```
getPageTypeData.js
1  let getPageTypeData =
2  async function(pageType) {
3    let database = firebase.firestore();
4    //==Get all data documents of ‘type’ from firestore.
5    try {
6      let result = await database
7        .collection(firebase.auth().currentUser.uid)
8        .doc('pages')
9        .collection(pageType)
10       .get();
11
12     return result;
13
14   } catch (error) {
15     console.log('Error getting documents: ', error);
16   }
17 };
```

Navigation

Routing a user between different Views within a single-page application needs to adhere to certain logical behaviors. The creator app allows the user to move to the next View by using cards and buttons, each associated with a navigation target, i.e., the View to go to (compare: **Figure 7.9**). Those elements are marked with the __nav_target utility CSS class, i.e., without any implications toward their appearance, and contain the identifier for the target View in the id field (**Listing 7.19**). Furthermore, from each View but the landing page, the user can return to the previous View using the back button.

Listing 7.19 Navigation Target HTML Element

```
target.html
<button id = "tartet-page" class = "__nav_target"></button>
```

As **Listing 7.20** illustrates, at the time the application is being initialized, those navigation target elements can be easily identified by a single query (querySelectorAll()) as the HTML scaffold for the entire application is delivered in a single file. By looping through those elements, an event listener can be added to each of those navigation targets for the onclick event to call the navigateTo() function (lines 4–8), delivering the invoking element (this).

Listing 7.20 Initiate Navigation Targets

```
navTargets.js
1 //==Find all target elements.
2 let nav_targets = document.querySelectorAll('.__nav_target');
3 //==Add event listener to each nav target.
4 for (let div of nav_targets) {
5     div.onclick = function() {
6         //--Invoke the UI logic.
7         navigateTo(this);
8     };
9 }
```

Then, the navigateTo() function (**Listing 7.21**) is invoked whenever the user clicks on a navTarget element. By using a switch(){} statement for the id of the element object (line 3), the user can be routed toward the desired destination View. This is achieved mostly by toggling CSS classes to hide or show certain container elements within the HTML DOM. In each case but the back, before changing Views, the target for the back button is set by remembering the current_id (line 6). In the case of the back target, the previous_id relative to the current target is set as the back target.

Listing 7.21 Page Navigation

```
navigateTo.js
let navigateTo =
  function(element) {
    switch (element.id) {
        case 'target-page':
          //-Remember the current view for back button.
          setBackTarget(current_id);
          //-NAVIGATION LOGIC GOES HERE
          break;
       //--MORE NAVIGATION TARGET CASES
       case 'back': //-Return to the pervious view.
          setBackTarget(previous_id);
       default: //-Error Case: Navigation Target is not defined!
    }
  };
```

Localization

To allow for localization between different languages, labels, i.e., on-screen text to guide the user, should not be included in the HTML file and thus need to be added when the application is initialized. To do that, those HTML elements, which are supposed to contain labels, are identified by the __string utility CSS class and contain the STRING_ID within their id field (**Listing 7.22**).

Listing 7.22 Label HTML Element

```
label.html
<div id = "STRING_ID" class = "__string"></div>
```

Comparable to the View navigation discussed above, those label elements can be identified by the querySelectorAll() method at the time the app is initialized (**Listing 7.23**). By looping through those elements (lines 4–9) and using the

STRING_ID as the key (line 6), the value of each element (strings[index]. innerHTML) can be set to the appropriate string to be accessed (line 8). This assumes that prior to this operation, the appropriate language JSON document has been retrieved from the server (compare: **Listing 7.15**), and the labels object can be accessed using that key.

Listing 7.23 Initiate Text Labels of the GUI

```
setLabels.js
1   //==Find all label elements.
2   let strings = document.querySelectorAll('.__string');
3   //==Look up the corresponding string for each element.
4   for (let index = 0; index < strings.length; index++) {
5       //--Get the STRING_ID.
6       let key = strings[index].id;
7       //--Access pre-loaded labels object.
8       strings[index].innerHTML = labels[key];
9   }
```

For dynamically created elements like forms, the same mechanism is deployed. Label elements are populated based on their placeholders by looking their keys up in the appropriate language JSON document object (compare: **Listing 6.12**).

Forms and Editors

Because of the recurring nature of Input elements, forms can be generated fully automated based on the schema and layout of the target Screen. Editors, on the other hand, are similar in their goals, i.e., generating a data document. However, they greatly differ in their structure and behavior.

To create a form, the async createForm() function (**Listing 7.24**) expects the pageType and pageLayout strings, as well as the parentElement container. First, an element to display the name is created, added to the container, and filled with the name string for the pageType in the chosen language (lines 5–8).

Listing 7.24 Create Form

```
createForm.js
let createForm =
  async function(pageType, pageLayout parentElement)
  {
    //==Add nameBox to container.
    let nameBox = document.createElement('div');
    parentElement.appendChild(nameBox);
    //==Access pre-loaded labels object.
    nameBox.innerHTML = lables[pageType];
    //==Get the schema and template for the desired type.
    let promises = [];
    promises.push(getFile('data/', pageType + '.schema', 'json'));
    promises.push(getFile('templates/', pageLayout, 'html'));
    //==Resolve promises.
    await Promise.all(promises).then((values) => {
      //--Get the schema.
      let jsonSchema = values[0];
      //--Get the template element.
      let templateElement = values[1];
      //--Get the IDs from the element.
      let elementIDs = getIds(templateElements);
      //--Loop through properties and add corresponding input elements.
      for (let property in jsonSchema['properties']) {
          //-Check if property is included in template.
          if(elementsIDs.includes(property)){
              //Create Input element.
              addInput(property, parentElement);
          }
      }
    });
  };
```

Second, the files corresponding to the chosen pageType and pageLayout are requested from the server, and the Promises returned by the getFile() function are stored in the promises array (lines 10–12). By calling the static method all(), which expects an array of Promises, a single Promise is created, which resolves all Promises contained with an array of values (line 14). Therefore, the first element in the array delivers the jsonSchema for the pageType and the second entry the templateElement HTML for the pageLayout. The getIds() function expects an HTML and returns an array of IDs to be stored in the elementsIDs variable (lines 16–20). Third, a loop iterates through the jsonSchema properties to check if those are present within the pageLayout template (lines 22–24). Fourth, for each property, identified this way, the addInput() function is called (line 26). It expects the property and the form container parentElement to create the appropriate Input element (compare: **Figure 7.21–7.25**) and add it to that container. Those Input elements are observed by the ViewModel. Thus, every entry performed by the creator is directly shown in the PreviewPhone element displayed next to each form container (compare: **Figure 7.22**).

Editors go beyond the capabilities which can be provided by those input fields. They can add certain functionality to forms or enable other unique inputs. The model for data documents describing rooms to be created by the Room Editor introduced in **Figure 7.29** requires an interactable grid for the creator being able to outline the exhibition space. **Listing 7.25** demonstrates that by an excerpt from that Room Editor. The createRoom() function expects a size integer and returns an HTML element. First, a gridBox container element is created to hold the block elements (line 4). As the grid is square, based on the received size, the rows and columns of the grid are the same length. Therefore, second, through an outer loop, gridRow elements are created (line 8). Third, an inner loop populates those rows with the required number of blocks. Those block elements are created and added to the grindRow, which then is added to the gridBox (lines 12–15). Finally, an event listener is added to the gridBox to pass the click event to the blockSelect() function. Within that function, the necessary operations are performed to alter the block identified by the event that was selected by the user.

Listing 7.25 Create Room

```
createRoom.js
let createRoom =
  function(size){
    //==Create container element.
    let gridBox = document.createElement('div');
    //==Crete the room grid.
    for(let row = 0; row < size; row ++){
      //--Create grid row.
      let gridRow = document.createElement('div');
      //--Create room blocks.
      for(let col = 0; col < size; col ++){
        let block = document.createElement('div');
        gridRow.appendChild(block);
      }
      //--Add row to room container.
      gridBox.appendChild(gridRow);
    }
    //--Add click listener.
    gridBox.onclick = function(){
        blockSelect(event);
    }
    return gridBox;
  };
```

For both form and editor entries, the user can be guided through the application interface, and inputs can be validated against the underlying schemata. Yet, for certain aspects, this is not possible to check for "correctness". In the case of the Room Editor, it is not advisable to set each room facing true north but approach it from its entrance (i.e., put it on the bottom of the grid) because that is better geared toward the point of view of the consumer. However, that cannot be ratified programmatically if, for example, a room has doors on more than one side. This is a good example of why sufficient documentation is required beyond the prototype implementation at every level of engagement with the prototype.

To change any of the data documents created utilizing Input or Editor elements, the existing data document can be bound to the corresponding element to show the current values. Then, after the desired changes have been made, the document can be updated within the document store (compare: **Listing 7.16**).

Consumer Application and Analytics

The consumer application deploys the same navigation (compare: **Listing 7.20**) and localization (compare: **Listing 7.23**) mechanism as the creator application. The Screens are generated by requesting the pageLayout based on the pageType defined by the data document comparable to the PreviewPhone element attached to the form (compare: **Listing 7.24**). One unique addition to the implementation of the consumer app is page logging to be able to give analytical feedback to the creator.

Listing 7.26 Log Page Method

```
logPage.js
let logPage =
  function(pageType, documentReference){
    let newVisit = {
        pageId: documentReference,
        pageType: pageType,
        pageIndex: currentPage,
        timestamp: new Date().getTime()
    };
    //==Get the current visit.
    let currentVisit = JSON.parse(window.localStorage.getItem('currentVisit'));
    if(currentVisit === null){
      //--Create new visit.
      currentVisit = [newVisit];
    }else{
        //--Add current visit to current visits array.
        currentVisit.push(newVisit);
      }
    }
    //Store current visits locally.
    window.localStorage.setItem('currentVisit', JSON.stringify(currentVisit));
  };
```

Listing 7.26 introduces the logPage() function, which expects the pageType and documentReference strings. First, a newVisit object is created containing both of those parameter values and a timestamp. Additionally, the pageIndex of the currentPage is recorded, i.e., the numeric value representing the position of the page in case of a tour or the numeric value assigned to the page by the creator in case of a guide app (lines 3–8). Second, the currentVisit array is retrieved from the localStorage, basically a key-value store of the browser which can be utilized by a web application (line 10). Third, if no such array exists yet, it is created and initialized with the newVisit object created above (lines 11–13). If that array does exist, the newVisit is just added to the array (line 16). Finally, the array is written to the localStorage again (line 20).

In certain intervals (e.g., the session has expired) or triggered through dedicated events (e.g., a tour has been finished), that data gets transferred to the remote document store. It then can be requested by the creator application and presented to the creator by appropriate means. In the case of the prototype implementation, the Google Charts library is used to visualize certain metrics.

Offline Access

Two additional components are necessary for a website to become a web app. First, a manifest JSON file has to be created. While the specification suggests the *.webmanifest extension, in practice, the normal *.json extension is used and supported by browsers. It contains certain metadata about the application, such as its name, the URL, and the preferred display orientation. This allows the browser to prompt the user to 'install' the app, i.e., add an icon to the phone's home screen, which gives the app a more native look and feel (compare: Section 7.2). Second, a service worker has to be registered in the browser upon initialization (**Listing 7.27**). A service worker is a small JavaScript file that is able to execute certain event-driven tasks. Here it is responsible for retrieving and caching the required static files from the server for the application to work if no network connection can be established. Whenever a httpRequest would be sent to the server, first, that cache is checked if the resource is already available locally.

Listing 7.27 Register Service Worker

```
registerServiceWorker.js
navigator.serviceWorker
        .register('sw_cache_pages.js')
        .then((reg) => console.log('Service Worker: Registered'))
        .catch((err) => console.log(`Service Worker Error: ${err}`));
```

8 Evaluation

"[Design Science Research] is fundamentally a problem-solving paradigm. DSR seeks to create innovations that define the ideas, practices, technical capabilities, and products through which the analysis, design, implementation, management, and use of IS can be effectively and efficiently accomplished" (Hevner, Ram, March, & Park, 2004, p. 76). Therefore, DSR differs from social and natural sciences, as it goes beyond just trying to understand reality and actively aims to create new things and purposefully shape the existing world (March & Smith, 1995). That also makes it difficult to evaluate what exactly constitutes a contribution of an artifact, leading to limited acceptance and impact of DSR in the global IS community. While certain domain experts fully dismiss problem relevance in regard to industry problems, especially the German 'Wirtschaftsinformatik' urges recognizing the close working relationship between industry and academia throughout Europe (Gregor & Hevner, 2013) (Tallgren, 2018).

Thus, to initiate a coherent evaluation process, the seven guidelines suggested by Hevner et al. (2004)—introduced in section 4.3 and summarized in **Table 8.1**—are each examined and linked to their implementation throughout this thesis.

T. Baumgärtner, *A Software Framework for Mobile Apps in the Museum Application Domain*, Gabler Theses, https://doi.org/10.1007/978-3-658-44367-2_8

Table 8.1 Guidelines for Design Science Research

Guideline	Description
(1) Design as an Artifact	DSR must produce a viable **artifact** in the form of a construct, a model, a method, or an instantiation.
(2) Problem Relevance	The objective of DSR is to develop **technology-based solutions** to important and **relevant business problems.**
(3) Design Evaluation	The utility, quality, and efficacy of a design artifact must be rigorously demonstrated via **well-executed evaluation** methods.
(4) Research Contributions	Effective DSR must provide clear and **verifiable contributions** in the areas **of the design artifact**, foundations, and/or methodologies.
(5) Research Rigor	DSR relies upon the application of **rigorous methods** in both the construction and evaluation of the design artifact.
(6) Design as a Search Process	The search for an effective artifact utilizes available means to reach desired ends while **satisfying laws in the problem environment.**
(7) Communication of Research	Design-science research must be **presented effectively** both to **technology-oriented** as well as **management-oriented audiences.**

Guideline (1)—"Design as an Artifact" refers to the four forms of artifacts defined as follows. **Constructs** are the language by which shared knowledge is communicated. Those primarily include theories and meta-requirements to aid the "conceptualization used to describe the problems within the domain and to specify their solutions" (March & Smith, 1995) but also "vocabulary and symbols" (Hevner, Ram, March, & Park, 2004). **Models** are descriptions or representations of how things are. Most commonly, those constitute "a set of propositions or statements expressing relationships among constructs" (March & Smith, 1995) or are simply described as "abstractions and representations" (Hevner, Ram, March, & Park, 2004). **Methods** are formalized instructions on how to perform a certain task, including "algorithms and practices" (Hevner, Ram, March, & Park, 2004). **Instantiations** are the manifestations of those artifacts within their environment. Hence, the latter either implements certain constructs, models, and methods or can be developed to derive those other artifacts by observing the instantiation itself (March & Smith, 1995) (Cronholm & Göbel, 2019) (Tallgren, 2018).

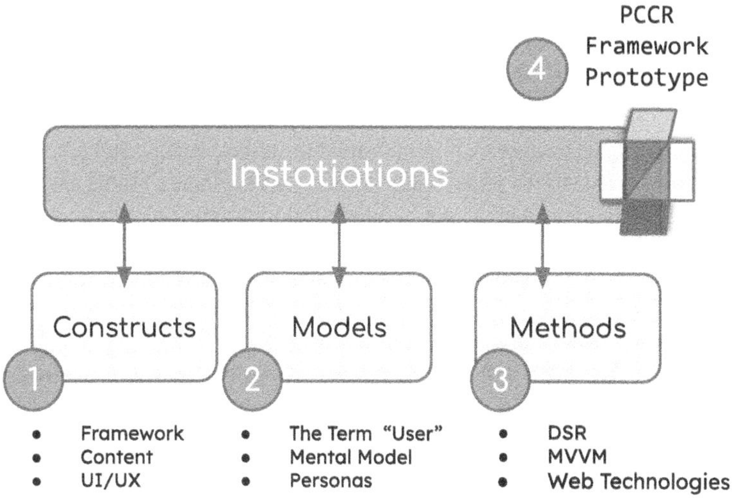

Figure 8.1 Design as an Artifact (cf. Tallgren, 2018, p. 15)

The impact of different artifacts can be identified throughout the progress of synthesizing *A Software Framework for Mobile Apps in the Museum Application Domain* in this thesis. **First**, the conceptual foundation and *fundamental ideas* are constructed; **second,** the procedures and roles to be addressed are thoroughly examined to address the *divide between technology, people, and organizational strategy* (chapter 5). **Third**, the framework design has been shaped to address the two central issues unifying both data inquiry and data visualization in the historico-cultural context by utilizing mobile applications with the *goal to derive those components to be included in the framework design* (chapter 6). **Finally**, the resulting prototype implementation of the PCCR framework converts those findings into an instantiation artifact *to be approachable by the target audience in the intended environment, as well as to provide grounds for further scientific and practical examinations* (chapter 7). **Figure 8.1** roughly contextualizes some prominent artifacts relevant to this thesis to satisfy this guideline. Also, **Figure 4.8** summarizes the research problems of this thesis.

Guideline (2)—"Problem Relevance" summarizes the objective of DSR to be concerned with developing technology-based solutions to important and relevant business problems. The requirements set by this guideline are clearly met by this dissertation. First, the problem relevance is highlighted throughout chapter 3.

Second, the prototype implementation of the Framework for Mobile Apps in the Museum Application Domain (chapter 6) utilizes web technologies to conceive an instantiation artifact in the form of a prototype implementation (chapter 7).

Guideline (3)—"Design Evaluation" requires the deployment of well-executed evaluation methods to rigorously demonstrate the utility, quality, and efficacy of a design artifact. Due to the issues summarized at the beginning of this chapter, the evaluation of those artifacts is not a simple task. Furthermore, while evaluation is part of the guidelines, there is little evidence on how to sufficiently perform it. That also highly depends on the artifact as well as its surrounding environment. Thus, to conduct a proper evaluation process, the Framework for Evaluation in Design Science Research (FEDS) suggested by Venable, Pries-Heje, and Bakersville (2016) has been utilized. It considers a two-dimensional characterization of DSR evaluation episodes to determine why, when, how, and what to evaluate. One dimension describes the functional purpose of the evaluation (*formative* or *summative*), and the other dimension describes the evaluation paradigm (*artificial* or *naturalistic*). **Formative episodes** often occur iterative or cyclic during the creation process and intend to improve characteristics or fit of the evaluand. By taking certain feedback into account, it becomes possible to adapt and pivot. **Summative episodes** occur close to the end of the creation process and determine the state or value of the evaluand. Based on specific contexts or applications, further decisions can be supported to properly appraise the situation before development or deployment. The continuum of the functional approach is represented along the x-axis in **Figure 8.2**. The orthogonally aligned y-axis emphasizes the practical approach to how to realize those functional episodes. In that sense, **artificial evaluation** deploys interpretive techniques, e.g., simulation or theoretical arguments, to test design hypotheses. Empirical as well as non-empirical means can aid in achieving an understanding of why an evaluand works or not. Better repeatability and falsifiability enable stronger scientific reliability. **Naturalistic evaluation** embraces the behavior of the evaluand in its real environment. This purely empirical approach is susceptible to the complexities introduced by the domain and observations based on the interactions within certain organizations, which drastically reduces repeatability. However, by exposing an artifact to its designated application domain, stronger internal validity can be achieved. Evaluation throughout a project usually follows a path from the bottom left to the top right.

Generally, artificial evaluation is based on abstractions; thus, it provides a simple, straightforward, and cost-effective way to synthesize precise findings in a controlled environment. It can reduce bias and room for interpretation while being inherently unrealistic. That may produce results that do not correspond well to the real use of the artifact. Naturalistic evaluation is affected by the environment itself; thus, as certain effects may disturb the observation, it is more difficult to obtain reliable insights about an artifact's utility or efficacy. While that exposure increases the validity and rigor of the approach, the results may lack precision or truthfulness (Venable, Pries-Heje, & Baskerville, 2016).

How to implement these suggestions and which evaluation strategies to pursue depends highly on the artifact in question, as well as on the needs and resources available. As DSR inherently is an iterative process, certain micro-evaluation episodes occur naturally alongside the research conducted, which are not necessarily noticeable or noteworthy. For the purpose of explicit design evaluation, three out of four distinct evaluation strategies suggested by Venable et al. (2016) to address particular goals and reduce design risks are pursued throughout this project, as shown in **Figure 8.2**. First, the "Quick and Simple" strategy (1, 2, 3) aims to achieve a quick evaluation trajectory to identify a holistic design that is both technically feasible and aligned sufficiently with the structural domain problem. To do that, the strategy starts out mostly artificial and gets progressively naturalistic to uncover incompatibilities between those goals and the core design. Second, the "Purely Technical" strategy (4, 5, 8) applies to the technical realization of the artifact. It is synthesized mostly at the artificial level, as naturalistic influences are almost irrelevant to the contemplation and selection of available technologies. Third, the "Human Risks and Effectiveness" strategy (6, 7, 9) is supposed to account for the social and user-oriented risks and to survey if the utility of the artifact does persist in real situations. Therefore, it is mostly naturalistic. The latter two processes are intertwined and form a hybrid evaluation strategy to be more efficient. Section 8.1 further elaborates on those three processes and the nine evaluation episodes displayed below. The fourth suggested strategy, "Technical Risk and Efficacy", would evaluate if the utility derived from the use of the new artifact is not evoked by other factors. As the design of the framework is mostly inventive (compare: Guideline 4), this is hardly applicable here.

Guideline (4)—"Research Contributions" demands clear and verifiable contributions in the areas of the design artifact. However, as Gregor and Hevner (2016) state, "a fundamental issue [of DSR] is that nothing is really *new*". Therefore, they have suggested the *DSR Knowledge Contribution Framework* to identify the potential of different research contributions in terms of "problem maturity"—concerned with the maturity of the problem context—and "solution

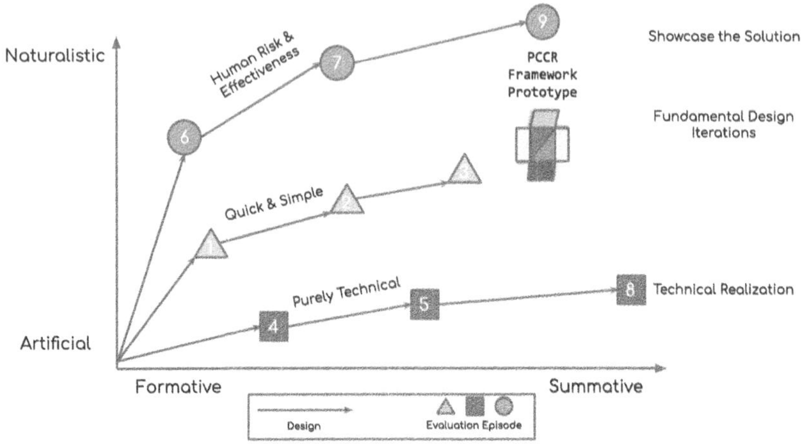

Figure 8.2 Design Evaluation Strategies: Episodes and Processes (cf. Venable, Pries-Heje, & Baskerville, 2016, p. 80)

maturity"—concerned with the current maturity of artifacts that exist as potential starting points. Those dimensions create the matrix presented in **Figure 8.3**, which consists of four cells.

Routine design, the bottom left cell, occurs when both "the existing knowledge for the problem area is well understood" and "when existing artifacts are used to address the [research] question". Usually, research methods are not required to apply best practices to organizational problems. That approach can be referred to as professional design and does not contribute to the knowledge base. **Exaptation**, the bottom right cell, applies existing solutions for a different purpose than it was originally intended for. As certain artifacts may already exist in one field and may just need to be extended or refined, it requires deep knowledge and experience in multiple domains to identify those solutions and their utility for other disciplines. It is important to demonstrate particular challenges of the new field for the research to be nontrivial and interesting to generate a contribution. **Improvement**, the top left cell, aims to create better solutions for the problem domain in terms of efficiency and effectiveness. Research is conducted within an established application context that either does not possess appropriate artifacts or operates on suboptimal solutions. Furthermore, the general understanding of the problem and solution space can be increased by introducing innovative solutions to important problems. The goal of increasing quality compared to existing

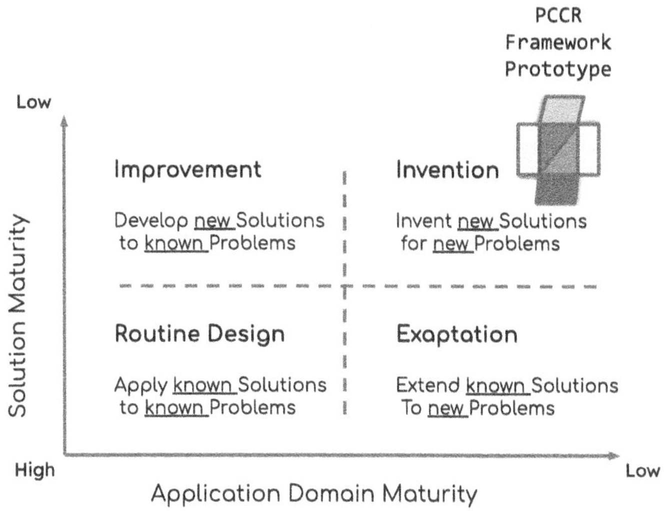

Figure 8.3 Design Science Contribution Framework (cf. Gregor & Hevner, 2013, p. 345)

solutions and genuinely advancing previous knowledge is the reason why most DSR contributions are located within this cell. **Invention**, the top right cell, is the result of "an exploratory search over a complex problem space" to find a feasible solution. It requires the application of cognitive skills, curiosity, creativity, and knowledge to depart from the accepted ways of thinking and doing. The goal is to create an artifact that can be applied and evaluated in the real world. Not only are effective artifacts unavailable for the domain, but the idea of the artifact itself is new. Thus, novel artifacts combat the fact that "a recognized problem may not necessarily exist" or "the value of a solution may be unclear" initially. Therefore, the research problem itself may not yet have been fully identified, and the conceptualization of the problem itself is part of the contribution. As Gregor and Hevner (2016) found, each instance of Invention manifests itself as an instantiation artifact. One of the most recognized inventions throughout the history of IS are Decision Support Systems (DSS) by Scott-Morton in 1967.

As identified throughout chapters 2 and 3, the application domain maturity of the MAD is particularly low, especially as its role alignment only recently has been transformed from a passive collector to an active communicator. Hence, as stated in section 4.1, because the domain itself has a protracted history, it is not easy to disrupt long-lasting traditions or innovate established processes to align them with those new goals (Culture Gap). Furthermore, no dedicated IT artifacts are in place to support museum professionals—especially in small and medium-sized cultural heritage institutions—for either task between data inquiry or data visualization (Implementation Gap). Therefore, the Routine Design can be eliminated, which in itself implies a certain degree of contribution. Moreover, it is difficult to improve something that is not yet available—neither in practice nor even conceptually. Certain internal tasks and processes related to archiving and administration are supported by fringe IT artifacts within the domain. However, those are hardly adopted by institutions nor translate well to support their newly accrued external responsibilities (compare: chapter 6).

The isolated solution maturity regarding mobile applications and data storage on a technical level is comparatively high, as both are well understood and successfully applied within many domains today. They increase productivity and solve a variety of other business problems. However, the issues related to the content complexity encountered in the Museum Application Domain, in conjunction with the low incentive for subjectively superfluous tasks (e.g., data inquiry) in a non-profit environment, make it impossible to extend any existing solution to effectively solve those problems recently introduced to that environment. The growth of top- or bottom-line profits does not matter for the most part within the Museum Application Domain. In small institutions, even organizational goals are mostly irrelevant and superseded by the values of the individual museum professional. Therefore, any suggested solution has to satisfy the needs of all stakeholders involved. That cannot be achieved by just implementing structurally complete databases or supplying collection or content management systems, overwhelming the capacity of those organizations and their members with internal complexities and promises of future returns or delayed gratification. That has immense implications for how the artifact should look like and what it is supposed to achieve.

The idea behind the suggested artifact to implicitly tie data documents to a template without making explicit assumptions about the appearance of the resulting content screen is original. It accomplishes to address many of the identified domain issues within the organizational context of small cultural heritage institutions. It creates an incentive for the museum professional to engage with data inquiry, even if it is not among their prioritized tasks. It yields data documents that can be processed, shared, and stored in a standardized manner. Those data documents can be instantly presented to consumers and creators in a way that is easily approachable, even for non-technical audiences. The framework also is easily extensible, both in regard to the data documents and from the presentation layer's perspective. Furthermore, the prototype implementation demonstrates the viability and the benefits listed above to be applicable in its intended environment. Those insights contribute to the classification of the Framework for Mobile Apps in the Museum Application Domain as an Invention. Additionally, the framework provides a solid foundation for future improvements, as briefly summarized in chapter 9.

Guideline 5—"Research Rigor" once more requires the application of rigorous methods during the design, development, and evaluation of the artifact. As this chapter demonstrates, the guidelines provided by Hevner et al. (2004) were faithfully followed. Furthermore, other established methods have been deployed throughout research and development episodes to ensure a rigorous conduct and comprehensible and replicable process throughout this dissertation.

Guideline 6—"Design as a Search Process" reiterates the importance of utilizing available means to reach design ends while satisfying the laws of the problem environment. This can be affirmed by the iterative nature of DSR itself, the prototyping approach deployed for the PCCR framework implementation, and is further underlined by the utilization of the FEDS framework in section 8.1 as well as the review of the following guideline.

Guideline 7—"Communication of Research" refers to the effective presentation of the research to both technology-oriented and management-oriented audiences. That requirement has been fulfilled, as this dissertation is accompanied by multiple peer-reviewed publications, both directly within the field of Information Systems and the cultural heritage community. Those papers were also presented at multiple symposiums and conferences to their respective audiences. Furthermore, from the early stages of the system's implementation onwards, feedback on design iterations could be obtained by communicating findings to domain experts involved in the ViSIT project (compare: *Preface*).

To further underline the proper conduct throughout the progress of research, this chapter presents the design evaluation episodes derived within Guideline (3) (*Section* 8.1—*Processes and Evaluation Episodes*). Beyond the mere methodological rigor, the integrity in regard to the conceptual scope defined for the framework is reviewed, and possible extensions are identified (*Section* 8.2—*Review of the Framework Concept*).

8.1 Evaluation Episodes and Processes

The evaluation episodes and processes following the suggestions of the FEDS framework—introduced above and illustrated in **Figure 8.2**—are further described below. The individual episodes for each of the processes, each following one of the three evaluation strategies, are discussed, and their outcome is presented with the common goals of the Framework for Mobile Apps in the Museum Application Domain in mind.

Quick and Simple

The evaluation episodes (1) through (3) in the predominately formative "Quick and Simple" evaluation strategy have been conducted to establish a match between certain design ideas and the actual problems identified within small institutions in the Museum Application Domain. The **first** design—Text Selection—has been dismissed as it had no grounds in terms of practical feasibility. The basic premise, which required available documents to function, could not be supported in practice (1). The **second** design—WYSIWYG Components—while solving certain issues related to visualization, presented internal and external structural issues. Visual components were to be selected by the creator simultaneously with the data input process. That added a layer of complexity, causing unnecessary confusion for inexperienced users, as well as inconsistencies within the data structures at the technical level (2). The **third** design—App Pages—put forth a promising foundation, as it achieved a reasonable alignment between the identified domain gaps, a technical solution, and the user goals. Therefore, it has been chosen as an effective design blueprint for the PCCR framework to construct the resulting artifact put forth by this dissertation (3). Those fundamental design iterations are analyzed in section 6.2.

Purely Technical

The "Purely Technical" strategy performs three mostly artificial evaluation episodes (4, 5, and 8) to determine the feasibility of the technical realization of the framework and the compliance with certain standards. Furthermore, this strategy also includes additional tests which involve static and automated unit testing that ensure particular code and documentation conventions regarding both the correctness and readability of files as well as error detection during software development. As those assessments are important continuously throughout the development process of the prototype implementation, there is no dedicated evaluation episode, but those tests are applied implicitly throughout the process.

Episode (4)—Selection of the Technology Stack

The earliest episode within the "Purely Technical" evaluation strategy has been concerned with the identification of those technologies best suited to realize the design identified in the previous process. The most important criteria were the minimization of external dependencies regarding both technologies and stakeholders, as well as resilience to changes in the future. While certain benefits could be identified for native application platforms in the Android and iOS ecosystems, the characteristics of the web were decisive (compare: Section 7.2). Most recently, the browser vendors have introduced 'baseline', a collection of features developers can expect to be implemented in all the major browser implementations to further solidify the web as a future-proof platform (Google, 2023). Furthermore, the capabilities of JSON and document stores to support almost any data structure ensures extensibility and also allows the adoption of existing Models in the future (compare: Subsection 6.4.1). The exclusively formative nature of this episode helps to determine a clear path for the following steps of the framework realization.

Episode (5)—Technical Mock-Up

Based on the previous evaluation episodes, a technical mock-up could be created to grasp the expected outcome for the consumer application, derive the necessary features for the creator application, and explore different possibilities for the data model as well as the document store. To ensure all goals could be achieved by the selected technologies, Screen elements for different page types have been manufactured. That made it possible to audit the entire process from a technical perspective as well as to exemplify the possibilities of data inquiry and visualization by directly assessing the coherence between the creator and consumer application as well as the structural implications for the underlying data model.

The starting point of the technical development has been the consumer application, as its primary purpose is the visualization of the data documents supposed to be generated within the creator application. **Figure 8.4** shows the six initial app page Screens, three for the basic pages (blue Screens elements at the top) and three for the advanced pages (green Screens elements at the bottom). At this stage, the layout and selection of the data to be displayed by those content pages have been prioritized.

Based on these preliminary outputs, the necessary input elements and mechanisms to be displayed within the creator application could be derived from those expected results. Hence, it becomes possible to render the preview phone in real-time next to the input form. **Figure 8.4** displays a form including the input fields for a 'person' page Screen.

The free-form ontology, for **one**, is capable of validating data documents by page type; **two**, enables the data model to establish an implicit connection between the individual data documents and their expected presentation; and **three**, is robust, flexible, as well as extensible, has been a direct result of the findings acquired by this evaluation episode.

Those observations between the mostly formative exploration of the chosen technology stack and the summative yet artificial confirmation of the feasibility of the underlying conceptual foundation enabled the further engineering of the framework components following the MVVM design pattern, described in section 6.5.

At this stage also tests regarding the technical infrastructure have been performed. The selection of Firebase as a BaaS solution is mostly based on the simple fact that it is capable of completely supporting all necessary tasks that go beyond the actual framework concept.

Episode (8)—Lighthouse Report

A fully automated Lighthouse Report has been generated for the consumer application, based on an instantiation of the "Campus Tour" app outlined in episode (6) below. The app was hosted through Firebase and loaded within an Incognito window of the Google Chrome browser to avoid any possible interference with other tools or applications. That brings the two major benefits of demonstrating the capabilities of Firebase as a reliable solution for hosting the web application and document store, as well as evaluating the requirements of modern web apps and PWAs. The resulting scores for the five categories summarized in **Figure 8.6** are briefly presented here.

The low score in the **Performance** category can be explained by the intended nature of the prototype implementation. The results in this category are based on metrics that depend mostly on speed and loading times encountered during the interaction with the application. Because the prototype implementation is deliberately verbose to be easily approachable by new developers, larger file sizes occur due to comments and code conventions that facilitate that goal. To reduce those loading times and improve the score, files and media resources could be minimized and compressed as well as certain improvements could be implemented to optimize resource loading chains. However, that has not been deemed worthwhile in this context. Nevertheless, one observation to note is that by utilizing asynchronous operations, low blocking times do successfully pass the audit.

All applicable audits for the **Accessibility** category, mostly suggested by the Web Accessibility Initiative's Accessible Rich Internet Applications (ARIA) specifications, have passed the automated tests performed by Lighthouse. ARIA aims

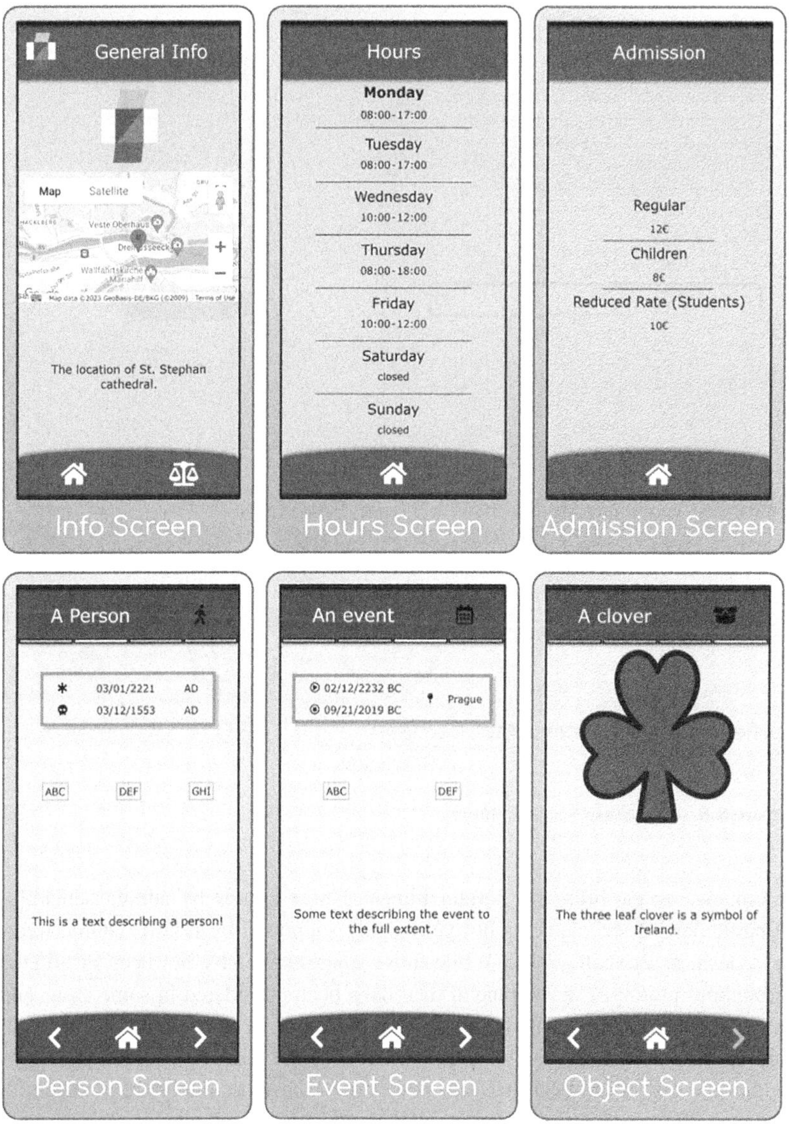

Figure 8.4 Examples of Basic and Advanced App Page Screens

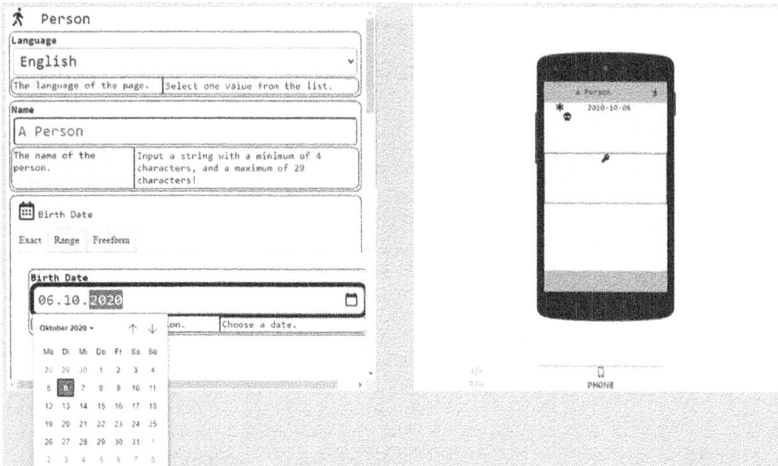

Figure 8.5 Form Input Mechanism for a 'Person' Page Screen

Figure 8.6 Lighthouse Score Summary

to enhance accessibility for certain impaired user groups by adding semantics to particular HTML elements not yet naively supported by HTML DOM (Kearney, Gash, & Boxhall, 2016). While those suggestions have not been prioritized throughout prototype development, they have been considered in some cases and offer opportunities to explore certain improvements in the future. Beyond that, this category also contains a variety of items that can only be checked manually. Additional tests have been performed to verify the most important elements to evaluate. Among those are that button elements are named appropriately and are keyboard-focusable, as well as that visual elements follow the order they appear in the DOM.

The **Best Practices** category includes tests to ensure security, web standards, and user expectations toward the application. Security audits check for measures like secure data transmission via HTTPS and actions to combat cross-site scripting (XSS), which are mostly enforced by Firebase as the hosting service provider. Tests to cover web standards to be followed are concerned with the aspect ratio of images and their resolution, as well as document-specific properties, like including the HTML doctype to the markup files. Measures to fulfill user expectations include avoiding unnecessary prompts or permission requests upon page load. This category also demonstrates the independence of the prototype implementation, as the only third-party library identified to be accessed by the app at runtime is Google Maps to render locations. All audits in this category have been performed successfully.

The **Search Engine Optimization** (SEO) category checks if basic SEO advice is being followed. Audits performed here include further document-specific properties and address certain important usability concerns. HTML documents should contain <title> and <meta> tags to summarize the content and purpose of the application. The <meta name = "viewport"> tag should define the width or an initial-scale to optimize the application for mobile screen sizes, which is also important for the PWA category. Furthermore, the page should only contain crawlable links and possess a valid robots.txt file to enable automated search engine indexing. Font sizes should be set to a legible size, and tap targets or interactable elements should be identifiable as such, both by size and appearance. This category also passed all audits performed by Lighthouse.

Most importantly, the **Progressive Web App** (PWA) category checks if all measures are taken by the web application to qualify as a PWA (compare: Section 7.2). Both the web app manifest containing descriptive information about the app and the service worker deployed by the web application meet the installability requirements. The additional requirements for an optimized PWA are fulfilled as well. Those include the proper use of service workers, the configuration of a custom splash screen within the custom manifest file (compare: Subsection 7.3.5), as well as appropriate content sizing relative to the viewport. Thus, the implementation of the consumer application of the PCCR framework can be truly classified as a PWA.

Those results can be extended toward the creator application, as it overall is less demanding than the consumer application while following the same principles. The Lighthouse Report, therefore, provides a solid conclusive episode as it yields a number of measures for conclusive summative evaluation results within the "Purely Technical" evaluation process underlying the solid foundation of the PCCR Framework prototype.

Human Risk and Effectiveness

The goals pursued by the evaluation episodes (6, 7, 9) conducted within the "Human Risk and Effectiveness" strategy are to expose the solution offered by the PCCR framework and to observe the artifact in its intended environment as well as to generate feedback on the design from the actual user's perspective. These mainly naturalistic trials, included in the implementation of the software framework, take place at several stages of progress during development. This includes the rather formative objective to consider the selection of the page types to include and to showcase the built-in capabilities of the consumer application. Furthermore, the summative appraisal of the utility of the creator application is performed by looking at certain mobile apps created by select domain experts.

Episode (6)—Showcase: "Campus Tour" App

This evaluation episode extends the precursory efforts explored in episode (5). It has been conducted primarily internally to set up the following episodes with external participants. The goal is to complement the purely technical considerations by reflecting a real-world use case to highlight the utility of the framework and its connected applications, as well as to uncover certain irregularities to straighten out before presenting them to actual users. Therefore, the "Campus Tour" app has been created by picking prominent landmarks around the campus of the University of Passau as a foundation to create compelling content pages.

To get a sense of the approachability of the creator application from the museum professional's perspective, the processes involved in creating those content pages were conducted in the following order. **First**, some basic research into the composition and the history of the selected objects has been conducted. **Second**, content pages have been created by applying the tools provided by the creator application to portray the objects and artists selected to be featured in the consumer application. **Third**, the content pages were assembled to create one coherent consumer application.

That examination has led to some minor and two primary adjustments within the implementation of the creator application to smoothen out the initial contact with the creator application. As creating a CUBE page requires a certain proficiency of interaction with the creator application, the process of creating those aggregate pages, introduced in subsection 6.2.4, has been moved from the 'pages' section directly into the App Editor, which considerably simplifies the initial contact.

Furthermore, in the course of that adaptation, the "text" page type has been added to allow for more flexibility for certain explanations and navigational aid, which is taken up again during the reflection of the scope within the next section.

Those chances applied to the system emphasize the formative character of these episodes.

As the technical mock-up does not include any actual content, it would have been difficult to fully encompass the capabilities of the framework. Therefore, the resulting consumer application of the "Campus Tour" app, in addition to the technical instantiation created earlier in episode (5), has been made available for the museum professionals and in the following episodes to grasp the intended concept of the software framework. Certain Screens of the resulting mobile app and those which are assembled to one CUBE are included in **Figure 8.7**. The CUBE Editor, which is embedded into the App Editor, is presented in **Figure 8.8**.

Episode (7)—Trial: "Kirchenmuseum Kößlarn" App

Initially, trying to conduct dedicated requirement engineering with different project partners, two very clear observations were made. First, the missing knowledge about the technology and its possibilities made it almost impossible for them to articulate tangible goals in general. Second, the capabilities of their own organization were not well reflected when suggesting certain examples of solutions offered by other prestigious institutions. That, on the one hand, emphasizes the important goal pursued in this thesis to create an entry point for those institutions and their members; on the other hand, it is necessary to carefully source requirements and features and to showcase products in a way accessible for their respective audiences. The conception of abstract personas (compare: Section 5.3) has been a direct result of those observations. Those can also be clearly monitored throughout this evaluation episode, which takes the step away from a purely internal review and introduces expert users within the intended environment of use for the framework. This naturalistic trial results in the "Kirchenmuseum Kößlarn" app and yields both formative and some summative insights about the suggested software framework.

Nobody at this stage of the ViSIT project strongly took the role of the "Repudiator", as the opportunities of a digital strategy were actively demonstrated throughout the collaboration between those involved. However, the initial interest in the ability to publish their own mobile applications came to a grinding halt for some "Reserved" members after the introduction of the PCCR framework prototype. The reasons, however, were not related to shortcomings of the framework's concept, its implementation, nor the required resources. Their concerns rather were associated with open access and the distribution model of the resulting consumer application via the internet. The fear of theft of their intellectual property as well as uncertainties on how to handle third-party rights of multimedia content, mostly photographs, overshadowed their affinity toward the

Figure 8.7 "Campus Tour" App

solution. Therefore, they could not be convinced to even engage in the initial process of creating content pages just to get acquainted with the general idea of the framework. This underlines the necessity of examining the legal implications as well as enhancing communication and advocating digital outlets. As a lot of those concerns do already exist within the analog world, i.e., printed information outlets, it would be interesting to examine the perceived risks associated with the digital counterpart.

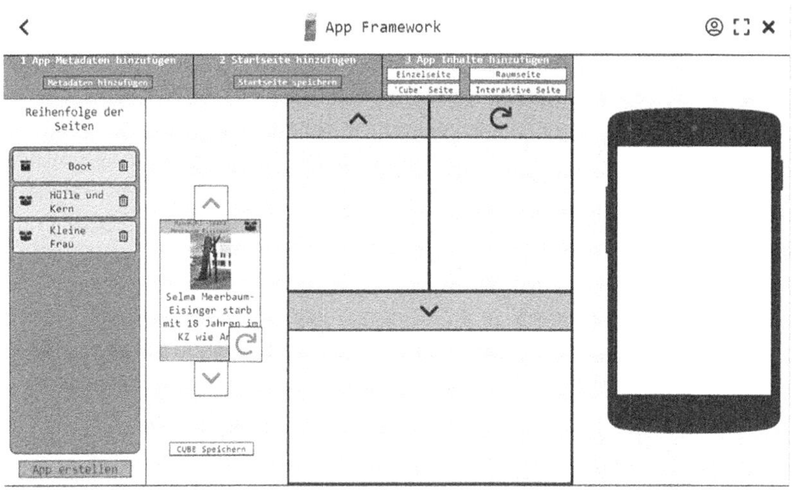

Figure 8.8 CUBE Compilation in the App Editor

Similarly, it has been difficult to convince certain members to be best categorized as "Movers" to commit the necessary resources, mostly their time, to fully unleash the potential of the software framework. While they were eager to get their hands on the implementation, some had not even finished creating a handful of content pages before requesting additional features and presenting "ideas" already included within the PCCR framework prototype implementation. Others were simply distracted by different aspects of the ViSIT project that may not have any long-term implications but were only to be experienced within the larger context of the project, e.g., 3D or CT scanning or of certain exhibits. As the fundamental sympathy toward is present with those museum professionals, they do not need to be convinced to try out innovative solutions but to develop long-term goals and strategies to funnel their resources and also to recognize the constraints of their environment. That could be achieved by establishing better communication between museum professionals, as well as realizing some network effects via a common platform to share ideas and results. Connecting small museums also would generate trust and comfort for those unsure if they should engage in such a digital strategy.

Furthermore, beyond those useful observations, the outbreak of the global COVID pandemic did eliminate the ability of certain institutions and other project members to conduct trials for the PCCR framework implementation. The circumstances surrounding those events, like lockdowns and the closure of many cultural heritage institutions, were devastating, to say the least. A digital strategy, while it may not solve all issues that accompany that situation, could at least mitigate the effects by providing a remote engagement opportunity.

While the concept is simple enough to require as little effort as possible, it cannot be engaged with by not dedicating at least some resources. Primarily the museum professionals from Kirchenmuseum Kößlarn—also a partner in the ViSIT project—demonstrated the most interest in the framework and could be categorized as "Enthusiasts". Therefore, providing them with the tools to create their own mobile apps has been prioritized for this evaluation episode.

To do that, the museum professionals were granted access to the creator application as well as the necessary documentation, primarily the user manual, via a link. That did allow them to follow the steps to execute the tasks necessary to create Screens for all page types and also to assemble a guide application without any further intervention or training. They were able to create coherent data documents to be utilized by both the creator and the consumer application to render Screens for each page type and layout. This has been a great opportunity to see the framework in action and to gain valuable insights from both the consumer's and the creator's perspectives.

To allow for a better understanding of the manifestation of those insights, **Figure 8.9** contains a selection of six Screens from the "Kirchenmuseum Kößlarn" app. Overall, it consists of 22 pages across all available page types and utilizes almost all available layouts for the resulting Screen elements. The internal structure has been compiled independently to great success. Each area of the exhibition is first introduced by a room page, indicating those exhibits featured in the following content pages. The subsequent Screens then are dedicated to each of those announced exhibits. Some offer additional information beyond the objects themselves. After each exhibit of the current room has been traversed through the app, a short quiz makes a reference to the most important facts presented to the visitor. One improvement directly resulting from this trial has been the addition of numbers to the objects or POIs of room pages. That grants the ability to reference those elements in other pages and descriptions. Further upgrades closely related to that are discussed in the following section.

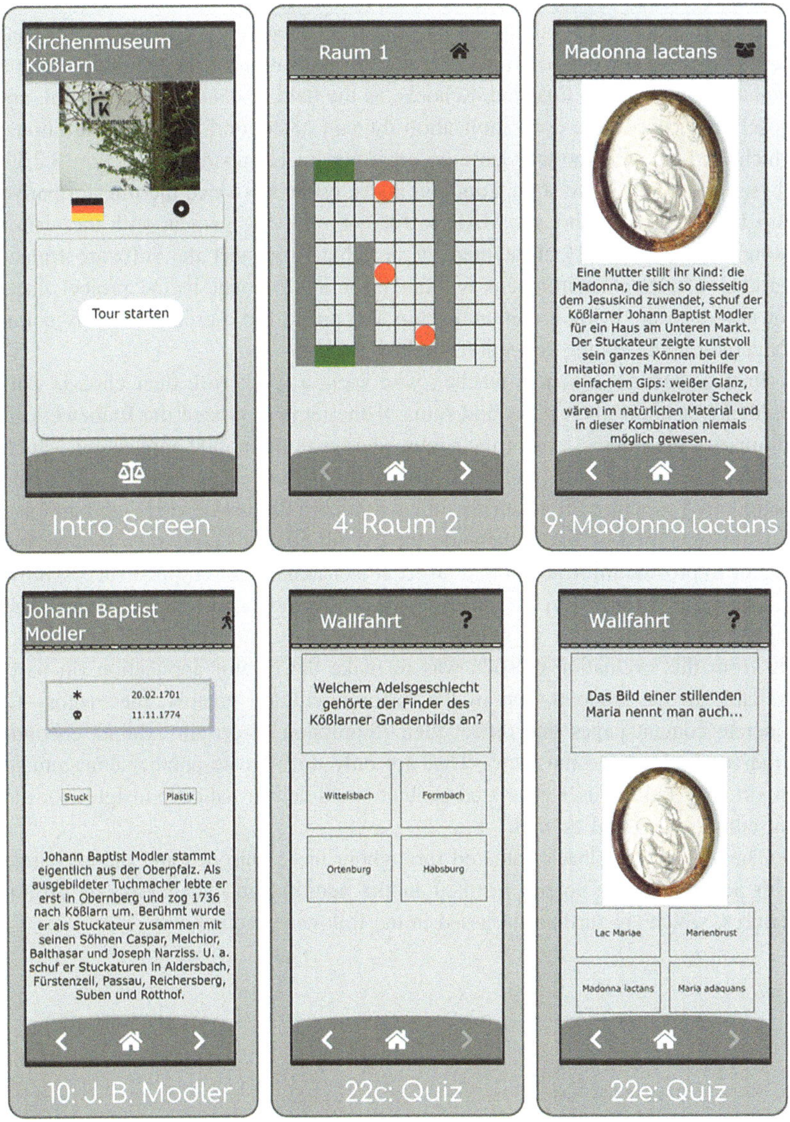

Figure 8.9 "Kirchenmuseum Kößlarn" App

Episode (9)—Case Study: "Burgruinen im Altmühlthal" App

To further extend the validity of the entire evaluation process, an additional case study was performed after the technical realization of the PCCR prototype implantation had been finalized. Schools, as the field of education in general, are closely adjacent to the core application domain of cultural heritage institutions, which itself is an important learning environment (compare: Subsection 3.2.1). These institutions share some common goals, especially since the transformative shift has occurred within the MAD to focus on the engagement with the visitor (compare: Section 3.1). That made it possible to subject the software framework to a testing environment without prior involvement in the project itself nor any exposure to the traditional setup encountered in museums, mostly being concerned with existing collections and exhibitions.

In this scenario, a school teacher, who spent a week with their class in Altmühltal to explore the castles and ruins of the region, utilized the framework to summarize the impressions of their tour. The resulting mobile application, which also has been made available to the students, is portrayed in **Figure 8.10**. While the required structure for a data document to record data associated with buildings was not supported by the framework, the overall goal of supplying a tool for the creator to provide information to a target audience has been fulfilled successfully.

This demonstrates that the utility of the software framework can be invoked beyond just the MAD or its initial scope. One useful suggestion directly resulting from this evaluation episode was to make the creator application (in part) available to the students—or, in the historico-cultural context, the visitor—to generate content pages that reflect their impression of certain exhibits encountered (throughout the museum). That not only does create another engagement opportunity, but the user-generated content could deliver valuable insights for the museum professional as well.

The valuable feedback gathered throughout these episodes and the exchange with actual domain experts resulted in the addition and adaptation of certain features, which are further discussed in the following section.

Figure 8.10 "Burgruinen im Altmühltal" App

8.2 Review of the Framework Concept

To conclude the evaluation process, it is important to also review if the scope of the framework has been fully realized within the resulting artifact, independently of its evident utility. Therefore, in this section, an audit is performed to check if all the requirements initially defined within the scope for *A Software Framework for Mobile Apps in the Museum Application Domain*, introduced in section 6.3, were fulfilled. Certain extensions and refinements based on the feedback gathered during development and the evaluation episodes discussed above are outlined. **Figure 8.11** reiterates the set goals and highlights the fulfilled areas as well as those elements which can be improved upon.

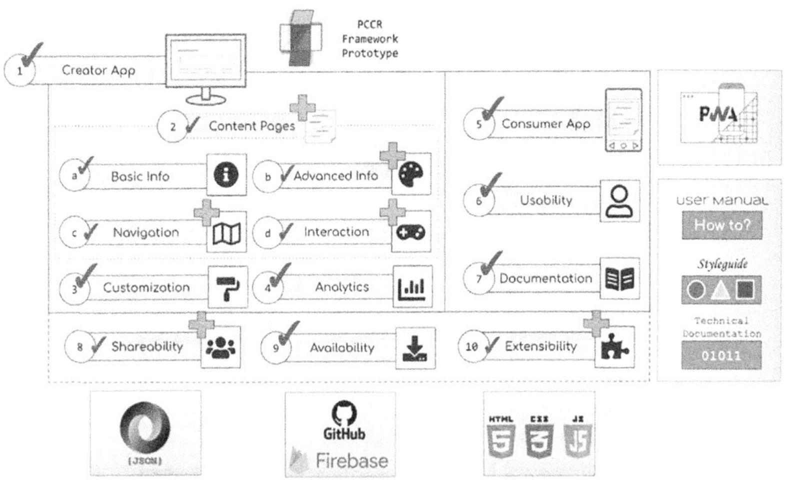

Figure 8.11 Delivery of the Framework Scope

(1) Creator App

The *creator app* does positively fulfill its intended purpose to enable the museum professional to access the necessary tools and enables them to create content pages and mobile applications, as well as to deploy random-access guides for their visitors. That has been successfully demonstrated during the related evaluation episodes and processes above. The intuitive input mechanism facilitates the development of structured data documents as well as their visualization. The museum professional is presented with linear processes, which can be easily understood and can be followed without extensive training.

(2) Content Pages

The software framework is primarily meant to enable cultural heritage institutions to represent themselves and their collections in the digital realm for a casual audience and to create structured data documents in the process. Those data documents, which represent the architectural backbone of the framework and its prototype implementation, are based on four categories of *content pages.*

These content pages can be created by the museum professional by interacting with the creator application (*1*) and displayed by the visitor in a random-access guide using their own smart mobile device via the consumer application (*5*).

Here is where the most utility is generated, and at the same time, exactly for that same reason, many additions to the framework could be realized to satisfy the needs and wants communicated from within the problem domain, by its members, and other stakeholders.

(a) Basic Info

The content pages to convey the essential *'Basic Info'* including "information" about the museum itself, "opening hours", and "admission fees" are available within the framework implantation.

Those could be extended by offering certain elements which represent a calendar suggesting upcoming events or contain information about services adjacent to the core exhibition, like shops or restaurants. However, those are often not necessary, as they are not applicable to many small or medium-sized museums.

(b) Advanced Info

The assortment of content pages represented in the *'Advanced Info'* category includes those entities encountered within the context of exhibitions, like "object", "person", "event", and "place".

As that selection included in the framework implementation primarily has been based on the wants and needs initially requested by those museum professionals involved in the ViSIT project as well as common entities of the MAD. However, the potential for future extensions is limitless. Given the free-form ontology, capable of mapping data structures by utilizing objects and arrays in any composition, the content included within those four categories can be broadened, and new content pages can be added at will. The most obvious example of a page type to be added is Building or Architecture in general, as can be derived from evaluation *Episode (9).*

Other such entities can be extracted from existing classification models or schemata existing within the Museum Application Domain. As an example, the LIDO schema, suggested by ICOM, introduces descriptive and administrative elements, like "material", "appellation", and "resource", which could support the available content pages or create entirely new ones.

(c) Navigation
The *'Navigation'* category foremost includes "room" content pages. While these could be improved by more realistic or granular maps, as well as positioning or way-finding systems (i.e., blue-dot navigation), the sourcing of the necessary information or the required additional hardware remains difficult and poses particular questions which cannot be answered by the software framework alone.

Other improvements are simple, yet compelling, and can easily be included within the framework and the prototype implementation, without additional requirements, like RFID beacons or Wi-Fi Routers.

One idea which has already been added during development is numbers for objects (indoor) or POIs (outdoor) within the room page to communicate the intended logical order of those elements and signal a path the room is supposed to be traversed by. Similarly, this page type could be further improved by making those markers interactable to present additional information directly within the room page, comparable to the CUBE concept. This could be implemented either by directly accessing the related content pages of those objects or simply by displaying a picture of those objects to establish a clear visual connection between the application and the physical environment. Also, certain descriptors could benefit those room pages regarding either specific architectural insights or other information that might be of interest to the visitor, e.g., the average time spent in the vicinity.

Another improvement, which can be added even more easily, is Guide or Signpost content pages to improve way-finding, orientation, and navigation in a more simplistic but effective manner, like outlined in **Figure 8.12**.

(d) Interaction
The *'Interaction'* category can also be improved in various ways. The most effective way to extend the gamification approach, like the quiz, is to allow consumers to enter their name or a pseudonym to be displayed in a scorecard or ranked list to compete with other participants. While comparatively, that does contribute the least amount to the general scope of the software framework of creating structured data documents, implications regarding user experience from this category could drastically improve the adoption of the consumer application.

Figure 8.12 Guide Navigation Screen

Those contemplations even could be extended to the creator application by introducing certain gamification elements to museum professionals, e.g., introducing a leaderboard for most pages created.

The possibility to combine certain content pages from different categories to create a more compelling and coherent experience, facilitated by the CUBE concept, has been demonstrated above. Further improvements in regard to content are also contingent upon the demand of the institution or the specific context. Those, however, are also, to a lesser extent, connected to structured data documents and require more specific or independent code beyond the core functionality provided by the prototype implementation, which makes those efforts less directional and more complex to materialize.

(3) Customization

As initially stated, the *customization* options are addressed mostly by the ability of the creator to change the visual appearance of the consumer application in such a way as to best represent the creator's desires. Furthermore, it is possible to determine certain parameters regarding the intended audience for the resulting random-access guide, whereas those selections have to resonate with the content created for that purpose.

The customization of the color scheme of the consumer application is possible without any technical implications and independently of the content pages. That is demonstrated by the figures provided throughout the evaluation episodes above.

It is facilitated through the separation of themes from the layout of each Screen element, as well as their general style (compare: Subsection 6.5.2). Thus, the available options can be freely extended.

Further customization or personalization opportunities could be expedited by the framework in the future. If consumer accounts were to be introduced, a wide array of opportunities could be opened up, e.g., bookmarking or the exchange of favorite content pages and user-generated content, like comments or ratings. Those have not been explored because of certain legal implications as well as the main goal to primarily aid the museum professional in getting acquainted with the opportunities associated with mobile apps and structured data.

(4) Analytics

Ongoing analysis of the visitor's behavior and their interaction with the collection is not commonly pursued by many cultural heritage institutions. Thus, the gathering of data related to the usage within the consumer application as well as the display of an aggregate of the collected data in the creator application has to be pursued diligently.

There are also some legal implications involved in connection with constructing the imprint of the consumer application that would need to be resolved by consulting a legal professional. At the time of development and during the evaluation episodes of the "Human Risk and Effectiveness" strategy, anonymized data was collected from the resulting mobile applications, which were published by the creators involved to assess the collection and the display of the usage statistics. An excerpt of how the gathered data is utilized within the creator application is displayed in **Figure 8.13**.

This approach can also be refined if consumer accounts were to be introduced, subject to the same issues discussed previously. Furthermore, the data collection could be extended toward the creator application to gather information about the usage and interaction of the museum professionals acting as creators to gather fundamental data and generate feedback for future improvements or developments.

(5) Consumer Application

The *consumer application* enables the delivery of micro-content to consumers, facilitated by the content pages conceived by museum professionals through the creator application. As stated before, the software framework is not meant to replace solutions to engage with the visitor already existing within an exhibition, like labels or in-person tours, nor systems supporting the administration of the collection. The goal is to complement and extend the overall portfolio

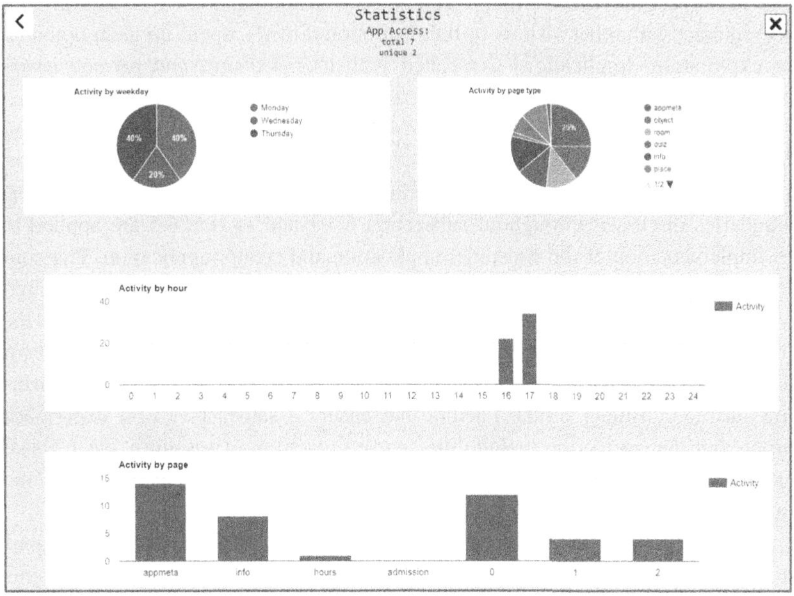

Figure 8.13 Analytics Utilization in the Creator Application

or, especially for small institutions, to facilitate the first steps toward a digital strategy.

The minimal viable prototype, as illustrated in **Figure 6.27**, can be successfully operated. The prototype implementation even goes beyond that demonstration of the utility of the framework, as it actually grants the ability for cultural heritage institutions to publish and distribute mobile apps to operate individual random-access guides for visitors. Certain shortcomings regarding the performance of the resulting mobile application—to be expected from a prototype implementation—were identified. Nevertheless, the implementation of the consumer app fulfills the benchmarks and requirements to qualify as a PWA. That does primarily demonstrate the feasibility of web technologies to deliver a smooth user experience for mobile applications to be operated on smart mobile devices via a BYOD strategy in the MAD.

In the future, it would be interesting to explore possibilities for content co-creation and individualization, the integration of social plug-ins, as well as other engagement opportunities. The possibilities to enable the visitor to fully engage with the experience offered by the app and the surrounding environment, as well as to interact with other visitors or the institution directly, opens up great potential for exploration. Implications associated with user accounts and privacy issues have been indicated throughout this section.

(6) Usability

Both the *usability* principles discussed in subsection 5.2.1 and the technological boundaries discussed throughout subsection 6.4.1 and section 6.5 are applied to the implementation of the consumer application and creator application. The content pages proved to be useful as they were indicative of the intended and desired outcome, both from the users' and the technical perspective. Furthermore, the limitations invoked by that fundamental design prevents technology overload for the museum professional or at the creator's side, as well as information overflow on the consumer's side. Factors that ensure a satisfactory user experience throughout the interaction include the sparse utilization of scrolling, clear visual cues, and navigational elements that guide the user through linear and atomic processes.

The extension or the inclusion of gamification elements to the applications of both user groups, e.g., rewarding different tasks or actions by virtual points which can be compared to other individuals, could further enhance the user experience while interacting with the connected applications enabled by the software framework.

(7) Documentation

The three critical levels of *documentation* are vital components of the software framework. The three levels between the 'User Manual', 'Styleguide', and 'Technical Documentation' summarize and extend the findings presented throughout this dissertation to be easily available for their respective audiences.

The *User Manual*—available both in German and English—contains step-by-step, cookbook-style guides to enable novice users to set up the system and how to interact with the connected applications of the software framework.

The *Styleguide* presents the recurring Views and UI elements utilized throughout the connected applications independently of the prototype implementation. This is a great resource for creators and designers, enabling them to get a surface-level impression of the system without the necessity of diving deep into the implementation details. This is primarily achieved by the KSS documentation syntax for CSS.

Similarly, the *Technical Documentation* utilizes documentation comments throughout the JavaScript source code. Those comments are based on JSDoc, which allows to automatically generate a comprehensive API documentation. That has the inherent advantage of making sure of proper and standardized comments throughout the codebase, as well as a presentable documentation output, suitable for both engineers and developers.

(8) Shareability

The explicit goal of the framework and its implementation has not been to provide a highly specialized product that rivals the state of the art, which is set by high-level individual institutions to be only available to a select few. It is supposed to act as an entry point to approach a digital strategy for most museum professionals, primarily in small institutions. Thus, shareability also is a category that can drastically enhance the quality of the software framework and its prototype implementation. Most of the possible improvements are rooted within the *(10) Extensibility* considerations and the efforts made to avoid proprietary technology throughout design and development.

Therefore, from the technical point of view, the framework is set up fairly well. As the underlying data model is based on a well-defined ruleset, the resulting data documents based on JSON can be utilized by most programming languages. The existing applications can be accessed and shared very easily, as they do not possess any requirements beyond a device supporting a modern browser, standard peripherals, and internet access. New applications can be connected directly by accessing the API provided by the prototype implementation. A dedicated import/export mechanism or a library to publish and access existing content pages, to enable the exchange between intra- and inter-institutional creators, would help to increase immediate shareability in the future.

It is also possible to further extend the framework to act as a platform to also share other resources like Screens, Templates, or Themes, as well as finished content pages or entire apps across institutions. Those practical implications may aid in cultivating a network that can enable the exchange of best practices and other know-how.

Additionally, the support for localization and multilingual distribution already enhances the shareability of the suggested software framework. The prototype implementation initially supports English and German creators. Beyond that, simply adding dictionaries for other languages can open up accessibility for different communities.

For each content page they create, creators also can select the desired language to allow for maximum flexibility and to reach their visitors. At the beginning of the app creation process, the language for the app is determined, and only pages of that language can be added to the resulting mobile application to also ensure a coherent experience for the consumer.

(9) Availability

Most of the insights previously highlighted for *(8) Shareability* can be extended to the *availability* category as well. The intent to provide an entry point for museum professionals to create digital content and structured data, as well as to provide access to information for the visitor, presupposes the availability of the content and the general components of the software framework. That also includes the provisioning of digital information in spaces, which could not have been supported by traditional means.

Furthermore, the applications associated with that PCCR prototype implementation and the connected document store were hosted through Firebase to grant accessibility for museum professionals by offering them Software as a Service (SaaS) that does not require any additional resources.

(10) Extensibility

The *extensibility* category has implications on each aspect of the suggested Software Framework for Mobile Apps in the Museum Application Domain, and, therefore, could be expanded indefinitely. Hence, the suggestions made here aim only at the core concepts of the framework, while propositions beyond that are targeted at the end of the concluding chapter of this dissertation.

Those core concepts of the framework are based on technology-agnostic ideas and avoid external dependencies. The general design has been composed with future adaptations, changes, and extensions in mind. That also is supported by the selection of services and tools (compare: Subsection 7.3.1) as well as the web technologies (compare: Section 7.2) involved throughout design and development.

Generally, the framework is extensible in both directions to expand the capabilities of the connected applications (View-Driven) and to connect different storage and archiving solutions (Model-Driven), as shown in **Figure 8.14**. The MVVM design pattern allows the necessary abstraction layer to be able to avoid data being stored in the exact form it would be needed for the consumption of the information contained. The ViewModel acts as a filter between the stencil—enforced by the View—and the standardized notation—required by the Model—to enable the best outcome for both intents and purposes.

A conscious decision has been made against adhering to the complexity of certain existing structures during the design and development process to explore the possibilities within the MAD without any initial bias.

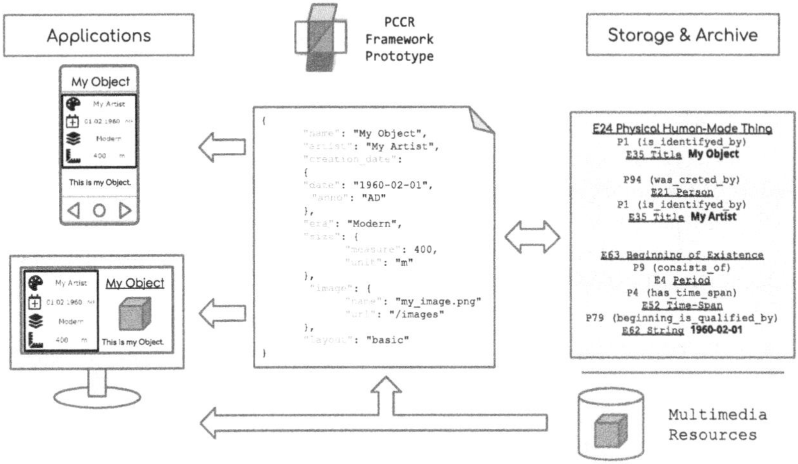

Figure 8.14 View- and Data-Driven Extensibility

From the Model-Driven point of view, the translation of the existing data documents is possible if it were explicitly required in the context of new applications. Relational data structures to perform more efficient queries or semantic path modeling to construct RDF-triples to allow for compositional data structures that accommodate additional metadata can be achieved by mere technical means, which can be addressed separately. Nevertheless, certain improvements could be achieved in the future by establishing compatibility with other systems. Adopting select classes suggested by CIDOC CRM within the free-form ontology of the software framework or utilizing LIDO to provide an export format between the framework's data model and existing archive and storage solutions, could further enhance its utility, e.g., creating an interface to connect the content pages to Linked Open Data (LOD). That, however, is contingent upon the adoption of a standard format throughout the cultural heritage domain, as well as the willingness or the of a legal framework that facilitates the shareability of digital assets between institutions. Therefore, it would not have been resourceful to introduce nor apply complex 'standards', that are not well adopted in the Museum Application Domain in the first place. One possibility to achieve that is the adoption of Blockchain technology, as briefly summarized in the concluding chapter of this dissertation. That also might aid the utilization of multimedia resources already available to cultural heritage institutions.

If the View-Driven perspective is the frame of reference, the modular concept of the interface elements—both for the creator and the consumer application—provides almost limitless possibilities for creating the design for different Views for the user interface of applications targeting different audiences or devices. Those considerations are supported by the *(7) Documentation* documents as well. Overall, there are almost no limitations for content customization within the bounds of the framework scope as they are only limited by the imagination.

Beyond that rather technical angle, certain extensions to or adaptations of the software framework could help to fulfill the demand for digital aides generated by the classical roles of the museum professionals or neighboring assignments commonly encountered within the MAD—like research or curation.

For the curator, the connection between the collection and past and current exhibitions held in the museum is essential. The framework could support the associated processes by introducing a Collection or Exhibition page type document. In that sense, it could be operationalized similarly to the app or CUBE page document to enable the museum professional to enter extensive metadata of collections or exhibitions and to organize related content pages based on their relevance or affiliated topics.

From the researcher's perspective, tools suited for scientific and scholarly work are necessary. Because of the close proximity to certain academic processes, some elements can be borrowed to support the existing software framework. For example, a tool to allow the museum professional to record references associated with certain information contained within the data documents or specific properties thereof could enhance the user experience of that audience. Similar to the extensions previously suggested, those citations could support certain citation standards—like MLA or APA—to offer standardized interfaces to other tools widely adapted by that workspace, e.g., Citavi or Mendeley. A mockup of such an extension is shown in **Figure 8.15**.

A similar feature for taking notes or exchanging ideas would be useful to enable multiple creators to collaborate in the creation process of content pages and mobile consumer applications.

Those insights uncovered throughout the evaluation episodes as well as this section, further consolidate the utility of the framework. Beyond the practical implications of the connected applications, the framework implementation facilitates clear communication and the ability to discover features, which in the ex-ante vacuum—without the suggested IT artifact—were not identifiable.

Overall, it can be established that the scope and the goals set for the Software Framework for Mobile Apps in the Museum Application Domain have been fulfilled throughout this dissertation.

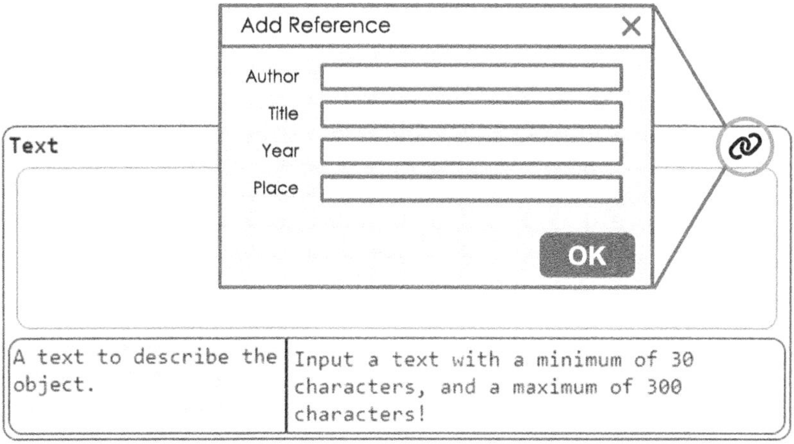

Figure 8.15 Input References

Conclusion

9

In the context of doctoral theses Davis (2005) describes design science research as "developing and demonstrating new or improved design of a conceptual or physical artifact. The contribution may be demonstrated by reasoning, proof of concept, proof of value added, or proof of acceptance and use" (Davis, 2005, p. 18). This dissertation applies rigorous methods supplied by the field of Information Systems to synthesize an innovative instantiation IT artifact that contributes to the knowledge base of both Information Systems and the Museum Application Domain. The practical utility is demonstrated by providing a dedicated prototype implementation.

The realization of *A Software Framework for Mobile Apps in the Museum Application Domain* has been conducted as an iterative search process and in alignment with the other guidelines suggested by the design science research paradigm conceived by Hevner et al. Considering the extraordinary circumstances encountered within the Museum Application Domain today and the unique starting situation associated with that environment, the design and development have been accompanied by the careful selection of components as well as the precise characterization of a common vocabulary to establish the gateway for communication as implied by domain-driven design, suggested by Evans.

Throughout this dissertation, several crucial issues have been examined to discover a holistic and sustainable solution. The primary consideration of small cultural heritage institutions (*where?*) throughout Chapter 3 is motivated based on the heavy restrictions of the domain in general and, in particular, the limited access to critical resources (*why?*).

T. Baumgärtner, *A Software Framework for Mobile Apps in the Museum Application Domain*, Gabler Theses, https://doi.org/10.1007/978-3-658-44367-2_9

The fundamental analysis of the conceptual duality of the 'user' in section 5.2 provides a valuable perspective to answer the questions considerably related to the interaction with the envisaged information system, which is directly based on the subsequent framework architecture (*who?*).

The expectations voiced by museum visitors, as the consumer of content, are introduced in subsection 5.2.2, and the tasks associated with museum professionals, as the creator of content, are examined in subsection 5.2.3. These insights, on top of the hereditary identity of museums, characterized in section 3.1, and the building blocks for random access guides, presented in section 3.2, provide the corner points of the design space explored by the software framework (*what?*).

Especially the tasks along the Customer Experience Value Chain, introduced in subsection 3.1.2, in particular the moment of data inquiry by the creator, as well as the utilization of the content offered to the consumer in the exhibition, are critical (*when?*) (compare: Section 5.2).

The technical foundation and its influence on the transport medium are discussed in subsection 3.1.2. The types of content to be offered, or more specifically, how information needs to be best prepared to be accessed and processed, are characterized in subsection 5.1.2. These insights highlight the challenging complexity of the creation and distribution processes related to random-access guides distributed by a BYOD strategy through mobile applications (*how?*).

Based on the preliminary analysis of the Museum Application Domain and the identified gaps within the discovered problem areas, three research problems were derived and addressed throughout this thesis. The main findings are summarized below. Subsequently, to conclude this thesis, certain limitations are considered, and future research potential is pointed out.

> *RP1. "Which fundamental ideas need to be considered to reduce the persistent inconsistencies emerging from the divide between technology, people, and strategy in the MAD?"*

To address the **Culture Gap** between the long-term organizational goals and the generally more nearsighted individual user goals, fundamental terms and concepts have to be identified and defined. Furthermore, the people involved within and outside the historico-cultural organizations in question have to be recognized as individuals rather than a uniform entity representing the institution to establish an understanding of their motivations. The tasks and roles involved in the organizational processes may not be aligned well with the long-term organizational strategy, which in turn may not reflect their actual wants and needs. Only if a clear and holistic path forward can be established, it becomes possible to address change by purposefully developing or introducing technological aides for the identified problems instead of enforcing transformation to adhere to alleged existing solutions.

Beyond those general insights, in the context of the MAD, it is important to not only be concerned with the traditional processes dominated by collection and exhibition management but also to explore interaction and engagement opportunities throughout the community, including visitors and members of other institutions. Museum professionals need to be enabled to learn about the available possibilities and their own capabilities, but also to recognize their own limitations to be able to fulfill their societal role now and in the future. Thus, the common goal of this dissertation is to provide an information system that is easily accessible via a graphical user interface, which utilizes mobile applications as an anchor for museum professionals to take their first step toward a digital strategy. It is supposed to yield structured data and deliver content to the visitor without overwhelming inexperienced users with either information or technology.

> *RP2. "From a socio-technical perspective, which components need to be considered in a framework design to cover basic expectations towards mobile applications within the MAD?"*

Therefore, to address the **Implementation Gap** between the IT-system quality and the IT requirements, an audit to identify those components most beneficial for the context provided by the historic-cultural institutions had to be performed. The challenge to appeal even to those individuals who critically observe technical innovation, threatening to disrupt the Museum Application Domain, had an immense formative impact on the design and development.

The fundamental socio-technical expectations and needs of the identified user groups have to be matched. Specifically, those prospects include first the consumer point of view regarding their assumptions associated with mobile applications; second, the creator's responsibilities, their technical rapport, as well as their individual capabilities and those of their institutions. To facilitate those mandatory tasks, primarily related to the data inquiry, depends heavily on the context and the ability to recognize the reasons and benefits of the effort required to create structured data (Baumgärtner, 2019.1).

Those aspects discussed here and during the evaluation in Chapter 8 also satisfy those requirements set by the framework definition introduced in subsection 5.1.1. To reiterate, a framework needs to be *generic* relative to its application domain so that it can be adopted across multiple organizations and applicable to their problems. Because of many of the same reasons, it needs to be *easy to use* to be approachable by those who are genuinely supposed to use it. Also, it needs to be *complete* in the sense that it provides everything necessary to construct applications, including documentation and instructions on both how to use it and the skeleton architecture underneath. That should not prohibit the framework from being *extensible* but rather include instructions on how to modify the default behavior and its composition. While it is required to be *flexible* regarding the initially intended application, it is required to be *robust* from both a conceptual and a technical perspective.

The core idea of the software framework suggested by this dissertation and its components has been to facilitate the content creation process for mobile applications to yield structured data, has been emphasized (Baumgärtner, 2019.2). The influence of human-centered design (compare: Subsection 5.1.3), as well as the psychological phenomena related to the mental model (compare: Subsection 5.2.1), offer valuable insights for the following design and development processes (Stojmenovic, Pilgrim, & Lindgaard, 2014).

> *RP3. "What architectural choices and data structures are necessary to compose A Framework for Mobile Apps in the MAD to reflect the academic urgency as well as the practical feasibility?"*

The suggested solution accommodates an extensible design by introducing a free-form otology at its conceptual core. It is based on schemata, which allow the dissipation of well-defined and easy-to-use entry mechanisms for the creation and verification of structured data documents. Those data documents can be stored, distributed, and rendered to support both the creation process and the consumption of content pages without being tied to any one specific implementation or technology.

Furthermore, the architectural model of the framework has been established in a mostly technology-agnostic manner by taking recourse to the MVVM design pattern (compare: Subsection 6.4.2). That allows to define individual visual components like input fields or screens (View) and implicitly tie them to their associated data types or data documents (Model). The mechanisms required to conflate these two layers can be described abstractedly and realized separately at the time of implementation.

The selection of standardized web technologies for the implementation of the framework prototype applications does unburden the practical operation from proprietary implications. Furthermore, it eliminates the requirements for additional infrastructure to deploy or access the resulting information system (compare: Section 7.2).

Beyond suggesting solutions to those three research problems, the PCCR prototype implementation and the suggested framework provide an effective vehicle to further investigate the issues encountered within the Museum Application Domain. Nevertheless, certain limitations of the dissertations need to be addressed as well, the four most significant of which are summarized here.

Limitations

The **first** and most obvious limitation can be attributed to the clash between the *innovative nature* of the approach suggested by this dissertation and the *unique application domain* surrounding historico-cultural institutions. As there are no suitable technical solutions to the identified problems available today and the overall situation is very particular in a narrow area of application, it is difficult to draw a comparison to different products or domains. This also is the primary cause for the small sample of experts who were able to trial the resulting instantiation of the suggested software framework. This, however, is the very reason that warrants the investigation to begin with.

The **second** constraint is rooted within the approach pursued throughout this dissertation. As museums are mostly considered non-profit organizations, the activities are focused primarily on the *organizational value* and the benefits for individual users. One resulting issue that needs to be addressed in the future is how to extract *economic value* from the suggested software framework. A certain return on investment can be attributed to the resulting data documents. However, without a monetary component, it becomes difficult to establish a sustainable platform that is able to maintain its utility or extend its capabilities even in a domain not measured by output or yield.

Another critical problem associated with the non-profit nature of cultural heritage institutions is that those who would benefit the most by utilizing the suggested software framework do not actively seek out a solution. Most museum professionals are simply not aware of the underlying problems; hence they are not able to benefit from the suggested software framework.

The **third** limitation is associated with choosing mobile applications as the conceptual anchor for the affiliated processes. A screen that does not even exceed five inches can only hold a certain amount of information before it becomes incomprehensible. Too much text or excessive media content on the phone screen may also distract the visitor from experiencing the real-life exhibits they are primarily there to admire anyway. While this works well for the processes supported by the chosen content types, the challenge for future extensions, targeting tasks not directly associated with mobile applications or the visitor, is equally challenging.

The conceptualization and integration of suitable applications need to be examined to purposefully support those processes in a suitable manner.

Fourth, IT in general and, more specifically, applications targeting end users or customers outside the business entity (B2C) create a broad array of *legal and privacy issues* that were hinted at throughout this thesis. The same holds true for the MAD, relevant to the content, information, and data available to museum professionals that may implicate *3ed party rights*. As these issues were not properly addressed, this point of view has to be further examined in the future.

Additionally, one strength of the PCCR prototype implementation has surfaced disguised as a weakness. Since the connected applications exceed the usual developmental state of a *prototype* in both functionality and appearance, the expectations often supersede their actual intent. Hence, they have been pointed out as simplistic or underdeveloped rather than decent prototypes on multiple occasions.

Future Research Potential

This dissertation captures the desire of cultural heritage institutions to offer mobile applications for their visitors and grants them the ability to generate structured data documents in that specific course of action. The contribution made by the Software Framework for Mobile Apps in the Museum Application Domain and the subsequent PCCR framework prototype implementation could be exaptated to other domains.

While the specific constraints and dependencies are unique to the MAD in the context of galleries, libraries, archives, and museums, the basic setup does occur in various other disciplines, e.g., the field of medicine. Medical practitioners do encounter similar problems as museum professionals, as they are surrounded by structured data related to patrons, examinations, and tests, that have to be accessed by different members in the field, while those people are preoccupied with tasks generally not related to IT or information systems. As the legal implications are even more severe in this context because very sensitive personal data is involved, veterinary medicine could act as a domain for testing out the concepts suggested by the software framework in the future.

Nevertheless, the framework can act primarily as the jumping-off point for new inventions and provide a proving ground for other concepts to be deployed to or explored within the Museum Application Domain. Furthermore, it can help to identify future research potential within cultural heritage institutions and facilitate the further adoption of pioneering and trend-setting technologies, such as in the following four examples. The framework does provide the ideal platform to quickly test and evaluate certain ideas in the intended environment and involves real users via the extensible prototype implementation available.

First, *new mobile devices*, both with smaller screens—e.g., wearables, like smartwatches—or more space to display content—e.g., phablets or foldables—create advanced challenges and offer new opportunities to be explored. As browsers do possess their own ecosystem independent of the underlying hardware or operating system of the user, web technologies can be deployed to examine these possibilities. By virtue of the standardization of the underlying technology, foremost the inevitable influence of JavaScript, few adoptions have to be applied to the application code, as most changes purely manifest themselves in the visualization layer. While the web as a platform, like any other software environment, is not immune to sudden changes, it is distinctly more resilient than native approaches, as backward compatibility is preserved as new features are introduced. While hardware enabling VR and AR also becomes more and more accessible as well, the experiences they are able to provide may be supported through the general approach suggested by this thesis but inevitably require additional components because of the higher level of content complexity.

Second, *Natural Language Processing (NLP)* and *conversational user interfaces* facilitate new approaches for the interaction with certain applications and the construction and composition of the UI. While classic UX design can be administered such that human-computer interaction seamlessly integrates into specific business processes, most UI elements cannot compete with natural language as the primary medium of communication. This also enables opportunities to provide targeted access to content, user manuals, or documentation in a more approachable manner or just-in-time delivery, e.g., by utilizing *chatbots*.

Third, those insights can be extended to *Large Language Models (LLM)* and *Generative Artificial Intelligence (GenAI)*. Recent developments have introduced unprecedented technical advances, which offer disruptive potential to the entire industry. Those newly available opportunities prompt the revisitation of the initial design iterations of the framework and to apply those possibilities alongside the insights gained throughout this dissertation. For example, the general idea of 'Text Selection' could be extended to the training of dedicated LLMs to identify certain structures in more extensive publications—like catalogues—to supply data documents for existing or new page types.

GenAI could enable the implementation of small or menial elements without the involvement of a dedicated developer or manual coding (*No Code/Low Code*). Therefore, a similar attempt could be applied to 'WYSIWYG Components' as well. As demonstrated, the framework does allow museum professionals to expand their knowledge base and, as a direct result, more clearly articulate their desires for additional features. On this basis, new Screen elements could be created simply by providing conversational user interfaces to the creator to enter dedicated prompts.

Moreover, a unified approach could be deployed within the current design as well. The analysis of available data sources and existing presentation outlets could offer the grounding to either derive additional schemata or Screen elements to extend and enhance the software framework; the attempt to take the leap to automatically generate complete content pages for museum visitors could be an interesting approach as well.

Blockchain, as the **fourth** and probably most interesting item of future curiosity, could enhance the general approachability of the framework. Concerns and uncertainties associated with certain transactions can be eliminated by introducing well-organized and tracked processes. That would allow communities to share resources more openly and practice knowledge transfer by providing transparency and peace of mind without the necessity of a trusted third party.

Furthermore, mobile applications, in conjunction with *smart contracts,* could support small cultural heritage institutions to escape their traditional setup and embrace certain opportunities for micro-transactions or other monetization potential. This also allows distributed engagement in specific assignments beyond their traditional curatorial tasks, like design and development, without relying on a trusted third party. The extended possibilities of collaboration within their community would prove advantageous to everybody involved.

Overall, it can be concluded that the leading research motive of this dissertation

> *"How to provide guidance for small cultural heritage institutions to govern digital transformation, and how to align the possibilities with the available capabilities by creating A Software Framework for Mobile Apps in the Museum Application Domain?"*

has been answered by a thorough examination of the surrounding environment, the rigorous application of suitable methods, and the development of an innovative IT artifact.

References

Abdullah, H. M., & Zeki, A. M. (2014). Frontend and Backend Web Technologies in Social Networking Sites: Facebook as an Example. *International Conference on Advanced Computer Science Applications and Technologies*, 85–89.

Aborujilah, A., Adamu, J., Shariff, S., & Long, Z. (2022). Descriptive Analysis of Built-in Security Features in Web Development Frameworks. *International Conference on Ubiquitous Information Management and Communication*, 1–8.

Accenture. (2022, 08 10). *What is edge computing?* Retrieved 08 10, 2019, from accenture.com: https://www.accenture.com/us-en/insights/cloud/edge-computing-index

Ackoff, R. (1989). From Data to Wisdom. *Journal of Applied Systems Analysis, 16*, 3–9.

Addis, M. (2005). New Technologies and Cultural Consumption–Edutainment is Born! *European Journal of Marketing*, 729–736.

Adepu, S., & Adler, R. F. (2016). A Comparison of Performance and Preference on Mobile Devices vs. Desktop Computers. *IEEE 7th Annual Ubiquitous Computing, Electronics & Mobile Communication Conference (UEMCON)*, 1–7.

Afreen, R. (2014). Bring Your Own Device (BYOD) in Higher Education: Opportunities and Challenges. *International Journal of Emerging Trends & Technology in Computer Science, 3*(1), 233–236.

Albert, I., Charaf, H., & Lengyel, L. (2013). Layout Definition Considerations for a Content Driven Template-Based Layout System. *EuroCon 2013*, 543–549.

Alexander, E. P., & Alexander, M. (2008). *Museum in Motion: An Introduction to the History and Functions of Museums*. Plymouth, United Kingdom: AltaMira Press.

Alexander, J., Barton, J., & Goeser, C. (2013). Transforming the Art Museum Experience: Gallery One. *In Museums and the Web 2013*. doi:https://mw2013.museumsandtheweb.com/paper/transforming-the-art-museum-experience-gallery-one-2/

Amadeo, R. (2018, 02 27). *Google starts a push for cross-platform app development with Flutter SDK*. Retrieved 12 16, 2019, from arsTechnica.com: https://arstechnica.com/gadgets/2018/02/google-starts-a-push-for-cross-platform-app-development-with-flutter-sdk/

Antill, L. (1985). Selection of a Research Method. In E. Mumford, R. Hirschheim, G. Fitzgerald, & T. Wood-Harper, *Research Methods in Information Systems*. (pp. 191–204). Amsterdam.

T. Baumgärtner, *A Software Framework for Mobile Apps in the Museum Application Domain*, Gabler Theses, https://doi.org/10.1007/978-3-658-44367-2

Appel, G., Libai, B., Muller, E., & Shachar, R. (2018). On the Monetization of Mobile Apps. *International Journal of Research in Marketing*. doi:https://doi.org/10.1016/j.ijresmar.2019.07.007

Apple Inc. (2007). *Apple Reinvents the Phone with iPhone*. Retrieved 10 2019, from apple.com: https://www.apple.com/newsroom/2007/01/09Apple-Reinvents-the-Phone-with-iPhone/

appypie. (2019). *App builder to make your app without coding*. Retrieved 12 16, 2019, from appypie.com: https://www.appypie.com/app-builder/appmaker

Arendt, L. (2008). Barriers to ICT Adoption in SMEs: How to Bridge the Digital Divide? *Journal of Systems and Information Technology, 10*(2), 93–108. doi:https://doi.org/10.1108/13287260810897738

Arhippainen, L., & Tähti, M. (2003). Empirical Evaluation of User Experience in Two Adaptive Mobile Application Prototypes. *Proceedings of the 2nd International Conference on Mobile and Ubiquitous Multimedia., 11*, 27–34.

Atkinson, L. (2013). Smart Shoppers? Using QR Codes and 'green' Smartphone Apps to Mobilize Sustainable Consumption in the Retail Environment. *International Journal of Consumer Studies, 37*, 387–393.

Babich, N. (2017, 07 17). *4 Ways Friction Can Improve UX*. Retrieved 12 16, 2019, from uxplanet.org: https://uxplanet.org/when-friction-in-design-is-good-for-ux-e2dd82cfab67

Bamberger, Y., & Tal, T. (2009). The Learning Environment of Natural History Museums: Multiple Ways to Capture Students' Views. *Learning Environments Research, 12*(2), 115–129.

Bandi, A., & Fellah, A. (2017). Design Issues for Converting Websites to Mobile Sites and Apps: A Case Study. *Proceedings of the IEEE 2017 International Conference on Computing Methodologies and Communication*, pp. 652–656.

BankGiro Lottery. (2019, 12 16). *BankGiro Lottery*. Retrieved from rijksmuseum.n: https://www.rijksmuseum.nl/en/join-us/funds/bankgiro-lottery

Baumgaertner, T., & Lehner, F. (2017.1). The Technical Aspects of Museum Information vs. the Museum Professionals Point of View: a Conceptual Change of Perspective on Data Processing. *Proceedings of the 21st Museums and the Web conference.*

Baumgärtner, T. (2019.1). A Software Framework for Mobile Apps within the Museum Application Domain. *Demonstration at the 23rd Museums and the Web conference (MW19), Boston, Massachusetts, USA, April 2–6, 2019.*

Baumgärtner, T. (2019.2). Conceptualizing a Mobile App Framework for the Museum Application Domain. *Proceedings of the 27th European Conference on Information Systems (ECIS), Stockholm & Uppsala, Sweden, June 8–14, 2019.* https://doi.org/978-1-7336325-0-8

Baumgärtner, T., & Lehner, F. (2017.2). Entwicklung mobiler Applikationen im Anwndungsbereich von Museen—Customer Experience Value Chain. *HMD Praxis der Wirtschaftsionformatik, 54*(5), 808–820.

Baumol, W., & Bowen, W. (1966). *Performing arts. The Economic Dilemma.* New York: The Twentieth Century Fund.

bavarikon. (2019). *Über bavarikon.* Retrieved 12 16, 2019, from bavarikon.de: https://www.bavarikon.de/object/bav:BSB-CMS-0000000000000605

Bellis, M. (2018, 07 12). *The Inventor of Touch Screen Technology*. Retrieved 12 16, 2019, from thoughtco.com: https://www.thoughtco.com/who-invented-touch-screen-technology-1992535

Berners-Lee, T., Fielding, R., & Masinter, L. (1998). Uniform Resource Identifier (URI): Generic Syntax. *The Internet Society—Network Working Group*.

Bevan, N. (2009). What is the Difference between the Purpose of Usability and User Experience Evaluation Methods. *Proceedings of the Workshop UXEM, 9*, 1–4.

Bevan, N., Kirakowski, J., & Maissel, J. (1991). What is Usability? *Proceedings of the 4th International Conference on HCI*.

Bianchini, R. (2019, 11 15). *Kunstmuseum Basel*. Retrieved 12 16, 2019, from inexhibit.com: https://www.inexhibit.com/mymuseum/kunstmuseum-basel/

Bianco, P., Kotermansk, R., & Merson, P. (2007). Evaluating a Service-Oriented Architecture. *Software Architecture Technology Initiative Report*.

Bishop, T. (2020, 01 15). *Why Microsoft embraced Chromium, and what the new Edge says about the state of web browsers*. Retrieved 06 01, 2020, from geekwire.com: https://www.geekwire.com/2020/microsoft-embraced-chromium-new-edge-says-state-web-browsers/

Bitgood, S., Patterson, D., & Benfield, A. (1992). Using Handouts to Increase Label Reading. *Visitor Behaviour, 7*(1), 15–17.

Bitkom. (2019). *Smartphone-Markt: Konjunktur und Trends*. Retrieved 10 2019, from bitkom.org: https://www.bitkom.org/sites/default/files/2019-02/Bitkom-Pressekonferenz%20Smartphone-Markt%2020%2002%202019%20Pr%C3%A4sentation_final.pdf

Blaug, M. (2001). Where are We Now on Cultural Economics? *Journal of Economic Surveys, 15*(2), 123–143.

Bloom, D., Cuadra, R., Fassbender, J., Weldesn-Smith, E., & Graham, S. (2012). Museums as Third Place. *California Association of Museums—Foresight Research Report*.

Bongio, A., Ceri, S., Fraternali, P., & Maurino, A. (2000). Modeling Data Entry and Operations in WebML. *International Workshop on the World Wide Web and Databases*, 201–214.

Borun, M., & Millep, M. (1980). What's in a Name? A Study of the Effectiveness of Explanitory Labels in a Scinece Museum. *The Franklin Institute Science Museum*.

Bott, E. (2011, 09 08). *The real history of Java and Android, as told by Google*. Retrieved 12 16, 2019, from ZDNet.com: https://www.zdnet.com/article/the-real-history-of-java-and-android-as-told-by-google/

Boukhary, S., & Colmenares, E. (2019). A Clean Approach to Flutter Development through the Flutter Clean Architecture Package. *International Conference on Computational Science and Computational Intelligence*, 1115–1120.

Box, D., Ehnebuske, D., Kakivaya, G., Layman, A., Mendelsohn, N., Frystyk Nielson, H., . . . Winer, D. (2000). Simple Object Access Protocol (SOAP) 1.1. *W3C*. Retrieved from https://www.w3.org/TR/2000/NOTE-SOAP-20000508/

Broadbent, J., & Marti, P. (1997). Location Aware Mobile Interactive Guides: Usability Issues. *ICHIM*, 88–98.

Bruck, P., & Foerster, F. (2012). Mobile Learning with Micro-content: A Framework and Evaluation. *25th Bled eConference eDependability: Reliable and Trustworthy eStructures, eProcesses, eOperations and eServices for the Future*.

Bughin, J., LaBerge, L., & Mellybye, A. (2017). The Case for Digital Reinvention. *McKinsey Quarterly*.

Bullinger, H.-J., Auernhammer, K., & Gomeringer, A. (2004). Managing Innovation Networks in the Knowledge-Driven Economy. *International Journal of Production Research, 42*(17), 3337–3353. doi:https://doi.org/10.1080/00207540410001695970

Cain, A. (2017, 01 23). *How the White Cube Came to Dominate the Art World.* Retrieved 12 16, 2019, from artsy.net: https://www.artsy.net/article/artsy-editorial-white-cube-dominate-art

Camarero, C., Garrido, M., & Vicente, E. (2011). How Cultural Organizations' Size and Funding Influence Innovation and Performance: The Case of Museums. *J Cult Econ, 35.* doi:https://doi.org/10.1007/s10824-011-9144-4

Cambridge Dictionary: Bring your own Device. (2019). Retrieved from https://dictionary.cambridge.org/dictionary/english/byod

Cambridge Dictionary: Tourism. (2019). *Tourism.* Retrieved 10 2019, from https://www.dictionary.cambridge.org/.

Capgemini Consulting. (2011). The Challenges of the Digital Revolution. *Digital Transformation Review.*

Cartwright, S. (1996). *Pre-production Planning for Video, Film, and Multimedia.* Taylor & Francis. doi:https://doi.org/9780240802718

Cascaval, C., Ortego, P., Robatmili, B., & Gracia, D. (2015). Concurrency in Mobile Browser Engines. *IEEE Pervasive Computing, 14*(3), 14–19.

CHA, K., Gregor, S., & Fernandez, W. (2008). Towards a Deeper Understanding of IT-Enabled Transformation. *Australian Conference on Information Systems, 71*, 207–217.

Chadgar, A. (2015, 05 18). *Dieter Rams and the Relevance of Functionalism.* Retrieved 12 16, 2019, from medium.com: https://medium.com/%40amarchadgar/dieter-rams-and-the-relevance-of-functionalism-65bf7c1af064

Champeon, S. (2001, 04 06). *JavaScript: How Did We Get Here?* Retrieved 12 16, 2019, from Web DevCenter: https://web.archive.org/web/20160401081302/http://archive.oreilly.com/lpt/a/754

Charsky, D. (2010). From Edutainment to Serious Games: A Change in the Use of Game Characteristics. *Games and culture, 5*(2), 177–198.

Chauhan, D., & Bansal, K. (2017). Using the Advantages of NOSQL: A Case Study on MongoDB. *International Journal on Recent and Innovation Trends in Computing and Communication, 5*(2), 90–93. doi:ISSN: 2321–8169

Chen, C.-Y., Chang, B., & Huang, P.-S. (2014). Multimedia Augmented Reality Information System for Museum Guidance. *Personal and Ubiquitous Computing, 18*, 315–322.

Christensen, J. (2011). Four Steps in the History of Museum Technologies and Visitors' Digital Participation. *Journal of Media and Communication Research*, 7–29.

Cockburn, A. (2005, 01 04). *Hexagonal Architecture.* Retrieved 09 18, 2019, from alistair.cockburn.us: https://alistair.cockburn.us/hexagonal-architecture/

Conn, S. (2010). *Do Museums Still Need Objects?* University of Pennsylvania Press.

Conway, M. (1968). How do Committees Invent? *design organization criteria*, 28–31.

Cox, A., Cecchinato, M., Gould, S., Iacovides, I., & Renfree, I. (2016). Design Frictions for Mindful Interactions: The Case for Microboundaries. *Late-Breaking Work: Designing Interactive Systems*, 1389–1397.

Cox, S. J. (2016). Time Ontology Extended for non-Gregorian Calendar Applications. *Semantic Web, 7*(2), 201–209.

Crockford, D. (2006). *JSON: The fat-free alternative to XML*. Retrieved 12 16, 2019, from json.org: http://www.json.org/xml.html

Cronholm, S., & Göbel, H. (2019). Design Science Research Constructs: a Conceptual Model. *Proceedings Twenty-Third Pacific Asia Conference on Information Systems, 6*.

Crossler, R., Long, J., Loraas, T., & Trinkle, B. (2014). Understanding Compliance with Bring Your Own Device Policies Utilizing Protection Motivation Theory: Bridging the Intention-Behavior Gap. *Journal of Information Systems, 28*(1), 209–226. doi:https://doi.org/10.2308/isys-50704

Cutting, J. (2003). Gustave Caillebotte, French Impressionism, and mere exposure. *Psychonomic Bulletin & Review, 10*(2), 319–343.

Däßler, R. (1999). Informationsvisualisierung—Stand Kritik Perspektiven. *Methoden/Strategien der Visualisierung in Medien, Wissenschaft und Kunst*.

Davis, G. (2005). Advising and Supervising. In D. Avison , & J. Pries-Heje, *Research in Information Systems: A Handbook for Research Supervisors and Their Students*. Amsterdam: Elsevier Butterworth Heinemann.

de Clercq, S., & Lourenço, M. (2004). A Note in Musum Resarch. *Focus ICOM News*.

Debnath, S. (2022). *Why java for android development?* Retrieved 05 30, 2022, from shibajidebnath.com: https://www.shibajidebnath.com/java-android-development

Decker, J. (2015). *Technology and Digital Initiatives: Innovative Approaches for Museums*. London: Rowman & Littlefield.

Dee, C. (2022, 08 10). *What is a headless website? A definition and examples*. Retrieved 10 08, 2022, from algolia.com: https://www.algolia.com/blog/ux/what-is-a-headless-website-a-definition-and-examples/

Devaraj, S., & Kohli, R. (2003). Performance Impacts of Information Technology: Is Actual Usage the Missing Link? *Management Science, 49*(3), 273–289.

DeVoe, J. (2011). *Objectve-C Developers Guide*. doi:https://doi.org/10.1002/9781118257692.ch1

Dickerson, G. (2018, 02 26). *Learn the History of Web Browsers*. Retrieved 12 16, 2019, from washingtonindependent.com: https://washingtonindependent.com/learn-the-history-of-web-browsers/

Domingo, M. (2020, 06 28). *Dieter Rams: 10 Timeless Commandments for Good Design*. Retrieved 07 01, 2020, from interaction-design.org: https://www.interaction-design.org/literature/article/dieter-rams-10-timeless-commandments-for-good-design

Drechsler, A., & Hevner, A. (2016). A Four-Cycle Model of IS Design Science Research: Capturing the Dynamic Nature of IS Artifact Design. *Breakthroughs and Emerging Insights from Ongoing Design Science Projects: Research-in-progress papers and poster presentations from the 11th International Conference on Design Science Research in Information Systems and Technology*, 1–8.

Dürrenmatt, F. (1958). *Elektronische Hirne* (30 Bände über Dürrenmatts Dramatisches Werk und Prosawerk (1980) ed., Vol. 27). Zürich: Diogenes-Verlag.

Dwyer, L. (2015). Globalization of Tourism: Drivers and Outcomes. *Tourism Recreation Research*. doi: https://doi.org/10.1080/02508281.2015.1075723

ecma. (1994). *History*. Retrieved 06 30, 2021, from ecma-international.org: https://www.ecma-international.org/about-ecma/history/

ecma. (2021). *Members*. Retrieved 06 30, 2021, from ecma-international.org: https://www.ecma-international.org/about-ecma/members/

Edinger, E.-C., & Reimer, R. T. (2015). Thirdspace als Hybride Lernumgebung. Die Kombination Materieller und Virtueller Lernräume. *Erwachsenenbildung und Raum. Theorie und Praxis der Erwachsenenbildung.*, 205–216.

Eghbal-Azar, K., Merkt, M., Bahnmueller, J., & Schwan, S. (2016). Use of Digital Guides in Museum Galleries: Determinants of Information Selection. *Computers in Human Behavior, 57*, 133–142. doi:https://doi.org/10.1016/j.chb.2015.12.035

Eich, B. (2005, 12 20). *Holiday Links and Trees.* Retrieved 06 30, 2021, from brendaneich.com: https://brendaneich.com/2005/

Eppler, M., & Mengis, J. (2004). The Concept of Information Overload: A Review of Literature from Organization Science, Accounting, Marketing, MIS, and Related Disciplines. *The Information Society, 20*(4), 325–344.

Erlangen CRM. (2019). *About.* Retrieved 12 16, 2019, from erlangen-crm.org/: http://erlangen-crm.org/

Erskine, A. (1995). Culture and Power in Ptolemaic Egypt: The Museum and Library of Alexandria. *Greece & Rome, 42*(1), pp. 38–48.

Evans, E. (2003). *Domain-Driven Design: Tackling Complexity in the Heart of Software.* Addison Wesley.

Excolo. (2014). *Between Data, Information and Content.* Retrieved 12 16, 2019, from http://excolo.com/: http://excolo.com/information-v-content/

fabulapp. (2019). *Frequently Asked Questions.* Retrieved 12 16, 2019, from fabulapp.de: https://fabulapp.de/de/faqs/

Fernando, N., Loke, S., & Rahayu, W. (2012). Mobile Cloud Computing: A Survey. *Future Generation Computer Systems, 29*(1), 84–106.

Fielding, R., & Taylor, R. (2002). Principled Design of the Modern Web Architecture. *ACM Transactions on Internet Technology, 2*(2), 115–150.

Floerecke, S., & Lehner, F. (2016). Cloud Computing Ecosystem Model: Refinement and Evaluation. *Research Papers, 138.* doi:https://aisel.aisnet.org/ecis2016_rp/138

Forbes. (2009). Strategy and Operations in the Enterprise: Closing the Alignment Gap. *Forbes | Insights*, 1–14.

Forbes, N., & Fresa, A. (2015). Museum Education with Digital Technologies: Participation and Lifelong Learning. *RICHES resources.*

Fowler, M. (2006, 7 18). *GUI Architectures.* Retrieved 12 06, 2019, from martinfowler.com: https://www.martinfowler.com/eaaDev/uiArchs.html

Frické, M. (2019). The Knowledge Pyramid: the DIKW Hierarchy. *Official Journal of the International Society for Knowledge Organization, 46*(1), 33–46. doi:10.5771/0943-7444-2019-1-33.

Friedrich, T., Schlauderer, S., Weidinger, J., & Raab, M. (2017). On the Research Paradigms and Research Methods Employed in the BISE Journal—A Ten-Year Update. *13th International Conference on Wirtschaftsinformatik. February 12–15, 2017, St. Gallen, Switzerland*, 1111–1125.

Fruth, M., Baazizi, M.-A., Colazzo, D., Ghelli, G., Sartiani, C., & Scherzinger, S. (2020). Challenges in Checking JSON Schema Containment over Evolving Real-World Schemas. In G. Grossmann, & S. Ram, *Advances in Conceptual Modeling* (pp. 220–230). Springer International Publishing. doi:https://doi.org/10.1007/978-3-030-65847-2-20

Garling, C. (2012, 06 09). *iPhone Coding Language Now World's Third Most Popular*. Retrieved 12 16, 2019, from wired.com: https://www.wired.com/2012/07/apple-objective-c/

Garrett, J. (2005). Ajax: A New Approach to Web Applications. *adaptivePath*, 1–4.

Gebbensleben, S., Dittmann, J., & Vielhauer, C. (2006). Multimodal Audio Guide for Museums and Exhibitions. *Multimedia on Mobile Devices II, 6074*.

Ghobakhloo, M., Benitez-Amado, J., & Arias-Aranda, D. (2011). Reasons for Information Technology Adoption and Sophistication within Manufacturing SMEs. *POMS 22nd Annual Conference: Operations Management: The Enabling Link*.

Goebelbecker, E. (2019, 01 10). *Service Oriented Architecture: A Dead Simple Explanation*. Retrieved 09 12, 2020, from dzone.com: https://dzone.com/articles/service-oriented-architecture-a-dead-simple-explan

Gold, M., & Klein, L. (2016). *Debates in the Digital Humanities 2016*. University of Minnesota Press. doi:https://web.archive.org/web/20190512181840/http://dhdebates.gc.cuny.edu/debates/2

González García, C., Espada, J., Pelayo G-Bustelo, B., & Cueva Lovelle, J. (2015). Swift vs. Objective-C: A New Programming Language. *International Journal of Artificial Intelligence and Interactive Multimedia, 3*(3), 74–81.

Google. (2023, 05 10). *Baseline*. Retrieved 05 15, 2023, from web.dev: https://web.dev/baseline/

Gorgels, P. (2013). Rijksstudio: Make Your Own Masterpiece! *Museums and the Web 2013*.

Gorgels, P. (2018). Rijksmuseum Mobile First: Rijksstudio Redesign And The New Rijksmuseum App. doi:https://mw18.mwconf.org/paper/rijksmuseum-mobile-first-redesign-rijksstudio-the-new-rijksmuseum-app/

Graf, B., & Noschka-Roos, A. (2009). Stichwort: Lernen im Museum Oder: Eine Kamerafahrt mit der Besucherforschung. *ZfE, 12*, 7–27.

Gregor, S., & Hevner, A. (2013). Positioning and Presenting Design Science Research for Maximum Impact. *MIS Quarterly, 37*, 337–356.

Gries, C. (2017). *Museen*. Passau.

Grove, R., & Ozkan, E. (2011). The MVC-Web Design Pattern. *Proceedings of the 7th International Conference on Web Information Systems and Technologies*, pp. 127–130. doi:https://doi.org/978-989-8425-51-5

Gruber, M. R. (2009). *E-Learning im Museum und Archiv. Vermittlung von Kunst und Kultur im Informationszeitalter*. doi:https://doi.org/10.13140/RG.2.1.4434.3289

Haesler, S., Obernesser, K., Raupp, T., Jahnke, C., Stapf, J., Bräker, J., . . . Steinicke, F. (2016). Edutainment & Engagement at Exhibitions: A Case Study of Gamification in the Historic Hammaburg Model. *Mensch und Computer 2016-Tagungsband*.

Haffner, D., & Schweibenz, W. (2017). Ergebnisse der Online-Umfrage zur Nutzung von kontrolliertem Vokabular in Museen im Herbst 2016. *Fachgruppe Dokumentation im DMB*.

Harms, H., Rogowski, C., & Iacono, L. (2017). Guidelines for Adopting Frontend Architectures and Patterns in Microservices-Based Systems. *11th Joint Meeting on Foundations of Software Engineering*, 902–907. doi:https://doi.org/10.1145/3106237.3117775

Hasan, S. (2019, 05 26). *Pipe and Filter Architecture*. Retrieved 09 19, 2019, from syedhasan010.medium.com: https://syedhasan010.medium.com/pipe-and-filter-architecture-bd7babdb908

Hasselbring, W., & Steinacke, G. (2017). Microservice Architectures for Scalability, Agility and Reliability in E-Commerce. *International Conference on Software Architecture Workshops*, 243–246.

Heavin, C., & Power, D. J. (2018). Challenges for Digital Transformation—Towards a Conceptual Decision Support Guide for Managers. *Journal of Decision Systems, 27*(1), 38–45. doi:https://doi.org/10.1080/12460125.2018.1468697

Hellerman, J. (2019, 04 26). *What Companies Does Disney Own?* Retrieved 12 16, 2019, from nofilmschool.com: https://nofilmschool.com/What-does-Disney-own

Hess, T., Matt, C., Benalian, A., & Wiesböck, F. (2016). Options for Formulating a Digital Transformation Strategy. *MIS Quarterly Executive, 15*(2), 123–139.

Hevner, A., & Chatterjee, S. (2010). Design Science Research in Information Systems. *Design Research in Information Systems.*, 9–22.

Hevner, A., Ram, S., March, S., & Park, J. (2004). Design Science in Information Research. *MIS Quarterly, 28*(1), 75–105.

Hick, E., & Hyman, R. (2020, 05). *Hick's Law.* Retrieved from lawsofux.com/: https://lawsofux.com/hicks-law.html

Hinrichs, U., Schmidt, H., & Carpendale, S. (2008). EMDialog: Bringing Information Visualization into the Museum. *IEEE Transactions on Visualization and Computer Graphics, 14*(6), 1181–1188.

Ho, R. C., & Chua, H. K. (2015). The Influence of Mobile Learning on Learner's Absorptive Capacity: A Case of Bring-Your-Own-Device (BYOD) Learning Environment. (T. S. Logonnathan, Ed.) *Taylor's 7th Teaching and Learning Conference 2014 Proceedings*, 471–479.

Hoffmann, A. (2020). Smart Art—Museen und Asstellungshäuser in einer digitalisierten Gesellschaft. *Handbuch Kulturmanagement* (69).

Hoffmann, J. (2020, 07 07). *The Browser Engine That Could.* Retrieved 02 12, 2021, from thehistoryoftheweb.com: https://thehistoryoftheweb.com/how-a-browser-engine-dominates-the-market/

Holman, N., Reynolds-Haertle, R., Griffin, C., & Dunham Kroes, L. (2022, 1 15). *Templates and layouts overview.* Retrieved from docs.microsoft.com: https://docs.microsoft.com/en-us/dynamics365/commerce/templates-layouts-overview#:~:text=Whereas%20a%20template%20defines%20all,selection%20and%20arrangement%20of%20modules.

Hooper-Greenhill, E. (1999). Communication in Theory and Oractice. In E. Hooper-Greenhill, *The Educational Role of the Museum—second edition* (pp. 28–43). New York: Routledge.

HTC. (2008). *T-Mobile Unveils the T-Mobile G1—the First Phone Powered by Android.* Retrieved 10 2019, from htc.com: https://web.archive.org/web/20110712230204/http://www.htc.com/www/press.aspx?id=66338

Hu, H., Wang, S., Bezemer, C.-P., & Hassan, A. (2019). Studying the Consistency of Star Ratings and Reviews of Popular Free Hybrid Android and iOS Apps. *Empirical Software Engineering, 24*, 7–32.

Hubackova, S. (2015). History and Perspectives of Elearning. *Procedia—Social and Behavioral Sciences, 191*, 1187–1190.

Hufenbach, Y. (2014). Referenzmodelle im Mobile Business—Analyse und Entwicklung neuer Rollen, Szenarien und Geschäftsmodelle. *PhD thesis.*

Hume, M., & Mills, M. (2011). Building the Sustainable iMuseum: is the Virtual Museum Leaving our Museums Virtually Empty? *International Journal of Nonprofit and Voluntary Sector Marketing*, 275–289. doi:https://doi.org/10.1002/nvsm.425

Hunt, J., & McManus, A. (1998). Frameworks. In J. Hunt, *Key Java* (pp. 103–118). London: Springer Science & Business Media.

Ianbi. (2010, 12 21). *Issue 67743: Access-Control-Allow-Origin: * doesn't match localhost.* Retrieved 12 16, 2019, from chromium.org: https://bugs.chromium.org/p/chromium/issues/detail?id=67743

ICOM. (2014). *What is the CIDOC CRM?* Retrieved 12 16, 2019, from cidoc-crm.org: http://www.cidoc-crm.org/

ICOM. (2017). *INTERNATIONAL COUNCIL OF MUSEUMS (ICOM)—Statutes.* Paris.

ICOM. (2019, 04 01). *Creating the new museum definition: over 250 proposals to check out!* Retrieved 12 20, 20119, from icom.museum: https://icom.museum/en/news/the-museum-definition-the-backbone-of-icom/

IPSOS. (2019). Holiday Barometer among Europeans & Americans . *IPSOS/EUROP ASSISTANCE SURVEY 19 TH EDITION.*

Jacksi, K., & Abass, S. (2019). Development History Of The World Wide Web. *International Journal of Scinetific & Technology Research, 8*(9), 75–79.

Jaffe, J. (2013). *FACTS ABOUT W3C.* Retrieved 12 16, 2019, from w3.org: https://www.w3.org/Consortium/facts

Jaffe, J. (2015). *W3C MISSION.* Retrieved 12 16, 2019, from w3.org: https://www.w3.org/Consortium/mission.html

Jaffe, J. (2018). *STANDARDS.* Retrieved 12 16, 2019, from w3.org: https://www.w3.org/standards/

Jaffe, J. (2019, 05 28). *W3C AND WHATWG TO WORK TOGETHER TO ADVANCE THE OPEN WEB PLATFORM.* Retrieved 12 16, 2019, from w3.org: https://www.w3.org/blog/2019/05/w3c-and-whatwg-to-work-together-to-advance-the-open-web-platform/

Jang, H.-C., & Lien, Y.-N. (2014). Educational Exhibition System and the Application of APP on Museum Mobile Learning—National Palace Museum as an Example. *International Conference on e-Commerce, e-Administration, e-Society, e-Education, and e-Technology.*

Jazayeri, M. (2007). Some Trends in Web Application Development. *Future of Software Engineering*, 199–213.

Jeffers, C. (2003). Museum as Process. *The Journal of Aesthetic Education, 37*(1), 107–119.

Jeurgens, C. (2013). Scent of the Digital Archive: Dilemmas with Archive Digitisation. *BMGN—Low Countries Historical Review, 128*(4), 30–54. doi:https://doi.org/10.18352/bmgn-lchr.9348

Johnson, P., & Thomas, B. (1998). The Economics of Museums: A Research Perspective. *Journal of Cultural Economics, 22*(2/3), 75–85. Retrieved from https://www.jstor.org/stable/41810659

Jose, R., & Davies, N. (1999). Scalable and Flexible location-based Services for Ubiquitous Information Access. *International Symposium on Handheld and Ubiquitous Computing*, 52–66.

Kahlert, H. (1988). Museen als Unternehmen. *Journal for Public and Nonprofit Services, 11*(1), 30–42. doi:https://www.jstor.org/stable/20763226

Kaidalova, J., Seigerroth, U., & Persson, A. (2017). Enterprise Modeling for Business and IT Alignment—A Framework and Recommendations. *Complex Systems Informatics and Modeling Quarterly*(12), 66–85. doi:https://doi.org/10.7250/csimq. 2017-12.04

Kaluza, M., Troskot, K., & Vukelic, B. (2018). Comparison of front-end Frameworks for Web Applications Development. *Zbornik Veleučilišta u Rijeci, 6*(1), 261–282.

Karczewski, D. (2020, 08 19). *Swift vs Objective-C: Which One to Consider For Your Next iOS App?* Retrieved 05 30, 2022, from ideamotive.co: https://www.ideamotive.co/blog/swift-vs-objective-c-which-should-you-pick-for-your-next-ios-mobile-app

Kearney, M., Gash, D., & Boxhall, A. (2016, 10 04). *Introduction to ARIA*. Retrieved 12 16, 2019, from web.dev: https://web.dev/semantics-aria/

Kelly, B., Ellis, M., & Gardler, R. (2008). What Does Openness Mean To The Museum Community? *Museums and the Web 2008 Conference Proceedings*.

Kendall Adams, G. (2019, 07 31). *Icom unveils new museum definition*. Retrieved 12 20, 2019, from https://www.museumsassociation.org/: https://www.museumsassociation.org/museums-journal/news/31072019-icom-reveals-updated-museum-definition

Keyul. (2019, 11 27). *10 Most Popular Web Frameworks in 2020*. Retrieved 12 16, 2019, from medium.com: https://medium.com/front-end-weekly/10-most-popular-web-frameworks-in-2020-167b9103e08a

Khaddage, F., Lattemann, C., & Acosta-Díaz, R. (2014). Mobile Gamification in Education: Engage, Educate and Entertain via Gamified Mobile Apps. *Society for Information Technology & Teacher Education International Conference*, 1654–1660.

Khruahong, S., Kong, X., Sandrasegaran, K., & Liu, L. (2017). Multi-Level Indoor Navigation Ontology for High Assurance Location-Based Services. *2017 IEEE 18th International Symposium on High Assurance Systems Engineering*, pp. 128–131.

Kienle, H. (2010). It's About Time to Take JavaScript (More) Seriously. *tools of the trade*, 60–62.

Klettke, M., Störl, U., & Scherzinger, S. (2015). Schema Extraction and Structural Outlier Detection for JSON-based NoSQL Data Stores. *BTW 2015*, 425–444.

Knežević Cvelbar, L., Dwyer, L., Koman, M., & Mihalič, T. (2016). Drivers of Destination Competitiveness in Tourism: a Global Investigation. *Journal of Travel Research, 55*(8), 1041–1050.

Knight, D. (2014, 04 26). *Personal Computer History: 1975–1984*. Retrieved 12 16, 2019, from lowendmac.com: https://lowendmac.com/2014/personal-computer-history-the-first-25-years/

Kohnke, O. (2016). It's not just about Technology: The People Side of Digitization. (Springer, Ed.) *Shaping the Digital Enterprise*, 69–91.

Kolter, N., & Kolter, P. (2000). Can Museums be All Things to All People?: Missions, Goals, and Marketing's Role. *Museum Management and Curatorship, 18*(3), 271–287.

Komarac, T., Ozretic-Dosen, D., & Skare, V. (2017). Understanding Competition and Service Offer in Museum Marketing. (E. P. Limited, Ed.) *Academia Revista Latinoamericana de Administración, 30*(2), 215–230. doi:1012–8255 https://doi.org/10.1108/ARLA-07-2015-0159

Kontiza, K., Loboda, O., Deladiennee, L., Castagnos, S., & Naudet, Y. (2018). A Museum App to Trigger Users' Reflection. *International Workshop on Mobile Access to Cultural Heritage*.

Kotler, N., & Kotler, P. (2000). Can Museums be All Things to All People?: Missions, Goals, and Marketing's Role. *Museum Management and Curatorship, 18*(3), 271–287.

KPN. (2019, 12 16). *KPN—Main Sponsor.* Retrieved from rijksmuseum.nl: https://www.rijksmuseum.nl/en/join-us/our-sponsors/kpn

Kraemer, H., & Kanter, N. (2015). Use and Re-Use of Data: How Collection Management Systems, Transmedia and Augmented Reality impact the Future of Museum. *International Conference on Virtual Systems & Multimedia (VSMM),* 214–216.

Krempels, K.-H., Ohler, F., & Terwelp, C. (2019). The Missing Link between Requirements Engineering and Architecture Design for Information Systems. *Proceedings of the 15th International Conference on Web Information Systems and Technologies (WEBIST 2019),* 161–166. doi: 978-989-758-386-5

Kruger, W. (2012). Strategic business–IT Alignment of Application Software Packages: Bridging the Information Technology Gap. *South African Computer Journal, 49,* 1–11.

Kuflik, T., Stock, O., Zancanaro, M., Gorfinkel, A., Jbara, S., Kats, S., . . . Kashtan, N. (2011). A Visitor's Guide in an Active Museum: Presentations,Communications, and Reflection. *Journal on Computing and Cultural Heritage, 3*(3), 1–25.

Kuflik, T., Wecker, A. J., Lanir, J., & Stock, O. (2014). An Integrative Framework for Extending the Boundaries of the Museum Visit Experience: Linking the pre, during and post Visit Ohases. *Inf Technol Tourism,* pp. 17–47. doi:https://doi.org/10.1007/s40558-014-0018-4

Kwon, M., & Stoneman, P. (1995). The Impact Of Technology Adoption On Firm Productivity. *Economics of Innovation and New Technology, 3*(3–4), 219–234. doi:https://doi.org/10.1080/10438599500000004

Laine, M., Nakajima, A., Dayama, N., & Oulasvirta, A. (2020). Layout as a Service (LaaS): A Service Platform for Self-Optimizing Web Layouts. *Web Engineering—20th International Conference,* 19–26.

Laskey, K., & Laskey, K. (2009). Service Oriented Architecture. *Wiley Interdisciplinary Reviews: Computational Statistics, 1*(1), 101–105.

Lassnig, M., Stabauer, P., & Friebel, L. (2019). Geschäftsmodell-Konzept für nachhaltige IT-unterstützte kulturtouristische Angebote von Burgen, Schlössern und Residenzen. *Salzburg Research.*

Law, E. L., Roto, V., Hassenzahl, M., Vermeeren, A. P., & Kort, J. (2009). Understanding, Scoping and Defining User Experience: A Survey Approach. *Proceedings of the SIGCHI Conference on Human Factors in Computing Systems,* 719–728.

Lawler, B. (2017, 08 2016). *Domain-first vs. Schema-first Architecting.* doi:https://softwareengineering.stackexchange.com/questions/377275/what-is-an-example-giving-the-difference-between-domain-model-and-data-model

Lee, P. (1997). The Musaeum of Alexandria and the Formation of the Muséum in Eighteenth-Century France. *The Art Bulletin, 3,* pp. 385–412. Retrieved from https://www.jstor.org/stable/3046259

Lepouras, G., & Vassilakis, C. (2005). Virtual Museums for All: Employing Game Technology for Edutainment. *Virtual Reality, 8,* 96–106.

LIDO. (2019). LIDO (Lightweight Information Describing Objects): Making it easier to deliver information to portals. *CIDOC Resources.*

Lourenco, M. (2003). Contributions to the History of University Museums and Colections in Europe. *MUSEOLOGIA, 3,* pp. 17–26.

Löw, M. (2001). *Raumsoziologie.* Frankfurt am Main: Suhrkamp.

Luftman, J., & Kempaiah, R. (2007). An Update on Business-IT Alignment: "A Line" has beend Drawn. *MIS Quarterly Executive, 6*(3), 165–177.

MacPherson, M. (2019, 07 26). *Website vs Web App: What's the Difference?* Retrieved 05 30, 2022, from medium.com: https://medium.com/@essentialdesign/website-vs-web-app-whats-the-difference-e499b18b60b4

Malraux, A. (1954). Museum Without Walls. In A. Malraux, *Voices of Silence* (pp. 13–130). Norwich: Fletcher & Son.

Manes-Rossi, F., Allini, A., Spanò, R., & Dainelli, F. (2016). Changing Performance Measurement Towards Enhanced Accountability: Insights from the British Museum. *International Journal of Public Sector Performance Management, 2*(4).

Mapanga, I., & Kadebu, P. (2013). Database Management Systems: A NoSQL Analysis. *International Journal of Modern Communication Technologies & Research*, 12–18. doi:https://doi.org/2321-0850

March, S. T., & Smith, G. F. (1995). Design and Natural Science Research on Information. *Decision Support Systems, 15*(4), 251–266.

Martinez, M., & Mateus, B. (2021). Why did Developers migrate Android Applications from Java to Kotlin? *arXiv*.

Marty, P. F., & Burton Jones, K. (2008). *Museum Informatics, People, Information and Technology in Museums.* New York: Routledge Taylor & Francis Group.

Matt, C., Hess, T., & Benlian, A. (2015). Digital Transformation Strategies. *Business and Information Systems Engineering, 57*(5), 339–343.

Mavisakalyan, A., & Weber, C. (2016). Linguistic Relativity and Economics. *Bankwest Curtin Economics Centre Working Paper*.

McGrath, G., & Brenner, P. (2017). Serverless Computing: Design, Implementation, and Performance. *International Conference on Distributed Computing Systems Workshops, 37*, 405–410.

Mehdi, J. (2007). Some Trends in Web Application Development. *Future of Software Engineering*, 199–213.

Melton, J. (1996). SQL Language Summary. *ACM Computing Surveys, 28*(1), 141–143.

Mertens, P. (1995). Wirtschaftsinfonnatik: Von den Moden zum Trend. In W. König, *Wirtschaftsinformatik '95* (pp. 25–66). Berlin Heidelberg: Springer.

Mertens, P., Bodendorf, F., König, W., Picot, A., Schumann, M., & Hess, T. (2001). *Grundzüge der Wirtschaftsinformatik.* Berlin: Springer.

Miaskiewicz, T., & Kozar, K. (2011). Personas and user-centered Design: How can Personas benefit Product Design Processes? *Design Studies, 32*(5), pp. 417–430. doi:https://doi.org/10.1016/j.destud.2011.03.003

Miller, G. (2020, 11). *Miller's Law.* Retrieved from lawsofux.com/: https://lawsofux.com/millers-law.html

Moniruzzaman, A., & Hossain, S. (2013). NoSQL Database: New Era of Databases for Big data Analytics—Classification, Characteristics and Comparison. *International Journal of Database Theory and Application, 6*(4), 1–13.

Morrill, D. (2008, 09 23). *Announcing the Android 1.0 SDK, release 1.* Retrieved 12 19, 2019, from Android Developers Blog: https://android-developers.googleblog.com/2008/09/announcing-android-10-sdk-release-1.html

Moussouri, T., & Roussos, G. (2014). Mobile Sensing, BYOD and Big Data Analytics: New Technologies for Audience Research in Museums. *Journal of Audience and Reception Studies, 11*(1), 270–285.

Müller, J., Buliga, O., & Voigt, K.-I. (2018). Fortune Favors the Prepared: How SMEs Approach Business Model Innovations in Industry 4.0. *Technological Forecasting and Social Change, 123*, 2–17.

Museumsforschung, I. f. (1981–2018). *Materialien aus dem Institut für Museumsforschung*. Retrieved from Staatliche Museen zu Berlin: https://www.smb.museum/en/museums-institutions/institut-fuer-museumsforschung/research/publications/materialien-aus-dem-institut-fuer-museumsforschung.html

Najda-Janozka, M., & Sawczuk, M. (2018). Musums as a Research Object in the Strategic Management Field. In A. Nalepka, & A. Ujwary-Gil, *Business and non-profit Organizations Facing Increased Competition and Growing Customers' Demands* (pp. 51–68). Tomaszowice.

netmarketshare.com. (2020, 05 31). *Browser Market Share*. Retrieved 06 01, 2020, from netmarketshare.com: https://netmarketshare.com/browser-market-share.aspx

Ng, W. (2015). Mobile Learning: BYOD and Personalised Learning. *New Digital Technology in Education*, 171–189.

Nielsen, J. (1994, 04 24). *10 Usability Heuristics for User Interface Design*. Retrieved 12 16, 2019, from nngroup.com: https://www.nngroup.com/articles/ten-usability-heuristics/

Nielsen, J. (2020, 05 01). *Jakob's Law*. Retrieved 07 01, 2020, from lawsofux.com: https://lawsofux.com/jakobs-law

Nix, U. (2021, 04 09). *KOTLIN VS. JAVA: WHICH IS THE WINNER?* Retrieved 05 30, 2022, from nix-united.com: https://nix-united.com/blog/kotlin-vs-java-which-is-the-winner/

Noce, V. (2019, 09 09). *Vote on Icom's new museum definition postponed*. Retrieved 12 20, 2019, from https://www.theartnewspaper.com/: https://www.theartnewspaper.com/news/icom-kyoto

Nochlin, L. (2005, 05 01). Opinion: Museum Without Walls. *The New York Times*, 6.

Noschka-Roos, A., & Kapschulte, L. (2020). Digitales Medium und analoge Ausstellung Zur Analyse von Museums-Apps aus besucher_innenorientierter Perspektive. *Institut für Museumsforschung*, 1–97.

Nuanez, J., & Myers, A. (2022, 05 01). *Introduction to progressive web apps*. Retrieved 05 20, 2022, from developer.mozilla.org: https://developer.mozilla.org/en-US/docs/Web/Progressive_web_apps/Introduction

O'Dell, J. (2012, 01 07). *Case study: How & why to build a consumer app with Node.js*. Retrieved 05 30, 2022, from venturebeat.com: https://venturebeat.com/2012/01/07/building-consumer-apps-with-node/

Odobasic, L. (2017). Early Museum as Symbol of National Identity. *International Journal of Engineering Research and Development, 4*, pp. 67–75. doi: https://doi.org/2278-067X

O'doherty, B. (1986). *Inside the white cube: the ideology of the gallery space*. Lapis Press.

Ollila, R., Makitalo, N., & Mikkonen, T. (2022). Modern Web Frameworks: A Comparison of Rendering Performance. *Journal of Web Engineering, 21*(3), 789–814.

Open Handset Alliance. (2007). *Industry Leaders Announce Open Platform for Mobile Devices*. Retrieved 10 2019, from openhandsetalliance.com: http://www.openhandsetalliance.com/press_110507.html

Osmani, E. (2015, 12 15). *Getting started with Progressive Web Apps*. Retrieved 05 20, 2022, from developer.chrome.com: https://developer.chrome.com/blog/getting-started-pwa/

Othman, M., Petrie, H., & Power, C. (2013). Measuring the Usability of a Smartphone Delivered Museum Guid. *Procedia—Social and Behavioral Sciences*, 629–637.

Othman, M., Petrie, H., & Power, C. (2011). Engaging Visitors in Museums with Technology: Scales for the Measurement of Visitor and Multimedia Guide Experience. *IFIP Conference on Human-Computer Interaction*, 92–99.

Oxford Dictionary: Psychology. (2019). *Psychology*. Retrieved from Lexico, powered by OXFORD: https://www.lexico.com/en/definition/psychology

Oxford Dictionary: Smartphone. (2019). *Smartphone*. Retrieved from Lexico, powered by OXFORD: https://www.lexico.com/en/definition/smartphone

Özgen, E., & Davies, I. (2002). Acquisition of Categorical Color Perception: A Perceptual Learning Approach to the Linguistic Relativity Hypothesis. *Journal of Experimental Psychology*, 477–493. doi:https://doi.org/10.1037//0096-3445.131.4.477

Pallud, J. (2017). Impact of Interactive Technologies on Stimulating Learning Experiences in a Museum. *Information and Management, 54*(4). doi:https://doi.org/10.1016/j.im.2016.10.004

Palumbo, F., Dominici, G., & Basile, G. (2014). The Culture on the Palm of your Hand: How to Design a User Oriented Mobile App for Museums. *Handbook of research on management of cultural products: E-relationship marketing and accessibility perspectives*, 225–244.

Paraskakis, I. (2005). Ambient Learning: a New Paradigm for e-Learning. *Recent Research Developments in Learning Technologies*.

Parasuraman, A. (2000). Technology Readiness Index (TRI)—A Multiple-Item Scale to Measure Readiness to Embrace New Technologies. (Springer, Ed.) *Journal of Service Research, 2*(4), pp. 307–320.

Parmentier, M. (2005). Die Kunst und das Museum. Stationen eines didaktischen Dilemmas. *Zeitschrift für Pädagogik, 51*, 756–773. doi:urn:nbn:de:0111-opus-47796

Patrick, T. (2017, 02 16). *The Relationship Between Android and Java*. Retrieved 12 16, 2019, from theiconic.tech: https://theiconic.tech/android-java-fdbd55aadc51

Paulheim, H. (2017). Knowledge Graph Refinement: A Survey of Approaches and Evaluation Methods. *Semantic Web, 8*(3), 489–508.

Paulson, L. (2005). Building Rich Web Applications with Ajax. *Computer*, 14–17.

Pavlov, R., Paneva-Marinova, D., Goynov, M., & Pavlova-Draganova, L. (2010). Services for Content Creation and Presentation in an Iconographical Digital Library. *Serdica Journal of Computing, 4*(2), 279–292.

Pedamkar, P. (2018, 08 12). *MVVM vs MVC*. Retrieved 12 14, 2019, from educba.com: https://www.educba.com/mvvm-vs-mvc/

Pedamkar, P. (2019, 03 26). *MVC vs MVP vs MVVM*. Retrieved 12 14, 2019, from educba.com: https://www.educba.com/mvc-vs-mvp-vs-mvvm/

Pederson, T. (1997). A Cup of Tea & a Piece of Cake—Integration of Virtual Information Workspaces Inspired by the Way We May Think.

Peng, D., Cao, L., & Xu, W. (2011). Using JSON for Data Exchanging in Web Service Applications. *Journal of Computational Information Systems, 7*(16), 5883–5890.

Perkinson, R., Bischoff, J., & Burke, M. (2003). Defining the Conservator: Essential Competencies. *American Institute for Conservation of Historic and Artistic Works*.

Pescarin, S. (2014). Museums and Virtual Musuems in Europe: Reaching Expectations. *SCIentific RESearch and Information Technology*, 131–140. doi:https://doi.org/10.2423/i22394303v4n4p131

Petrelli, D., & O'Brien, S. (2018). Phone vs. Tangible in Museums: A Comparative Study. *Proceedings of the 2018 CHI Conference on Human Factors in Computing Systems*, 1–12.

PHP. (2004, 2022 05). *History of PHP*. Retrieved 30, from php.net: https://www.php.net/manual/en/history.php.php

PHP. (2015). *PHP Documentation -Preface*. Retrieved 05 30, 2022, from php.net: https://www.php.net/manual/en/preface.php

Plaza, B. (2000). Evaluating the Influence of a Large Cultural Artifact in the Attraction of Tourism—The Guggenheim Museum Bilbao Case. *Urban Affairs Review, 36*(2), 264–274.

Plaza, B. (2006). The Return on Investment of the Guggenheim Museum Bilbao. *International Journal of Urban and Regional Research, 30*(2), 452–467.

Powell, A. (1997, 12 19). *Web 101: A History of the GUI*. Retrieved 12 16, 2019, from wired.com: https://www.wired.com/1997/12/web-101-a-history-of-the-gui/

Prahalad, C., & Hamel, G. (1994). Strategy as Field of Study: Why Search for a new Paradigm? *Strategic Management Journal, 15*, 5–16.

Que, P., Guo, X., & Zhu, M. (2016). A Comprehensive Comparison Between Hybrid and Native App Paradigms. *International Conference on Computational Intelligence and Communication Networks*, 611–614.

Rajaa, R. (2020, 01 17). *Microsoft Edge 79: What's new in the Chromium-based Edge?* Retrieved 02 12, 2021, from browserstack.com: https://www.browserstack.com/blog/chromium-based-edge/#:~:text=With%20the%20Edge%2079%20release,for%20its%20own%20Chrome%20browser.

Rams, D. (2019). *The power of good design*. Retrieved 12 16, 2019, from vitsoe.com: https://www.vitsoe.com/rw/about/good-design

Ray, A. (2020, 07 13). *3 Common UX Mistakes Killing Good Design*. Retrieved 07 14, 2020, from uxplanet.org/: https://uxplanet.org/3-common-ux-mistakes-killing-good-design-97cedf1474e1

Reimer, H. (2016). EU-Datenschutz-Grundverordnung erfordert zusätzliche Ressourcen für Datenschutzbehörden. *DUD—Datenschutz und Datensicherheit,* 543–550.

Reinheimer, S., & Robra-Bissantz, S. (2014). Business-IT-Alignment—Kernaufgabe der Wirtschaftsinformatik. *HMD*, 526–548. doi:https://doi.org/10.1365/s40702-014-0078-0

Rengman, H. (2008). Standardization of Museum Data—A Threat to the Heritage? *2008 Annual Conference of CIDOC*.

Richard, S., & LePage, P. (2020, 02 24). *What are Progressive Web Apps?* Retrieved 05 20, 2022, from web.dev: https://web.dev/what-are-pwas/

Richly, K. (2021). Memory-Efficient Storing of Timestamps for Spatio-Temporal Data Management in Columnar In-Memory Databases. *International Conference on Database Systems for Advanced Applications*, 542–557.

Rivero, J., Grigera, J., Rossi, G., Luna, E., Montero, F., & Gaedke, M. (2014). Mockup-Driven Development: Providing Agile Support for Model-Driven Web Engineering. *Information and Software Technology, 56*(6), 670–687.

Rodley, E. (2013, 09 23). *REVIEW: CLEVELAND MUSEUM OF ART'S GALLERY ONE—PART ONE.* Retrieved from thinkingaboutmuseums.com: https://thinkingaboutmuseums.com/2013/09/23/review-cleveland-museum-of-arts-gallery-one-part-one/

Rodrigues, J., Pereira, J., Sardo, J., de Freitas, M., Cardoso, P., Gomes, M., & Bica , P. (2017). Adaptive Card Design UI Implementation for an Augmented Reality Museum Application. In M. Antona, *Universal Access in Human–Computer Interaction* (pp. 433–443). Vancouver, BC, Canada: Springer.

Rodriguez, A. (2008). RESTful Web Services: The Basics. *IBM—developer works.*

Rosewater, M. (2011, 12 05). *New World Order.* Retrieved 12 16, 2019, from magic.wizards.com/: https://magic.wizards.com/en/articles/archive/making-magic/new-world-order-2011-12-02

Rothwangl, S. (2002). The Last Day Calculation at the Base of Anno Domini. 105–106.

Rounds, J. (2004). Strategies for the Curiosity-Driven Museum Visitor. *Curator: The Museum Journal, 47*, 389–412. doi:https://doi.org/10.1111/j.2151-6952.2004.tb00135.x.

Rowley, J. (2007). The Wisdom Hierarchy: Representations of the DIKW Hierarchy. *Journal of Information Science, 33*, 163–180. doi:https://doi.org/10.1177/0165551506070706

Russell, A. (2015, 08 12). *Progressive Web Apps: Escaping Tabs Without Losing Our Soul.* Retrieved 05 20, 2022, from medium.com: https://medium.com/@slightlylate/progressive-apps-escaping-tabs-without-losing-our-soul-3b93a8561955

Samimi, H., Schafer, M., Artzi, S., Millstein, T., Tip, F., & Hendren, L. (2012). Automated Repair of HTML Generation Errors in PHP Applications Using String Constraint Solving. *International Conference on Software Engineering*, 277–287.

Sanders, J. (2018, 04 18). *Why it's finally time to give up on the name JavaScript.* Retrieved 06 30, 2021, from techrepublic.com: https://www.techrepublic.com/article/why-its-finally-time-to-give-up-on-the-name-javascript/

Sandoval, K. (2020, 08 19). *The Difference Between Tight Coupling and Loose Coupling.* Retrieved 12 13, 2022, from nordicapis.com: https://nordicapis.com/the-difference-between-tight-coupling-and-loose-coupling/

Sarkar, S., Sarker, B., & Hossain, S. (2016). Cross Platform Interactive Programming Learning Environment for Kids with Edutainment and Gamification. *19th International Conference on Computer and Information Technology (ICCIT)*, 218–222.

Sarwar, A. (2020, 01 06). *What is Service Oriented Architecture.* Retrieved 09 12, 2020, from medium.com: https://medium.com/@adeelsarwarblog/what-is-service-oriented-architecture-9b4406fcedeb

Scandi, P. (2019, 07 19). *History of Progressive Web Apps.* Retrieved 05 20, 2022, from medium.com: https://medium.com/progressivewebapps/history-of-progressive-web-apps-4c912533a531

Schmid, S. (2020, 08 21). *Was ist eigentlich ein Headless System.* Retrieved 12 16, 2022, from unchained.shop: https://unchained.shop/de/blog/headless

Schön, E., Winter, D., Escalona, M., & Thomaschewski, J. (2017). Key Challenges in Agile Tequirements Engineering. *International Conference on Agile Software Development*, 37–51.

Shead, S. (2019, 12 18). *Facebook owns the four most downloaded apps of the decade.* Retrieved 12 18, 2019, from bbc.com: https://www.bbc.com/news/technology-50838013

Shenton, H. (2003). Life Cycle Collection Management. *Liber Quarterly*, 254–272.

Shukla, S. (2017, 06 17). *Framework vs Library vs Platform vs API vs SDK vs Toolkits vs IDE*. Retrieved 12 16, 2019, from medium.com: https://medium.com/@shashvatshukla/framework-vs-library-vs-platform-vs-api-vs-sdk-vs-toolkits-vs-ide-50a9473999db

Skinner, S., Ekelund Jr., R., & Jackson, J. (2009). Art Museum Attendance, Public Funding, and the Business Cycle. *American Journal of Economics and Sociology, 68*(2).

Sladeczek, F.-J. (2011). «Cabinet mit Bibliothec und übrigen Raritäten…» Basels frühe Rolle als Kunststadt im Spiegel seiner Privatsammlungen. *Kulturtransfer,* pp. 16–28.

smaato.com. (2020, 03 15). *2020 App Monetization Guide: Strategies, Techniques, Tips*. Retrieved 03 15, 2020, from smaato.com: https://www.smaato.com/app-monetization-guide/

Small, Z. (2019, 08 19). *A New Definition of "Museum" Sparks International Debate*. Retrieved 12 20, 2019, from https://hyperallergic.com/: https://hyperallergic.com/513858/icom-museum-definition/

Snell, J., & Cohen, P. (2008). *Apple opens iTunes App Store*. Retrieved 10 2019, from Macworld: https://www.macworld.com/article/1134380/app_store.html

Soegaard, M. (2020, 05 02). *Usability: A part of the User Experience*. Retrieved 06 29, 2020, from https://www.interaction-design.org/: https://www.interaction-design.org/literature/article/usability-a-part-of-the-user-experience

Søndergaard, M., & Veirum, N. (2012). Museums and culture-driven innovation in public–private Consortia. *Museum Management and Curatorship, 27*, 341–356.

Sourour, B. (2016, 10 26). *Code dependencies are the devil*. Retrieved 12 16, 2019, from freecodecamp.org: https://www.freecodecamp.org/news/code-dependencies-are-the-devil-35ed28b556d/

Staatliche Antikensammlungen und Glyptothek. (2019). *Antike am Königsplatz*. Retrieved 12 16, 2019, from antike-am-koenigsplatz.mwn.de: https://www.antike-am-koenigsplatz.mwn.de/index.php/de/glyptothek

Stam, D. (1996). Spiders across the Stars—A Web-based Model for Providing Access to multi-institutional Museum Information. *Archives and Museum Informatics, 10*(4), 374–384.

Statcounter. (2019). *Mobile Operating System Market Share Worldwide 2009–2019*. Retrieved 12 2019, from statcounter.com: https://gs.statcounter.com/os-market-share/mobile/worldwide/#monthly-200901-201912

Statista. (2019). *Global smartphone penetration rate as share of population from 2016 to 2020*. Retrieved 10 2019, from statista.com: https://www.statista.com/statistics/203734/global-smartphone-penetration-per-capita-since-2005/

Stein, M.-K., Galliers, R., & Whitley, E. (2016). Twenty Years of the European Information Systems Academy at ECIS: Emergent Trends and Research Topics. *European Journal of Information Systems, 25*, 1–15.

Steiner, T. (2018). What is in a Web View? An Analysis of Progressive Web App Features When the Means of Web Access is not a Web Browser. *Companion Proceedings of the The Web Conference 2018*, 789–796.

Stigler, G. (1958). The Economies of Scale. *The Journal of Law and Economics, 1*, 54–71.

Stojmenovic, M., Pilgrim, C., & Lindgaard, G. (2014). Perceived and Objective Usability and Visual Appeal in a Website Domain with a Less Developed Mental Model. *Proceedings of the 26th Australian Computer-Human Interaction Conference on Designing Futures: the Future of Design*, 316–323. doi:https://dl.acm.org/doi/10.1145/2686612.2686660

Stonebraker, M. (2010). SQL Databases vs. NoSQL Databases. *communications of the acm*, 10–11. doi:https://doi.org/10.1145/1721654.1721659

Stormer, H., Meier, A., & Lehner, F. (2005). Mobile Business—eine Übersicht. *HMD—Mobile Anwendungen, 244.*

Su, C., & Cheng, C. (2015). A Mobile Gamification Learning System for Improving the Learning Motivation and Achievements. *Journal of Computer Assisted Learning, 31*(3), 268–286.

Takahashi, D. (2020, 01 15). *App Annie: Mobile game spending will top $100 billion in 2020.* Retrieved 03 15, 2020, from /venturebeat.com/: https://venturebeat.com/2020/01/15/app-annie-mobile-game-spending-is-expected-to-top-100-billion-in-2020/

Tallgren, M. (2018). Developing a Collaborative Planning Tool for Construction. *Chalmers University of Technology.*

Tallon, L. (2009, 05 19). *About that 1952 Sedelijk Museum audio guide, and a certain Willem Sandburg.* Retrieved 12 15, 2019, from MuseMatic.net: https://web.archive.org/web/20110319044115/http://musematic.net/2009/05/19/about-that-1952-sedelijk-museum-audio-guide-and-a-certain-willem-sandburg

Tamburri, D., Bersani, M., Mirandola, R., & Pea, G. (2018). DevOps Service Observability By-Design: Experimenting with Model-View-Controller. *Service-Oriented and Cloud Computing*, 49–64. doi:https://doi.org/10.1007/978-3-319-99819-0_4

The Open Group. (2009). *SOA Source Book.* Van Harlen Publishing, Zaltbommel.

The Radicati Group. (2020). Mobile Statistics Report, 2020–2024. *Press Release.*

Themed Entertainment Association. (2019). TEA/AECOM 2018 Theme Index and Museum Index. *The Global Attractions Attendance Report.*

Thönes, J. (2015). Microservices. *IEEE Software*, 112–115.

Tombs, K. (2004). Knowlege Management is Dead: Long Live Records Management. *Records Manamgement Journal*, 90–93. doi:https://doi.org/10.1108/09565690410546145

Tu, S. (2019). Analysis on the Development Trend and Application Technology of Digital Museum. *Proceedings of the 1st International Symposium on Innovation and Education, Law and Social Sciences*, 2352–5398. doi:https://doi.org/10.2991/ielss-19.2019.26

van Roy, R., & Zaman, B. (2017). Why Gamification Fails in Education and how to Make it Successful: Introducing nine Gamification Heuristics Based on self-determination Theory. *Serious Games and Edutainment Applications*, 485–509.

Van Ruymbeke, M., Hallot, P., Nys, G., & Billen, R. (2018). Implementation of Multiple Interpretation Data Model Concepts in CIDOC CRM and Compatible Models. *Virtual Archaeology Review, 9*(19), 50–65.

Venable, J., Pries-Heje, J., & Baskerville, R. (2016). FEDS: a Framework for Evaluation of Design Science Research. *European Journal of Information Science, 25*, pp. 77–86.

Vino Online. (2019). *VINO—die browserbasierte Datenbanklösung zur Inventarisierung auf Einzelplatz-PC, Intranet oder Internet.* Retrieved from vino-online.net/: https://www.vino-online.net/index1.html

W3C. (2004, 04). *Position Paper for the W3C Workshop on Web Applications and Compound Documents.* Retrieved 12 16, 2019, from w3.org: https://www.w3.org/2004/04/webapps-cdf-ws/papers/opera.html

W3C. (2021, 06 28). *W3C/WHATWG Relationship update.* Retrieved 06 30, 2021, from https://www.w3.org/2021/06/WHATWG-W3C-MOU_2021_update.html

w3schools. (2019). *XML RDF.* Retrieved 12 16, 2019, from www.w3schools.com/: https://www.w3schools.com/xml/xml_rdf.asp#:~:text=RDF%20Schema%20(RDFS)%20is%20an,such%20extension%20is%20RDF%20Schema.

W3Tech. (2022, 06 09). *Usage statistics of PHP for websites.* Retrieved 06 09, 2022, from w3techs.com: https://w3techs.com/technologies/details/pl-php

Waibel, G., & Erway, R. (2009). Think Global, Act Local—Library, Archive and Museum Collaboration. *Museum Management and Curatorship, 24*(4).

Walker, K. (2008). Structuring Visitor Participation. In L. Tallon, & K. Walker, *Digital Technologies and the Museum Experience: Handheld Guides and Other Media* (pp. 109–124). Lanham: AltaMira Press.

Wang, Y., Wei, J., & Vangury, K. (2014). Bring Your Own Device Security Issues and Challenges. *The 11th Annual IEEE CCNC- Mobile Device, Platform and Communication*, 80–85.

Warwick, C., Mahony, S., Nyhan, J., Ross, C., Terras, M., Tiedau, U., & Welsh, A. (2011). UCLDH: Big Tent Digital Humanities in Practice . *Digital Humanities 2011 Conference Abstracts*, 387–389.

Wei, X., & Jianping, Z. (2015). Mobile Application used in Museum Learning and Its Case Study. *2015 International Conference of Educational Innovation through Technology*, 90–93.

Wein, L. (2014). Visual Recognition in Museum Guide Apps: Do Visitors Want It? *CHI 2014, One of a CHInd*, 635–638. doi:https://dl.acm.org/doi/10.1145/2556288.2557270

Westerhoff, J. (2001). A World of Signs: Baroque Pansemioticism, the Polyhistor and the Early Modern Wunderkammer. *Journal of the History of Ideas, 4*, pp. 633–650.

Westerman, G., Bonnet, D., & McAfee, A. (2014, Jan 07). *The Nine Elements of Digital Transformation.* Retrieved 01 01, 2020, from MIT Management Review: https://sloanreview.mit.edu/article/the-nine-elements-of-digital-transformation/

WHATWG. (2017). *WHATWG—FAQ.* Retrieved 12 16, 2019, from whatwg.org: https://whatwg.org/faq

Wiegers, K., & Beatty, J. (2013). *Software Requirements* (3 ed.). Washington: Microsoft Press. doi:https://doi.org/978-0-7356-7966-5

Winick, E. (2018, 03 15). *Bridging the communications gap between human and machine.* Retrieved 12 16, 2019, from technologyreview.com: https://www.technologyreview.com/2018/03/15/144653/bridging-the-communications-gap-between-human-and-machine

Winn, T., & Calder, P. (2002). Is This a Pattern? *IEEE SOFTWARE*(January/February), pp. 59–66. doi:0740-7459/02

WissKi. (2019). *Welcome to WissKI.* Retrieved 12 16, 2019, from wiss-ki.eu/: http://wiss-ki.eu/

World Tourism Organization. (2019). International Tourism Highlights, 2019 Edition. *UNWTO.* doi:https://doi.org/10.18111/9789284421152

Wu, S., & Chua, P. (2008). Museum Collection Management On-Demand. *Proceedings of the 2nd international conference on Theory and practice of electronic governance*, 310–315.

Zan, L. (2000). Managerialisation Processes and Performance in Arts Organisations: The Archaelogical Museum of Bologna. *Scandinavian Journal of Management*, 431–454.

zetcom. (2019). *museum plus- Browserbasiertes Museum Management—Jederzeit und überall.* Retrieved from zetcom.com: https://www.zetcom.com/museumplus_de/

Zheng, Y., Li, M., Lou, W., & Hou, Y. (2017). Location Based Handshake and Private Proximity Test with Location Tags. *IEEE Transactions on Dependable and Secure Computing, 14*(4), 406–419.

SPRINGER NATURE

GPSR Compliance

The European Union's (EU) General Product Safety Regulation (GPSR) is a set of rules that requires consumer products to be safe and our obligations to ensure this.

If you have any concerns about our products, you can contact us on ProductSafety@springernature.com

In case Publisher is established outside the EU, the EU authorized representative is:

Springer Nature Customer Service Center GmbH
Europaplatz 3
69115 Heidelberg, Germany

The manufacturer's authorised representative in the EU is Springer Nature Customer Service Centre GmbH, Europaplatz 3, 69115 Heidelberg, Germany. If you have any concerns regarding our products, please contact ProductSafety@springernature.com

Printed and bound by CPI Group (UK) Ltd, Croydon, CR0 4YY
30/09/2026
02225301-0002